# Integrating AI and Machine Learning into Business and Management Education

Manjunath B. R.
*Tecnológico de Monterrey, Mexico*

Sunil Kumar R.
*Shoolini University, India*

IGI Global
Scientific Publishing
Publishing Tomorrow's Research Today

Published in the United States of America by
IGI Global Scientific Publishing
701 East Chocolate Avenue
Hershey, PA, 17033, USA
Tel: 717-533-8845
Fax: 717-533-7115
Website: https://www.igi-global.com E-mail: cust@igi-global.com



Library of Congress Cataloging-in-Publication Data

LCCN: 2025005800 (CIP Data Pending)
ISBN13: 979-8-3373-2150-9
Isbn13Softcover: 979-8-3373-2151-6
EISBN13: 979-8-3373-2152-3

British Cataloguing in Publication Data
A Cataloguing in Publication record for this book is available from the British Library.

# Table of Contents

# Detailed Table of Contents

AI tools and technologies are transforming management education by improving learning experiences, teaching efficiency, and preparing students for the future workforce. Personalized learning carried out by AI commutes educational content to students' individual needs, promoting better commitment and understanding. AI control simulations can provide students with a realistic, risk-free environment, practice decision-making and problem-solving, and bridge the gap between theory and practice. Additionally, AI-based assessment tools automate ratings and feedback, store trainers, and provide students with instant, personalized answers. Predictive analytics allow educators to monitor student performance and actively intervene in combat learners. While AI is developing, integration into management curriculums is becoming increasingly important, offering new ways to improve educational outcomes, enhance management tasks, and ensure business school graduates produce in a digitally controlled business world.



Artificial Intelligence (AI) is driving the evolution of management education, and India has the potential to be the pioneer of this digital transformation. In an era where Digitization and Gen AI are set to transform industries. B-Schools have a crucial role in bridging the skills gap and reshaping the corporate sector. The Gen AI and the sectors like electric vehicles, renewable and climate change are driving the dynamism of management education. The management graduate start-ups are also challenging the conventional way of doing business, and Gen AI will significantly impact traditional job roles will also emerge. With the changing pace of the world today, the change in hiring practices is about building a workforce that is agile, diverse, and capable of meeting the needs of a tech-driven world. The curriculum on sustainability, ESG, Circular Economy, which MBA graduates learn the fundamentals for sustainability, social development, Deglobalization, geopolitical diversity, and sensitivities. This paper focuses the how sustainable technology solutions are useful in Education.

# Preface

Artificial Intelligence (AI) and Machine Learning (ML) are redefining the boundaries of traditional education paradigms across disciplines. Their application in business and management education has emerged as a transformative force, enabling personalized learning, enhanced data-driven decision-making, and a curriculum grounded in future-ready competencies. This book, titled "Integrating AI and Machine Learning into Business and Management Education" serves as a comprehensive examination of how AI technologies are shaping pedagogical innovation, institutional strategy, and learner outcomes in business schools.

In the current global educational landscape, business schools face the dual challenge of equipping students with domain knowledge while fostering innovation, agility, and digital fluency. With the rapid proliferation of AI-driven platforms, tools such as ChatGPT, predictive analytics engines, recommendation systems, and intelligent tutoring systems have become integral to reimagining teaching methodologies. This book positions itself at the confluence of this revolution, offering actionable insights, frameworks, and case studies to facilitate successful adoption and integration of AI into the teaching-learning process.

This book is targeted toward a wide range of academic and professional stakeholders, including educators in business and management schools, academic administrators, EdTech developers, curriculum designers, corporate trainers, researchers, and graduate students. It offers both foundational concepts and advanced perspectives, making it suitable for those implementing AI in educational practice, as well as those conducting research in the domains of management education and educational technology.

Chapter 1 Turing to Transformation: The Journey of AI and ML, lays the groundwork by exploring the evolution of artificial intelligence and machine learning. It highlights key breakthroughs, from symbolic AI to generative AI, and reflects on their implications for management education. The chapter emphasizes how understanding the history of AI prepares educators to integrate emerging technologies strategically.

Chapter 2 AI Innovations in Higher Education and Management of Students, investigates AI's transformative role in enhancing student experience and institutional efficiency. It covers ethical considerations such as bias, data privacy, and responsible AI adoption. This chapter sets a conceptual framework for understanding AI's value across educational touchpoints.

Chapter 3 Generative AI in Business Education Transforming Teaching and Learning, emphasizes the practical integration of tools like ChatGPT and DALL·E in curriculum delivery. It critically examines the opportunities and challenges of generative AI for lesson planning, assessment, and interactive learning. The chapter calls for ethical integration and capacity-building for faculty.

Chapter 4 Generative AI in Management Education: A Conceptual Framework for Transforming Teaching and Learning Practices, introduces a conceptual framework to embed generative AI in management education. Based on literature reviews and expert interviews, it proposes four pillars: Strategic Alignment, Adaptive Learning Models, Reflective Practice, and Stakeholder Engagement. The framework bridges theory and practice, enhancing student engagement and institutional readiness.

Chapter 5 AI Tools and Technologies for Management Education, provides an in-depth analysis of how AI applications like business simulations, predictive analytics, and automated feedback are reshaping pedagogy. It illustrates how AI supports personalized learning, real-time student tracking, and competency-based instruction.

Chapter 6 From Chalkboards to Chatbots, documents the paradigm shift in educational delivery, from traditional classrooms to AI-supported ecosystems. The chapter analyzes India's evolving management education system and evaluates how generative AI, sustainability trends, and digitization are influencing new-age learning practices.

Chapter 7 Leveraging AI to Create Personalized Learning Experiences, explores adaptive education models empowered by AI. It shows how curriculum design and learning pathways can be dynamically adjusted based on learner analytics, creating inclusive and responsive educational environments.

Chapter 8 Revolutionising Business and Management Education with Generative AI, examines how generative AI fosters innovation, problem-solving, and decision-making in business education. It underscores the need for rethinking curriculum structure to incorporate AI-driven creativity, agility, and ethical thinking. The chapter highlights both pedagogical and institutional shifts needed for successful implementation.

Chapter 9 Machine Learning vs Traditional Models - A Comparative Analysis of LSTM and ARIMA for Stock Prediction with Management Education Applications, offers a comparative evaluation of LSTM and ARIMA models for stock price prediction and their instructional applications in finance education. It underscores experiential learning through real-time datasets, enabling students to grasp algorithmic trading, financial forecasting, and data interpretation in practice.

Chapter 10 Enhancing Data Analytics and Forecasting Education through Machine Learning Algorithms, focuses on the integration of machine learning in analytics and forecasting courses. It highlights pedagogical strategies like gamification, project-based learning, and hands-on labs to make complex algorithms more accessible. The chapter outlines how to overcome challenges like algorithm complexity and faculty training.

Chapter 11 Machine Learning and Management Education: A Pathway to Sustainability, connects machine learning and sustainability by aligning educational practices with Sustainable Development Goals (SDGs). It emphasizes AI-powered adaptive learning, inclusive practices, and ethical data usage, showing how sustainability and technology can co-evolve in modern classrooms.

Chapter 12 Emerging Trends and Innovation in AI for Business and Management Education - A Future Ready Approach, outlines innovations in AI for business education through global case studies. It reflects policy, ethics, and strategy while evaluating emerging instructional models in institutions like MIT, INSEAD, and ISB. The chapter guides readers on how to balance innovation with responsible AI integration.

Chapter 13 AI-Driven Business Systems, Pioneering Innovation and Transformation, synthesizes how AI is transforming business systems in real-world sectors like retail, healthcare, and finance. It showcases how machine learning, NLP, and predictive analytics streamline operations and decision-making. This chapter bridges academic theory with corporate implementation of AI.

In conclusion, this book stands as a timely, scholarly contribution to the evolving discourse on artificial intelligence in management education. Each chapter not only explores current technologies and strategies but also charts the path for future innovations. By compiling multidisciplinary perspectives and applications, this book aims to guide educators, administrators, and policymakers in embedding AI effectively into business education frameworks. The collective insights offer a roadmap for transforming management education to be more adaptive, inclusive, and aligned with the digital economy.

# Chapter 1
# Turing to Transformation:
## The Journey of AI and ML

**Vinayak Anand Anand Teli**
https://orcid.org/0009-0006-5961-691X
*Dayananda Sagar College of Engineering, India*

**H. P. Ramya**
https://orcid.org/0000-0002-2048-807X
*Dayananda Sagar College of Engineering, India*

## ABSTRACT

*This chapter explores the evolution of Artificial Intelligence and Machine learning, tracing their development from the foundation period to the modern era of generative AI, highlighting key milestones and breakthroughs. It also anticipates future advancements, focusing on AI's role in automation, decision-making, and AI-human collaboration. The challenges of AI adoption, including implementation barriers and ethical concerns, are also discussed. Additionally, the chapter explores AI's transformative impact on business, enhancing efficiency, predictive analytics, and customer engagement. The importance of AI and ML knowledge in management education is emphasized, preparing future professionals for AI-driven industries. The purpose of this chapter is to provide insights into AI's evolution and its relevance in business and education. By integrating AI into learning, professionals can adapt to digital transformations, fostering innovation, competitiveness, and strategic leadership.*

DOI: 10.4018/979-8-3373-2150-9.ch001

## INTRODUCTION

Artificial intelligence (AI) is the simulation of human intelligence in a machine. With the growing importance of data-driven decisions, AI plays a vital role in various fields, from diagnosis and treatment to planning, control, automation, and execution of decisions. In contrast, machine learning (ML) is a branch of AI that learns from existing data and inputs and predicts new outputs based on existing patterns. This learning can be supervised, unsupervised, or reinforcement learning. AI and ML, in their current state, are the results of a series of experiments and improvements dating back to the 1950s (Turing, 2009). As a result of these experiments and innovations, technologies have evolved to be in such an intelligent state of performing tasks autonomously. The improved technology is acting as a breakthrough and transforming the traditional industries, which was hardly anticipated. Business-related fields are the most favored with the invention and evolution of AI, automating production to customer query addressing using chatbots the businesses have come far and are anticipating much more. As a person studying management, staying relevant to such breakthroughs and their future ambitions in society, country, and world is essential to reap the benefits for betterment and improvements. This study dwells on these concepts, providing detailed information regarding the advent and evolution of these intelligent technologies and their relevance to management education.

The period between 1950 and 1970 formed the basis for Artificial Intelligence (AI) and Machine Learning (ML) facilitated by theoretical innovations combined with some early experimentation. The Turing test, introduced in Alan Turing's seminal paper "Computing Machinery and Intelligence" (1950), formed a primary basis of AI in considering whether machines can exhibit intelligent behavior equivalent to that of a human being (Jannai et al., 2023). The formal foundation for this field was laid during the Dartmouth conference in 1956, where the term 'artificial intelligence' was introduced (Cordeschi, 2006). The major technological advancements during this period include Arthur Samuel's self-teaching checker's program (Samuel, 1960), Rosenblatt's Perceptron (Rosenblatt, 1961), MENACE (Michie, 1963), and Shakey the Robot (Raphael, 1972) had prepared the ground for machine learning and neural networks. Research centers like MIT, Stanford, and Carnegie Mellon became the hubs for AI supported by generous funding, particularly from ARPA (now DARPA) (Delipetrev et al., 2020). While the expectations were high for AI, the technical limitations, underwhelming progress, and negative evaluations led to the first AI winter during the 1970s. The ALPAC report in 1966 (ALPAC, 1966) and the Lighthill report in 1973 (1973) assessed the downside of machine translation in general AI research and highlighted the lack of appreciable progress and scalability of methods from the combinatorial explosion (Delipetrev et al., 2020). This disinvestment, coupled with negative assessments, resulted in a decline in government and institutional funding, interrupting the advancement of AI for a while.

The period of symbolic AI (1970s to 1980s) was a vital period of AI, where the focus was on transferring human expert knowledge into a computer system that incorporated human-like reasoning through rule-based expert systems (Delipetrev et al., 2020). Major projects such as MYCIN (Shortliffe et al., 1975) and SHRDLU (Winograd, 1971) helped establish the concept of AI in diagnosis and natural language processing. The invention of the Prolog (Rouchy, 2006), Stanford Cart (Moravec, 1983), and the Hopfield network (Rumelhart et al., 1985) marked progress in the areas of logic programming and robotics. However, despite the significant investments from countries like USA, UK, and Japan the period faced obstacles as the expert systems suffered many setbacks (Delipetrev et al., 2020), and problems like brittleness, difficulty in knowledge acquisition, and maintenance issues led to the second AI winter (Hayes-Roth et al., 1983). The downfall of specialized machines such as Lisp computers further compounded the recession.

AI evolved significantly from symbolic AI to data-driven machine learning and deep learning between 1990 and 2020. The earliest inventions belonging to this age comprise convolutional neural networks for image recognition (LeCun et al., 1989) and quantum (Watkins, 1989). LSTM (Hochreiter & Schmidhuber, 1997), and IBM Deep Blue (IBM Deep Blue, 2025) represented the potential capabilities of AI. In 2009, ImageNet catalyzed advances in image recognition (Deng et al., 2009), and in 2011, IBM Watson won the competition of Jeopardy! (Ferrucci, 2012), demonstrating artificial intelligence's prowess in natural language processing. Remarkable progress in deep learning and AI was accomplished from 2012 to 2019. Some of the highlights included the 2012 AlexNet breakthrough in image classification (Krizhevsky et al., 2012); the introduction of generative adversarial networks (Goodfellow et al., 2014); and reinforcement learning successes like DeepRL (Mnih et al., 2015); and AlphaGo (Silver et al., 2016). Transformers and BERT (Ashish, 2017) further improved advancements in natural language processing. The increasing investments pouring into AI, particularly by major tech companies like Google and Microsoft fueled the growth (Delipetrev et al., 2020); while adversarial attacks, data poisoning, and privacy leakage (Wang et al., 2024) have presented new challenges. Ethical concerns, including biases in AI models and data availability, also became critical issues (Talaei Khoei et al., 2023).

The recent period witnessed a considerable step forward in the form of Generative AIs. The invention of GPT–3 in 2020 revolutionized text generation, achieving remarkable capabilities in summarization and translation tasks (Floridi & Chiriatti, 2020). AlphaFold 2, by DeepMind in 2020, greatly advanced protein structure prediction to near-X-ray accuracy (Stevens & He, 2022). The emergence of DALL·E (2021) and GPT – 3 applications in text and image generation expanded the frontier of AI with promising results (Ramesh et al., 2022). In 2023, GPT-4 unfurled human-level performance on a multitude of tasks (Achiam et al., 2023), while Google Bard rolled out high-intensity NLP-driven solutions in real-time (Aydın, 2023). Meta's LLaMA (Touvron et al., 2023) and Microsoft with Copilot improved the productivity powered by AI (Microsoft Copilot, 2025). The year 2025 marked the rise of DeepSeek as a powerhouse in the AI industry, having overshadowed its competition and rival ChatGPT (Times of India news on DeepSeek, 2025).

Generative AI offered a transformative prospect in various industries like manufacturing, healthcare, automotive, and media, through operational efficiencies and new business models. Gartner Inc. (Gartner – Impact of AI in future, 2025) forecasted that AI-augmented development strategies will be adopted by 30% of enterprises by 2025, while by 2026, generative design AI will be working on 60% of web and app design. The rapid developments and growth of AI make it necessary to have regulatory oversight, leading to the introduction of the AI Act in the European Union by 2024 to ensure safe and ethical AI use (EU - AI Act, 2025).

In present days, the integration of AI into business is observed transforming areas like predictive analytics, customer relationship management (CRM), fraud detection, and supply chain optimization, thereby favoring improved decision-making and operational efficiency (Chowdhury, 2024). AI also integrates human resource management, like enhancing recruitment and employee performance analysis (Chowdhury et al., 2023). Therefore, business schools must keep up with the new developments in AI to prepare their students with the necessary skill sets in AI and data analytics considered important for industries. This must also include the development of interdisciplinary approaches in data management, predictive analytics, and decision-making to equip the students to work with AI agents in the business domain (Stine et al., 2019).

## Research Gap

While numerous advancements have been accomplished in AI and ML, the majority of existing studies mainly emphasize their technical or domain-specific applications with little consideration given to their blend into the management curriculum. There is a noticeable gap in addressing how business schools prepare current managers to work with AI, comprehend algorithmic insights, and lead in AI-driven environments. Another neglected area is how the newly born generative AI instruments can facilitate strategic thinking and decision-making in business education. The present study intends to fill this gap by signaling the specific relevance of AI evolution in contemporary management learning.

## Objectives of the Study

1. To trace the historical evolution and key milestones in Artificial Intelligence and Machine learning.
2. To analyze the impact of AI advancements on business operations and managerial functions.
3. To evaluate the relevance of AI and ML integration into management education.

## METHODOLOGY

Qualitative-descriptive research has been adopted for this study by means of secondary data analysis. The research draws from academic journals, historical documentation, published articles, and trustworthy internet sources such as IBM, OpenAI, Google AI Blog, and Gartner. The study creates a cohesive narrative of the evolution and relevance of AI in management education by blending the chronic journey of AI whereby it is discussed from past to present and speculative future.

## Evolution of Artificial Intelligence and Machine Learning

The intelligence is defined as "the ability to learn, understand, and make judgments or have opinions that are based on reason" (Cambridge Dictionary, 2025). Whereas Professor John McCarthy defined AI as "the science and engineering of making intelligent machines." AI pioneer Arthur Samuel in the 1950s defines machine learning as "the field of study that gives computers the ability to learn without explicitly being programmed." The evolution of AI is studied under different time periods as explained below.

### 1. AI Foundation (1950 -1970)

The foundation for the evolution of AI was rooted in the 1950s, led by Alan Turing with his seminal work "Computing Machinery and Intelligence" (Jannai et al., 2023). In his paper, Turing considered the fundamental question "Can machines think?" and put forth the Turing test, an imitation game. The Idea behind Turing's machine test game was a male-female imitation game where there were three persons involved: a human interrogator, one male (A), and one female (B). Through questions and answers, the interrogator must ascertain which of the A and B the male is. In the game, the A's goal was to fool the interrogator into giving the incorrect identification. Three people participated in the imitation game: a human "foil," a human interrogator, and a computer. The interrogator interacts with both humans and the machine during the test without knowing which is which. All the communication took place through a keyboard and screen or a similar setup (Turing recommended a teleprinter link). The interrogator may ask questions as penetrating and wide-ranging as he or she likes to figure out if they're talking to a human or a computer, and the computer was permitted to do everything possible to force a wrong identification. (So, the computer might answer the question 'Are you a computer?' as 'No' or if it is asked to do a math problem it might pretend to take a long time to think and give wrong answers to seem more like a human). The foil must help the interrogator to make a correct identification. Since Alan Turing first conceived the Turing Test in 1950, it has been carried out numerous times. Depending on the implementation and the AI systems under test, the outcomes have varied. Some early AI programs controversially claimed to have passed the test by limiting themselves to scripted situations or by presenting excuses for poor reasoning and conversational abilities.

The Dartmouth conference in 1956 marked the beginning of the first AI period, where John McCarthy first introduced the word Artificial Intelligence. The primary aim of the conference was "Every aspect of any other feature of learning or intelligence should be accurately described so that the machine can simulate it" (Cordeschi, 2006). The conference provided discussions on foundational concepts like neural networks and machine learning. It laid the groundwork for AI research and led to the establishment of major AI research centers and institutions like Carnegie Mellon University, MIT, and Stanford University.

*Table 1. The notable AI breakthroughs (1950-1970)*

| Year | Developments |
|---|---|
| 1957 | Frank Rosenblatt presented the perceptron in his paper. The perceptron was an artificial neural network that imitated human cognitive functioning. The perceptron contains input nodes, weights, a summation processor, and an output node; the weights were adjusted using a learning algorithm to correct the errors. This model was successfully applied to the solution of a simple pattern recognition task and provided the foundations for deep learning and neural networks (Rosenblatt, 1961). |
| 1961 | MENACE (Machine Educable Noughts and Crosses Engine) was an early example of machine learning, designed to play and learn Tic-Tac-Toe. MENACE used matchboxes representing game states, with colored beads for different moves. By adjusting beads based on game outcomes, MENACE improved its strategy over time. This system demonstrated the potential of reinforcement learning and was a pioneering example of AI applied to game-playing (Michie, 1963). |
| 1965 | Joseph Weizenbaum introduced ELIZA, one of the first computer programs with natural language processing that was capable of conversing with people and responding using simple patterns. The most famous version of ELIZA, Called DOCTOR, mimicked a Rogerian psychotherapist and responded to the user questions like a psychotherapist (Weizenbaum, 1966). |
| 1969 | Shakey the Robot, developed at the Stanford Research Institute, was the first general-purpose mobile robot with the ability to reason its actions. It was a pioneering project in AI and robotics as it combined research in robotics, natural language processing, and computer vision (Raphael, 1972). |

**Source:** Compiled by Author(s).

***Investments in AI during the period:*** The US government, inspired by scientists' optimism, invested hugely in research on Artificial Intelligence. The director of ARPA, J.C.R. Licklider was convinced to fund researchers instead of particular projects, allowing for a loose research environment with a lot of funding but no tight deliverables. ARPA (Advanced Research Projects Agency) subsequently became the Defense Advanced Research Projects Agency (DARPA), which invested millions in sponsoring academic AI research centers including MIT, Stanford University, and Carnegie Mellon University, as well as commercial research facilities like SRI International (Delipetrev et al., 2020). One of the notable investments made by DAPRA was Project MAC (Mathematics and Computation), which was founded at the Massachusetts Institute of Technology, in 1963. The objective of the project MAC was to enable multiple users from different locations to access a single computer program.

***The first AI winter 1970s:*** The first AI winter period was caused by large expectations, financial difficulties, and technological limitations and led to reductions in interest and funding for AI research (Delipetrev et al., 2020). This period saw a significant drop in AI activities in both industry and academia.

## 2. **Symbolic AI (1970 – 1990)**

The symbolic AI period had the intention of converting human-like expert knowledge into computer form. The expert systems contained two components: 1) The knowledge base - a set of rules, facts, and relationships for a specific domain, 2) The inference engine- described how to handle and combine these symbols. By the 1980s, various businesses began to create software packages known as 'inference engines', but they could not capture the breadth of human knowledge to function satisfactorily (Delipetrev et al., 2020).

*Table 2. The breakthroughs of this period (1970-1990)*

| Year | Developments |
|---|---|
| 1972 | Alain Colmerauer and Philippe Roussel developed and implemented Prolog, a symbolic programming language, in Marseille, France. It allowed programmers to specify the tasks using logical statements instead of conventional instructions (Rouchy, 2006). |
| 1979 | The Stanford cart was a mobile robot that navigated a room by itself while avoiding obstacles. It gained knowledge of its environment from images broadcast by an onboard TV system and used stereopsis for locating objects in three dimensions and planning its path to reach the destination (Moravec, 1983). |
| 1982 | John Hopfield introduced the 'Hopfield network' a type of recurrent artificial neural network that consists of binary state neurons connected by symmetric weights and functions as an associative memory system and it was capable of storing and recalling patterns demonstrating the potential of the simple neurons to perform the complex computations (Hopfield, 1982). The introduction of the 'backpropagation algorithm', a key method for training artificial neural networks. Hopfield network and backpropagation algorithm restored the AI field of connectionism (Rumelhart et al., 1985). |
| 1983 | J. R. Quinlan developed the ID3 algorithm, which creates a decision tree from the dataset. ID3 is the predecessor to the C4.5 algorithm utilized in machine learning and natural language processing. (Quinlan, 1986). |

**Source:** Compiled by Author(s).

***Investments in AI during the period:*** The symbolic AI period witnessed different significant investments and projects. From 1980 to 1986, XCON, an expert system, saved Digital Equipment Corporation's $40 million per year. By 1985, the US had committed more than $1 billion to AI expert systems. The UK started the £350 million Alvey project. In 1981, Japan's Ministry of Economy, Trade, and Industry invested $850 million in a fifth-generation computer project to produce machines capable of communicating, translating languages, analyzing visuals, and thinking like humans (Delipetrev et al., 2020).

***Issues faced during the period (Second Winter of AI):*** The significant reduction in the funding and enthusiasm for AI research led by unfulfilled expectations and technological limitations marked the second AI winter. Specialized computers like Lisp machines, which were developed heavily for AI programming were very expensive and the development of general-purpose computers doomed these specialized machines (Steele & Gabriel, 1996). The corporate funding for research dried up during winter and the companies invested in AI began to doubt the return on their investments. This period was also characterized by the downfall of the expert systems (Hayes-Roth et al., 1983) for reasons like:

- *Brittleness:* The expert systems failed to solve the situations beyond the programmed rules.
- *Knowledge acquisition bottleneck:* The transferring of human expertise into the rule-based systems was expensive and time-consuming.
- *Maintenance complications:* Updating these rule-based systems was complicated indeed, as during adding new rules there were always interactions between old rules.

## 3. Machine Learning and Deep Learning (1990 – 2020)

The period from 1990 to 2020 marked a significant evolution in the field of artificial intelligence with the rise of deep learning and machine learning. The focus of the research during this period had shifted from symbolic AI and expert systems to the data-driven approach. Machine learning is an AI application that allows a system to learn and improve on its own without being explicitly programmed. Deep learning is a part of machine learning that relies on artificial neural networks to learn from data. Artificial neural networks are inspired by the human brain and can be utilized to solve a wide range of problems including natural language processing, image recognition, and speech recognition (Google Cloud – Deep learning, Retrieved 12:33, February 21, 2025).

The contemporary understanding of machine learning can be traced back to psychologist Frank Rosenblatt of Cornell University, who developed a machine capable of recognizing letters of the alphabet. This innovation was inspired by the functioning of the human nervous system and is detailed in his 1957 work, "The Perceptron: A Perceiving and Recognizing Automaton" (Fradkov, 2020). In 2006,

Fei-Fei Li, a professor of computer science at Stanford University, played a pivotal role in shifting paradigms within the field. She hypothesized that "AI's main limitation is the data quantity to reflect the real-world scenarios, and that more data will produce better models."

*Table 3. The AI breakthroughs of this period (1990-2020)*

| Year | Developments |
|---|---|
| 1993 | Schmidhuber, a German computer scientist, accomplished a 'Very deep learning' task utilizing a hierarchy of recurrent neural networks, allowing the system to find compact internal representations of long sequences of data across multiple time scales and levels of abstraction. This approach successfully solved the problem requiring over 1,000 subsequent computational layers or stages (Schmidhuber, 1993). |
| 1995 | Support vector machines were utilized for handwritten character recognition, text categorization, and image classification and the algorithm was found to exhibit very fine performance in contrast with other classical algorithms (Cortes et al., 1995). |
| 1995 | The 'No Hands Across America' project was a significant milestone in autonomous driving involving a journey from Pittsburgh, PA, to San Diego, CA, in a 1990 Pontiac Trans Sport minivan by Research scientist Dean Pomerleau and Ph.D. student Todd Jochem from Carnegie Mellon. The vehicle included RALPH (Rapidly Adapting Lateral Position Handler), and some 'optional' equipment called the Navlab 5. The semi-autonomous car was piloted independently for 2,797 miles, about 98.2% of the total journey with a human driver controlling the throttle and brakes (Jochem et al., 1995). |
| 1997 | IBM's Deep Blue was the first computer system to defeat Garry Kasparov, who was then world chess champion, in a six-game marathon under standard tournament controls. Deep Blue's success was credited to its ability to examine 200 million chess positions every second, using 32 processors to perform high-speed computations in parallel (IBM Deep Blue, Retrieved 10:32, February 21, 2025). |
| 1997 | Long Short–Term Memory (LSTM) network architecture improved by addressing the challenge of learning long-term reliance in recurrent neural networks (RNNs). It used special units called constant error carousels and multiplicative gates to maintain a constant error flow control information flow, and improved efficiency (Hochreiter & Schmidhuber, 1997). |
| 1998 | The gradient-based learning was improved and applied for document recognition highlighting the effectiveness of multilayer neural networks trained with the backpropagation algorithm, a gradient-based learning technique (LeCun et al., 1998). |
| 2002 | TD – Gammon, a neural network-based program achieved remarkable success using temporal difference (TD) learning. It trained itself to play backgammon by playing against itself. Starting from a random initial play, the self-teaching methodology of the program resulted in a highly skilled player, which when combined with a shallow lookahead surpassed even the finest human players demonstrating the potential of reinforcement learning and neural networks and complex decision-making tasks (Tesauro, 2002). |
| 2005 | Stanford's robot, Stanley won the DARPA Grand Challenge on October 8, 2005. Stanley, a modified 2004 Volkswagen Touareg R5, was equipped with state-of-the-art AI technologies, including probabilistic reasoning, and machine learning and the software architecture relied heavily on sensor data acquisition, environment modeling, and real-time decision-making. It successfully navigated a 132-mile course through the Mojave Desert in 6 hours, 53 minutes, and 58 seconds, finishing ahead of all other competitors (Thrun et al., 2006). |
| 2009 | ImageNet was published, with 3.2 million annotated photos organized into 5,247 categories and 12 subtrees such as "mammal," "vehicle," "furniture," and so on, where on average over 600 images were collected for each synset (Deng et al., 2009). |
| 2011 | IBM Watson defeated champions Ken Jennings and Brad Rutter in a game of Jeopardy. Watson was created as a question-answer computing system that employed advanced natural language processing, knowledge representation, information retrieval, machine learning, and automated reasoning technologies in the field of open-domain question answering. Watson's architecture, known as DeepQA, allowed it to explore a broad range of hypotheses and their associated evidence, making it a powerful tool for knowledge discovery and problem-solving (Ferrucci, 2012). |
| 2012 | The cat experiment was conducted where the deep neural network was trained to recognize cats from Ten million randomly selected YouTube video thumbnails. The system, which was based on unsupervised learning, learned to distinguish and recognize the cats without labeled data. The program outperformed earlier attempts at unsupervised learning by about 70% (Le, 2013). |
| 2014 | In 2014, Generative Adversarial Networks (GANs) were introduced, which had two neural networks, a generator, and a discriminator. Both networks were trained simultaneously through an adversarial process. The generative model (analogous to counterfeiters) attempts to produce fake data samples, while the discriminative model (analogous to the police) aims to detect whether a sample is real or generated. This minimax game drives both networks to improve their performance, resulting in the production of highly realistic data by the generator. GANs were capable of learning to replicate any data distribution and generate content in any domain, including images, music, and voice (Goodfellow et al., 2014). |

continued on following page

*Table 3. Continued*

| Year | Developments |
|---|---|
| 2015 | The DeepRL (Deep Reinforcement Learning) model successfully learned control policies directly from high-dimensional sensory input via reinforcement learning. The model's only input was raw pixels, and its output was a value function that estimated future rewards. It mastered a varied range of Atari 2600 games to superhuman levels, where Atari games became the usual benchmarks for AI algorithms, and the AI exceeded human players in the majority of them (Mnih et al., 2015). |
| 2016 | AlphaGo was developed by DeepMind to play the game of Go and it defeated the world's top Go player, Lee Sedol. These networks evaluated board positions to predict the winning probability from a given state and to select the most promising moves to play. AlphaGo achieved a 99.8% winning rate against other Go programs and defeated the European Go champion by 5 games to 0 (Silver et al., 2016). The AlphaGo Zero achieved superhuman performance and defeated the Champion AlphaGo with 100 – 0. It used a general reinforcement learning algorithm. It started from random play and learned to master the game by solely relying on the rules of the game, without any human knowledge, and achieved superhuman performance in the Game of Go, chess, and shogi (Japanese chess) (Silver et al., 2017). |
| 2017 | The transformer structure revolutionized deep learning by leveraging the self–attention mechanism, which enabled the model to measure the value of distinct words in a phrase by computing attention scores for each word, regardless of their position, and allowed it to capture long-range dependencies more effectively than conventional recurrent neural networks (RNNs) (Ashish, 2017). |
| 2017 | Libratus, an AI program designed to play heads-up no-limit Texas hold 'em poker marked a significant achievement by defeating four top professional human poker players in a 120,000–hand competition. It analyzed the game's rules and devised its own strategy in an imperfect-information game. It also identified and fixed the potential weakness in the blueprint strategy based on the opponents' gameplay (Brown & Sandholm, 2018). |
| 2018 | The OpenAI Five defeated the amateur human teams at Dota 2 (one of the most difficult and popular esports games in the world). It learned by playing 180 years' worth of games against itself every day, demonstrating AI's potential in sophisticated, real-time strategic games (Open AI research, https://openai.com/index/openai-five/). In July, Open AI introduced Dactyl, a robotic hand that resembles a human hand and was designed to manipulate actual things with unparalleled dexterity. The Dactyl was fully trained in simulation using reinforcement learning techniques before transferring its expertise to the real world. The system used a Shadow Dexterous Hand to perform tasks such as reorienting objects in its palm and its training involved domain randomization in which the robot was exposed to different simulated environments with subtle differences enabling its effective adaption to the real-world conditions (Open AI research Dactyl- https://openai.com/index/learning-dexterity/). |
| 2018 | Google AI language laboratory introduced Bidirectional Encoder Representations from Transformers (BERT). It was designed to understand text context from both directions (left and right). Using deep learning the model predicts the missing word and determines the sentence sequence (Koroteev, 2021). |
| 2019 | DeepMind's AlphaStar defeated a top professional player in StarCraft II, the success of which was attributed to its use of deep neural networks trained directly from the raw game data through supervised and reinforcement learning. It won with a 5 – 0 score against Team Liquid's Grzegorz "MaNa" Komincz, one of the world's strongest professional StarCraft players (Arulkumaran et al., 2019). |
| 2019 | GPT – 2 (Generative Pre-trained Transformer – 2) was introduced, which was a large–scale unsupervised language model with 1.5 billion parameters and was trained on a dataset called Web Text that consists of text from 45 million website links. It was able to perform tasks without any task-specific fine-tuning and delivered a strong performance in tasks like text generation, machine translation, question answering, and summarization (Radford et al., 2019). |

**Source:** Compiled by Author(s).

***Investments in AI during the period:*** During this period, private companies became the primary Investors in AI. Major internet companies invested significant funds and hired leading AI scientists: Google hired Geoffrey Hinton and acquired DeepMind for $500 million in 2014, Facebook hired Yann LeCun, Microsoft Invested $1 billion in OpenAI, DeepMind received investments of $570 million in 2018, $341 million in 2017, and $154 million in 2016 and other companies like Apple, Amazon, Uber, and Tesla made similar investments and hiring strategies. In China, companies like Tencent, Baidu, Alibaba, and Huawei have also announced substantial AI strategic plans (Delipetrev et al., 2020). The annual funding for AI by venture capital firms increased dramatically.

***Issues highlighted during the period:*** The evolution of machine learning and deep learning had revolutionized the field of AI, meantime, exposed to different threats and risks as critical security challenges, including data poisoning, adversarial attacks, privacy leakage, and model theft (Wang et al., 2024), Deepfake (Kietzmann et al., 2020) and also faced the challenges like data availability and interpretability of models.

- *Adversarial attacks:* Adversarial attacks involve input data manipulation to deceive deep learning models and force them to make inaccurate predictions. Such issues can be dangerous in safety-critical applications like medical diagnostics and autonomous vehicles (Security Intelligence, retrieved 6:36, February 21, 2025).
- *Data poisoning:* In this type of attack, adversaries inject harmful data into the training dataset, which makes the model learn incorrect patterns leading the compromises in model integrity and incorrect predictions (Wang et al., 2024).
- *Privacy leakage:* Privacy leakage in machine learning algorithms is one of the critical issues that compromise the confidentiality of personal information as such models are trained on sensitive personal data like health records, personal photos, or transaction history that can inadvertently reveal this information (Pan et al., 2019).
- *Deepfake:* Deepfakes are the creation of highly realistic fake content, including images, videos, and audio using advanced Artificial intelligence and Machine learning techniques, and make it difficult for human observers to distinguish between real and fake content. Deepfakes pose significant risks including identity theft, the spread of misinformation, and reputational damage (Kietzmann et al., 2020).
- *Ethics and fairness:* The ethical and fairness concerns deep learning models concentrate on dealing with the model's prejudice and biases. These algorithms learn from enormous datasets that may be skewed, resulting in unfair outcomes. Such concerns may lead to disparities, particularly in areas like hiring, financing, and criminal justice, where fairness and openness are critical. (Talaei Khoei et al., 2023).
- *Data availability and quality:* The deep learning model requires large amounts of labeled data for training. However, gathering such high-quality labeled data may turn out time-consuming, expensive, or difficult. Approaches such as data augmentation can be utilized to generate huge volumes of data, however they may not always meet the model's requirements. On the contrary, having a small amount of data causes overfitting concerns (Talaei Khoei et al., 2023).

- *Interpretability and explainability:* The models of deep learning pose complexity and difficulty in understanding the workings of the model. As deep neural networks have numerous layers and parameters, their decision-making process is like 'black boxes', making it difficult to interpret how a specific decision is made. Such a lack of transparency hinders trust in the adoption of these models (Talaei Khoei et al., 2023).

## 4. Generative AI and Autonomous AI (2020 – Present)

"Generative AI refers to deep-learning models that can generate high-quality text, images, and other content based on the data they were trained on" (IBM GEN AI, retrieved 6:50, February 21, 2025). These models learn the underlying patterns and the structures from the training data and use them to produce new data. Autonomous intelligence refers to Artificial Intelligence that is capable of acting without human intervention, input, or direct supervision (Nord VPN, retrieved 7:25, February 21, 2025). The introduction of AI applications like ChatGPT (2022) and Google Bard (2023) has provided a wide scope in various sectors through diagnosis assistance, report generation, and tailored explanations.

*Table 4. The important evolutions in generative AI of this period (2020 – present)*

| Year | Developments |
|---|---|
| 2020 | GPT 3, a third-generation autoregressive language model that leverages deep learning to produce human-like text. It was capable of generating a sequence of words, codes, or other information based on an input source known as the prompt, and it was widely used in machine translation, summarization, grammatical correction, question-answering, chatbots, and email composition. It was trained on the unlabeled dataset that comprised texts from Wikipedia and other websites and had 175 billion parameters. The training for this model was conducted on Microsoft Azure's AI supercomputer and at a cost estimated at $12 million (Floridi & Chiriatti, 2020). |
| 2020 | DeepMind's AlphaFold 2 led advancement in protein structure prediction and achieved near X-ray resolution accuracy in the 2020 Critical Assessment of Protein Structure Prediction (CASP 14) competition. It surpassed other protein structure prediction methods, accurately predicting short-loop regions (Stevens & He, 2022). |
| 2020 | Tesla introduced the Full Self-Driving (FSD) Beta program. It extended Tesla's Autopilot from highways to non-highway roads, allowing the car to drive autonomously under the supervision of the driver. This system was classified as an SAE Level 2 partially automated driving system (Nordhoff et al., 2023). |
| 2021 | Open AI introduced DALL·E, a neural network capable of generating images from text descriptions. It was a 12 billion parameter version of GPT – 3 which was specifically trained to generate images from the text descriptions, using a dataset of text–image pairs (Open AI DALL·E, Retrieved 7:10, February 24, 2025). |
| 2021 | Google introduced the Multitask Unified Model (MUM) that leveraged the T5 text-to-text framework and was 1,000 times better than BERT. It was trained across 75 different languages and multiple tasks simultaneously and was capable of understanding language and also generating it (Google AI blog, Retrieved 12:33, February 21, 2025). |
| 2022 | DALL-E 2 was an image generation system created by OpenAI that could generate high-resolution images that combine various concepts and art styles (Ramesh et al., 2022). |
| 2022 | Open Artificial Intelligence(Open AI) introduced an AI chatbot tool called ChatGPT, it was based on the Generative Pre-trained Transformer (GPT) architecture as its foundation. The users were able to interact with the Chatbot by inputting the prompts, and it was capable of producing the results for writing stories, songs, essays, and other things (Haleem et al., 2022). |

continued on following page

*Table 4. Continued*

| Year | Developments |
|---|---|
| 2023 | GPT 4 was introduced, which was capable of handling both images and text, creating text outputs. It was a transformer-based model pre-trained to predict the next token in the document. It exhibited human-level performance on various benchmarks including passing a simulated bar exam with a score around the top 10% of test takers. GPT 4 was used in a wide range of applications like chatbots, translating languages, and summarizing texts (Achiam et al., 2023). |
| 2023 | Google introduced Google Bard, which was a text-based chatbot that used natural language processing and machine learning to provide real-time answers. It helped in retrieving information from different online sources and explaining complex tasks (Aydın, 2023). |
| 2023 | Meta introduced LLaMA (Large Language Model Meta AI), a collection of foundation language models ranging from 7 billion to 65 billion parameters. It was trained on trillions of tokens using publicly available datasets. The model supported multiple languages and excelled in tasks like sentiment analysis, text classification, and language translation (Touvron et al., 2023). |
| 2023 | Microsoft integrated copilot into Microsoft 365, It used natural language processing to understand commands and generate the relevant content and enhanced productivity of the Microsoft 365 tool with AI-powered assistance. It provides real-time assistance like analyzing the document, drafting the document, managing emails, and organizing notes (Microsoft Copilot, Retrieved 7:25, February 22, 2025). |
| 2024 | Google DeepMind released Gemini 1.5 Pro and Gemini 1.5 Flash, members of the Gemini 1.5 family, with notable improvements in sparse and dense scaling, training efficiency, distillation, and serving infrastructure. These models demonstrated better reasoning, planning, multi-linguality, function calling, and long-context processing capabilities. One of the most important advances in the Gemini 1.5 line was their capacity to process very long contexts, remembering and reasoning over subtle details over as many as 10 million tokens—unmatched among modern large language models (LLMs). This allowed for the processing of entire document libraries, hours of video, and almost five days of audio (Team et al., 2024). |
| 2024 | Sora was an OpenAI text-to-video generative AI model, launched in February 2024, that produced videos based on text prompts, which can be employed to create realistic or fictional scenes and mimic the physical world. It had applications in areas like filmmaking, learning, and advertising (Liu et al., 2024). |
| 2025 | In January 2025 DeepSeek released the chatbot, which was based on the DeepSeek-R1 model and was capable of answering questions, writing computer programs similar to other Chatbots, and solving logical problems. The DeepSeek surpassed ChatGPT to become the most downloaded freeware app on Apple's App Store in the U.S.A. It was trained in around 55 days and for US$5.58 million and claimed to have needed only about 2000 Graphics processing units (GPUs) namely the H800 series chip from Nvidia (Times of India news on DeepSeek, Retrieved 7:27, April 12, 2025). |

**Source:** Compiled by Author(s)

## FUTURE PREDICTIONS

Generative AI is expected to have an impact on a broad range of sectors like manufacturing, architecture, engineering, aerospace, medical, pharmaceutical, media, interior design, automotive, electronics, defense, and energy by enhancing core operations through the use of AI models (Gartner – Impact of AI in future, retrieved 6:06, February 22, 2025). The research conducted by Okeleke, and Patrick Azuka provides a scope of AI in Predictive analytics for market trends. The information published on the Times of India's website dated Oct 25, 2023, states that AI's advancements are expected to cover a wide variety of sectors like healthcare, Education, creativity, Ethics, and Automobiles (The Times of India, October 25, 2023). Gartner Inc. predicted that the utilization of generative AI will have a significant impact on enterprises in the future and stated that (Gartner – Impact of AI in future, retrieved 6:06, February 22, 2025):

- By 2025, the proportion of enterprises embracing an AI-augmented development and validation strategy is expected to rise to 30%, compared to just 5% in 2021.
- The generative design AI, by 2026, is expected to take care of 60% of the design work for new websites and mobile apps.
- By 2026, more than 100 million people will enlist robo-colleagues to assist with their work.
- By 2027, AI will create nearly 15% of new applications on autopilot without any human intervention.

As stated by Bernard Marr (2024) in Forbes (Forbes Media LLC), in the article "The Future of Generative AI: 6 Predictions Everyone Should Know About," generative AI is expected to make significant advancements in different domains, and forecasted the following breakthroughs (Forbes – Future of Gen AI, retrieved 7:00, February 22, 2025):

- *Multi-Modal AI:* Artificial intelligence systems are evolving to become more multi-tasking, allowing them to simultaneously see, hear, speak, read, and generate content. Tools like DALL-E 3 can generate text within images, and ChatGPT has also included voice and vision functionality. Generative AIs are expected to advance the development of multi-modal AIs that are capable of generating content in real-time in multiple formats, similar to the processes of the human brain.
- *Interactive AI:* The role of AI is evolving from generating content to performing tasks. Mustafa Suleyman of DeepMind envisions "interactive AI," with bots not only responding to questions but also assigning tasks. In the future, AI might be capable of independently developing apps, managing projects, or even planning trips by reserving hotels and arranging restaurant bookings that consider dietary preferences.
- *AI-equipped Robots:* Generative AI enhances cognitive and creative tasks, but when combined with robotics, it could revolutionize physical labor. AI-powered robots might fill roles in factories, construction sites, retail environments, and the hospitality sector, potentially transforming entire industries.
- *AI for Social Good:* Generative AI has a significant potential for addressing global challenges like climate change, inequality, hunger, and healthcare. By increasing agricultural productivity, predicting epidemics, and expanding the availability of mental health support, AI can be viewed as a revolutionary instrument for social advancement.
- *Regulation and Oversight:* The potential threats of AI, including misinformation and autonomous weapons, require regulatory action. Some oversight

is developing, such as Meta's requirement that political ads generated by AI disclose their origins. However, formal regulations and ethics guidelines are needed to ensure the responsible and safe use of AI.

- *AI Delegation and the Future of Work:* Through the automation of repetitive tasks, AI will enable humans to focus on more strategic and creative pursuits. Although certain jobs may disappear, numerous others will be upgraded. Workers in the future will need to excel at delegating tasks to AI—deciding which tasks should be given to machines and which work to do manually.

## European Union Artificial Intelligence Act

The European Union (EU) enacted the Artificial Intelligence (AI) Act in 2024 which was the first substantial AI regulations law. The legislation targets harmonizing the rules on AI within the EU to make sure that artificially intelligent systems are created and used safely and reliably. The AI Act uses a risk-based approach to identify AI systems based on their risk to society. High-risk AI technology must meet tight restrictions, yet some AI activities, such as cognitive behavior manipulation and social scoring, are disallowed. The law centers on reliability, openness, and responsibility in AI technologies. (EU - AI Act, 2025).

## Relevance of Artificial Intelligence to Business

The evolution of AI and ML has brought a dramatic change in traditional business practices and activities like predictive analytics, Customer relationship management, chatbots and virtual assistants, supply chain optimization, Fraud detection and security, Human resources, and recruitment leading to the efficiencies in business operations, enhanced customer experience, Cost efficiency, Privacy and Ethical considerations, and skill and workforce transformation (Chowdhury, 2024). These applications are explained below:

- *Predictive analytics:* AI helps businesses harness the power of predictive analytics, thereby predicting future trends and behaviors based on historical data. This application is very useful in forecasting demand, predicting the financial market, and planning maintenance strategies in industries like manufacturing (Chowdhury, 2024).
- *Customer Relationship Management:* The incorporation of AI into CRM systems improves customer experience by providing personalized interactions. The AI algorithm, by analyzing the customer data, helps the business to tailor their services, predict the needs of the customer, and build strong customer relationships (Chowdhury, 2024).

- *Chatbots and virtual assistants:* Businesses are leveraging chatbots and virtual assistants to streamline communication and improve customer service, thereby helping to achieve operational efficiency. These applications help businesses in real-time interaction with customers, addressing routine inquiries, and providing support (Chowdhury, 2024).
- *Supply chain optimization:* AI technologies help make the supply chain leaner and more efficient by optimizing the processes and reducing wastage. AI helps in reducing the time needed for decisions. Process automation reduces the requirement of human resources for repetitive tasks and provides real-time guidance to help improve capacity utilization rates (Helo & Hao, 2022).
- *Fraud detection and security:* AI helps in detecting unusual patterns and potential threats in financial institutions. It identifies fraudulent activities, protects against cyber threats, and ensures integrity in financial transactions (Chowdhury, 2024).
- *Human resource management:* AI in human resource management enhances productivity by understanding and predicting human behavior, offering value through HR analytics. AI-enabled HR software collects and analyzes employee data to make informed decisions involving strategic workforce capability and performance measurement. It aids in recruitment processes, selection of candidates suitable for jobs, decision-making regarding hiring, and making recommendations for an appropriate salary, thus helping organizations gain a competitive edge (Chowdhury et al., 2023).

## Artificial Intelligence and Management Education

The ongoing emergence of knowledge in the economy is leading to a mismatch between the rate of change in the business curriculum and the rate of change in the desired skill set by employers. With the evolution of AI, companies need employees who can understand AI concepts and methods and use such knowledge to manage the AI-augmented workspace and collaborate with AI agents (Ransbotham et al., 2017). While fields like computer science and engineering have long been offering AI courses, students from the management field are also expected to be relevant in the age of AI. Equipping them with AI knowledge and skills as part of their degree program can help them improve their chance of employment (Stine et al., 2019). Thus, the emergence of AI demands a change in the existing paradigm of business education concerning how and what is delivered in the classroom. AI is increasingly impacting many aspects of business, including areas like information technology, human resources, marketing, and finance. Business students must be capable of gathering proper or correct information and applying logical reasoning and appropriate problem-solving methodology to analyze real-world business problems. AI is becoming a crucial tool in this process. There is a necessity to switch from the silos of focusing on specialized managerial functions in business schools. Ackoff stated in the inaugural issue of the Academy of Management Learning and Education, "There is no such thing as a marketing problem or a financial problem or a production problem. These are points of view, not kinds of problems" (Detrick, 2002).

One of the key reasons for this shift is the increasing focus on overall business processes rather than narrowly focused functions. This is because the business operates through numerous interconnected business processes. For example, launching a new product involves collaboration from departments like R&D, production, information systems, accounting, finance, and marketing, among others. The business landscape today is far more competitive compared to previous decades. Factors like deregulation, globalization, and the internet have created a competitive landscape where companies produce similar products and employ similar technologies. Hence, companies need to differentiate their business processes. A key part of this differentiation is utilizing business analytics effectively, which is important for better decision-making. AI is a rapidly growing science that handles multiple challenges at once. It meets the rigorous analytical requirements expected by business schools while also solving practical challenges. It focuses on business processes, which encompass a variety of activities. This focus is critical since it is one of the few opportunities for organizations to differentiate themselves and create a competitive advantage. Employers value the capacity to communicate with data above all else. The second most valuable ability is data management and statistics using spreadsheets. Employers continue to choose students with strong conventional skills and the ability to effectively express technological material (Sollosy & McInerney, 2022).

Data is everywhere. With advances in technology, particularly AI, data collection is growing rapidly. Data analytics and AI are transforming many industries. Companies today are looking to hire people who possess the ability to handle big datasets to assist their business decision-making processes. This has led to a higher demand for individuals with these skills in the job market (Clayton & Clopton, 2019). Ultimately, all students, irrespective of their field of study, need to acquire knowledge of AI and data analytics. Students must understand how and when to use data analytics tools. There's a significant demand for enhancing data ability in students who aren't majoring in data analytics. This demand exists for all majors, including accounting, entrepreneurship, finance, management, and marketing. Business schools are facing a high demand for people skilled in three key areas of business decision-making: prescriptive, descriptive, and predictive analytics. AI is an interdisciplinary field that requires the integration of database systems, data management, data warehousing, network analysis, natural language processing, social networking, statistical analysis, and optimization. These skills are often part of a business curriculum. The primary opportunity for business schools is to prepare students to comprehend business requirements, interpret AI-analyzed big data, and lead data-driven decision-making within their enterprises. To make meaningful contributions and aid decision-makers, experts must first comprehend business concerns. This understanding is critical for developing appropriate analytical solutions. Professionals must listen to and understand business needs, as well as be familiar with the company's goals. They require expertise in finance, marketing, accounting, transportation and logistics, and operations management. Additionally, they should also be able to successfully communicate and work with the rest of the business team. This is only possible if you work as part of a team rather than on your own. Organizations must foster an environment of informed decision-making. Communication skills are vital for implementing such a culture. AI analysts must describe their findings in terms that their business companions can grasp. They must transmit the appropriate message and lessons gained so that the entire organization may benefit from the information. In the context of business education, AI entails understanding, interpreting, thinking, and acting to achieve organizational goals. Management practitioners derive insights from data and algorithms developed by technologists. This viewpoint suggests that training for these talents should be part of a business school. However, the specific department and talents required may vary depending on how industries apply these skills. AI is frequently used across multiple departments, including finance, marketing, R&D, and logistics. As a result, these abilities should be covered in all functional areas taught in the institution (Chiang et al. 2012).

## CONCLUSION

From the Turing test to today's advanced generative models, Artificial intelligence has demonstrated dramatic improvements. With the evolution in the time frame, AI-related technologies not only transformed industries but also had a strong impact on business, education, healthcare, and other sectors by enabling automation, productivity gains, and data-driven decision-making. The developments have also seen pitfalls in terms of funding and interest in the early years as well as the serious challenges to which it is vulnerable today. Companies must learn and embrace these technologies to differentiate themselves from the pack in today's competitive business world, while in management education it is necessary for prospective managers to be trained to deal with and harness such complex technologies. The future of AI is not only about automation but also about how human beings and smart systems work together to create new avenues for innovation and advancement.

## REFERENCES


Achiam, J., Adler, S., Agarwal, S., Ahmad, L., Akkaya, I., Aleman, F. L., . . . McGrew, B. (2023). Gpt-4 technical report. *arXiv preprint arXiv:2303.08774.*

Act, E. U.-A. I. https://digital-strategy.ec.europa.eu/en/policies/regulatory-framework-ai, Retrieved 11:00, February 22, 2025.

ALPAC, L. (1966). Machines: Computers in Translation and Linguistics, Report by the Automatic Language Processing Advisory Committee, Division of Behavioral Sciences. *National Academy of Sciences, National Research Council, Publication, 1416.*

Arulkumaran, K., Cully, A., & Togelius, J. (2019, July). Alphastar: An evolutionary computation perspective. In *Proceedings of the genetic and evolutionary computation conference companion* (pp. 314-315). DOI: 10.1145/3319619.3321894

Ashish, V. (2017). Attention is all you need. *Advances in Neural Information Processing Systems*, *30*, I.

Aydın, Ö. (2023). Google Bard generated literature review: Metaverse. *Journal of AI*, *7*(1), 1–14. DOI: 10.61969/jai.1311271

Brown, N., & Sandholm, T. (2018). Superhuman AI for heads-up no-limit poker: Libratus beats top professionals. *Science*, *359*(6374), 418–424. DOI: 10.1126/science.aao1733 PMID: 29249696

Chiang, R. H., Goes, P., & Stohr, E. A. (2012). Business intelligence and analytics education, and program development: A unique opportunity for the information systems discipline. [TMIS]. *ACM Transactions on Management Information Systems*, *3*(3), 1–13. DOI: 10.1145/2361256.2361257

Chowdhury, R. H.Rakibul Hasan Chowdhury. (2024). The evolution of business operations: Unleashing the potential of Artificial Intelligence, Machine Learning, and Blockchain. *World Journal of Advanced Research and Reviews*, *22*(3), 2135–2147. DOI: 10.30574/wjarr.2024.22.3.1992

Chowdhury, S., Dey, P., Joel-Edgar, S., Bhattacharya, S., Rodriguez-Espindola, O., Abadie, A., & Truong, L. (2023). Unlocking the value of artificial intelligence in human resource management through AI capability framework. *Human Resource Management Review*, *33*(1), 100899. DOI: 10.1016/j.hrmr.2022.100899

Clayton, P. R., & Clopton, J. (2019). Business curriculum redesign: Integrating data analytics. *Journal of Education for Business, 94*(1), 57–63. DOI: 10.1080/08832323.2018.1502142

Cordeschi, R. (2006). AI's half century. On the thresholds of the Dartmouth conference. *IA Retrospettiva, 3*, 1–2.

Cortes, C., & Vapnik, V. (1995). Support-vector networks. *Machine Learning, 20*(3), 273–297. DOI: 10.1023/A:1022627411411

Delipetrev, B., Tsinaraki, C., & Kostic, U. (2020). Historical evolution of artificial intelligence.

Deng, J., Dong, W., Socher, R., Li, L. J., Li, K., & Fei-Fei, L. (2009, June). Imagenet: A large-scale hierarchical image database. In *2009 IEEE conference on computer vision and pattern recognition* (pp. 248-255). Ieee. DOI: 10.1109/CVPR.2009.5206848

Detrick, G. (2002). Russell L Ackoff: Interview by Glenn Detrick. *Academy of Management Learning & Education, 1*(1), 56–63. DOI: 10.5465/amle.2002.7373640

Ferrucci, D. A. (2012). Introduction to "this is watson". *IBM Journal of Research and Development, 56*(3.4), 1-1.

Floridi, L., & Chiriatti, M. (2020). GPT-3: Its nature, scope, limits, and consequences. *Minds and Machines, 30*(4), 681–694. DOI: 10.1007/s11023-020-09548-1

Forbes – Future of Gen AI. https://www.forbes.com/sites/bernardmarr/2024/03/05/the-future-of-generative-ai-6-predictions-everyone-should-know-about/, retrieved 7:00, February 22, 2025.

Fradkov, A. L. (2020). Early history of machine learning. *IFAC-PapersOnLine, 53*(2), 1385–1390. DOI: 10.1016/j.ifacol.2020.12.1888

Gartner – Impact of AI in future, https://www.gartner.com/en/topics/generative-ai#:~:text=of%20Gen%20AI-,Which%20industries%20are%20most%20impacted%20by%20generative%20AI%3F,-Generative%20AI%20will, retrieved 6:06, February 22, 2025.

Goodfellow, I., Pouget-Abadie, J., Mirza, M., Xu, B., Warde-Farley, D., Ozair, S., & Bengio, Y. (2014). Generative adversarial nets. *Advances in Neural Information Processing Systems*, •••, 27.

Google, A. I. Blog. (2021). Introducing MUM: A new AI milestone for understanding information. https://blog.google/products/search/introducing-mum/, Retrieved 12:33, February 21, 2025.

Haleem, A., Javaid, M., & Singh, R. P. (2022). An era of ChatGPT as a significant futuristic support tool: A study on features, abilities, and challenges. *BenchCouncil transactions on benchmarks, standards and evaluations, 2*(4), 100089.

Hayes-Roth, F., Waterman, D. A., & Lenat, D. B. (1983). *Building expert systems.* Addison-Wesley Longman Publishing Co., Inc.

Helo, P., & Hao, Y. (2022). Artificial intelligence in operations management and supply chain management: An exploratory case study. *Production Planning and Control, 33*(16), 1573–1590. DOI: 10.1080/09537287.2021.1882690

Hochreiter, S., & Schmidhuber, J. (1997). Long short-term memory. *Neural Computation, 9*(8), 1735–1780. DOI: 10.1162/neco.1997.9.8.1735 PMID: 9377276

Hopfield, J. J. (1982). Neural networks and physical systems with emergent collective computational abilities. *Proceedings of the National Academy of Sciences of the United States of America, 79*(8), 2554–2558. DOI: 10.1073/pnas.79.8.2554 PMID: 6953413

IBM Deep Blue https://www.ibm.com/history/deep-blue, Retrieved 10:32, February 21, 2025.

IBM GEN AI. https://research.ibm.com/blog/what-is-generative-AI#:~:text=is%20generative%20AI%3F-,Generative%20AI%20refers%20to%20deep%2Dlearning%20models%20that%20can%20generate%20high%2Dquality%20text%2C%20images%2C%20and%20other%20content%20based%20on%20the%20data%20they%20were%20trained%20on.,-Explore%20what%20you, retrieved 6:50, February 21, 2025.

Jannai, D., Meron, A., Lenz, B., Levine, Y., & Shoham, Y. (2023). Human or not? A gamified approach to the Turing test. *arXiv preprint arXiv:2305.20010.*

Jochem, T., Pomerleau, D., Kumar, B., & Armstrong, J. (1995, September). PANS: A portable navigation platform. In *Proceedings of the Intelligent Vehicles' 95. Symposium* (pp. 107-112). IEEE. DOI: 10.1109/IVS.1995.528266

Kietzmann, J., Lee, L. W., McCarthy, I. P., & Kietzmann, T. C. (2020). Deepfakes: Trick or treat? *Business Horizons, 63*(2), 135–146. DOI: 10.1016/j.bushor.2019.11.006

Koroteev, M. V. (2021). BERT: a review of applications in natural language processing and understanding. *arXiv preprint arXiv:2103.11943.*

Krizhevsky, A., Sutskever, I., & Hinton, G. E. (2012). Imagenet classification with deep convolutional neural networks. *Advances in Neural Information Processing Systems*, •••, 25.

Le, Q. V. (2013, May). *Building high-level features using large scale unsupervised learning. In 2013 IEEE international conference on acoustics, speech and signal processing*. IEEE.

LeCun, Y., Boser, B., Denker, J. S., Henderson, D., Howard, R. E., Hubbard, W., & Jackel, L. D. (1989). Backpropagation applied to handwritten zip code recognition. *Neural Computation, 1*(4), 541–551. DOI: 10.1162/neco.1989.1.4.541

LeCun, Y., Bottou, L., Bengio, Y., & Haffner, P. (1998). Gradient-based learning applied to document recognition. *Proceedings of the IEEE, 86*(11), 2278–2324. DOI: 10.1109/5.726791

Liu, Y., Zhang, K., Li, Y., Yan, Z., Gao, C., Chen, R., . . . Sun, L. (2024). Sora: A review on background, technology, limitations, and opportunities of large vision models. *arXiv preprint arXiv:2402.17177.*

Michie, D. (1963). Experiments on the mechanization of game-learning Part I. Characterization of the model and its parameters. *The Computer Journal, 6*(3), 232–236. DOI: 10.1093/comjnl/6.3.232

Microsoft Copilot https://www.microsoft.com/en-us/microsoft-365/blog/2025/01/16/copilot-is-now-included-in-microsoft-365-personal-and-family/, Retrieved 7:25, February 22, 2025.

Mnih, V., Kavukcuoglu, K., Silver, D., Rusu, A. A., Veness, J., Bellemare, M. G., ... & Hassabis, D. (2015). Human-level control through deep reinforcement learning. *nature, 518*(7540), 529-533.

Moravec, H. P. (1983). The Stanford cart and the CMU rover. *Proceedings of the IEEE, 71*(7), 872–884. DOI: 10.1109/PROC.1983.12684

Newell, A. (1962). The processes of creative thinking. *Contemporary approaches to creative thinking/Atherton.*

Nord, V. P. N. https://nordvpn.com/cybersecurity/glossary/autonomous-intelligence/#:~:text=Autonomous%20intelligence%20is%20artificial%20intelligence,care%20robots%20for%20the%20elderly., Retrieved 7:25, February 21, 2025.

Nordhoff, S., Lee, J. D., Calvert, S. C., Berge, S., Hagenzieker, M., & Happee, R. (2023). (Mis-) use of standard Autopilot and Full Self-Driving (FSD) Beta: Results from interviews with users of Tesla's FSD Beta. *Frontiers in Psychology, 14,* 1101520. DOI: 10.3389/fpsyg.2023.1101520 PMID: 36910772

Open, A. I. DALL·E, https://openai.com/index/dall-e/, Retrieved 7:10, February 24, 2025

Open AI research. Five, https://openai.com/index/openai-five/, Retrieved 7:27, February 24, 2025

Open AI research Dactyl. https://openai.com/index/learning-dexterity/, Retrieved 7:27, February 24, 2025

Pan, X., Wang, W., Zhang, X., Li, B., Yi, J., & Song, D. (2019). How you act tells a lot: Privacy-leakage attack on deep reinforcement learning. *arXiv preprint arXiv:1904.11082*.

Quinlan, J. R. (1986). Induction of decision trees. *Machine Learning*, *1*(1), 81–106. DOI: 10.1023/A:1022643204877

Radford, A., Wu, J., Child, R., Luan, D., Amodei, D., & Sutskever, I. (2019). Language models are unsupervised multitask learners. *OpenAI blog, 1*(8), 9.

Ramesh, A., Dhariwal, P., Nichol, A., Chu, C., & Chen, M. (2022). Hierarchical text-conditional image generation with clip latents. *arXiv preprint arXiv:2204.06125, 1*(2), 3.

Ransbotham, S., Kiron, D., Gerbert, P., & Reeves, M. (2017). Reshaping business with artificial intelligence: Closing the gap between ambition and action. *MIT Sloan Management Review*, *59*(1).

Raphael, B. (1972). *Robot Research at Stanford Research Institute*. Stanford University.

Rosenblatt, F. (1961). *Principles of neurodynamics. perceptrons and the theory of brain mechanisms.* Cornell Aeronautical Lab Inc Buffalo NY. DOI: 10.21236/AD0256582

Rouchy, P. (2006). Aspects of PROLOG History: Logic Programming and Professional Dynamics. *Blekinge Institute of Technology, Sweden).(English). TeamEthno-Online*, (2), 85-100.

Rumelhart, D. E., Hinton, G. E., & Williams, R. J. (1985, September). *Learning internal representations by error propagation.*

Samuel, A. L. (1960). Programming computers to play games. [). Elsevier.]. *Advances in Computers*, *1*, 165–192. DOI: 10.1016/S0065-2458(08)60608-7

Schmidhuber, J. (1993). Habilitation thesis: System modeling and optimization. *Credit assignment across the equivalent of 1200 layers in an RNN*, 150.

Shortliffe, E. H., Davis, R., Axline, S. G., Buchanan, B. G., Green, C. C., & Cohen, S. N. (1975). Computer-based consultations in clinical therapeutics: Explanation and rule acquisition capabilities of the MYCIN system. *Computers and Biomedical Research, an International Journal*, *8*(4), 303–320. DOI: 10.1016/0010-4809(75)90009-9 PMID: 1157471

Silver, D., Huang, A., Maddison, C. J., Guez, A., Sifre, L., Van Den Driessche, G., ... & Hassabis, D. (2016). Mastering the game of Go with deep neural networks and tree search. *nature, 529*(7587), 484-489.

Silver, D., Schrittwieser, J., Simonyan, K., Antonoglou, I., Huang, A., Guez, A., ... & Hassabis, D. (2017). Mastering the game of go without human knowledge. *nature, 550*(7676), 354-359.

Sollosy, M., & McInerney, M. (2022). Artificial intelligence and business education: What should be taught. *International Journal of Management Education*, *20*(3), 100720. DOI: 10.1016/j.ijme.2022.100720

Steele, G. L., & Gabriel, R. P. (1996). The evolution of Lisp. In *History of programming languages---II* (pp. 233-330). DOI: 10.1145/234286.1057818

Stevens, A. O., & He, Y. (2022). Benchmarking the accuracy of AlphaFold 2 in loop structure prediction. *Biomolecules*, *12*(7), 985. DOI: 10.3390/biom12070985 PMID: 35883541

Stine, J., Trumbore, A., Woll, T., & Sambucetti, H. (2019). Implications of artificial intelligence on business schools and lifelong learning. *Final Report at Academic Leadership Group*, 19-2.

Talaei Khoei, T., Ould Slimane, H., & Kaabouch, N. (2023). Deep learning: Systematic review, models, challenges, and research directions. *Neural Computing & Applications*, *35*(31), 23103–23124. DOI: 10.1007/s00521-023-08957-4

Team, G., Georgiev, P., Lei, V. I., Burnell, R., Bai, L., Gulati, A., . . . Batsaikhan, B. O. (2024). Gemini 1.5: Unlocking multimodal understanding across millions of tokens of context. *arXiv preprint arXiv:2403.05530.*

Tesauro, G. (2002). Programming backgammon using self-teaching neural nets. *Artificial Intelligence*, *134*(1-2), 181–199. DOI: 10.1016/S0004-3702(01)00110-2

Thrun, S., Montemerlo, M., Dahlkamp, H., Stavens, D., Aron, A., Diebel, J., Fong, P., Gale, J., Halpenny, M., Hoffmann, G., Lau, K., Oakley, C., Palatucci, M., Pratt, V., Stang, P., Strohband, S., Dupont, C., Jendrossek, L.-E., Koelen, C., & Mahoney, P. (2006). Stanley: The robot that won the DARPA Grand Challenge. *Journal of Field Robotics*, *23*(9), 661–692. DOI: 10.1002/rob.20147

Touvron, H., Lavril, T., Izacard, G., Martinet, X., Lachaux, M. A., Lacroix, T., . . . Lample, G. (2023). Llama: Open and efficient foundation language models. *arXiv preprint arXiv:2302.13971.*

Turing, A. M. (2009). *Computing machinery and intelligence.* Springer Netherlands. DOI: 10.1007/978-1-4020-6710-5_3

Wang, T., Bi, Z., Zhang, Y., Liu, M., Hsieh, W., Feng, P., . . . Niu, Q. (2024). Deep Learning Model Security: Threats and Defenses. *arXiv preprint arXiv:2412.08969.*

Watkins, C. J. C. H. (1989). Learning from delayed rewards.

Weizenbaum, J. (1966). ELIZA—A computer program for the study of natural language communication between man and machine. *Communications of the ACM, 9*(1), 36–45. DOI: 10.1145/365153.365168

# Chapter 2
# AI Innovations in Higher Education and Management of Students

**Sunil Kumar**
https://orcid.org/0000-0002-2362-1972
*Shoolini University, India*

**Komal Thakur**
*Shoolini University, India*

**Dushyanth Kumar**
https://orcid.org/0000-0002-9483-9274
*Lovely Professional University, India*

## ABSTRACT

*This chapter will explore Artificial Intelligence innovation and management in Higher Education. Artificial Intelligence (AI) is a pivotal technology that profoundly affects the learner's experience. Ethical concerns such as bias, fair use, privacy, and data security are paramount when implementing AI in Higher Education. Educational institutions and platforms are utilizing AI tools for teaching and student evaluation. AI is notably enhancing the efficiency and outcomes of the educational system. This study explores the thematic and conceptual development of AI in Higher Education and emphasizes the role of ethics in its implementation and development. The analysis indicates that all stakeholders in higher education increasingly recognize the importance of ethical applications and tools in AI.*

DOI: 10.4018/979-8-3373-2150-9.ch002

## INTRODUCTION

Lockdowns gave birth to work-from-home culture across many industries. Digital technologies took center stage and helped students, working professionals, and gig workers to continue their education/learning, even during the lockdown. Mobile devices, along with the internet, are changing the education landscape. Artificial Intelligence is at the center stage of providing superior learning experience to learners, among many other educational technologies. Artificial Intelligence (AI) is not a new term. John McCarthy introduced it in the mid-1950s at a conference on the Dartmouth College campus. John McCarthy is also widely known as the father of AI. Alan Turing, a mathematician, proposed a test (known as the Turing Test) that measured a machine's ability to repeat actions to a level the same as a human being. AI is a subset of computer science focusing on machine-driven intelligence (i.e., non-humane).

AI has been of interest to scientists. In the current century, also termed by some people as the century of the mind, AI applications are being seen in many areas – driverless cars, self-healing cyber security systems, Robots extracting data elements from scanned images, interpreting and analyzing, and natural language processing. AI in education is just the tip of the iceberg, and AI has enormous potential to enable learners. According to Klutka et al. (2018), the goals of AI in education are to increase outcomes, access, and retention and to lower costs and time. Zawacki-Richter et al. (2019), in their review of published research papers, classified that AI in education will be used in four key areas: profiling and prediction, intelligent tutoring systems, assessment and evaluation, and adaptive and personalization. These indicate that AI will have a role in content presentation, content management, testing of content comprehension (assessment), learning analytics, prediction, and personalization. Many factors impact learning, such as appropriate content, learner motivation, skill level, time available, access/readiness to/of facilities/infrastructure, and emotional state of the learner.

El-Seoud et al. (2014) studied the use of e-learning in higher studies. Studies were done at Carnegie Mellon University (CMU), America. Their research showed that the results of e-learning students were better than those who were studying traditionally. El-Seoud et al. (2014) did the study across five years (2004-2009). There was a rise in 12-14% annual student enrollment for online courses. The benefit of online courses is that learners can study from anywhere and anytime. E-learning is transforming the educational sector. Priatna et al (2020) focused on essential factors that are key to successful e-learning. The key success factors were grouped into three categories–Organization, Technology, and Human Resources. Availability, Reliability, Accessibility, Usability, and Content are critical components of technology that enable learner learning. Learners' knowledge, skills, and attitudes are categorized under human resources.

The role of Artificial Intelligence (AI) in education has gained significant attention in recent years. AI has the potential to transform education by providing personalized and adaptive learning, automating administrative tasks, and enabling efficient feedback mechanisms. The application of AI in education can enhance the learner's experience by creating engaging and immersive learning experiences that cater to the individual needs of the learners. The use of AI in education has gained significant attention in recent years. AI-based tutoring systems can provide personalized and adaptive learning experiences. These systems can analyze learner data and provide customized learning paths based on the learner's strengths and weaknesses. Additionally, AI can help educators to create an engaging learning environment by creating immersive learning experiences. For example, virtual reality (VR) and augmented reality (AR) can be used to create immersive learning experiences that enhance the learner's experience.

The application of AI in education has evolved significantly since its inception in the mid-20th century. Initially, AI in education was focused on basic automation, such as grading systems and adaptive learning environments that responded to student inputs. One of the earliest AI systems in education was the "PLATO" computer-based education system developed in the 1960s. It used a rudimentary form of AI to provide instructional content to learners based on their responses to quiz questions.

As AI technology advanced, so did its potential applications in education. In the late 1990s and early 2000s, intelligent tutoring systems (ITS) such as Cognitive Tutors and AutoTutor began to emerge. These systems utilize AI to adapt educational content to individual student's needs and performance levels, providing personalized feedback and hints during the learning process. These early efforts were foundational in demonstrating the potential of AI to tailor education to students' individual needs.

By the 2010s, AI applications expanded beyond adaptive learning systems to encompass many functions, from chatbots that assist students in navigating administrative processes to predictive analytics systems designed to identify at-risk students and improve retention rates. With advancements in machine learning, natural language processing (NLP), and big data analytics, AI systems are now more capable of supporting and enhancing teaching and learning in higher education.

## Evolution of AI in Education

The evolution of AI in education has occurred through four distinct stages:

1. Early Foundations (1950s-1970s): In this phase, the use of computers in education began with simple Computer-Assisted Learning (CAL) tools like PLATO and LOGO. These systems were designed for repetitive tasks and basic drills in subjects such as math and programming, enabling students to practice and repeat lessons on computers.
2. Intelligent Tutoring Systems (1980s-1990s): This stage introduced systems like SCHOLAR and GUIDON, which used AI expert systems to adapt learning based on the student's responses. These tools were able to simulate human tutors by modifying instructions based on learners' inputs. They provided a more personalized learning experience compared to earlier static systems.
3. Machine Learning & Data-Driven Education (2000s): With the rise of machine learning, AI systems such as ALEKS and Knewton became popular. These platforms leveraged student data to recommend personalized learning paths and provide predictive analytics for academic performance. This allowed institutions to identify struggling students and improve course outcomes in real-time.Moder
4. AI in Education (2010s–Present): Today, AI is deeply integrated into education through advanced technologies like Duolingo, ChatGPT, Gradescope, and Khanmigo. These tools offer virtual learning assistants, instant grading, essay feedback, generative AI-powered content, and predictive tools for student success. Education has become more personalized, efficient, and accessible globally.

*Figure 1. Stages of technologically enhanced education.*

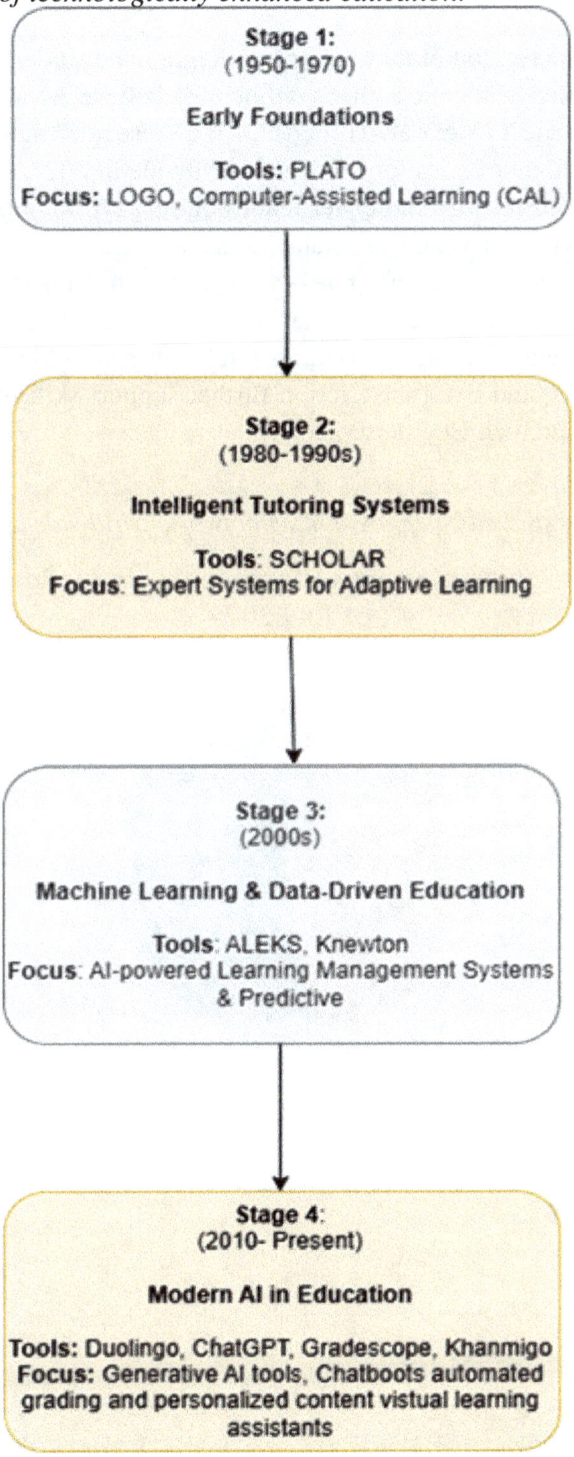

## Global Perspective of AI in Education

A 2023 U.S. survey found that 85% of undergraduate students prefer AI tools developed by trusted academic sources, while 65% believe AI will enhance learning rather than harm it (McGraw-Hill, 2023). The research highlights the top AI use cases among higher education students worldwide in 2024. The most popular application is AI for resume and cover letter building (76%), emphasizing career preparation. Tools like AI writing assistants, personalized content recommendations, and research tools each have a usage rate of 66%, aiding students in academic writing and tailored learning. Adaptive assessments (62%) and AI tutoring chatbots (59%) enhance personalized learning experiences, while other tools like mock interviews, career assessments, and live transcription further support skills development and accessibility (On EdTech Newsletter, 2024).

*Figure 2. Share of students using AI for schoolwork worldwide as of July 2024.*

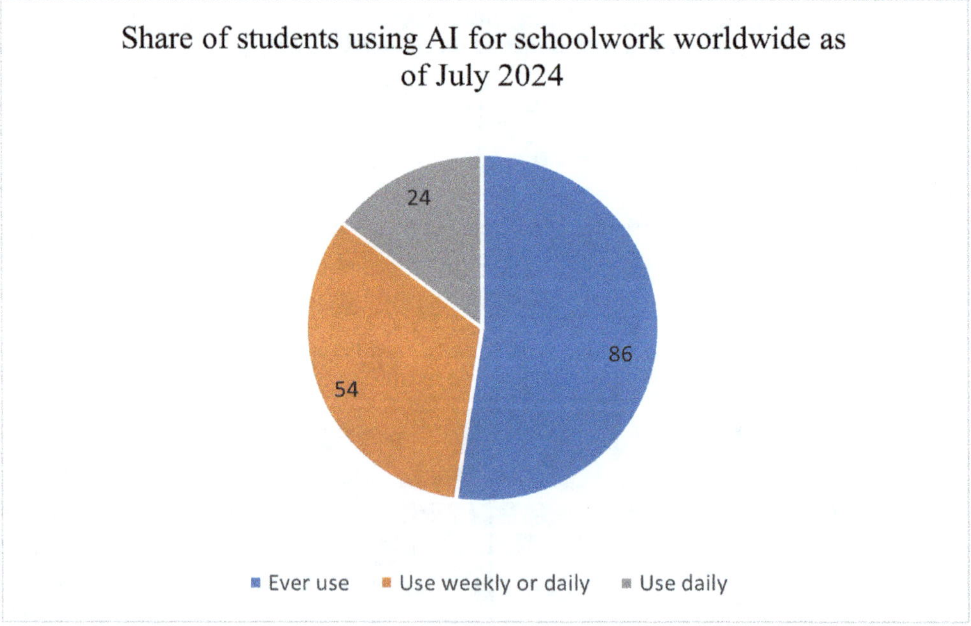


*Source:* Global student AI usage for schoolwork 2024 | Statista

## Benefits of AI in Education

AI has several benefits in education, including enhancing personalized learning, automating administrative tasks, and improving the quality of learning materials. One significant benefit of AI is its ability to personalize student learning experiences. AI-powered learning systems can analyze data on students' learning patterns and create personalized learning pathways for each student (Luo & Hsiao-Chin, 2023). This personalized approach can enhance the learner's experience by catering to each student's unique learning needs. Another significant benefit of AI in education is its ability to automate administrative tasks, such as grading and feedback. AI-powered systems can analyze student responses and provide instant feedback on assignments, reducing the workload on teachers and improving the efficiency of the learning process (Rekha et al., 2024). AI can also improve the quality of learning materials by analyzing student data and identifying areas where students struggle the most. This information can help teachers create more effective teaching materials that address students' specific needs. Additionally, AI-powered systems can enhance the accessibility of learning materials for students with disabilities by providing customized materials that meet their specific needs (Ramaiah et al., 2025).

One of the significant advantages of AI in education is the ability to provide personalized learning experiences. AI algorithms can analyze student data and provide tailored learning paths based on their learning styles, strengths, and weaknesses (Jafari & Shaterzadeh-Yazdi, 2024). This approach can significantly enhance students' learning experience by providing individualized attention and support. Moreover, AI-powered virtual assistants can provide immediate feedback and guidance to learners, which can help them address their misunderstandings and misconceptions in real time (Mohamed et al., 2024). This feedback loop can help learners identify their learning gaps and focus on areas that need improvement. AI-powered tools can automate many administrative tasks in education, such as grading, scheduling, and attendance tracking (Makinde et al., 2024). This automation can free up educators' time, allowing them to focus on more meaningful tasks such as providing feedback, facilitating discussions, and developing engaging learning activities. Additionally, AI algorithms can analyze large datasets and provide insights into student performance, learning outcomes, and engagement (Ouyang et al., 2023). This data-driven approach can help educators identify areas of improvement and develop evidence-based teaching strategies.

A study by Twabu and Nakene-Mginqi (2024) suggests that AI-based grading systems can provide accurate and efficient grading, reducing the workload of educators. AI-based scheduling systems can also automate the scheduling of classes and resources, reducing the administrative workload of educators (Taye et al., 2023). Moreover, AI can enable efficient feedback mechanisms that provide timely and constructive feedback to learners. AI-based feedback systems can provide feedback based on learner data, which can help learners identify their strengths and weaknesses. This feedback can enable learners to improve their performance and achieve their learning goals. However, the adoption of AI in education is still in its early stages, and there are concerns regarding its impact on employment and the need for ethical considerations. Adoption of AI in education may significantly impact employment, as some jobs may be automated. Additionally, there are ethical considerations regarding the use of AI in education, such as data privacy and bias. It is crucial to address these concerns to ensure AI's ethical and responsible use in education.

## Challenges of AI in Education

Despite the numerous benefits of AI in education, several challenges are associated with its integration into the learning process. One major challenge is the potential bias in AI systems. AI-powered learning systems rely on data to make decisions, and if this data is biased, it can perpetuate inequality and discrimination (Rouabhia, 2025). For example, an AI-powered system may recommend specific courses to female students based on their gender, perpetuating gender stereotypes and limiting their educational opportunities. Another significant challenge of AI in education is the potential loss of jobs for teachers. As AI systems automate administrative tasks, such as grading and feedback, the need for human teachers may decrease, leading to job losses (Igbokwe, 2023). Despite AI's potential benefits in education, several challenges and concerns need to be addressed. One of the significant concerns is the ethical use of AI algorithms. AI algorithms can perpetuate bias and discrimination if not designed and implemented carefully (Varona & Suárez, 2022). Educators and policymakers must be aware of the potential biases and ensure that AI algorithms are transparent and accountable. Another concern is the potential impact of AI on educators' roles and responsibilities. AI automation can replace many administrative tasks, but it cannot replace the human touch in education, such as empathy, creativity, and critical thinking (Kayyali, 2024). Educators must embrace AI as a tool that can enhance their teaching practices rather than a threat to their profession.

## Ethical Issues and Moral Concerns of AI in Higher Education

Nicolae and Nicolae (2018) review the challenges higher education faces amidst rapid global changes, especially regarding artificial intelligence. They highlight the unprecedented pace of change and the struggle of educational systems to keep up with advancements in AI. Educational leaders must ensure institutions stay current with AI developments despite concerns about job displacement and data control.

The article explores how leaders adapt to these challenges and the importance of the proactive integration of AI into education to prepare for its societal impacts.

Milton and Al-Busaidi (2023) discuss the need for education leaders to adapt to changes brought by artificial intelligence. They emphasize the increasing competitiveness of higher education and the crucial role of digital technology. As AI becomes a significant part of digital transformation, leaders must stay current with technology and understand AI's workings. The research examines how AI might alter leadership expectations, the new skills leaders need, and whether AI could take over some leadership roles. It seeks to understand the future of educational leadership as AI becomes more integrated.

Adopting AI in higher education presents several ethical and moral concerns, specifically over privacy, bias, transparency, and the overall impact on education. Privacy concerns arise from handling student data, including worries regarding data access and security. AI systems can reinforce existing biases in training data, leading to unequal educational outcomes (Holstein & Doroudi, 2021). The opaque nature of AI decision-making processes raises concerns about transparency and accountability. Furthermore, AI systems can exacerbate academic integrity difficulties, needing explicit criteria for their ethical application. The expanding significance of AI in decision-making raises challenges about the role of human judgment, emphasizing the need.

## Application of Artificial Intelligence in Education

- **Personalized Learning:** One of the techniques AI is employed in educational settings is through customized learning. Together with personalized learning, AI techniques are used to scrutinize a student's achievements and extend modified lesson plans and referrals to what a learner should learn next. Personalized Learning switches the role of learners from being a participant in education to co-creators and contributors to their learning track (Bates, 2014). Personalized learning systems assist in scrutinizing the expertise in skills, offer learners the finest academic activities, and motivate learners to learn at their rhythm (Tapalova & Zhiyenbayeva, 2022). A personalized learning atmosphere incorporates a variety of aids, learning resources, and programs personalized to the individual learner's needs. It uses innovations such as Web 2.0 or Web 3.0 to build cost-effective training, augment participant experience, and create individualized learner identity. Intelligent systems emphasize more on defined topics, revisiting concepts that were not fully comprehended (Klašnja-Milićević et al., 2021).
- **Assessment/grading:** Evaluating a learner means gathering, scrutinizing information, examining, and following up on data about his/her achievement

of learning goals (Redcay et al., 2019). There are several types of evaluation/assessment. For instance, educational organizations primarily use standard-based evaluation/assessment (Bennett, 2011), which is basically used for determining competencies, providing a review, increasing transparency, etc. On the one hand, the evaluation of many learners is in no way a simple task; on the other hand, it is one of the principal tasks of educators (Al-Amri & Ali, 2016). After the COVID pandemic, educational organizations have switched their activities to E-learning platforms, and it is very challenging for educators to manage everything digitally, specifically the grading of projects, tests, and examination papers. Many scientists have worked to advance unbiased and productive assessment systems using distinct types of digital technology (Brew & Leacock, 2013; Liu et al., 2019). Through computational learning techniques and self-regulating clustering methods, AI platforms can work productively and tackle these hurdles (Morris, 2003). It can be determined that AI platforms can greatly guide learner efficiency assessment and minimize educator duties. This process will boost unbiased and productive grading in contrast to the conventional/traditional assessment/grading (Ahmad et al., 2022).

- **Admission/Enrollment:** As AI has its supporting features in various fields, particularly in education, its implementation starts from enrollment. Many education organizations promote admissions on their portals, and the learners expect pleasing services like guidance and enrollment information (Kim et al., 2014). Currently, many educational institutions offer essential services to participants or guardians through web-driven service platforms. Consequently, this demands it to be designed as intuitively as possible, which is the primary factor developers consider during the technology adoption model (Ranoliya et al., 2017). AI tools, especially machine learning procedures/algorithms, are more frequently used in postsecondary applications (Van Busum & Fang, 2023). It can also assist universities in gaining a deeper understanding of enrollment requirements and their influence on the enrollment process (Young & Caballero, 2019), along with enrollment returns (Jamison, 2017). AI can also be employed to anticipate the probability of enrollment for individual learners (Acharya et al., 2019; Raghavendran et al., 2021) in certain circumstances and can, at times, confirm prejudice in the person-centered enrollment process (Alvero et al., 2020).
- **Smart Classrooms:** The acronym SMART in "SMART classroom" stands for Showing, Manageable, Accessible, Real-time Interactive and Testing (Huang et al., 2019). Smart classrooms are active learning areas that use data from the surroundings, learners, and educators and can offer well-timed and significant data to enhance the teaching and learning procedures and sup-

port decision-making (Figueroa et al., 2024). Smart classrooms are physical learning spaces that, using data from the environment, students and teachers can provide timely and valuable information to improve teaching and learning processes and foster decision-making. A Smart classroom merges educational system and innovation (Kinshuk et al., 2016), such as mobile devices, automated communication and educational resources, projection devices, photographic devices, detectors, face identification software, and other components that monitor the diversity of environmental influences (Mircea et al., 2021). Educators in the smart classroom are responsible for improving learners' performance, innovation, and thinking abilities while utilizing new edging approaches such as social education, wireless learning, and U-learning (Kinshuk et al., 2016). Most innovations utilized in an innovative class depend on artificial intelligence that enables the participatory, versatile, and innovative application of those innovations during knowledge-building (Dimitriadou & Lanitis, 2023). Post 1970, artificial intelligence in education has commenced to impact technology implementation to guide and acquire knowledge, enhance the knowledge acquisition process, and endorse the learner's achievements (Southgate et al., 2019).

- **Intelligent Tutoring Systems:** Intelligent tutoring systems are technology-driven learning systems that use artificial intelligence to provide personalized and flexible instructions for students (Lin et al., 2023). Technology empowers us to deliver real-time guidance and assessments to learners, typically without human engagement (Gupta & Singh, 2023). As a significant application of artificial intelligence in education, intelligent tutoring systems can assist educators in boosting teaching standards and scan boost and define occasional outcomes for students (Conati et al., 2018). They can also observe students' improvement, give evaluations, clues, and assistance, and identify relevant problems or tasks for students to practice (Lin et al., 2023).

## AI Tools for Education

There is a broad range of artificial intelligence applications in education, including the following types of educational technology tools.

- **Chatbots:** A chatbot is a typical illustration of an artificial intelligence system and one of the most fundamental and widespread examples of intelligent Human-Computer Interaction (Adamopoulou & Moussiades, 2020). A chatbot is "A computer program designed to stimulate conversation with human users, especially over the Internet." AI is a "software program that simulates a conversation with human users, using text, voice, or images or a combination of spoken and visual heuristics" (Argal et al., 2018). Chatbots are mentioned as technology-driven AI assistants, and they originate from written scripts/texts or AI. It functions 24/7, supplying essential information and responses regarding admission. It not only assists the visitors or inquirers all day and night to obtain what they require but also decreases the responsibility or duty of the enrollment staff (Cui et al., 2017). According to Wollny et al., (2021) chatbots in education deal with three guiding topics: self-directed learning, life skills, and learning capabilities, and three guiding techniques: scaffolding, suggesting, and notifying. Chatbots might be utilized in a tutorial function to structure questions and responses with student feedback, and they could also be used to facilitate family outreach to support their children's academic development (Garcia-Brustenga et al., 2018). Through their personalized learning support, chatbots offer sizable educational potential and a positive impact on student learning and satisfaction (Winkler & Soellner, 2018).

- **Expert Systems:** Expert systems are computer software that can advise, decide support, and work performance assistance based upon their embedded expertise in precise problem solving (McFarland, & Parker, 1990). Expert systems are a renowned area of Artificial Intelligence and profoundly impact various aspects of life (Khanna et al., 2010). AI in education research suggested that versatile and integrated expert systems can help with curriculum planning and fully liberate the capabilities of learning management systems (LMS) teaching and learning (Dias et al., 2015). The structural traits of an expert system can model how users engage with it, thus simplifying and enhancing the teaching and instructional experiences. In a recent study by Hwang et al., (2020) the impacts of the hard-to-please expert system on elementary students' math learning results in Taiwan were explored. The study found that the adaptive learning model affective and intellectual performance evaluation efficiently reduced math nervousness among fifth-grade learners in Taiwan (Hwang et al., 2020).
- **Machine Learning:** Machine learning aims to program computers to use illustrative data or experience to solve specific challenges (Alpaydin, 2020). Machine learning is programming computers to optimize productivity standards using dummy data from all experiences (Alpaydin, 2020). A machine learning algorithm means using a model that yields correct information given that we have provided input data (Kučak et al., 2018). There are plenty of other business Executions of machine learning, many of which are in the Academic area. One of the fascinating areas is predicting student productivity by learning about every individual learner. The machine learning model can identify vulnerability and suggest improvement pathways such as additional

lectures or studying additional literature (Anozie & Junker, 2006). Test and grade students impartially. Machine learning can help generate computerized adaptive assessments (Luckin & Holmes, 2016). Machine learning-based assessment provides continuous feedback to educators and learners about how the student learns, the assistance they need, and the improvement they are showing toward their learning goals (El-Alfy & Abdel-Aal, 2008). Improve retention of students. Machine learning, such as learning analytics, will help to improve the students' turnover rates (Đambić et al., 2016).

- **Virtual Learning Environments:** With the rise in virtual reality technologies, studies have begun investigating the potential of visualizations with AI in education (Zhang & Aslan, 2021). Undeniably, learners found the learning experience in VLE enjoyable and stated that it simplified learning and collaborations (Griol et al., 2014). In the same way, educators also observed that learners were better committed to learning (Griol et al., 2014). A combination of both technologies, AI and virtual reality (VR), was found productive for refining the learning experience and attracting the learners of the young generation in Australia (Ijaz et al., 2017). Undergraduate learners learning with the help of AI and virtual reality are also performing more effectively in comprehension, as evaluated by the researchers in this study (Ijaz et al., 2017).
- **Personalized Learning Systems:** Stretching out the educational concepts of differentiation and individualization to connect to the interests and experiences of learners and meeting the needs and interests of every learner by tailoring the structured set of courses and learning activities of each learner (Bartle, 2015). Kose and Arslan (2016) explored the impacts of personalized learning systems on 110 undergraduate students from two semesters of computer programming courses. The researchers found that with the help of personalized learning systems, learners can achieve desirable learning outcomes, and it also helps improve their learning experiences. Research conducted by Walkington & Bernacki (2019) in the USA with high school students found that learning within an intelligent tutoring system could be enhanced by linking math to students' interests beyond school. This level of tailored personalization could enhance learning and contribute to students' success.

## METHOD

The data was collected from 10 educationalists. The data collected was analyzed using Latent Dirichlet Allocation (LDA) technique of text analysis. 6 open ended questions given below were framed to collect anonymous responses. The data is collected in 2025.

- **Question 1:** How is AI transforming your role and the way you approach your work?
- **Question 2:** Which AI tools are you currently utilizing to enhance efficiency and achieve your tasks in your role?
- **Question 3:** Is your organization supporting the use of AI tools in your role? If yes, how are they providing this support?
- **Question 4:** What ethical considerations or challenges arise from using AI in your role?
- **Question 5:** Should the use of AI in education be banned? Please explain your perspective.
- **Question 6:** What do you envision as the future of AI in education, and how do you think it will shape learning and teaching experiences?

## Topic Modeling Results

Figure 3 presents the topics extracted with their beta values. The 5 topics are extracted using the LDA text analysis technique. *Topic 1- Privacy and Technology:* The topic analysis discussed the concerns around data privacy, digital security, and ethical AI practices. *Topic 2-Al Ethics:* Examines the role of AI in decision-making, fairness in machine learning, and ethical considerations. *Topic 3- Human-Technology Interaction:* Explores how humans interact with technology in workspaces and society. *Topic 4- AI Adoption Challenges:* Highlights obstacles in AI implementation and strategies for overcoming them. *Topic 5- Development & Future Trends:* Discusses ongoing AI advancements and future technological transformations.

*Figure 3. The five topics and their beta values.*

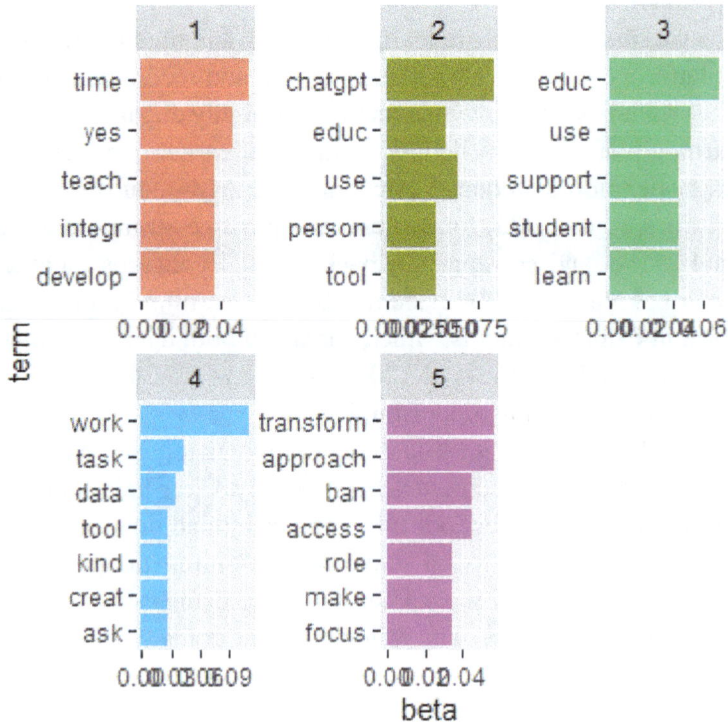


## DISCUSSION

Among many educational technologies, artificial intelligence (AI) has been contemplated as a critical technology for improving learners' learning outcomes. AI needs to be incorporated into e-learning systems to provide personalized, adaptive learning content, feedback for improvement, and recommendations for learning paths. AI learning systems provide learning guidance and associated supplementary content (Liu et al., 2019), thus considerably enhancing learning outcomes. Many AI programs are being developed and integrated into e-learning platforms. AI-led e-learning systems adapt to learners with different understanding levels and deliver appropriate content relevant to their understanding level. AI-based LMS has been helpful in training, refresher courses, professional development, and upskilling (Kavitha & Lohani, 2019).

AI will play a significant role in learner profiling and prediction, intelligent and interactive platforms, assessment, personalization, and recommendation to enable learners to get what is valuable to them and get it highly engaging. In other words, AI-led e-learning platforms will deliver unmatched learner experiences.

Research has explored students' perceptions of AI in education. Djokic et al. (2024) and Idroes et al. (2023) found generally positive attitudes, noting benefits like universal access and constant feedback, though concerns included reduced human interaction. Niu et al. (2022) studied Smart Learning Partner (SLP), an AI-aided platform in Chinese schools, which enhanced both teaching and learning by personalizing content. Labarthe et al. (2018) and Renz & Hilbig (2020) confirmed AI's role in expanding learning opportunities.

Sangapu (2018) revealed that while students appreciated AI-supported teaching, most rejected the idea of replacing teachers entirely. Over half believed AI could improve teacher performance but not fully replace human presence in classrooms. Similarly, Chan & Hu (2023) found students were optimistic about using GenAI tools like ChatGPT in learning and careers, but also expressed concerns over reliability, ethics, and data privacy. The following are the major outcomes of AI use in education management.

- **Filling Gaps in Explanation:** AI helps identify and address conceptual gaps in teaching. Platforms like Coursera alert educators when many students answer a question incorrectly and offer personalized hints to future learners, ensuring consistent understanding (Verma, 2018).
- **Support from AI Tutors:** AI-based tutors assist with fundamental subjects like math and writing. While helpful for foundational skills, they are currently limited in teaching higher-order thinking, where human teachers remain essential (Verma, 2018).
- **Feedback for Students and Educators:** AI systems provide tailored feedback, helping students improve and enabling teachers to target weak areas. Virtual schools use AI to track student progress and alert educators to potential issues (Verma, 2018).
- **Transforming Learning Environments**: AI enables learning anytime, anywhere, and can even substitute some teaching functions. AI-powered tools already support students worldwide, reshaping traditional education models (Verma, 2018).
- **Adaptive Learning and Personalization**: AI tailored content to individual learning needs. Adaptive platforms adjust material complexity and pac-

ing based on student performance, enhancing engagement and effectiveness (D'Souza, 2024; Murphy, 2019).

## CONCLUSION

Artificial Intelligence (AI) emerges as a transformative force in education, one that must be understood and adopted at both the student and teacher levels. To maximize its potential, there is a need for structured support systems and increased awareness about AI tools within the curriculum. Educators should be trained to integrate and use these tools effectively. AI-powered solutions such as intelligent tutors are gaining popularity in classrooms worldwide.

However, challenges persist—issues such as algorithmic bias, ethical usage, and the protection of student data privacy must be carefully addressed. The integration of AI in teaching and learning is expanding rapidly. Teachers are experimenting with various AI-driven applications to support neurodiverse learners, address gender inclusivity, assist second-language acquisition, and implement AI-based self-assessment methods.

Whether AI becomes a devil or an angel in education depends entirely on how it is used and by whom. Current literature and research suggest a growing inclination toward adopting AI tools in academic environments. In essence, AI offers *a "magic wand"* to educators—how they wield this tool will determine whether it creates confusion or catalyzes true transformation. The stage is set; let's see what magic unfolds!

## REFERENCES


Acharya, M. S., Armaan, A., & Antony, A. S. (2019, February). A comparison of regression models for prediction of graduate admissions. In *2019 international conference on computational intelligence in data science (ICCIDS)* (pp. 1-5). IEEE. DOI: 10.1109/ICCIDS.2019.8862140

Açıkgöz, A., & Latham, G. P. (2022). Self-Set learning goals and service performance in a gig economy: A Moderated-Mediation role of improvisation and mindful metacognition. *Journal of Business Research, 139*, 1553–1563. DOI: 10.1016/j.jbusres.2021.10.074

Adamopoulou, E., & Moussiades, L. (2020). An overview of chatbot technology. In *Artificial Intelligence Applications and Innovations: 16th IFIP WG 12.5 International Conference, AIAI 2020, Neos Marmaras, Greece, June 5–7, 2020* [Springer International Publishing.]. *Proceedings, 16*(Part II), 373–383.

Agudo-Peregrina, Á. F., Hernández-García, Á., & Pascual-Miguel, F. J. (2014). Behavioral intention, use behavior and the acceptance of electronic learning systems: Differences between higher education and lifelong learning. *Computers in Human Behavior, 34*, 301–314. DOI: 10.1016/j.chb.2013.10.035

Ahmad, S. F., Alam, M. M., Rahmat, M. K., Mubarik, M. S., & Hyder, S. I. (2022). Academic and administrative role of artificial intelligence in education. *Sustainability (Basel), 14*(3), 1101. DOI: 10.3390/su14031101

Al-Amri, S., & Ali, Z. (2016). Systematic review of computer based assessments in medical education. *Saudi Journal of Medicine & Medical Sciences, 4*(2), 79–88. DOI: 10.4103/1658-631X.178288 PMID: 30787703

Alpaydin, E. (2020). *Introduction to machine learning*. MIT press.

Alvero, A. J., Arthurs, N., Antonio, A. L., Domingue, B. W., Gebre-Medhin, B., Giebel, S., & Stevens, M. L. (2020, February). AI and holistic review: informing human reading in college admissions. In *Proceedings of the AAAI/ACM Conference on AI, Ethics, and Society* (pp. 200-206). DOI: 10.1145/3375627.3375871

Anozie, N., & Junker, B. W. (2006, July). Predicting end-of-year accountability assessment scores from monthly student records in an online tutoring system. Educational Data Mining: Papers from the AAAI Workshop. Menlo Park, CA: AAAI Press.

Argal, A., Gupta, S., Modi, A., Pandey, P., Shim, S., & Choo, C. (2018, January). Intelligent travel chatbot for predictive recommendation in echo platform. In *2018 IEEE 8th annual computing and communication workshop and conference (CCWC)* (pp. 176-183). IEEE. DOI: 10.1109/CCWC.2018.8301732

Ashford, S. J., Caza, B. B., & Reid, E. M. (2018). From surviving to thriving in the gig economy: A research agenda for individuals in the new world of work. *Research in Organizational Behavior*, *38*, 23–41. DOI: 10.1016/j.riob.2018.11.001

Bartle, E. (2015). Personalised learning: An overview. *The Institute for Teaching and Learning Innovation, Queensland University. Retrieved from* https://itali. uq. *edu. au/filething/get/1865/Personalised_learning_overview_Final_16_Mar_15.pdf.*

Bates, S. (2014). Personalised learning: Implications for curricula, staff and students. *Universitas (Accra)*, •••, 21.

Bennett, R. E. (2011). Formative assessment: A critical review. *Assessment in Education: Principles, Policy & Practice*, *18*(1), 5–25. DOI: 10.1080/0969594X.2010.513678

Brew, C., & Leacock, C. (2013). Automated short answer scoring: Principles and prospects. In *Handbook of Automated Essay Evaluation* (pp. 136–152). Routledge.

Bunjak, A., Černe, M., & Popovič, A. (2021). Absorbed in technology but digitally overloaded: Interplay effects on gig workers' burnout and creativity. *Information & Management*, *58*(8), 103533. DOI: 10.1016/j.im.2021.103533

Campus Technology. (August 27, 2024). Share of higher education students using artificial intelligence (AI) tools for schoolwork worldwide as of July 2024 [Graph]. In *Statista*. Retrieved January 16, 2025, from https://www.statista.com/statistics/1498309/usage-of-ai-by-students-worldwide/

Chan, C. K. Y., & Hu, W. (2023). Students' voices on generative AI: Perceptions, benefits, and challenges in higher education. *International Journal of Educational Technology in Higher Education*, *20*(1), 43. DOI: 10.1186/s41239-023-00411-8

Conati, C., Porayska-Pomsta, K., & Mavrikis, M. (2018). AI in Education needs interpretable machine learning: Lessons from Open Learner Modelling. *arXiv preprint arXiv:1807.00154.*

Cui, L., Huang, S., Wei, F., Tan, C., Duan, C., & Zhou, M. (2017, July). Superagent: A customer service chatbot for e-commerce websites. In *Proceedings of ACL 2017, system demonstrations* (pp. 97-102). DOI: 10.18653/v1/P17-4017

D'Souza, R. (2024). Scope of Artificial Intelligence in Education. *International Journal of Emerging Knowledge Studies, 03*(09), 670–678. DOI: 10.70333/ijeks-03-09-035

Đambić, G., Krajcar, M., & Bele, D. (2016). Machine learning model for early detection of higher education students that need additional attention in introductory programming courses. *International journal of digital technology & economy, 1*(1), 1-11.

Dias, S. B., Hadjileontiadou, S. J., Hadjileontiadis, L. J., & Diniz, J. A. (2015). Fuzzy cognitive mapping of LMS users' quality of interaction within higher education blended-learning environment. *Expert Systems with Applications, 42*(21), 7399–7423. DOI: 10.1016/j.eswa.2015.05.048

Dimitriadou, E., & Lanitis, A. (2023). A critical evaluation, challenges, and future perspectives of using artificial intelligence and emerging technologies in smart classrooms. *Smart Learning Environments, 10*(1), 12. DOI: 10.1186/s40561-023-00231-3 PMID: 40478141

Djokic, I., Milicevic, N., Djokic, N., Maleic, B., & Kalas, B. (2024). STUDENTS' PERCEPTIONS OF THE USE OF ARTIFICIAL INTELLIGENCE IN EDUCATIONAL SERVICES. *Amfiteatru Economic, 26*(65), 294–310. DOI: 10.24818/EA/2024/65/294

El-Alfy, E. S. M., & Abdel-Aal, R. E. (2008). Construction and analysis of educational tests using abductive machine learning. *Computers & Education, 51*(1), 1–16. DOI: 10.1016/j.compedu.2007.03.003

El-Seoud, M. S., Taj-Eddin, I. A., Seddiek, N., El-Khouly, M. M., & Nosseir, A. (2014). E-learning and students' motivation: A research study on the effect of e-learning on higher education. *International Journal of Emerging Technologies in Learning, 9*(4), 20. DOI: 10.3991/ijet.v9i4.3465

Figueroa, E., Batista, E., Palau, R., Unciti, O., Ferre, M., & Ballesté, A. M. (2024). The Use of Artificial Intelligence Techniques in Smart Classrooms is in its Infancy. *IEEE Access : Practical Innovations, Open Solutions, 12*, 125179–125193. DOI: 10.1109/ACCESS.2024.3454372

Garcia-Brustenga, G., Fuertes-Alpiste, M., & Molas Castells, N. (2018). Briefing paper: chatbots in education. DOI: 10.7238/elc.chatbots.2018

Griol, D., Molina, J. M., & Callejas, Z. (2014). An approach to develop intelligent learning environments by means of immersive virtual worlds. *Journal of Ambient Intelligence and Smart Environments, 6*(2), 237–255. DOI: 10.3233/AIS-140255

Gupta, M., & Singh, A. (2023). Emerging Trends in Artificial Intelligence Education: Advancements, Opportunities, and Impact on Educational Technology. *Quanta Research, 1*(1), 20–26.

Holstein, K., & Doroudi, S. (2021). Equity and artificial intelligence in education: will" aied" amplify or alleviate inequities in education? *arXiv preprint arXiv:2104.12920.*

Huang, L. S., Su, J. Y., & Pao, T. L. (2019). A context aware smart classroom architecture for smart campuses. *Applied Sciences (Basel, Switzerland), 9*(9), 1837. DOI: 10.3390/app9091837

Hwang, G. J., Sung, H. Y., Chang, S. C., & Huang, X. C. (2020). A fuzzy expert system-based adaptive learning approach to improving students' learning performances by considering affective and cognitive factors. *Computers and Education: Artificial Intelligence, 1*, 100003. DOI: 10.1016/j.caeai.2020.100003

Idroes, G. M., Noviandy, T. R., Maulana, A., Irvanizam, I., & Idroes, R. (2023). Student perspectives on the role of artificial intelligence in education: A survey-based analysis. *Journal of Educational Management and Learning, 1*(1), 8–15. DOI: 10.60084/jeml.v1i1.58

Igbokwe, I. C. (2023). Application of artificial intelligence (AI) in educational management. *International Journal of Scientific and Research Publications, 13*(3), 300–307. DOI: 10.29322/IJSRP.13.03.2023.p13536

Ijaz, K., Bogdanovych, A., & Trescak, T. (2017). Virtual worlds vs books and videos in history education. *Interactive Learning Environments, 25*(7), 904–929. DOI: 10.1080/10494820.2016.1225099

Jafari, D., & Shaterzadeh-Yazdi, Z. (2024). Transforming Education with AI: The Development of a Personalized Learning Algorithm for Individual Learning Styles. *Journal of Algorithms and Computation, 56*(2), 135–150.

Jamison, J. (2017, March). Applying machine learning to predict Davidson college's admissions yield. In *Proceedings of the 2017 ACM SIGCSE Technical Symposium on Computer Science Education* (pp. 765-766). DOI: 10.1145/3017680.3022468

Kavitha, V., & Lohani, R. (2019). A critical study on the use of artificial intelligence, e-Learning technology and tools to enhance the learners experience. *Cluster Computing, 22*(S3, Suppl 3), 6985–6989. DOI: 10.1007/s10586-018-2017-2

Kayyali, M. (2024). Future possibilities and challenges of AI in education. In *Transforming education with generative AI: Prompt engineering and synthetic content creation* (pp. 118–137). IGI Global Scientific Publishing. DOI: 10.4018/979-8-3693-1351-0.ch006

Khanna, S., Kaushik, A., & Barnela, M. (2010, March). Expert systems advances in education. In *Proceedings of the National Conference on Computational Instrumentation NCCI-2010. CSIO* (pp. 109-112).

Kinshuk, C., Chen, N.-S., Cheng, I.-L., & Chew, S. W. (2016). Evolution is not enough: Revolutionizing current learning environments to smart learning environments. *International Journal of Artificial Intelligence in Education, 26*(2), 561–581. DOI: 10.1007/s40593-016-0108-x

Klašnja-Milićević, A., & Ivanović, M. (2021). E-learning personalization systems and sustainable education. *Sustainability (Basel), 13*(12), 6713. DOI: 10.3390/su13126713

Klutka, J., Ackerly, N., & Magda, A. J. (2018). *Artificial intelligence in higher education: Current uses and future applications*. Learning House.

Kose, U., & Arslan, A. (2016). Intelligent e-learning system for improving students' academic achievements in computer programming courses. *International Journal of Engineering Education, 32*(1), 185–198.

Kučak, D., Juričić, V., & Đambić, G. (2018). MACHINE LEARNING IN EDUCATION-A SURVEY OF CURRENT RESEARCH TRENDS. *Annals of DAAAM & Proceedings, 29.*

Labarthe, H., Luengo, V., & Bouchet, F. (2018, June). Analyzing the relationships between learning analytics, educational data mining and AI for education. In *14th International Conference on Intelligent Tutoring Systems (ITS): Workshop Learning Analytics* (pp. 10-19).

Lin, C. C., Huang, A. Y., & Lu, O. H. (2023). Artificial intelligence in intelligent tutoring systems toward sustainable education: A systematic review. *Smart Learning Environments, 10*(1), 41. DOI: 10.1186/s40561-023-00260-y

Liu, X., Wang, S., Wang, P., & Wu, D. (2019, May). Automatic grading of programming assignments: an approach based on formal semantics. In *2019 IEEE/ACM 41st International Conference on Software Engineering: Software Engineering Education and Training (ICSE-SEET)* (pp. 126-137). IEEE. DOI: 10.1109/ICSE-SEET.2019.00022

Luckin, R., & Holmes, W. (2016). *Intelligence Unleashed: An argument for AI in Education*. UCL Knowledge Lab.

Luo, Q. Z., & Hsiao-Chin, L. Y. (2023). The influence of AI-powered adaptive learning platforms on student performance in Chinese classrooms. *Journal of Education, 6*(3), 1–12. DOI: 10.53819/81018102t4181

Makinde, A. I., Adeleye, S. A., Oronti, A. O., & Jimoh, I. T. (2024). Revolutionizing education. *Artificial Intelligence for Wireless Communication Systems: Technology and Applications, 103.*

McFarland, T. D., & Parker, R. (1990). Expert systems in education and training. *Educational Technology.*

McGraw-Hill. (October 24, 2023). Share of undergraduate students who have various opinions on the use of artificial intelligence (AI) tools in higher education in the United States in 2023 [Graph]. In *Statista.* Retrieved January 16, 2025, from https://www.statista.com/statistics/1445975/us-undergraduate-students-opinions-on-the-use-of-ai-in-education/

Milton, J., & Al-Busaidi, A. (2023). New role of leadership in AI era: Educational sector. In *SHS Web of Conferences* (Vol. 156, p. 09005). EDP Sciences.

Mircea, M., Stoica, M., & Ghilic-Micu, B. (2021). Investigating the impact of the internet of things in higher education environment. *IEEE Access : Practical Innovations, Open Solutions*, *9*, 33396–33409. DOI: 10.1109/ACCESS.2021.3060964

Mohamed, A., Faisal, R., & Shaalan, K. (2024, September). Exploring the Impact of AI-Driven Virtual Assistants in AR and VR Environments for Special Needs Education: A Quantitative Analysis. In *International Conference on Extended Reality* (pp. 113-127). Cham: Springer Nature Switzerland. DOI: 10.1007/978-3-031-71713-0_8

Morris, D. S. (2003, November). Automatic grading of student's programming assignments: an interactive process and suite of programs. In *33rd Annual Frontiers in Education, 2003. FIE 2003.* (Vol. 3, pp. S3F-1). IEEE. DOI: 10.1109/FIE.2003.1265998

Murphy, R. F. (2019). Artificial intelligence applications to support K-12 teachers and teaching. *Rand Corporation*, *10*(1), 1–20.

Nicolae, M., & Nicolae, E. E. (2018). Leadership in higher education–coping with AI and the turbulence of our times. In *Proceedings of the International Conference on Business Excellence* (Vol. 12, No. 1, pp. 683-694). Sciendo. DOI: 10.2478/picbe-2018-0061

Niu, S. J., Luo, J., Niemi, H., Li, X., & Lu, Y. (2022). Teachers' and students' views of using an AI-aided educational platform for supporting teaching and learning at Chinese schools. *Education Sciences*, *12*(12), 858. DOI: 10.3390/educsci12120858

On EdTech Newsletter. (August 6, 2024). Leading use cases for artificial intelligence (AI) tools in schoolwork among higher education students worldwide as of July 2024 [Graph]. In *Statista*. Retrieved January 16, 2025, from https://www.statista.com/statistics/1498323/use-cases-ai-by-students-worldwide/

Ouyang, F., Wu, M., Zheng, L., Zhang, L., & Jiao, P. (2023). Integration of artificial intelligence performance prediction and learning analytics to improve student learning in online engineering course. *International Journal of Educational Technology in Higher Education, 20*(1), 4. DOI: 10.1186/s41239-022-00372-4 PMID: 36683653

Priatna, T., Maylawati, D., Sugilar, H., & Ramdhani, M. (2020). Key success factors of e-learning implementation in higher education. [iJET]. *International Journal of Emerging Technologies in Learning, 15*(17), 101–114. DOI: 10.3991/ijet.v15i17.14293

Raghavendran, C. V., Pavan Venkata Vamsi, C., Veerraju, T., & Veluri, R. K. (2021). Predicting student admissions rate into university using machine learning models. In *Machine Intelligence and Soft Computing* [Springer Singapore.]. *Proceedings of ICMISC, 2020*, 151–162.

Ramaiah, M. S., Nagarajan, S. K. S., Whig, P., & Dutta, P. K. (2025). AI-Powered Innovations Transforming Adaptive Education for Disability Support. In *Advancing Adaptive Education: Technological Innovations for Disability Support* (pp. 73-100). IGI Global Scientific Publishing.

Ranoliya, B. R., Raghuwanshi, N., & Singh, S. (2017, September). Chatbot for university related FAQs. In *2017 International Conference on Advances in Computing, Communications and Informatics (ICACCI)* (pp. 1525-1530). IEEE. DOI: 10.1109/ICACCI.2017.8126057

Redcay, E., & Schilbach, L. (2019). Using second-person neuroscience to elucidate the mechanisms of social interaction. *Nature Reviews. Neuroscience, 20*(8), 495–505. DOI: 10.1038/s41583-019-0179-4 PMID: 31138910

Rekha, K., Gopal, K., Satheeskumar, D., Anand, U. A., Doss, D. S. S., & Elayaperumal, S. (2024, May). Ai-Powered Personalized Learning System Design: Student Engagement and Performance Tracking System. In *2024 4th International Conference on Advance Computing and Innovative Technologies in Engineering (ICACITE)* (pp. 1125-1130). IEEE.

Renz, A., & Hilbig, R. (2020). Prerequisites for artificial intelligence in further education: Identification of drivers, barriers, and business models of educational technology companies. *International Journal of Educational Technology in Higher Education, 17*(1), 14. DOI: 10.1186/s41239-020-00193-3

Rouabhia, R. (2025). Ethical Implications of AI: Examining Bias and Fairness in AI-Powered Education. In *Using AI Tools in Text Analysis, Simplification, Classification, and Synthesis* (pp. 411-438). IGI Global Scientific Publishing.

Southgate, E., Blackmore, K., Pieschl, S., Grimes, S., McGuire, J., & Smithers, K. (2019). *Artificial intelligence and emerging technologies in schools: Research report*. University of Newcastle. https://www.dese.gov.au/supporting-family-school-community-partnerships-learning/resources/ai-schools-report

Tapalova, O., & Zhiyenbayeva, N. (2022). Artificial intelligence in education: AIEd for personalised learning pathways. *Electronic Journal of e-Learning*, *20*(5), 639–653. DOI: 10.34190/ejel.20.5.2597

Taye, G., Sharma, S., Shah, P., & Nuriye, Y. G. (2023, October). Exploring the Role of Artificial Intelligence in Class Scheduling and Management: A Comprehensive Survey and Review. In *2023 International Conference on Computer Science and Emerging Technologies (CSET)* (pp. 1-11). IEEE. DOI: 10.1109/CSET58993.2023.10346898

Twabu, K., & Nakene-Mginqi, M. (2024, December). Developing a design thinking artificial intelligence driven auto-marking/grading system for assessments to reduce the workload of lecturers at a higher learning institution in South Africa. [). Frontiers Media SA.]. *Frontiers in Education*, *9*, 1512569. DOI: 10.3389/feduc.2024.1512569

Van Busum, K., & Fang, S. (2023, March). Analysis of AI models for student admissions: a case study. In *Proceedings of the 38th ACM/SIGAPP Symposium on Applied Computing* (pp. 17-22). DOI: 10.1145/3555776.3577743

Varona, D., & Suárez, J. L. (2022). Discrimination, bias, fairness, and trustworthy AI. *Applied Sciences (Basel, Switzerland)*, *12*(12), 5826. DOI: 10.3390/app12125826

Verma, M. (2018). Artificial intelligence and its scope in different areas with special reference to the field of education. *Online Submission*, *3*(1), 5–10.

Walkington, C., & Bernacki, M. L. (2019). Personalizing algebra to students' individual interests in an intelligent tutoring system: Moderators of impact. *International Journal of Artificial Intelligence in Education*, *29*(1), 58–88. DOI: 10.1007/s40593-018-0168-1

Winkler, R., & Söllner, M. (2018, July). Unleashing the potential of chatbots in education: A state-of-the-art analysis. In *Academy of management proceedings* (Vol. 2018, No. 1, p. 15903). Briarcliff Manor, NY 10510: Academy of Management. DOI: 10.5465/AMBPP.2018.15903abstract

Wollny, S., Schneider, J., Di Mitri, D., Weidlich, J., Rittberger, M., & Drachsler, H. (2021). Are we there yet?-a systematic literature review on chatbots in education. *Frontiers in Artificial Intelligence*, *4*, 654924. DOI: 10.3389/frai.2021.654924 PMID: 34337392

Young, N. T., & Caballero, M. D. (2019). Using machine learning to understand physics graduate school admissions. *arXiv preprint arXiv:1907.01570.*

Zawacki-Richter, O., Marín, V. I., Bond, M., & Gouverneur, F. (2019). Systematic review of research on artificial intelligence applications in higher education–where are the educators? *International Journal of Educational Technology in Higher Education*, *16*(1), 1–27. DOI: 10.1186/s41239-019-0171-0

Zhang, K., & Aslan, A. B. (2021). AI technologies for education: Recent research & future directions. *Computers and education. Artificial Intelligence*, *2*, 100025.

# Chapter 3
# Generative AI in Business Education Transforming Teaching and Learning


**Abida Ellahi**
https://orcid.org/0000-0003-2383-852X
*Abbottabad University of Science and Technology, Pakistan*

**Muhammad Farooq Jan**
https://orcid.org/0000-0002-6547-2469
*Abbottabad University of Science and Technology, Pakistan*

**Muddassar Khan**
*Abbottabad University of Science and Technology, Pakistan*



## ABSTRACT

*Generative AI is revolutionizing business education by making lesson planning easier, providing additional personalized instruction, and automating administrative tasks. ChatGPT, DALL-E, and Gradescope are tools that simplify the generation of content, adaptive learning, and grading issues, but with concerns over data privacy and bias. This makes the emergence of trends like AI-based virtual classrooms and gamification, the ones that can provide an immersive and future-ready learning experience. This chapter identifies how AI develops the power of educators, fuels engagement by students, and reorganizes the area of learning business, while controlling innovation and ethical obligations.*



DOI: 10.4018/979-8-3373-2150-9.ch003

## INTRODUCTION

Picture a business classroom where lessons mirror global markets, instruction adapts to each student, and professors prioritize mentorship over paperwork. Generative AI enables this vision, with ChatGPT drafting syllabi, DALL-E visualizing trade flows, and Gradescope automating grading (Chacko, 2024). For educators, researchers, and professionals, AI aligns education with a tech-driven economy, where 90% of business roles demand analytics and AI literacy (Mayer et al., 2025).

Business schools are beginning to weave generative artificial intelligence, or generative AI, into their curricula so graduates can tackle fast-changing workplaces. Generative AI tools, capable of drafting reports, running realistic simulations, and even producing video lessons, open fresh pathways for both teaching and learning. Instructors who adopt these technologies can reproduce authentic business challenges, tailor instruction to individual needs, and cultivate essential skills like problem-solving and strategic thinking. The present chapter reviews this change, drawing on practical classroom examples and evidence from both scholarly research and industry case studies.

However, AI's promise is not without pitfalls. High costs, faculty skepticism, bias, privacy risks, inequities, and over-reliance threaten its efficacy. While Harvard leverages AI for case preparation, and adaptive learning boosts outcomes (VanLehn & Chi, 2012), unchecked adoption could depersonalize learning or widen resource gaps. This chapter incorporating a detailed historical overview, expanded case studies, and educator testimonials offers a rigorous, practical roadmap for integrating AI thoughtfully.

**Key Points**: *AI transforms business education but requires careful management of costs, ethics, and human roles to ensure equitable, impactful learning.*

### Historical Context of AI in Education

***Early Foundations (1960s–1980s):*** AI's journey in education began with PLATO (Programmed Logic for Automatic Teaching Operations) in the 1960s at the University of Illinois, delivering interactive lessons via mainframes (Panda, 2024). By the 1970s, systems like SCHOLAR introduced basic question-answering for geography, laying groundwork for adaptive learning. The 1980s saw intelligent tutoring systems, such as Carnegie Mellon's LISP Tutor, which provided personalized feedback for coding (Anderson et al., 1985). These early tools were limited by hardware and narrow scopes but sparked interest in AI's educational potential.

***Growth and Integration (1990s–2000s):*** The 1990s brought broader AI applications, with tools like AutoTutor simulating human tutors for physics (Graesser et al., 1999). Learning management systems (LMS) like Blackboard emerged, integrating

AI for analytics by the 2000s. Business schools adopted early AI for data-driven courses, with MIT Sloan using predictive models for finance curricula in 1998 (Sircar, 2009). However, high costs restricted access, foreshadowing equity challenges.

***Rise of Generative AI (2010s–Present):*** The 2010s marked a turning point with machine learning advancements. The launch of GPT models in 2018 by OpenAI introduced generative AI, enabling dynamic content creation syllabi, cases, visuals. In October 2024, AACSB surveyed 236 deans and 429 faculty members from 60+ countries to learn about GenAI use in business schools. While 75% of deans and 69% of faculty were from AACSB-accredited schools, only 47% of deans said they had GenAI-related policies in place, and most users identified as novice or intermediate in terms of proficiency (AACSB, 2025). Some of the business schools may have resources constraints. This disparity underscores ongoing tensions between innovation and access.

*Table 1. Milestones in AI and Business Education*

| Decade | Development | Business Education Impact |
|---|---|---|
| 1960s | PLATO system | Early computer-based learning; limited access |
| 1980s | Intelligent tutoring (LISP Tutor) | Personalized feedback; narrow applications |
| 1990s | AutoTutor, predictive models | Data-driven finance courses at elite schools |
| 2000s | LMS (Blackboard, Moodle) | Analytics for enrollment, grading |
| 2010s | Machine learning, simulations | Market pilots |
| 2020s | Generative AI (GPT, DALL-E) | Business Schools adoption/Non Adoption, Resource Constraints |

**Source:** Author(s).

## The Evolution of Business Education

***Historical Shifts:*** Business education began with rote learning in the early 20th century, focusing on management principles via textbooks. Harvard's 1920s case method introduced real-world problem-solving, a cornerstone still used today (Barnes et al., 1994). The digital era shifted priorities, with most of the programs emphasizing tech skills by 2025.

***Current Demands:*** Globalization, AI, and blockchain require agility. McKinsey reports 90% of business roles demand digital transformation and analytics, (McKinsey, 2024), therefore, traditional methods lectures, static cases fall short. AI bridges this gap, crafting relevant simulations, but risks depersonalization and inequity if elite schools dominate adoption.

## LITERATURE REVIEW: GENERATIVE AI IN BUSINESS EDUCATION

The integration of generative AI into business education has sparked a growing body of research, encompassing peer-reviewed studies, industry reports, and institutional analyses. This literature review synthesizes key findings on AI's transformative potential, focusing on its effects on faculty workload, student learning outcomes, and ethical concerns such as algorithmic bias and data protection (Baig & Yadegaridehkordi, 2025).

Generative AI is now reshaping information and communication technology (ICT) teaching by making classes livelier, personalizing study paths, and giving students near-instant help. AI-enabled platforms spark curiosity and adjust lessons to each learner's speed, which helps them master tricky ICT ideas. Ruiz-Rojas et al. (2023) noted that when teachers weave such tools into course design, student interaction rises, and the delivery of technical material becomes smoother. The flip side, however, is that overdependence can dull independent thinking. Chugh et al., (2025) warn that leaning too much on AI helpers may erode crucial problem-solving abilities in ICT study. Privacy concerns add to the mix, as Lim et al. (2023) point out; unchecked data harvesting by AI raises ethical questions for both educators and learners. By deliberately mixing AI support with human oversight, instructors can tap their strengths while guarding against these pitfalls, creating active and responsible ICT classrooms.

Artificial intelligence (AI) has reconfigured professors' everyday duties on campus, easing some burdens while creating fresh demands that call for quick adjustment. Tools such as automated grading software and smart tutoring apps cut the hours spent on monotonous chores-grading tests or fielding the same student questions-over, letting instructors focus more on teaching and research. For example, a 2025 study showed that personalized tasks and instant feedback from AI reduced faculty effort by streamlining how assignments are evaluated (Liang et al., 2025). Even so, bringing these systems into the classroom requires substantial hours spent learning the technology and redesigning syllabuses-often with little help from the administration. As noted in a separate study, many educators cite mastering AI tools as a major hurdle and call for more training if the benefits are to be realized (Mah et al., 2025). This mixed picture shows that AI can lighten some workloads while simultaneously adding others.

Generative AI (GAI) is already changing business education by altering how faculty teach, how courses are built, and how students take part in class. Research shows that smart tutoring programs tailor lessons to each learner, guiding them through difficult real-world business cases (Bahroun et al., 2023). Applications like ChatGPT keep students engaged by producing lively text and debate prompts, sharpening the critical-thinking habits employers now demand (Zhang et al., 2023). At the same time, privacy worries and hidden cultural biases-specially for learners from abroad-cannot be brushed aside (Wang et al., 2023).

GAIs spread across campuses also forces instructors to rethink tests and assignments so they truly value originality and sound analysis (Smolansky et al., 2023). Although literature still lacks a step-by-step integration model, upcoming studies must weigh tech gains against ethical risks and design guides that do both (Kanbach et al., 2023). Meeting those challenges head-on will let business schools equip graduates for a job market that is changing by the month.

The literature collectively paints a nuanced picture: generative AI enhances efficiency and engagement but introduces risks that demand human oversight. Faculty workload reductions free time for innovation, yet training is critical to overcome resistance. Student outcomes improve with personalization, but dependency and bias threaten progress. Ethical concerns bias, privacy, inequity require robust solutions, while cross-disciplinary insights and trends point to evolving roles. This review synthesizes these themes, addressing a call for peer-reviewed rigor and ethical depth, providing a foundation for understanding AI's transformative role in business education.

## Understanding Generative AI

***Definition and Mechanics:*** Generative AI creates original content text, images, simulations using neural networks trained on vast datasets. Models like GPT-4 generate syllabi, DALL-E 3 produces visuals, and custom tools simulate markets. Unlike predictive AI, generative models excel in creativity but falter in subjective judgment.

***Relevance to Business Education:*** Generative artificial intelligence is genuinely revitalizing business education, and the shift offers a thrilling glimpse of tomorrow's classroom. Picture an environment where students stop reading theories and instead pilot AI-crafted simulations that mimic managing a live company. Such platforms replicate high-stakes events-a sudden stock plunge or a shipment delay-and challenge learners to respond on the spot. Intelligent Tutoring Systems (ITS) and GenAI provide customized, immediate feedback with flexible access for learners that can enhance learners disengagement and accommodate a range of ways of learning. Moreover, GenAI equips teachers with responsive tools to build multimedia learning content and facilitate integrated assessments. GenAI also supports teachers' effectiveness and collaborative learning in the classroom (Nguyen et al., 2024). Thus, its value lies in augmenting, not replacing, human expertise.

Generative AI is also reshaping how courses adapt to individual learners, and that shift could prove revolutionary. Each student processes material in a distinctive way: one grasps financial modeling almost instantly, yet another requires extra drills in marketing analytics. Intelligent learning platforms observe performance patterns and then generate targeted assignments or practice exercises that align precisely with those strengths and gaps. The effect resembles having a personal tutor who not only identifies your weak spots but also delivers the exact resource that will help you improve.

## Applications of Generative AI in Business Education

### Lesson Planning and Content Creation

- *AI-Generated Lesson Plans:* ChatGPT drafts syllabi, cutting planning time for teachers. In a study by Poet and Aston (2025), it was stated that 57% of teachers reported using at least one type of AI tool to support their work and teachers in the ChatGPT group saved time around 25 minutes per week on average. This is a 31% cut in lesson planning time, on average, compared to teachers asked not to use any GenAI.
- *Case Studies and Simulations:* AI can be practically applied to business education, as it will develop dynamic, real-time cases shaped by student learning levels and interests to facilitate higher engagement and relevance. It can create multimedia-rich, role-based scenarios to develop critical thinking and decision-making that is particularly effective in remote or hybrid learner situations. AI-generated simulation cases enable remote learners to engage with complex real-life problems (e.g., welfare, trauma, and systems issues), which cannot be replicated as experiences in the classroom (Asakura et al., 2020).
- *Multimedia Content:* Visuals provide undoubtedly critical value to the experience of comprehension and retention in the teaching of business content, such as market trends, financial models, or strategic frameworks. Research indicates that people retain only 10–20% of what they hear or read; and this goes up to 65% when combining visual elements (Macesar, 2023). DALL·E and similar tools create custom infographics to demonstrate and operationalize abstract concepts. Using AI-generated visuals can be particularly useful when conceptualizing business simulations, supply chain dynamics, and even economic cycles to make sense of the ideas for able learners.

## Personalized and Adaptive Learning

- *AI-Powered Tutoring Systems:* One of the most significant impacts of GenAI is hyper-personalized education. Traditional business courses often follow a one-size-fits-all approach, but AI enables adaptive learning paths based on individual student needs.

Examples:

- Khanmigo (Khan Academy) – An AI tutor that assists MBA students with financial modeling, case study analysis, and strategic decision-making in real time.

Benefits:

24/7 learning support: outside classroom hours
Instant clarification of complex concepts (e.g., NPV calculations, Porter's Five Forces)
Adaptive difficulty adjustment based on performance

## AI-Driven Curriculum Customization

Business schools are using GenAI to dynamically adjust course content based on:

- Student performance metrics (e.g., quiz scores, engagement levels)
- Industry trends (e.g., adding modules on AI ethics due to rising demand)

## Automated Content Generation for Business Education

**AI-Generated Case Studies:** Professors spend hundreds of hours developing case studies. GenAI can automate this process while ensuring relevance.

- **Harvard Business AI Tool**

Harvard Business Publishing provides an educator portal that includes case studies and simulations with a focus on AI tools to improve relevancy for teaching. Specifically, HBS's Data Science and AI for Leaders course allows students to work with an AI-based tutor bot that helps with case studies, using real-life small business examples (Sax, 2025). While the platform does not create cases from headline events or reduce the time to write a case to hours, it does allow for timely customization by subject area. The HBP simulations allow students to engage in strategic decision-making, for instance, examining markets, but there is little evidence of GenAI bringing immersive virtual company simulations.

## Case Study: IBM's AI-Powered Business Simulator

Students in MIT Sloans MBA program use IBMs sophisticated business simulator to rehearse high-stakes decision-making in a risk-free setting. The platform mirrors economic shifts-inflation, supply shocks, and changing consumer costs-and produces plausible competitor responses in real time. Participants compare the experience to a serious strategy video game, gaining tactile insight into markets without jeopardizing actual capital. Such simulation-based learning links abstract theory to practical know-how, equipping graduates to tackle tomorrow's complex business problems.

### AI in Business Research and Data Analysis

**AI Research Assistants:** GenAI tools like Elicit, Claude, and Scite.ai help students.

- Summarize academic papers (e.g., meta-analysis of 50+ papers on consumer behavior)
- Identify research gaps in business literature

Example: London Business School's AI Integration

## Automated Market and Financial Analysis

Bloomberg GPT (a finance-specific AI) is used in courses like:

- Investment Banking (generating equity research reports)
- Digital Marketing (predicting campaign ROI using AI-driven analytics)

## AI-Powered Assessment and Feedback

### Automated Grading Systems

- Turnitin's AI Detector – Flags AI-generated content in essays
- GPT-4 for Business Plan Evaluation – Assesses feasibility of student startup proposals

Ethical Debate:

- Pros: Faster grading, unbiased scoring
- Cons: Risk of over-reliance on AI, missing nuanced arguments

### Real-Time Presentation Feedback

- Otter.ai transcribes and critiques MBA pitches
- Zoom AI Companion suggests improvements in persuasion techniques

## Multidisciplinary Applications

- *Finance:* Stanford's AI simulates crashes, teaching risk analysis
- *Operations:* MIT Sloan's AI models disruptions, refining logistics skills.

*Table 2. AI Tools for Content Creation*

| Tool | Application | Strength | Weakness |
|---|---|---|---|
| ChatGPT | Syllabi, cases | Speed, coherence | Generic without edits |
| DALL-E | Infographics, visuals | Rapid visualization | Oversimplification risks |
| Jasper | Corporate training content | Tone customization | Slower than ChatGPT |
| Midjourney | Detailed visuals | High-quality art | Less suited for quick drafts |
| Manual | Custom curricula | Deep personalization | Time-intensive (4x longer) |

**Source:** Author(s)

## Case Study: Darden MBA Program

Darden's MBA program, via its AI, Data Analytics, and Decision Sciences concentration, will most likely incorporate AI in situational learning in case-based courses in Strategy starting in 2025, which personalizes educational content to specializations a student is pursuing, such as technology or sustainability, for example. In addition, Darden's courses in AI are hosted on Coursera.

*Table 3. Administrative AI Tools*

| Tool | Function | Strength | Weakness |
|---|---|---|---|
| Gradescope | Exam grading | Speed, consistency | Subjective errors |
| Turnitin | Essay grading, plagiarism | High accuracy | Limited creativity detection |
| ClassDojo | Attendance tracking | Real-time analytics | Privacy risks |
| Calendly | Scheduling | time savings | Over-reliance risks |
| Manual | Traditional admin tasks | Nuanced judgment | Slow, labor-intensive |

**Source:** Author(s)

## Future Directions

As Generative AI continues to evolve, its applications in business education are expanding into virtual classrooms, gamification, blockchain credentials, AI-driven career guidance, and educator upskilling. However, each innovation brings both opportunities and challenges, from accessibility barriers to ethical concerns. Below is a detailed exploration of these future trends, supported by real-world case studies, institutional reports, and industry data.

1. Virtual Classrooms & Immersive Simulations

*Current State & How It Works:* Virtual classrooms powered by AI, VR (Virtual Reality), and AR (Augmented Reality) allow students to engage in realistic business simulations. These environments replicate:

- Boardroom negotiations
- Global supply chain management
- Crisis leadership scenarios

### Case Study: London Business School (LBS) 2025 AI Simulations

London Business School introduced a ground-breaking, AI-powered virtual boardroom for its MBA cohort. There, students negotiated with lifelike avatars playing the roles of the CEO, investors, and government officials. According to the school, the practice boosted participants' average bargaining performance and quickened strategic decision-making by twenty percent (Cloudforce, 2025). In response, LBS is piloting cloud-based cases that run in standard browsers and pairing them with live facilitators, so discussions stay dynamic. By mixing digital and human elements, the school aims to keep cutting-edge training within reach while preserving the rich give-and-take of real boardroom talk.

## Gamification in Business Learning

*Current State & How It Works:* Gamification applies game mechanics (badges, leaderboards, challenges) to business education, increasing engagement. AI enhances this by:

- Personalizing quests based on student weaknesses (e.g., extra finance drills for struggling learners).
- Generating real-time business scenarios (e.g., a marketing campaign simulation where students compete for market share).

## Blockchain for Secure Academic Credentials

*Current State & How It Works:* Blockchain ensures tamper-proof diplomas, certificates, and micro-credentials. AI assists by:

- Automating credential verification (e.g., recruiters instantly validate degrees).
- Tracking lifelong learning (e.g., AI recommends upskilling courses based on career gaps).

## Case of IBM's Blockchain Courses

IBM offers courses related to block chain and NFT technologies across multiple platforms.

## LinkedIn's AI Career Coach (2025)

LinkedIn Learning's AI chatbot supports user learning by providing real-time and personalized feedback for learners' skill-based inquiries. The AI system draws from course content produced by experts to provide customized recommendations and responses for users, such as when users want advice about difficult workplace scenarios, such as delegation and having hard conversations. The AI uses an iterative feedback loop to improve its responses over time and provide more accurate and personalized feedback. The AI tool also demonstrates contextual intelligence using the user profile to provide different strategic courses of action for individual contributors and managers that are based on the context of the user inquiry. The AI tool also provides diagnostic follow-up questions. This contextual determination is like research on adaptive learning systems which aim to improve the learning outcomes of learners through AI based personalized recommendations for user learning.

## Evolving Educator Skills for the AI Era

Professors must now master:

- AI literacy (e.g., auditing ChatGPT outputs for bias).
- Prompt engineering (crafting queries to generate quality case studies).
- Ethics training (addressing AI plagiarism, data privacy).

## Case Study: Yale AI in Education

In August 2024, Yale University established a $150 million effort into becoming a national leader in artificial intelligence (AI) in higher education. The funding is earmarked for a variety of needs - to develop computational infrastructure, hire interdisciplinary faculty, and engage AI in the curriculum, particularly in relationship to ethical inquiry and responsible use. The initiative was developed with substantial investment from the university's 2024 Task Force on Artificial Intelligence on the role of AI within higher ed; it encourages the development of AI but also the critical inquiry related to it in new courses such as "AI Policy," "Neuro-AI," and programs like the Schmidt Program on Artificial Intelligence at the Jackson School of Global Affairs. The Poorvu Center has also funded faculty interested in teaching AI and provided teaching resources, grants for the group work, and student initiatives, such as the AI Policy Initiative, which went further by addressing the implications of AI on society. As AI tools like ChatGPT enter the mainstream and become ubiquitous amongst students, inconsistencies in classroom policy over the use of AI tools have sent up a red flag on academic integrity. With all of this disarray in the classroom, Yale is using its effort to rationalize their vision establishing the role of AI in education through invention, governance, and engagement across disciplines.

## Case Study: HEC Paris

In 2024, two students from HEC Paris qualitatively evaluated the evolving role of generative AI (GenAI) in academic research and business education. Through surveys administered to partner institutions and HEC Paris, the students discovered that 96% of the students had used either ChatGPT or some form of generative AI in the completion of their dissertations, including literature reviews, grammar editing, authoring text, and data analysis, which saved them the average of 38% more time. While students overwhelmingly saw efficiencies from the use of generative AI, 89%

of students did not report to their supervisors that they had used AI tools in their dissertation work, reflecting an absence of institutional clarity and standards, and challenges with respect to academic integrity. Generative AI was overwhelmingly seen as a tool to supplement human support, with most students editing and reviewing human content produced with respect to AI. A complementary project suggest an integration of AI in depth, foundational courses and specialized electives articulating the use practically through labs, and cross-institutional partnerships with industry. Within a professional context, this research was presented at HEC leadership, and they called for continued opportunities for dialogue involving students, faculty and administrators to ensure that the use of AI in education is ethical, effective, and future-based (HEC Paris, 2025)

## The Impact of Technology on Sustainability in Business Education

Advanced technologies are reshaping business education by embedding sustainability into curricula, research, and operations. Business schools employ data analytics to develop case studies on circular economies, simulate ESG (Environmental, Social, and Governance) decision-making, and optimize campus resource management, as seen at institutions like Wharton and INSEAD. Students use analytical tools to model sustainable supply chains, linking theory with practical applications. However, concerns arise about the energy demands of computational systems, necessitating energy-efficient solutions to reduce environmental impact. Additionally, unverified sustainability claims risk promoting "greenwashing," highlighting the need for robust data validation.

To counter these challenges, business schools are adopting ethical technology practices aligned with sustainability objectives, such as the UN Sustainable Development Goals. Programs at Stanford and MIT Sloan prioritize auditing tools for efficiency and accuracy to ensure responsible application. Technology enables advanced sustainability education through product life-cycle assessments and scenario analyses, enhancing decision-making skills. Over-reliance on unverified metrics could erode trust, requiring careful oversight. By balancing technological innovation with environmental and ethical considerations, business education prepares future leaders for responsible, sustainable management.

## CONCLUSION

Generative artificial intelligence is transforming business education by creating interactive, tailored, and hands-on learning environments. When teachers embed these AI tools, they ready students for data-rich workplaces while also promoting sharp analytical and imaginative thought. Yet, ethical dilemmas and unequal access still demand attention if schools wish to unlock AI's full promise. As technology advances, business programs must adjust their curricula and practices so that graduates can guide a most digital future.

Generative AI transforms business education, as seen at Kellogg, Darden, Ross, and HEC Paris, streamlining tasks and personalizing learning. Yet there are certain risks such as costs, bias, inequities, and dependency. Human oversight is critical, blending AI's efficiency with educator judgment. Educators must train in AI literacy, institutions subsidize access, and researchers probe long-term impacts.

Actionable Recommendations:

- **Educators**: Enroll in AI workshops to master tools while prioritizing mentorship.
- **Institutions**: Fund open-source AI to bridge gaps for smaller schools.
- **Researchers**: Study equity, dependency, and outcomes to guide adoption.
- **Professionals**: Pilot hybrid models for balanced results.

This approach ensures AI enhances the human connection central to business education.

### Questions for Reflection

1. How can educators balance AI with mentorship?
2. What policies ensure equitable AI access?
3. How does training enhance AI's impact?
4. What prevents student over-reliance?
5. How has business education evolved over the past few decades, and what role does technology play in this evolution?
6. What are the key challenges facing business educators today, and how can generative AI help address them?
7. How do you envision generative AI transforming your own teaching or learning experience in the next five years?
8. What ethical concerns might arise from the use of generative AI in education, and how can they be mitigated?

9. How can generative AI tools like ChatGPT and DALL-E enhance the efficiency and creativity of lesson planning?
10. What are the potential drawbacks of relying on AI-generated content, and how can educators ensure quality and relevance?
11. How might AI-generated case studies and simulations improve student engagement and learning outcomes?
12. Reflect on a lesson or course you've taught or taken. How could generative AI have been used to improve it?
13. How can adaptive learning platforms address the diverse needs of students in a business education setting?
14. What are the benefits and limitations of using AI tools like Grammarly and Turnitin for real-time feedback?
15. How can customized learning materials help bridge the gap between theoretical knowledge and practical application?
16. Reflect on a time when personalized instruction made a difference in your learning or teaching. How could AI have enhanced that experience?
17. How can automated grading systems like Gradescope improve the efficiency and fairness of assessments?
18. What are the potential risks of relying on AI for tasks like attendance tracking and scheduling?
19. How can educators balance the use of AI for administrative tasks with the need for human oversight?
20. Reflect on an administrative task that consumes a lot of your time. How could AI help streamline this process?
21. What steps can institutions take to ensure the privacy and security of student data when using AI tools?
22. How can educators identify and address biases in AI-generated content or recommendations?
23. What role should human judgment play in an AI-driven educational environment?
24. Reflect on a situation where ethical considerations were critical in education. How would you handle a similar situation involving AI?
25. How might AI-powered virtual classrooms and gamification change the way business concepts are taught and learned?
26. What are the benefits of collaborative efforts between educators, tech firms, and industry leaders in shaping the future of business education?
27. What skills and competencies will business educators need to thrive in an AI-driven world?
28. Reflect on the future of your own institution or workplace. How can you prepare for the changes brought by AI and other emerging technologies?

29. How do you see generative AI complementing, rather than replacing, the role of educators in business education?
30. What excites you most about the potential of generative AI in education, and what concerns you the most?
31. How can business schools ensure that the adoption of AI tools aligns with their mission and values?
32. What steps can you take today to start integrating generative AI into your teaching or learning practices?
33. How can business schools use data analytics to teach students about sustainable practices, like circular economies or ESG decision-making, and what challenges might they face in ensuring these tools are environmentally sustainable?
34. What steps can business schools take to prevent "greenwashing" when using technology to create sustainability case studies, and why is transparent data validation important for credibility?
35. How can technology, such as supply chain modeling tools, help students connect sustainability theory to real-world business practices, and what is one potential drawback of relying heavily on these tools?

## REFERENCES


AACSB. (2025, February). *GenAI adoption in business schools: Deans and faculty respond* [Report]. https://www.aacsb.edu/insights/reports/2025/genai-adoption-in-business-schools-deans-and-faculty-respond

Anderson, J. R., Boyle, C. F., & Reiser, B. J. (1985). Intelligent tutoring systems. *Science*, *228*(4698), 456–462. DOI: 10.1126/science.228.4698.456 PMID: 17746875

Asakura, K., Occhiuto, K., Todd, S., Leithead, C., & Clapperton, R. (2020). A call to action on artificial intelligence and social work education: Lessons learned from a simulation project using natural language processing. *Journal of Teaching in Social Work*, *40*(5), 501–518. DOI: 10.1080/08841233.2020.1813234

Bahroun, Z., Anane, C., Ahmed, V., & Zacca, A. (2023). Transforming education: A comprehensive review of generative artificial intelligence in educational settings through bibliometric and content analysis. *Sustainability (Basel)*, *15*(17), 12983. DOI: 10.3390/su151712983

Baig, M. I., & Yadegaridehkordi, E. (2025). Factors influencing academic staff satisfaction and continuous usage of generative artificial intelligence (GenAI) in higher education. *International Journal of Educational Technology in Higher Education*, *22*(1), 5. DOI: 10.1186/s41239-025-00506-4

Barnes, L. B., Christensen, C. R., & Hansen, A. J. (1994). *Teaching and the case method: Text, cases, and readings*. Harvard Business Press.

Chacko, A. S. (2024). *Exploring Design Education in the Age of Generative Artificial Intelligence: Opportunities and Challenges* (Master's thesis, Georgetown University).

Chugh, R., Turnbull, D., Morshed, A., Sabrina, F., Azad, S., Md Mamunur, R., Kaisar, S., & Subramani, S. (2025). The promise and pitfalls: A literature review of generative artificial intelligence as a learning assistant in ICT education. *Computer Applications in Engineering Education*, *33*(2), e70002. DOI: 10.1002/cae.70002

Cloudforce. (2025, June 12). *London Business School becomes first UK business school to provide AI for all* [Press release]. PR Newswire. https://www.prnewswire.com/news-releases/london-business-school-becomes-first-uk-business-school-to-provide-ai-for-all-302480049.html

Graesser, A. C., Wiemer-Hastings, K., Wiemer-Hastings, P., & Kreuz, R.Tutoring Research Group. (1999). AutoTutor: A simulation of a human tutor. *Cognitive Systems Research*, *1*(1), 35–51. DOI: 10.1016/S1389-0417(99)00005-4

Harvard Business Review. (2024). Gen AI's impact on the case classroom. Retrieved from https://hbsp.harvard.edu/inspiring-minds/gen-ais-impact-on-the-case-classroom

Kanbach, D. K., Heiduk, L., Blueher, G., Schreiter, M., & Lahmann, A. (2024). The GenAI is out of the bottle: Generative artificial intelligence from a business model innovation perspective. *Review of Managerial Science*, *18*(4), 1189–1220. DOI: 10.1007/s11846-023-00696-z

Liang, J., Stephens, J. M., & Brown, G. T. L. (2025). A systematic review of the early impact of artificial intelligence on higher education curriculum, instruction, and assessment. *Frontiers in Education*, *10*, 1522841. DOI: 10.3389/feduc.2025.1522841

Macesar, A. F. (2023, August 3). *How to create marketing images from AI*. The Sustainable Agency. https://thesustainableagency.com/blog/how-to-create-ai-images-for-marketing/

Mah, D. K., Knoth, N., & Egloffstein, M. (2025, March). Perspectives of academic staff on artificial intelligence in higher education: Exploring areas of relevance. [). Frontiers Media SA.]. *Frontiers in Education*, *10*, 1484904. DOI: 10.3389/feduc.2025.1484904

Mayer, H., Yee, L., Chui, M., & Roberts, R. (2025, January 28). Superagency in the workplace: Empowering people to unlock AI's full potential. McKinsey Digital. https://www.mckinsey.com/capabilities/mckinsey-digital/our-insights/superagency-in-the-workplace-empowering-people-to-unlock-ais-full-potential-at-work

McKinsey & Company. (2024, August 7). *What is digital transformation?* Retrieved from https://www.mckinsey.com/featured-insights/mckinsey-explainers/what-is-digital-transformation

Nguyen, A., Kremantzis, M., Essien, A., Petrounias, I., & Hosseini, S. (2024). Enhancing Student Engagement Through Artificial Intelligence (AI): Understanding the Basics, Opportunities, and Challenges. *Journal of University Teaching & Learning Practice*, *21*(6). Advance online publication. DOI: 10.53761/caraaq92

Panda, R. (2024). Artificial Intelligence in Educational Systems: From Early Computational Tools to Contemporary AI-Enhanced Learning Environments. *International Journal of Research Publication and Reviews*, *5*(8), 3756–3760. DOI: 10.55248/gengpi.5.0824.2213

HEC Paris. (2025, May 7). *Students massively adopt AI tools for schoolwork*. HEC Paris.

Poet, H., & Aston, K. (2025, June 9). *Teachers' use of ChatGPT in lesson preparation can save time*. Chartered College of Teaching. https://my.chartered.college/impact_article/teachers-use-of-chatgpt-in-lesson-preparation-can-save-time/#:~:text=Saving%20time,not%20to%20use%20any%20GenAI

Ruiz-Rojas, L. I., Acosta-Vargas, P., De-Moreta-Llovet, J., & Gonzalez-Rodriguez, M. (2023). Empowering education with generative artificial intelligence tools: Approach with an instructional design matrix. *Sustainability (Basel)*, *15*(15), 11524. DOI: 10.3390/su151511524

Sax, M. (2025, June 24). *Custom AI tutor bots are transforming learning at HBS: Here's how students are using them*. Harvard Business Publishing. https://hbsp.harvard.edu/inspiring-minds/ai-tutor-bots-harvard-business-school

Sircar, S. (2009). Business intelligence in the business curriculum. *Communications of the Association for Information Systems*, *24*(1), 17.

Smolansky, A., Cram, A., Raduescu, C., Zeivots, S., Huber, E., & Kizilcec, R. F. (2023, July). Educator and student perspectives on the impact of generative AI on assessments in higher education. In Proceedings of the tenth ACM conference on Learning@ Scale (pp. 378-382). DOI: 10.1145/3573051.3596191

van Lehn, K., & Chi, M. (2012). Adaptive expertise as acceleration of future learning. *Adaptive technologies for training and education*, 28-45.

Wang, T., Lund, B. D., Marengo, A., Pagano, A., Mannuru, N. R., Teel, Z. A., & Pange, J. (2023). Exploring the potential impact of artificial intelligence (AI) on international students in higher education: Generative AI, chatbots, analytics, and international student success. *Applied Sciences (Basel, Switzerland)*, *13*(11), 6716. DOI: 10.3390/app13116716

Zhang, C., Zhang, C., Zhang, M., & Kweon, I. S. (2023). Text-to-image diffusion models in generative ai: A survey. arXiv preprint arXiv:2303.07909.

# Chapter 4
# Generative AI in Management Education:
## A Conceptual Framework for Transforming Teaching and Learning Practices


**B. S. Sahana**
https://orcid.org/0000-0002-4831-7731
*Jain University, India*

**Kesavulu Poola**
https://orcid.org/0000-0002-6565-7666
*Jain University, India*

**Sara Elias**
https://orcid.org/0000-0003-2417-9474
*Jain University, India*

**Sana Saima**
*Jain University, India*



## ABSTRACT

*Generative AI is transforming management education by enhancing learning tools and experiences in today's digital market. While educators often use tools like ChatGPT and DALL·E, many fail to connect them to effective classroom strategies. This research reviews 65 academic studies (2016–2024) and includes 25 expert interviews from North America, Europe, and Asia to develop a practical framework. The proposed model includes four key elements: Strategic Alignment to integrate AI into institutional goals, Adaptive Learning Models to personalize learning through*


DOI: 10.4018/979-8-3373-2150-9.ch004

*data insights, Reflective Practice to improve critical thinking with AI tools, and Stakeholder Engagement to ensure ethical, transparent use. The study also addresses challenges like algorithmic bias and suggests solutions such as policy standards, skill-building, and pilot programs with clear goals and feedback loops. Results show GenAI increases student engagement, supports practical learning, and enhances teaching without replacing educators.*

## 1. INTRODUCTION

Modern management education experiences technical innovation by combining advanced technology with how students and teachers learn. GenAI shows exceptional ability to change education patterns because its technology creates tailored and intelligent learning experiences at personal and course levels. GenAI represents a category of artificial intelligence featuring ChatGPT and DALL·E among others that create human-like text images code and simulators. Modern business practices rooted in technology require education programs to upgrade their approach to train students for the digital market (Holmes, 2016). The new technology behind GenAI requires us to shift our teaching approach toward its strengths and weaknesses.

During the past few years, the world experienced rapid development and wide adoption of General Artificial Intelligence technologies. Educational background systems now use these cutting-edge technologies after they earned fame in artistic and technological areas (Jin et al., 2024). Students depend more on AI to produce ideas and summarize content for presentations of solved issues. Teachers and students across the world use technology tools to build better instructional methods and teach diverse student groups with less daily routine work. Management educators who teach multiple subjects should see AI tools as tools to help their students and as problems to solve (Jackson et al., 2024). Using AI technology students gain better access to real market situations. Besides developing AI-supported tactics teachers must assess AI safety concerns and maintain learning quality against robotic solutions.

This research sets out a thoughtful model that explains how General AI will change the ways teachers and students learn management subjects. Through this framework educators and institutions can analyze how GenAI works in education plus its disadvantages and professional rules (Biloslavo et al., 2024). Management education focuses on developing technology benefits to enhance student abilities in problem solving and critical thinking through interactive learning activities (Moravec & Martínez-Bravo, 2023). Most management school programs teach students ways to solve problems by thinking critically and strategically.

Integrating GenAI into management education creates new challenges about the future of teachers. As AI works on content production and exam evaluation tasks educators wonder if they will lose their professional value (Lim et al., 2023). The essay shows that teachers need to transform their duties instead of losing them altogether. Teachers turn into organizers and supervisors alongside ethical mentors as they use AI in their classrooms. They should train themselves to evaluate AI output and help students use technology properly while creating meaningful learning goals with AI tools. The new teaching approach needs educators to have both technology knowledge and updated education methods. Based on these four essential areas the study recommends using (1) better teaching methods (2) personalization in student learning (3) new educational content and (4) ethical teaching standards. The study explains different areas of application with helpful examples and academic suggestions.

The study provides institutions with a strategy for choosing new educational technology that values students and protects ethical standards. Our evaluation shows the risks of incorrect information use alongside AI tools plus study techniques and academic core standards weakening into our education system (Ruiz-Rojas et al., 2024). AI technology needs support through formal rules, team education and accepting proper AI standards. AI technology can enhance teacher methods to assess students in management education. Current grading methods are changing into AI systems that provide ongoing feedback and adjust to personal learning habits to help learners develop themselves (Jackson et al., 2024). To bring this change into action needs thoughtful planning coupled with moral evaluation approaches to ensure fairness and academic ethics

The research shows higher education needs to use GenAI within its designated framework and educational goals to develop students who can think critically and ethically. Professional use of AI learning tools requires institutions to research their impact on higher education. Educational professionals and learning centers need to study AI effects on teaching and make sure AI works alongside human relationships (Batista et al., 2024). Management programs need both modern technology systems and human training methods that help students think better and lead their organizations.

The research looks into how generative AI helps teach management subjects through current instructional methods to ultimately develop an AI-based educational framework. The study explains both the moral and real-world difficulties with AI programs and suggests ways to include them properly in management education.

## 1.1. Context and Rationale

Management education needs to face important changes between fast developing technology and changing needs for workers. Business leaders worldwide must know core skills like finance and strategy plus they need to adapt to data-based systems and new digital business patterns (Holmes, 2016). Students who come from digital interactions need education systems that match their digital interaction habits (Lim et al., 2023). Artificial Intelligence that creates new content helps us achieve better teaching methods in business education. OpenAI's GPT 4 and DALL·E display how GenAI can produce human-level texts handling cases, draw visual scenarios, and hold educational interactions with students.

Researchers (Chiu, 2023) show that AI generates business cases and adapts student learning dashboards while an AI system suggests educational activities based on student performance. The evidence shows GenAI works but most schools use these systems separately through experiments. Most educators use Artificial Intelligence (GenAI) for specific assignments rather than creating comprehensive learning plans that focus on detailed institutional plans (Batista et al., 2024). Independently adding GenAI tools to specific tasks creates weak connections to education goals and increases the risk of mistakes with ethical implications.

## 1.2. Research Gaps

Three main differences appear when strategic goals do not line up with the way teachers use GenAI. This misalignment manifests in three primary gaps:

1. **Strategic Disconnection**: The GenAI pilots do not follow company strategies or curriculum plans which leads to random new system use and wasted resources.
2. **Pedagogical Fragmentation**: Small use cases do not follow established theories of learning like adaptive, hands-on, or thoughtful approaches so they create limited educational outcomes.
3. **Ethical and Governance Vacuums**: Numerous technology projects do not have established rules to protect data security plus shield against bias-operate while keeping people responsible for their actions.

## 1.3. Objectives and Contributions

The overarching aim is to develop and validate a conceptual framework that integrates GenAI into management education across four dimensions:

- **Strategic Alignment**: Align AI initiatives with institutional vision, curriculum design, and resource planning.
- **Adaptive Learning Models**: Employ AI-driven analytics for personalized content delivery and formative feedback.
- **Reflective Practice**: Use AI-mediated journaling and simulations to deepen critical reflection and professional growth.
- **Stakeholder Engagement**: Establish inclusive governance structures encompassing educators, students, IT staff, policymakers, and vendors.

Key contributions include:

- A synthesized review of 65+ academic sources and insights from 25 expert interviews.
- A four-dimensional framework with practical exemplars and actionable guidelines.
- Ethical and governance templates (ethics charter, bias audit checklist).
- A pilot roadmap and research agenda targeting longitudinal outcomes and equity considerations.

### 1.4. Paper Organization

Section 2 reviews theoretical foundations and recent advancements in AI-driven education. Section 3 details our mixed-methods methodology. Section 4 presents the conceptual framework. Section 5 discusses implementation guidelines and pilot planning. Section 6 outlines limitations, future research directions, and concluding reflections.

## 2. REVIEW OF LITERATURE

### 2.1 Early Developments in AI and Education

AI entered education through Intelligent Tutoring Systems during the 1970s and 1980s period. The systems imitated human tutoring through personalized instructions defined by pre-established criteria. During the early period of ITS their functionality depended on knowledge-based systems which demanded major human involvement to establish domain knowledge structure (Leung et al., 2024).

The limited adaptability of these systems became the base for developing future AI-driven educational environments.

The scoping review integrates modern academic research about how Generative AI (GenAI) transforms education by focusing on three main effects: enhanced individualized instruction alongside automated grading techniques and decreased faculty labor involvement (Holmes, 2016). The introduction of Large Language Models (LLMs) under GenAI has brought extra layers of complexity to both educational design processes and student self-direction after researchers previously focused on machine learning development of adaptive learning systems (Ogunleye et al., 2024). The review focuses on vital socio-technical difficulties which involve algorithmic bias and data privacy together with digital inequality yet all these needs immediate attention for AI integration in educational contexts.

## 2.2 Advancements in AI-Powered Learning Tools

Advancement in machine learning coupled with big data analytics has enabled AI applications in education to evolve into more complex systems. AI algorithms in Carnegie Learning and Knewton analyse student results to adjust their educational materials in real time (Leung et al., 2024). Using personalized experiences based on individual needs enables better learning outcomes because it evaluates particular student abilities so education remains inclusive.

Educational institutions use Natural Language Processing (NLP) as they integrate this technology into their operations (Bahroun et al., 2023). Students experience assistance through machine-based systems such as IBM's Watson and OpenAI's ChatGPT along with virtual and chatbot assistants as they execute queries while providing solutions and leading intellectual conversations.

## 2.3 AI in Administrative Automation and Assessment

The implementation of AI strengthens educational operations so that instructors can focus their efforts on teaching activities. The evaluations performed by artificial intelligence software-based solutions automate educational program assessment to assist teachers with their grading responsibilities (Lim et al., 2023). AI analytics tools examine student papers to provide fast assessment information to students that helps develop their academic writing skills. Online proctoring solutions featuring artificial intelligence functions ensure academic integrity by detecting irregularities that appear in assessment procedure (Chiu, 2023). The practical application of substantial adaptive assessment becomes achievable through Artificial Intelligence technology. The artificial intelligence system determines how to change the question complexity for following tests based on student evaluation data. The testing method delivers a more effective measure of student abilities than conventional standardized assessment methods (Ogunleye et al., 2024). The educational industry is switching to Artificial Intelligence (AI) technology which provides individualized learning areas and flexible teaching models for teaching practices. Various research releases prove that educational platforms benefit from artificial intelligence systems like machine learning and natural language processing by delivering personalized educational content to individuals (Jackson et al., 2024).

## 2.4 Management Learning Theories and AI

Management education relies on various learning theories, including experiential learning, transformative learning, and constructivist approaches. AI enhances these models by offering interactive simulations and adaptive learning pathways. AI-enabled adaptive learning enhances decision-making skills and critical thinking among business students.

### 2.4.1 Experiential Learning and AI

The learning method of experiential learning helps students solve problems by allowing them to handle practical activities. Realistic immersive educational experiences have emerged through AI-powered business simulations and virtual reality (VR) platforms which transformed experiential learning (Lim et al., 2023). Artificial intelligence tools create risk-free training environments for students to develop their decision-making skills through realistic business scenario analysis and strategic thinking development. These instruments establish direct relations between theoretical insights and practical implementations which results in more efficient education. The paper develops a conceptual model which unites Generative AI (GenAI) capabilities with adult education theories andragogy and transformative learning for application in higher education learning. The objective is to use GenAI tools (Adarkwah, 2024) to provide customized material alongside immediate remarks and interactive educational features for adult learners' digital learning experience enhancement.

### 2.4.2 Transformative Learning and AI

Transformative learning focuses on critical reflection and the development of new perspectives. Artificial intelligence enhances transformative learning by generating customized educational pathways which provide data-based information about student advancement in real-time (Jin et al., 2024). Technical platforms enabled by AI deliver enhanced capabilities for critical thinking and decision-making abilities in students of business studies (Batista et al., 2024). The platforms process student-specific learning data to supply customized educational material which boosts cognitive engagement between students and drives personal changes in their management education paths. Conducting research on the developing effects of generative artificial intelligence (GenAI) tools including ChatGPT on higher education represents the core subject of the paper (Wood & Moss, 2024). Different research investigations demonstrate how GenAI maintains an ambivalent role between disruption of pedagogies and their enhancement. The benefits of GenAI tools including customized learning and automated tasks and instant feedback lead us to these powerful risks against academic rules as well as next-generation thinking deterioration (Moravec & Martínez-Bravo, 2023). The review promotes fundamental changes (Leung et al., 2024) in education methodologies and curricular structures by suggesting teaching professionals should merge technological gains together with moral evaluations. Research findings demonstrate extensive evidence that teachers lack competency and proper training in GenAI implementation for their educational practices. The acceptance level toward GenAI (Biloslavo et al., 2024) varies among educators depending on their discipline area and age group alongside their digital literacy skills because computer science faculty demonstrates higher openness to adoption compared to social science instructors. Research by (Ruiz-Rojas et al., 2024) et al. creates a knowledge base which enables evaluation of educator acceptance for GenAI adoption in actual academic environments.

### 2.4.3 Constructivist Learning and AI

Student participation with team-based education constitutes the core approach of constructivist learning methods. The constructivist learning receives assistance through artificial intelligence-based chatbots along with discussion forums and intelligent tutoring systems (ITS) that enable interactive student-to-student communication (Ogunleye et al., 2024). Through AI platforms peer-to-peer learning becomes achievable by allowing users to get immediate feedback and develop appropriate discussion material and measure participant engagement. Students develop their understanding better in AI-supported collaborative learning platforms due to the environments that drive useful dialogue which expands existing suggestions between participants (Mittal et al., 2024). GenAI brings two main capabilities through its ability to optimize assessment processes in student learning and to reduce teaching tasks and generate dynamic educational systems. The use of GenAI encounters lengthy disputes regarding its impact on fairness visibility and participant protection and privacy. Colleges need to develop AI governance systems that establish ethical guidelines for monitoring user accountability regarding AI-based practices. Recent academic opinions agreed with Bahroun et al., (2023) that GenAI serves best to strengthen traditional higher education operations without seeking their replacement. Research suggests that GenAI becomes advantageous for educational institutions when they utilize it to reach their goals and enhance both performance outcomes and student satisfaction levels.

## 2.5 AI in Business Education and Corporate Training

In business education, AI applications extend beyond traditional learning models. AI-powered learning management systems (LMS) offer real-time analytics, personalized course recommendations, and automated assessments. Corporate training programs leverage AI to design competency-based learning modules, ensuring employees acquire relevant skills efficiently. AI-driven performance analytics help organizations track employee progress and identify skill gaps, leading to more effective workforce development (Mittal et al., 2024). Generative AI (GenAI) is revolutionizing supply chain optimization, enhancing decision support, scenario simulation, and demand forecasting beyond traditional AI applications. Educational institutions have faced substantial discussion about ChatGPT (Chiu, 2024) because it helps develop creative ideas yet triggers questions about plagiarism in academic work. The adoption of AI writing tools like Grammarly and Turnitin has created the foundation for general educational AI use. Researchers indicate that generative models pose a risk to critical thinking processes since they might automate intellectual work.

## 2.6 Stakeholder Involvement in AI-Driven Education

The four groups that participate in AI-driven education are educators and students and policymakers together with technology developers. Successful collaborations between these groups facilitate the implementation of AI technology while resolving possible learning model biases caused by artificial intelligence. The essential aspect for implementing ethical artificial intelligence in education stands in effective stakeholder collaboration. Teacher education reforms in developing countries align with global education reforms that focus on advancing the Sustainable Development Goals (Risang Baskara, 2024) especially through SDG 4 that supports inclusive and equitable quality education according to Nedungadi et al., (2024). Evidence shows that developing countries previously implemented broken and slow teacher education policies that did not create links between policy objectives and the classroom. Systemic change necessitates alliances among governments and higher education institutions and international development agencie. Schools need well-developed capabilities along with sufficient financial support and efficient leadership systems to achieve effective teaching education changes. Continued teacher development through modern practices of professional teaching alongside reflective learning contributes significantly to improving instructor quality and skills (Omran Zailuddin et al., 2024).

## 2.7 Ethical and Practical Considerations

The many benefits of AI coexist with ongoing ethical problems about data protection along with machine learning prejudices and educational trustworthiness. The successful adoption of AI in educational systems depends on both open AI decision processes and human-aided institutional directions. Academic institutions demonstrate a general move towards implementing natural language models by adopting ChatGPT. However, the advent of generative AI calls for a revaluation of traditional academic practices and assessment methods (Lotherington et al., 2024). Academic integrity challenges together with the effects of AI de-skilling as well as the implications AI generates for knowledge formation dominate the ongoing dialogue (Aure & Cuenca 2024). The learning community should embrace ChatGPT through a balanced outlook that sees it partner with students in their academic work. The digital pedagogy together with ethical standards argue that academic institutions need to move away from content reproduction assessments because GenAI tools promote creativity and language development and self-directed learning (Calleja & Camilleri, 2025). The educational institutions should develop comprehensive policies to teach both students and faculty about AI literacy and ethical matters.

Studies demonstrate that GenAI serves three primary functions as content producer and as educational tool and operational enhancer. The adoption of GPT needs careful ethical management since it raises privacy challenges and bias risks and potential improper utilization. The GenAI (Bell & Bell, 2023), has broad transformative capacity yet its deployment must follow strict regulations because digital literacy (Ivanov & Soliman, 2023), institutional rules, and inter-disciplinary groupwork provide the best path to ethical and effective use.

## 2.8 AI-Driven Learning Environments

AI platforms help students navigate complex management situations through which they gain improved insight into business operations (Thottoli et al., 2025). GAI marks a revolutionary period through its transformation of content creation services alongside customer support processes and decision-making strategies. GPT-3 operates as an advanced language technology to produce textual output with human simulation abilities which helps programming while benefiting education and healthcare industries (Nyaaba et al., 2024). The initial studies of modern GAI systems founded the framework which enhanced business and personal efficiency and creative output. GAI influences digital transformation through its application of interactive tools such as ChatGPT DALL·E and GitHub Copilot (Dai et al., 2023) which cause disruptions to conventional operational procedures. The high-level automated capabilities of GAI receive widespread praise yet problems with ethical conduct together with job loss and information falsity and programmed partiality remain unresolved (Lee et al., 2024). Research indicates that innovation strategies should align with enhanced responsibility measures since effective frameworks of transparency and accountability help reduce these risks according to Leoni et al., (2024).

The potential of GenAI to offer personalized feedback derives from Vygotsky's zone of proximal development and Bloom's mastery learning model according to existing literature. A body of research (Nyaaba, 2024) and other studies verified chatbots and intelligent tutoring systems and virtual agents as means for learning improvement. Literature documents frequent issues about ethical problems including software bias and teacher professional devaluation and excessive technological dependency (Xia et al., 2024).

## 2.9 Challenges in AI Implementation

Educational institutions need to establish formal guidelines which combine training programs to improve AI competence among teaching faculty and their students (Katsamakas et al., 2024). GenAI demonstrates its capability to improve student learning while helping create content and deliver real-time tutoring yet it poses potential risks to academic integrity with plagiarism as one main concern (Ghobakhloo et al., 2024) accompanied by misinformation and ethical issues. Similar studies on virtual language education demonstrate that students need adaptable platforms for learning foreign languages (Lao & You, 2024) which makes GenAI work as an instrument to establish realistic conversations and boost student interest (Wang et al., 2023). An optimal solution requires proper utilization of GenAI capabilities together with regulatory standards and ongoing trainer education alongside institutions that establish academic ethical frameworks.

# 3. CONCEPTUAL FRAMEWORK FOR AI-DRIVEN EDUCATIONAL TRANSFORMATION

This paper presents a conceptual framework for implementing generative AI in management learning. The framework comprises:

## 3.1 Strategic Planning

The strategic planning process is equally crucial when it comes to the effective and responsible endowment of generative AI elements in the process of the management education. It encompasses a conscious process of integrating the use of AI in line with the vision of the institution and its educational objectives as well as the law. Thus, by having a clear understanding of the formation of an AI strategy, institutions help in the implementation of technology to improve on the delivery system, faculty interaction, and ultimately the quality of student learning (Lee et al., 2024). Its advantages include use of analytical tools in efficiency enhancement in various areas such as timetabling, human resource or student enrolment forecasting. These can help in the making of conclusions when time is of essence to make a change concerning the management academic resources. Such a plan should also name additional goals concerning AI implementation, timescales to improve IT infrastructure, and readiness checks among the faculty. Furthermore, there is a need to instil proactive risk assessment, ethical compliance measures and, data management guidelines within this roadmap in order to fight misuse while maintaining organizational morality (Chiu, 2024). Close collaboration between academic departments, IT support teams and other organisational leaders is essential for the sustainability of such endeavors. Lastly, this planning should be cyclical and include structures for feedback, tourism policy change and expansion to allow institutions to adjust for the use of technology and education as these change with time.

## 3.2 Adaptive Learning Models

Adaptive learning models is one of the modern approaches within the management education aimed at providing student-centered, flexible and AI-driven learning environment(Nedungadi et al., 2024). These models depend on the analysis of data and the advanced algorithms of machine learning to present the lessons, the sequences of the lessons, and quizzes just to mention but few, based on the learner characteristic. Using LMSs as tools for artificial intelligence have adapted the system to track the learner performance, identify any learning gaps, and make course content changes in real-time to cater for all students. The approach opens up the possibility to achieve course objectives, work at one's own pace, increase course involvement, and develop a deeper understanding of concepts (Omran Zailuddin et al., 2024). Other forms of AI like the AI tutors and the chatbots can be very useful in the provision of feedback to the several learners who find it difficult to grasp certain management concepts thus creating an environment that mimics real life scenarios with feedback after achieving a particular level. These intelligent systems also relieve faculties from routine teaching and academic related tasks such as grading, generating feedback, and creating content. Some of the courses that could greatly benefit from adaptive learning are those that are associated to case analysis and decision-making exercises (Wood & Moss, 2024). However, in enhancing and improving on the curricula, institutions can as well analyze the analysis and behavior of the student/learner in the process as the data will help to point out on behaviors that require to be created to fit the societal needs.

## 3.3 Reflective Practice Methodologies

The reflective approaches to AI-supported management learning provide for the critical, ethical and judgmental elements in the learning process. Despite the ability of generative AI to generate the response content, feedback delivery, and even feedback assessment, the feedback recipient and provider must reflect to verify the analysis and relevance of the outputs generated by the AI. The reflective practices help the learners to evaluate the reliability and authenticity of the information provided by the AI tools (Lotherington et al., 2024). This fosters analysis, synthesis and metacognition which are important in the build-up of managerial skills. Some of the approaches that are implemented in learning include journaling where learners document their learning activities and self-reflection for evaluation. The necessity of learning by scenarios can be an intriguing subject for future research since it is a consistent practice in terms of providing an elaborated context close to the realistic one and using AI technologies to create iterations and reflections upon the learners' decision-making strategies and their consequences of actions. Learners can also use reflective tools to judge the applied by the faculty teaching strategy and adjust it with the help of AI tools (Ivanov & Soliman, 2023). Moreover, it identifies the responsibility of incorporating reflective practice for improving AI training, thus enhancing the awareness of ethics, data, and critical thinking in the students. When AI is integrated in educational contexts, the teaching-learning portfolios reflect on cycles that put humans as key to construction of knowledge and professional development (Nyaaba, 2024).

## 3.4 Stakeholder Engagement

Students, academic staff, employers and other members of organizational stakeholders' groups are important in ensuring effective and sustainable incorporation of generative AI in management education. Incorporation of all the stakeholders such as teachers, learner, university administrators, computer personnel, artificial intelligence designers, and the policy makers ensures that the Artificial intelligence as a teaching aid is both properly implemented and has the right ethic consideration (Xia et al., 2024). Students are the main beneficiaries who should be involved in co-designing AI solutions that would address their needs and incorporate their input regarding the use of AI in education (Lee et al., 2024). It is observed that institutional leaders are central in allocating resources, developing policies for the governance of AI, and driving AI adoption across the units. In particular, the technologists developing technologies and the AI vendors who are reselling such technologies should, therefore, engage with educators to fine-tune the technologies for fit within academic contexts and adherence to the values of education.

## 4. METHODOLOGY AND DISCUSSION

### 4.1 Research Design

This study adopts a qualitative research design to explore the incorporation of Generative AI (GenAI) in management education. Guiding an interpretivist philosophy, this research seeks to gain knowledge of educators' and experts' understandings of the pedagogical, ethical, and institutional issues of GenAI. A conceptual framework was developed based on theories of digital pedagogy, educational technology, and transformative learning. The design makes it possible to examine closely how GenAI transforms professorial roles, learning processes, and teaching practices. Through literary review, specialist opinion, and situational facts, the study offers insights worthwhile for policy building, curriculum remapping, and ethical higher education management.

### 4.2 Data Collection Methods

The data collection used a mixed-methods strategy, entailing structured interviews, close-ended questionnaires, and secondary data analysis. Primary data were collected from AI practitioners and educators to elicit first-hand experiences, perceptions, and concerns of integrating GenAI in management education. The questionnaires yielded quantifiable data, whereas interviews yielded rich, context-dependent stories. Secondary data were peer-reviewed studies, policy reports, and cross-country case studies to put findings into perspective. Thematic coding was utilized for qualitative data to allow for the identification of patterns that were repetitive in nature. The triangulated approach brought rich insights regarding theoretical and practical aspects of GenAI adoption in education.

## 5. FINDINGS AND DISCUSSION

**Questionnaire Analysis:** The questionnaire component of the study consists of closed-ended questions, to measure important themes like perceived usefulness, readiness of institutions, ethical issues, and pedagogical innovation.

*Table 1. Summary of Questionnaire Responses (N = 100)*

| Item | Agree (%) | Neutral (%) | Disagree (%) |
|---|---|---|---|
| GenAI tools can personalize and enhance student learning | 78% | 12% | 10% |
| I am confident using GenAI in my teaching | 45% | 30% | 25% |
| GenAI raises serious ethical concerns (e.g., bias, privacy) | 62% | 20% | 18% |
| Institutions are adequately prepared for AI integration | 28% | 35% | 37% |
| Training on GenAI use should be mandatory for faculty | 84% | 10% | 6% |
| GenAI will replace traditional teaching roles | 22% | 38% | 40% |
| GenAI improves engagement in management subjects | 69% | 19% | 12% |

***Source:*** Compiled by author(s)

Based on the questionnaire findings, while the educators embrace the value of GenAI in improving personalized learning and student engagement, concerns are huge when it comes to ethical risks, institutional preparedness, and employee training. Most of them favor organized implementation and compulsory training, reflecting guarded optimism towards embracing AI tools for management education.

Thematic Analysis:

*Table 2. Thematic Analysis Summary*

| Theme | Description | Sample Code |
|---|---|---|
| Pedagogical Transformation | GenAI supports adaptive learning, simulations, personalized feedback | "It helps me tailor lessons to each student." |
| Ethical Ambiguity and Risk | Concerns about plagiarism, data privacy, and bias | "AI makes it too easy for students to cheat." |
| Institutional Preparedness | Faculty feel undertrained and lack guidance | "There's no roadmap on how we should use it." |
| Faculty Role Redefinition | AI shifts instructors from content deliverers to mentors and facilitators | "We're becoming more like guides than lecturers." |
| Curriculum Realignment | Need to integrate AI tools into course objectives and assessments | "Courses need redesigning around AI capabilities." |

***Source:*** Compiled by author(s)

Thematic analysis yielded three overarching themes: pedagogical change through individualized and experiential learning; ethical issues of bias, privacy, and academic integrity; and institutional issues like undertraining and policy shortfall. These themes highlight the necessity of balanced, ethically informed AI adoption augmented by faculty capacity development and strategic alignment.

The literature sources included in the review has led to the following discussions and findings were developed

## 5.1 The Emergence of Generative AI in Education

The generative AI is slowly finding its place in the educational management system with its features of generating human-like responses and content. Some of them are being used in writing aids, writing feedbacks, writing assistance as tutors, and writing administrative jobs such as writing emails, preparing documents, and creating contents. The studies earlier discussed point that it is not simply the trend, but an evolution that will revolutionalise not only the means of instruction delivery but also the assessment (Aure & Cuenca 2024). The literature further supports these findings asserting that the generative AI advancement is part of a transformation brought about by digital technologies in the higher learning institutions. AI does, therefore, present itself as a solution to the goals that institutions have set for the development of a relevant curriculum for students, academic advice, and instruction.

## 5.2 Redefining the Role of Educators

The second transition area identified by the writers across all the papers reviewed is the Transformed Role of Educators. Since generative AI can help generate quizzes, outline content, even grades students' papers, teachers are left with the role of learning designers. Teachers need to foster under student's critical thinking skills, moral understanding and knowledge application across content areas (Thottoli et al., 2025). This type of use of AI tools is particularly emphasized in the review as well as the importance of intervention strategies aimed at helping faculty know how to integrate such tools into their programs in a way that the tools are partners in the teaching and learning process rather than tools being used for teaching by the faculty (Katsamakas et al., 2024).

## 5.3 Pedagogical Innovation Through Generative AI

Generally, generative AI gives room for the development of new pedagogy especially the learning models of choice. On the authors' note AI tools can customised contents in a strategy that reaches out to different learners' preferences and abilities on how they learn at their own pace, which is quite important in management learning bearing in mind that practical and cases form the basis of content.

The review outlines the following uses of AI in teaching and learning:

- Hypothetical case solving: It provides an environment where hypothetical cases can be adapted to give a student a feel of real-life business environment (Ghobakhloo et al., 2024).
- Flipped classrooms: In class assignments, teachers can use AI for providing contents therefore, making the class time more useful, informative and effective in cases such as discussions, solving of questions or problems in groups (Wang et al., 2023).
- Course credit: This comes handy as students can receive feedback instantly on assignments and this could lead to faster learning loop (Lao & You, 2024).

*Figure 1. Conceptual Framework for GenAI Integration in Management Education*

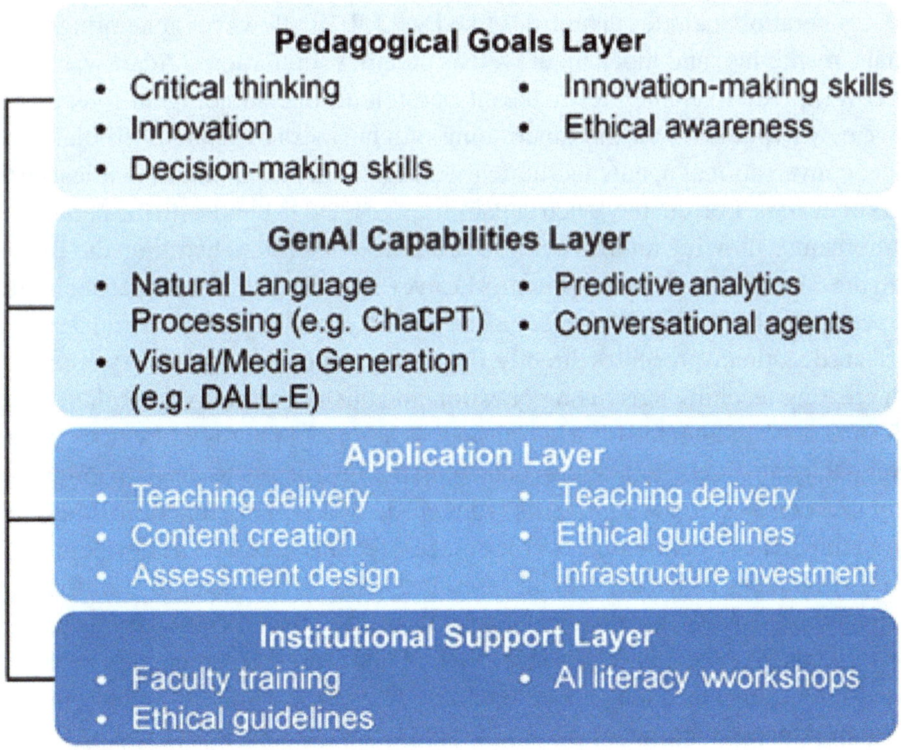

Figure 1 represents a detailed conceptual map about how Management Education can decentrally incorporate GenAI in order to alter the teaching-learning process. The model is designed with four linked layers, all of which are aimed at making improvements to the educational process while focusing on the employment of the best ethics, efficacy and sustainability in its practice.

The first layer of the framework is the **Pedagogical Goals Layer** and the goals signify the general purpose of management education in the context of AI. This is aimed at boosting proficiency in required competencies for the 21st century including critical thinking skills, creativity, ethics and innovation skills, problem solving skills and technological skills. These competencies are quite different from rote memorization or mastery of concepts and theories as most of the competencies aim at preparing the learners for practical business problems where critical thinking and ethical decision-making skills are important.

Below that there is the **GenAI Capabilities Layer** which enables to highlight the technological advantages of the GenAI tools. This includes components as simple as Natural Language Processing (NLP) that enables text-based creatives like generating reports, answering questions or summarizing the content. Skills of visualization and media generation include capabilities like DALL·E, it allows for generating custom visuals, marketing, and mock up as well as creating simulations (Adarkwah, 2024). Moreover, predictive analytics makes it possible to make intelligent forecasts and derive new hypotheses for the functioning of a business by using Artificial Intelligence; conversational agents facilitate the usage of artificial intelligent learners as tutors or avatars. Fortunately, such capabilities go hand in hand with the pedagogical requirements, allowing an instructor to promote or facilitate learning and interest.

In the current study, **the Application Layer** is a connection between technology and pedagogy. It identifies these instances where GenAI in particular can be applied to affect educational processes directly. For example, in teaching delivery, it can assist with creating teaching aids, using question and answer sessions to explain lessons and come up with interactive material such as animated photos and videos. In tasks relating to content development, AI can help the instructors to develop unique case study and content, and assignments (Lim et al., 2023). This function is helpful in automating the evaluation process for quizzes, feedback as well as developing peer review simulators which are crucial for improving performance. In addition, it can be applied in real-life in a manner of role plays and business simulations as it will give students the practical experience. Virtual tutors are instrumental in backing up students' learning since they are able to support your learning on an ongoing basis as required by each learner.

The only one on the lower level of the proposed framework is the **Institutional Support Layer**, which reflects the importance of educational institutions for successful integration of the GenAI. This involves the provision of faculty development to help teachers on how best to incorporate the use of these tools in their process and gain an understanding on the impact these have on their students. Another area institutions must dedicate their efforts is setting standards that will deter the abuse, fraudulent content, or dependence on the AI programmes. Support for such requirements as availability of AI tools and platforms that require maintenance of secure environments, and AI experimentation is also essential (Biloslavo et al., 2024). Training of both the faculty members and the students can go a long way in increasing confidence and more importantly; would ensure responsible incorporation of AI technologies in the learning process.

In combined, the four layers make up a coherent architecture which not only guides the implementation of GenAI in management education, it also incorporates necessary considerations for goals, ethics, pedagogy and institutions. This framework is useful for guide universities, educators and policymakers to understand and implement Generative AI for enhancing the capabilities of future business professionals.

## 5.4 Enhancing Student Engagement and Motivation

One of the main points presented is how the dissemination of generative AI can benefit students. This paper shows that the actual use of AI tools in classroom makes management theories come alive through the simulation of real-life scenarios. To this end, AI presentation of arguments to the students will foster curiosity and motivation in students to have dialogues (Ogunleye et al., 2024). Among the mentioned approaches, there are gamification, case studies with AI learning, and the use of scenarios as advanced learning more effective by their integration with AI assistance. This has been proven to enhance motivation and learning among the students particularly in management courses that can best be taught and understood in context with practical application as well as problem solving skills (Batista et al., 2024).

*Table 3. GenAI Tools and Their Use Cases in Management Education*

| Tool/Platform | Function | Use in Education |
|---|---|---|
| ChatGPT | Text generation, Q&A, summarization | Generating case studies, answering queries, essay reviews |
| DALL·E | Visual media generation | Creating marketing ads, infographics, branding visuals |
| Synthesia | AI-generated video presenters | Teaching videos in multiple languages |
| Grammarly | Writing assistance | Enhancing student reports and project submissions |
| MidJourney | Creative image generation | Design thinking and creativity in innovation courses |

**Source:** Compiled by Author(s)

## 5.5 Addressing Skill Gaps in Management Education

In the studies explored in the literature, it is shown that generative AI can be useful in fulfilling a powerful role in facilitating the transfer of skills. The students lack practical experiences and interpersonal skills, and although they are well armed with theoretical knowledge. Due to the availability of advanced technology, simulations and virtual role plays can be used in the learning process by the AI tools (Ogunleye et al., 2024). In turn, AI tools may also take on coaching roles for students and help them enhance interpersonal skills in communication and leadership or perhaps negotiation. For instance, virtual reality allows mimicking such scenarios as an interview, a board meeting or a working or business meeting with a client, and provides real time coaching and assessment. It also supports the argument in this regard that the manner indicated above makes the management education more relevant to marketplace expectations and improves employment prospects of graduates.

## 5.6 Ethical and Privacy Considerations

Several studies highlighted the problems of data privacy, the misuse of information by students, and presence of bias in algorithms (Jackson et al., 2024). It can be seem from the literature that use of AI has many benefits, yet it poses some issues like dependency, misuse that includes issues like plagiarism by the AI models. This means that there are certain rules and provisions for how generative AI should be used that needs to be defined and laid down by institutions (Lim et al., 2023). Teachers and learners require not only the skills of using such a tool but also familiarization with the probable drawbacks of their applications.

## 5.7 Challenges and Barriers to Implementation

However, the following challenges have been noted according to the review that may hinder proper integration of artificial intelligence into corporate planning:

- Change resistance: The teaching faculty and institutions will not support the use of new teaching technologies.
- Facilitating inequity in a learning setting: Students' access to technology is another factor that might widen the gap.
- Inadequate skills: Student teachers do not possess adequate skills to incorporate AI gadgets into their deliveries.
- Limited usage: Institutions may not have implemented the use of IT systems that facilitate AI in education.

Such issues must be approached through change management where the organization has to invest in training, structures and people.

## 5.8 Conceptual Framework for Integration

The outline of the study revolves around a conceptual framework that would present a coherent structure on how generative AI may be systematically infused in management education.

Based on the context given below, the framework is made up of the following parts:

1. Input Layer – Curriculum, institutional readiness, faculty capabilities.
2. Process Layer – utilization of AI in delivering various forms of instructional practices (personalized instruction, formative assessments, etc.).
3. Output Layer – Enhanced student learning outcomes, engagement, and skill development.
4. Feedback Loop – Continuous improvement through analytics, faculty feedback, and student evaluations.

This structured approach helps to avoid the situation when AI is implemented in some ill-conceived and irrelevant manner but is properly contextual and fits into the educational environment.

## 5.9 Impact on Curriculum Design

The curriculum in the management education process needs to be adjusted in order to include AI literacy and data-driven decision making. Excerpt, from the literature, are the following principles that have been identified as having a concern with the following courses:

- AI in business and decision-making.
- Data analytics and visualization.
- Digital transformation strategies.

For that reason, generative AI also facilitates the generation of real-time curriculum. The educators are also bound to revise case, integrate current affairs and even co-author with the help of AI making the approach very current.

## 5.10 Assessment and Evaluation Transformations

Some of the generative AI applications are today transforming the assessment designing and conducting process. Standard tests are no longer considered effective to assess the higher order thinking skills as well as students' creativity.

Instead, AI allows for:

- Continuous formative assessments.
- Project-based evaluations.
- AI-generated quizzes and practice exercises.
- Peer assessments facilitated through AI.

The educators need to gauge more open- ended, problem-based activities where students have to use the knowledge assimilated in a new way rather than reproduce it.

## 5.11 Faculty Development and Training Needs

Faculty development as an enabler for AI integration is the topic under consideration which appears to be rather critical. The review suggests that there is a continuous training requirement with regard to AI literacy, ethical use, and integrating instructions with AI (Jin et al., 2024). Education institutions must provide not only content knowledge based on software applications to be used in education but also encourage intellectual enhancements in terms of learning delivery. In addition, cooperation between the educators, technologists as well as instructional designers is critical to optimize the use of generative AI.

## 5.12 Managerial Applications of GenAI-Enhanced Education

Incorporating Generative AI (GenAI) into business school education not only revolutionizes pedagogy but influences managerial practice in the business, as well. Learners who have been trained using GenAI tools in their educational program show a spectacular advantage when confronted with the realities of business in current times (Biloslavo et al., 2024). Such students gain skill-by-skill mastery that relates to core managerial activities in marketing, operations, HR, and strategic planning.

The students, exposed to AI simulations and adaptive learning technologies, are employment-ready with enhanced skills in data analysis, scenario development, and stakeholder management. For instance, they are able to develop market-entry simulations, develop customer personas, and produce decision-supporting insights out of real-time data through AI, which are all minimum expectations of early- to mid-level managers.

In addition, companies that hire such GenAI-exposed graduates enjoy higher onboarding effectiveness, innovative potential, and digital resilience (Moravec & Martínez-Bravo, 2023). Feedback from industry stakeholders reveals that GenAI-exposed graduates can deliver to roles like customer service automation, internal communications planning, and AI-led financial modelling within weeks of recruitment.

## 6. CONCLUSION

The research papers are quite successful in describing the possibility of using generative AI in management education. In doing so, it gives useful information about the possible ways of making the implementation of AI in teaching and learning worthwhile. Nevertheless, in order to achieve such change, it is necessary to have clear vision, involve key players, and focus on innovations. The application of AI in education can only be effective in the presence of educators, institutions and policymakers who take up the responsibility of enhancing its virtues while scanning for vices. It is for this reason that the future of management education does not seem to lie in a future of displacing human knowledge gurus but enhancing it through innovative technologies aimed at making the learning process interactive, accessible, and resourceful for the current fast-changing world of business.

### 6.1 AI-Enhanced Teaching Strategies

Cognitive AI has presented positive changes to a traditional approach to teaching methods through the use of learning. Business simulations in which artificial intelligence plays a role help students solve real-life problems and think, therefore making decisions. Possibility of getting instant feedback through AI ensures that students enhance the ways of solving business cases as they practice with actual real-life enhanced situations. Also, due to the intervention of artificial intelligence, most learning platforms adapt to the educational material depending on learning modes and pace. These platforms also assess the performance data of the students and then facilitate the presentations based on the most suitable method. Such a level of individual attention makes students to be more receptive and greatly encourages the provision of individualized help to every learner in line with their difficulties. Machine learning algorithms also help in coordination and coopetition among learners. Educational chatbots and assistants assist students / respond to the questions and explain concepts that may have been confusing. This has helped in freeing up the instructors from responding to routine questions which could be responded without much difficulty hence allowing them to engage in activities that require human input.

## 6.2 Role of Stakeholders

The integration of AI in management education cannot be realized without commitment from the management systems, academicians, policymakers, and all the other relevant stakeholders. Teachers have a valuable function to play in the context of applying the advancements of AI technology that need to support and uphold teaching practices. This has ensured that the appreciation for AI innovations in learning environment is effectively enhanced among learners. This entails using artificial intelligence for the enhancement of learning management systems and the training of teachers in artificial intelligence literacy alongside the formulation of policies relative to the acceptable use of artificial intelligence. It is, therefore, essential to address challenges which relate to the technological and the financial resources required in the institution to spur the uptake of AI in education. As such, policy makers must set the right standards that govern the use of AI to ensure the same is done responsibly without compromising on academic integrity. Policies should also include sections regarding privacy of data, reducing biases in algorithms, and how the executed algorithms match with the educational objectives and guidelines. In this way, enlarging cooperation between practitioners and scholars, the policymakers may promote harmonious approaches to using artificial intelligence in education for the benefit of all the parties involved.

## 6.3 Ethical Considerations

Ensuring ethical AI adoption in management education requires addressing key concerns such as algorithmic bias, data privacy, and transparency. To this effect, institutions have to adopt measures that will make them provide information on how the artificial intelligence systems are making decisions and also have to include bias-detection mechanisms. One drawback, again the implications of which will be discussed in what follows, is the more general issue of data privacy since such AI solutions capture and synthesize significant amounts of information concerning students. It is therefore crucial for institutions to develop strict data protection measures in line with the GDPR, and other data protection acts and regulations in the respective regions. It is therefore necessary and paramount that clear guidelines are followed in the use and storage of the data and this must be communicated to the student and educators. The principle of academic integrity has to be upheld also in the learning process which is enhanced by artificial intelligence. With the help of AI in research and content creation, students can be taught on the appropriate ways of using AI to avoid being paralyzed or engaging in cheating. It is on this basis that institutions should come up with the right regulations and standards that are balancing between the use of AI in learning, and the general desire for achieving valid learning and critical thinking.

## 6.4 Challenges and Future Directions

Among the predominant issues facing the integration of generative AI into management education is the technological infrastructure gap that still exists within institutions. It is found that many of these college and university education systems in the developing world do not possess some of the basic components of edtech such as fast internet connection, updated learning management systems that are compatible with Artificial Intelligence devices. This bars the educators and the students from taking advantage of what AI has to offer in learning processes. This is so because the support that university faculty brings also poses a challenge through offering resistance and lack of technical competency. Current approaches towards artificial intelligence have most educators anxious for several reasons which include; fear of losing their jobs, poor awareness of emerging technologies, and infrequent professional development. This is usually masked by poor competencies in key competencies like AI literacy, data analysis, and the overhauling on how to integrate AI in teaching and learning. Concerns in the ethical and legal aspect also form as components of the compelling issues in the current societies. There are cognitive and social concerns connected with the use of AI tools, for example, issues of plagiarism, information privacy, and authorship. Currently there are no frameworks that guide the learners when using AI in a manner that does not violate course policies or which do not produce assignments with the help of AI; or which themselves do not violate copyright laws or which compromise the learners' data.

Also, excessive use of AI can prove to be disadvantageous to students, for example, the level of critical thinking and creative problem solving reduces significantly. One of the drawbacks of the use of the AI tools in generating responses is that it demotivates students, and they end up finding only basic material to work on in their courses. This is relevant in areas such as management, where one needs to employ analytics and logic in decision making. The current curriculum in most management educating programs has not prepared for this disruption that is brought by AI applications on learning. To integrate such application in courses, time, effort, and approval from the institution is needed. This comprises modifying the learning outcomes, revising the curriculum, modifying the assignments, and making them relevant to the current world market. Hence, assessing students using time-honoured assessment techniques like exams and papers is not efficient anymore, not to mention that it cannot determine actual knowledge and learning outcomes, especially when new tools like AI can help in writing the content. Teachers are therefore challenged to come up with techniques that will make the evaluations genuine as far as the students are concerned. The lack of access to AI tools is a daunting task that must be covered through some policies and which requires policy interventions.

While Generative AI provides rich enrichments to management education—e.g., customized learning and capable content generation—it also introduces sophisticated problems requiring careful scrutiny. These are threats to **pedagogical nuance**, wherein AI threatens to foster surface learning at the cost of dialogue-centered, human-agent pedagogy. On top of that, ubiquitous **privacy and surveillance** issues are born of analytics and proctoring technologies enabled by AI that can erode trust and agency. AI applications are prone to algorithmic bias, discriminatory against minority students in a negative way and exacerbating structural inequalities. Black-box model impenetrability compromises accountability, as challenging or comprehending AI-made decisions becomes more difficult. Institutions also have other exposure risks, such as vendor lock-in and non-alignment with accrediting standards, in addition to emerging regulatory uncertainty. These issues demand robust governance: transparency regulations, bias screenings, stakeholder monitoring panels, well-defined policy guidelines, ethics training, and data security protocols.

## 6.5 Implications for Industry and Professional Practice

The use of GenAI-based learning models has immediate support for business demands by making graduates ready to encounter the changing digital work environment. The need for businesses is increasing as they need professionals who are capable of operating with AI systems, utilizing not just them for job automation but for creation of innovations, creative solutions, and possessing ethical procedures for embracing technology.

By integrating GenAI into business school curriculum, schools bridge the skills gap between learning and work. Furthermore, collaborations between academia and business sponsors—through internships, project learning, and co-designed curricula—convert classroom skills into tangible business value.

These advances also imply that GenAI-based management training is not only an educational innovation but also a training strategy for the workforce with real managerial implications.

## REFERENCES


Adarkwah, M. A. (2024). GenAI-Infused Adult Learning in the Digital Era: A Conceptual Framework for Higher Education. *Adult Learning*. Advance online publication. DOI: 10.1177/10451595241271161

Aure, P. A., & Cuenca, O. (2024). Fostering social-emotional learning through human-centered use of generative AI in business research education: An insider case study. *Journal of Research in Innovative Teaching and Learning*, *17*(2), 168–181. DOI: 10.1108/JRIT-03-2024-0076

Bahroun, Z., Anane, C., Ahmed, V., & Zacca, A. (2023). Transforming Education: A Comprehensive Review of Generative Artificial Intelligence in Educational Settings through Bibliometric and Content Analysis. In *Sustainability (Switzerland)* (Vol. 15, Issue 17). Multidisciplinary Digital Publishing Institute (MDPI). DOI: 10.3390/su151712983

Batista, J., Mesquita, A., & Carnaz, G. (2024). Generative AI and Higher Education: Trends, Challenges, and Future Directions from a Systematic Literature Review. In *Information (Switzerland)* (Vol. 15, Issue 11). Multidisciplinary Digital Publishing Institute (MDPI). DOI: 10.3390/info15110676

Bell, R., & Bell, H. (2023). Entrepreneurship education in the era of generative artificial intelligence. *Entrepreneurship Education*, *6*(3), 229–244. DOI: 10.1007/s41959-023-00099-x

Biloslavo, R., Edgar, D., Aydin, E., & Bulut, C. (2024). Artificial intelligence (AI) and strategic planning process within VUCA environments: A research agenda and guidelines. *Management Decision*. Advance online publication. DOI: 10.1108/MD-10-2023-1944

Calleja, J., & Camilleri, P. (2025). Primary school teachers' perceptions towards the use of generative AI in teaching using lesson study. *International Journal for Lesson and Learning Studies*. DOI: 10.1108/IJLLS-11-2024-0268

Chiu, T. K. F. (2023). The impact of Generative AI (GenAI) on practices, policies and research direction in education: A case of ChatGPT and Midjourney. *Interactive Learning Environments*. Advance online publication. DOI: 10.1080/10494820.2023.2253861

Chiu, T. K. F. (2024). Future research recommendations for transforming higher education with generative AI. *Computers and Education: Artificial Intelligence*, *6*, 100197. Advance online publication. DOI: 10.1016/j.caeai.2023.100197

Dai, Y., Liu, A., & Lim, C. P. (2023). Reconceptualizing ChatGPT and generative AI as a student-driven innovation in higher education. *Procedia CIRP*, *119*, 84–90. DOI: 10.1016/j.procir.2023.05.002

Ghobakhloo, M., Fathi, M., Iranmanesh, M., Vilkas, M., Grybauskas, A., & Amran, A. (2024). Generative artificial intelligence in manufacturing: Opportunities for actualizing Industry 5.0 sustainability goals. *Journal of Manufacturing Technology Management*, *35*(9), 94–121. DOI: 10.1108/JMTM-12-2023-0530

Holmes, W. (2016). *Intelligence Unleashed: An argument for AI in Education.* https://www.researchgate.net/publication/299561597

Ivanov, S., & Soliman, M. (2023). Game of algorithms: ChatGPT implications for the future of tourism education and research. *Journal of Tourism Futures*, *9*(2), 214–221. DOI: 10.1108/JTF-02-2023-0038

Jackson, I., Ivanov, D., Dolgui, A., & Namdar, J. (2024). Generative artificial intelligence in supply chain and operations management: A capability-based framework for analysis and implementation. *International Journal of Production Research*, *62*(17), 6120–6145. DOI: 10.1080/00207543.2024.2309309

Jin, Y., Yan, L., Echeverria, V., Gašević, D., & Martinez-Maldonado, R. (2024). *Generative AI in Higher Education: A Global Perspective of Institutional Adoption Policies and Guidelines*. DOI: 10.1016/j.caeai.2024.100348

Katsamakas, E., Pavlov, O. V., & Saklad, R. (2024). Artificial Intelligence and the Transformation of Higher Education Institutions: A Systems Approach. *Sustainability (Basel)*, *16*(14), 6118. Advance online publication. DOI: 10.3390/su16146118

Lao, Y., & You, Y. (2024). *Unraveling generative AI in BBC News: application, impact, literacy and governance. Transforming Government: People*. Process and Policy., DOI: 10.1108/TG-01-2024-0022

Lee, D., Arnold, M., Srivastava, A., Plastow, K., Strelan, P., Ploeckl, F., Lekkas, D., & Palmer, E. (2024). The impact of generative AI on higher education learning and teaching: A study of educators' perspectives. *Computers and Education: Artificial Intelligence*, *6*, 100221. Advance online publication. DOI: 10.1016/j.caeai.2024.100221

Leoni, L., Gueli, G., Ardolino, M., Panizzon, M., & Gupta, S. (2024). AI-empowered KM processes for decision-making: Empirical evidence from worldwide organisations. *Journal of Knowledge Management*, *28*(11), 320–347. DOI: 10.1108/JKM-03-2024-0262

Leung, C. K., Ursino, D., Sajja, R., Erazo Ramirez, C., Li, Z., Demiray, B. Z., Sermet, Y., & Demir, I. (2024). *Integrating Generative AI in Hackathons: Opportunities.* Challenges, and Educational Implications., DOI: 10.3390/bdcc8120188

Lim, W. M., Gunasekara, A., Pallant, J. L., Pallant, J. I., & Pechenkina, E. (2023). Generative AI and the future of education: Ragnarök or reformation? A paradoxical perspective from management educators. *International Journal of Management Education, 21*(2), 100790. Advance online publication. DOI: 10.1016/j.ijme.2023.100790

Lotherington, H., Pegrum, M., Thumlert, K., Tomin, B., Boreland, T., & Pobuda, T. (2024). Exploring opportunities for language immersion in the posthuman spectrum: Lessons learned from digital agents. *Interactive Technology and Smart Education.* Advance online publication. DOI: 10.1108/ITSE-02-2024-0038

Mittal, S. Sai, V. Chamola and D. Sangwan. (2024). A Comprehensive Review on Generative AI for Education," in *IEEE Access.* 12, 142733-142759, DOI: 10.1109/ACCESS.2024.3468368

Mittal, U., Sai, S., Chamola, V., & Member, S. (n.d.). (2024). *A Comprehensive Review on Generative AI for Education.* https://doi.org/DOI: 10.1109/ACCESS.2017.DOI

Moravec, J. W., & Martínez-Bravo, M. C. (2023). Global trends in disruptive technological change: Social and policy implications for education. *On the Horizon, 31*(3–4), 147–173. DOI: 10.1108/OTH-02-2023-0007

Nedungadi, P., Tang, K. Y., & Raman, R. (2024). The Transformative Power of Generative Artificial Intelligence for Achieving the Sustainable Development Goal of Quality Education. *Sustainability (Basel), 16*(22), 9779. Advance online publication. DOI: 10.3390/su16229779

Nyaaba, M. (2024). *Transforming Teacher Education in Developing Countries: The Role of Generative AI in Bridging Theory and Practice.*

Nyaaba, M., Zhai, X., & Faison, M. Z. (2024). Generative AI for Culturally Responsive Science Assessment: A Conceptual Framework. *Education Sciences, 14*(12), 1325. Advance online publication. DOI: 10.3390/educsci14121325

Ogunleye, B., Zakariyyah, K. I., Ajao, O., Olayinka, O., & Sharma, H. (2024). A Systematic Review of Generative AI for Teaching and Learning Practice. In *Education Sciences* (Vol. 14, Issue 6). Multidisciplinary Digital Publishing Institute (MDPI). DOI: 10.3390/educsci14060636

Omran Zailuddin, M. F. N., Nik Harun, N. A., Abdul Rahim, H. A., Kamaruzaman, A. F., Berahim, M. H., Harun, M. H., & Ibrahim, Y. (2024). Redefining creative education: A case study analysis of AI in design courses. *Journal of Research in Innovative Teaching and Learning*, *17*(2), 282–296. DOI: 10.1108/JRIT-01-2024-0019

Risang Baskara, F. X. (2024). *British Journal of Teacher Education and Pedagogy Generative AI as an Enabler of Sustainable Education: Theoretical Perspectives and Future Directions*. https://doi.org/DOI: 10.32996/bjtep

Ruiz-Rojas, L. I., Salvador-Ullauri, L., & Acosta-Vargas, P. (2024). Collaborative Working and Critical Thinking: Adoption of Generative Artificial Intelligence Tools in Higher Education. *Sustainability (Basel)*, *16*(13), 5367. Advance online publication. DOI: 10.3390/su16135367

Thottoli, M. M., Cruz, M. E., & Al Abri, S. S. S. (2025). The incubation revolution: Transforming entrepreneurial education with artificial intelligence. *Asia Pacific Journal of Innovation and Entrepreneurship*, *19*(1), 2–23. DOI: 10.1108/APJIE-11-2023-0221

Wang, H., Dang, A., Wu, Z., & Mac, S. (2023). *Generative AI in Higher Education: Seeing ChatGPT Through Universities' Policies*. Resources, and Guidelines., DOI: 10.1016/j.caeai.2024.100326

Wood, D., & Moss, S. H. (2024). Evaluating the impact of students' generative AI use in educational contexts. *Journal of Research in Innovative Teaching and Learning*, *17*(2), 152–167. DOI: 10.1108/JRIT-06-2024-0151

Xia, Q., Weng, X., Ouyang, F., Lin, T. J., & Chiu, T. K. F. (2024). A scoping review on how generative artificial intelligence transforms assessment in higher education. In *International Journal of Educational Technology in Higher Education* (Vol. 21, Issue 1). Springer Science and Business Media Deutschland GmbH. DOI: 10.1186/s41239-024-00468-z

## KEY TERMS AND DEFINITIONS

**Adaptive Learning:** A learning model that uses AI and data analytics to tailor educational content to individual student needs, providing real-time feedback and support to enhance learning outcomes.

**Assessment Transformation:** The shift from traditional assessments to AI-driven evaluations, including continuous formative assessments, automated feedback, and project-based learning—enhancing authenticity and learner development.

**Constructivist Learning:** A student-centered approach where learners build knowledge through active engagement and collaboration. AI supports this with intelligent tutoring systems, discussion forums, and real-time feedback.

**Digital Pedagogy:** The use of technology—including AI—to design and implement teaching strategies. It focuses on enhancing interactivity, engagement, and personalization in the digital learning environment.

**Experiential Learning:** An educational approach that emphasizes learning through direct experience. AI facilitates this by enabling virtual simulations and business scenario modeling for hands-on learning in management.

**Generative AI (GenAI):** Artificial intelligence systems (e.g., ChatGPT, DALL·E) capable of producing human-like content such as text, images, code, and simulations. In education, GenAI supports personalized learning, automated feedback, and content creation.

**Management Education:** An academic discipline focused on teaching principles of business management, leadership, decision-making, and organizational behavior.

**Transformative Learning:** A theory of adult learning that involves deep, reflective thinking leading to a shift in perspective. AI tools support this by customizing learning paths and enabling critical reflection.

Chapter 5
# AI Tools and Technologies for Management Education:
## Enhancing Learning Through Innovation

**Muhammad Usman Tariq**
https://orcid.org/0000-0002-7605-3040
*Abu Dhabi University, UAE & University College Cork, Ireland*

## ABSTRACT

*AI tools and technologies are transforming management education by improving learning experiences, teaching efficiency, and preparing students for the future workforce. Personalized learning carried out by AI commutes educational content to students' individual needs, promoting better commitment and understanding. AI control simulations can provide students with a realistic, risk-free environment, practice decision-making and problem-solving, and bridge the gap between theory and practice. Additionally, AI-based assessment tools automate ratings and feedback, store trainers, and provide students with instant, personalized answers. Predictive analytics allow educators to monitor student performance and actively intervene in combat learners. While AI is developing, integration into management curriculums is becoming increasingly important, offering new ways to improve educational outcomes, enhance management tasks, and ensure business school graduates produce in a digitally controlled business world.*

DOI: 10.4018/979-8-3373-2150-9.ch005

## INTRODUCTION

Integrating AI tools into business and management training will transform how learning is delivered and received, offering significant possibilities for enhancing teaching methods and fostering student engagement. Artificial intelligence is transforming various fields, including education, by providing innovative solutions that personalize learning, improve efficiency, and offer valuable knowledge beyond the reach of traditional methods.

While, AI is developing, its role in business and management training will improve, creating new opportunities to better equip students with the skills and knowledge they require to succeed in a rapidly changing world. AI tools don't just replace traditional methods. It is to improve them and explore new teaching and learning methods for educators and students. Traditional classroom environments often have problems reducing the diverse needs of students, especially in large classes. AI-controlled technologies such as learning management systems (LMS) and adaptive learning platforms aim to assess learning progress, as well as the strengths and weaknesses of individual students. These systems can adjust the speed of education, suggest additional resources, and even provide real-time feedback to students. It allows for a more personalized learning approach. For example, AI tools can track student progress in real-time and provide recommendations and adjustments to course materials based on a particular learning pace and preferences. This level of adaptation is challenging in traditional educational settings. It is a great promise to improve student commitment and commitment.

AI-powered analytics tools can search large data records and recognize patterns and trends that will help educators make decisions that control the data about how curriculum design and curriculum strategies can be improved. For example, predictive analytics can help identify which students are at risk, allowing trainers to intervene actively. Not only will this help improve individual student outcomes, but it also provides valuable insight into the general effectiveness of the curriculum, allowing institutions to adapt their offers to evidence rather than adapting and improving them. In the digital age, students need to be familiar with the technology that develops industries such as AI, data analytics, and machine learning (Adeleye et al., 2024). By including these technologies in the curriculum, institutions can ensure that students are prepared for today's world of data-controlled business. AI-operated tools allow students to provide real-world experience in data analysis, knowledge, and decisions based on solving complex problems in real-world business scenarios. This exposure to AI in an educational setting links the gap between academic knowledge and practical skills. It helps students prepare for the challenge of being within their careers (Leong & Sung, 2025).

AI tools facilitate active learning and enable students to cope with course material interactively and more effectively. AI-run simulations, virtual environments, and interactive case studies allow students to use theoretical knowledge in a realistic environment and promote deeper understanding and bonding. For example, AI can create a virtual business environment where students can experiment with decision-making and see the outcomes of decisions in a simulated market. These experiences are especially valuable in business and management training, where understanding the impact of strategic decisions is very important. Cooperation is central to many business environments, and the ability to effectively cooperate with others is important for management professionals (Amdan et al., 2024).

AI-powered platforms can facilitate group projects and discussions by providing collaboration tools, real-time feedback, and peer review systems. These platforms can also monitor group dynamics, ensuring that all members contribute and that work is evenly distributed. In this way, AI helps students create a more integrated and effective learning environment where they can deal with colleagues, learn from each other, and develop important teamwork and communication skills. One of the most important obstacles to change is educators, institutions, and students. Many educators can be hesitant to use new technologies, especially if they are unfamiliar with AI or have a sense of hindering established educational practices (Clegg and Sarker, 2024). Similarly, students are skeptical about the effectiveness of AI-controlled learning tools, especially if they are new to teaching technical operations. Overcoming this resistance cannot be overlooked through comprehensive training for educators and students, and the possibility of AI not to fatigue and improve traditional learning methods. Institutions must invest in the necessary infrastructure and resources for AI-controlled technologies to effectively integrate into the curriculum. It includes acquiring AI tools, developing personnel functions, and training faculty to use AI-equipped systems effectively. Additionally, institutions need to tackle data protection and security issues, particularly when using AI to pursue student progress and analyze sensitive information. Ensuring that AI tools are used responsibly and ethically is an important concern for educational institutions, and regulatory frameworks and best practices must be carefully considered (Creely, 2024).

Furthermore, using AI in business education raises questions about the learning itself. As AI tools become more demanding, there is growing concern about whether their educational experience could deteriorate. While AI can provide personalized feedback and support, it lacks the emotional intelligence and understanding that a human trainer can provide. When looking for efficiency and personalization, there is a risk of losing the human aspect of education. Educators must increase the balance between using AI technology and maintaining personal connections with students, which are crucial to motivation and commitment (Clegg & Sarker,2024).

One central question is: How do AI-driven tools support business education? Researchers found that AI tools can improve learning by providing personalized feedback, promoting active learning, and enabling data-driven insights that inform lessons and curriculum design. There is still much to consider, particularly regarding the long-term impact of AI on student outcomes in terms of skill development and employment ability. As mentioned, resistance to change from educators and students is a significant hurdle.

Furthermore, the challenges to address are the complexity of implementing AI systems in an educational setting, the potential for data protection issues, and the need for ongoing professional development for educators (Demartini et al., 2024). Research findings are needed to understand these obstacles better and develop strategies to overcome them. Integrating AI tools offers opportunities for personalized learning, data-controlled decision-making, and the development of key skills essential to today's business world. However, successfully implementing these technologies requires significant challenges, including resistance between educators and students, the need for infrastructure and training, and ethical considerations related to data protection and security. As research continues to explore these issues, it is clear that AI may revolutionize business and management training and provide new opportunities to meet the requirements of the modern workforce (Ellikkal and Rajamohan, 2024; Tariq, 2025).

## AI-Driven Technologies in Business Education

Rapid advances in artificial intelligence (AI) will significantly change the educational environment, particularly in economic and management training. AI integration into learning management systems (LMS), AI-based tutoring systems, automated screening and evaluation equipment, and AI-controlled games and simulations revolutionize teaching and learning experiences. These innovations optimize the learning process and are more personalized, efficient, and committed to students. Using AI, educational institutions can meet the diverse needs of students, improve educational outcomes, and provide future business professionals with the skills they need in a rapidly developing business environment (Essien et al., 2024). Traditional LMS platforms have been used for delivery, communication, and management functions. However, they cannot often adapt to students' unique needs and learning styles. However, AI's improved LMS platform takes the skills of these systems to the next level by enabling a more personalized learning experience. These platforms use data-controlled knowledge and algorithms for machine learning to adapt the content and pace of learning based on the progress and performance of each student (Tariq, 2024). For example, suppose students must struggle with a particular concept. The system can automatically adjust the course material to provide additional resources, explanations, or exercise questions to reinforce this concept.

Similarly, AI can provide active intervention by notifying instructors when students risk retreating at a good time and allowing support. Additionally, the AI Amplifier LMS platform can provide the flexibility to identify individual student learning tensions and process course materials with the flexibility to optimize them through videos, interactive modules, reading materials, and quizzes. This personalized approach allows students to learn independently and improve bonding and understanding. By analyzing data from student interactions with the platform, AI generates insight into areas requiring more attention and helps trainers make sound decisions about adapting their educational strategies (Nguyen et al., 2024). For example, suppose most classes need to address a particular module. In that case, the instructor can change approaches or provide additional support without waiting for a formal review to indicate the issue. In this way, AI improves LMS adaptability and creates a dynamic learning environment catering to students' and trainers' needs. These systems provide personalized, real-time student support, providing interactive alternatives to traditional personalized tutoring. Operated by AI, virtual teaching assistants can address students through natural language processing, answer questions, explain concepts, and give instructions (Kaggwa et al., 2024). These AI-powered tutors can simulate individual lessons and allow students to find help rather than waiting for opening hours or a human trainer's availability. For example, suppose a student is working on a business case study or mathematical problem. In that case, the AI tutor can evaluate the student's response and provide corrective feedback if necessary. This feedback is not limited to correct or incorrect answers. However, it can also provide a deeper learning experience, including information, explanations, and suggestions for improvement (Gama and Magistretti, 2025).

Additionally, AI tutors pursue student progress over time, learning difficulty levels accordingly, and identifying patterns as they adapt. This dynamic interaction promotes growth and deductions and encourages students to improve and learn about their mistakes in a non-evaluative and supportive environment. Based on student performance on various topics, AI systems can propose areas for further improvement, recommend additional learning resources, and adjust the learning pace. For example, suppose theoretical concepts characterize students but must fight against practical applications. In that case, AI tutors can provide more realistic business scenarios and simulations so that students can build on the knowledge used (Grájeda et al., 2024). This ability goes beyond the scope of traditional personalized instruction by providing a highly individualized pedagogical approach to adapt to each student's unique learning track. This assessment is essential but time-consuming for educators, especially in large classes and online courses. Traditional classifications often include manual reviews that can lead to delays in providing feedback and are exposed to human error and distortion. AI-based rating systems streamline this process by automating the evaluation of tasks, tests, tests, and other forms (Singh et al., 2025). These systems use algorithms for machine learning to evaluate student submissions, compare them with preset criteria, and assign grades accordingly. However, AI also evaluates more complex tasks such as essays, projects, and case studies. With the help of NLP, AI can analyze text-based answers, assess their consistency, relevance, and overall quality, and assign classes based on predefined categories. While people may continue to be categorized for certain subtle or subjective aspects of the task, AI-based assessment systems reduce the time and effort required for assessments, allowing trainers to focus on providing more detailed and constructive feedback when needed (Gupta et al., 2024). Table 1 provides an overview of AI-driven technologies in business education.

*Table 1. Overview of AI-driven technologies in business education.*

| AI Tool | Application | Educational Area |
|---|---|---|
| AI-Powered LMS | Adaptive course pacing, feedback | General/All disciplines |
| Predictive Analytics | Identifying at-risk students, performance trends | Strategy & Performance |
| AI-Driven Simulations | Business scenario analysis, decision-making | Operations, Strategy |
| NLP Tools | Market trend analysis, sentiment detection | Marketing, Finance |
| AI Chatbots | Student support, Q&A | General/All disciplines |
| Automated Grading Tools | Essay and quiz assessment | All modules with coursework |

**Source:** Compiled by Author

Automated grading and assessments also allow for real-time feedback. Instead of waiting days or weeks, students can quickly learn how to cut off tasks, quizzes, or exams, helping them understand their strengths and weaknesses. Real-time feedback allows students to enter new material and modify and adjust their learning strategies before promoting continuous improvement. Additionally, AI systems provide personalized recommendations for further research based on performance, helping students focus on areas where maximum improvement is needed (Ruiz-Rojas et al., 2024).

Formative assessments promote a more holistic approach to learning, where students receive consistent feedback and have several ways to improve over time. AI allows educators to assess student progress in real-time, identify learning gaps, and provide timely support to help them create a more likely and dynamic learning environment. Gamification includes incorporating game elements such as points, levels, and rewards in the learning process and converting education into a more interactive, committed, and motivated experience (Adeleye et al., 2024). AI control simulation continues this concept by creating a realistic and interactive environment where students can apply theoretical knowledge to real scenarios. These simulations mimic real business scenarios such as market competition, organizational decision-making, financial management, and more, allowing students to experience the complexities of business operations without financial or professional risk. AI plays an essential role in these simulations by adapting virtual environments based on student decisions, feedback, and student decisions based on performance. AI responds to that decision by simulating market changes, competitive behaviors, and customer preferences (Amdan et al., 2024). By dealing with simulations, students can experiment with different approaches, see the outcomes of their actions, and learn from experience. These simulations provide a deeper understanding of business dynamics, improve critical thinking, and enable students to practice decisions in a safe and controlled environment.

Using rewards, achievements, and competition makes learning more comfortable, encourages students, exists in research, and allows more effort to be invested in material proficiency. AI-powered gamification platforms can create personalized learning paths based on student performance, providing rewards and assignments tailored to your progress. These systems also encourage collaboration as students can compete with each other and collaborate in a team-based manner to achieve common goals in simulation and gaming environments. The competitive and collaborative aspects of gamification help students develop the teamwork, communication, and leadership qualities essential for success in the business world. AI control systems can dynamically adapt to the complexity of business simulations to ensure that students are still involved and that decision-making skills are gradually developed. Including AI in the Gamified Learning Experience enables institutions to create a more urgent, interactive, and effective learning environment that improves academic performance and promotes the practical skills needed for real-world success (Sedkaoui & Benaichouba, 2024).

These AI-controlled innovations provide personalized, real-time, adaptive learning experiences previously unreachable with traditional teaching methods. By using the power of AI, educators can provide tailor-made support to their students, engage them more effectively, and prepare them better for the requirements of the modern business world. However, successfully integrating these technologies requires careful consideration of data protection, ethical concerns, and the ongoing need for human interaction in education. While AI is developing, it will undoubtedly play an increasingly central role in the design of future education, changing student learning and gaining the skills necessary to succeed in a world of business and management (Tariq, 2025).

## AI Tools for Data Analytics and Decision-Making

Business analytics is transforming by integrating AI and machine learning (ML) technologies. As organizations increasingly rely on data-controlled knowledge for decision-making, the focus is on teaching corporate students how to apply AI to predictive modeling, decision analysis, and other analytical techniques. Machine learning is central to transforming raw data into valuable predictions and knowledge, enabling business professionals to make better decisions. For business analytics students, learning is the creation of tools and algorithms needed to communicate how these methods are used and help data flourish in an environment directed toward decision-making (Jin et al., 2025).

Predictive models include using historical data to create models that predict future outcomes. It is essential to business decisions as companies can forecast market trends and demand, and optimize resources. For example, retailers can use forecasting models to predict sales based on previous data that optimizes stock levels. Students learn machine learning in business analytics, gain real-world experience using these models, understand how algorithms work, and recognize the importance of data quality in forecasting. These methods allow students to analyze complex data records, identify patterns, and predict future trends accurately. For example, students may use learning algorithms such as linear regression or decision trees to predict customer behavior and identify factors influencing sales services. Unsupervised learning techniques such as clustering allow students to group similar data points and discover hidden patterns that are not immediately apparent (Keskar, 2024).

Additionally, the increased enrichment, a subgroup of machine learning, allows you to teach algorithms, make decisions through interaction with the environment, maintain feedback, and optimize actions that optimize results. In business analysis, decision analysis involves assessing various options, considering potential risks, and choosing the best procedure. Machine learning algorithms can simulate and evaluate various decision scenarios, incorporate historical data, and predict future outcomes. Using machine learning technology, students learn to assess various options, predict outcomes, and make informed decisions, including marketing, finance, operations, and supply chain management. Simply creating a model is not enough (Leelavathi and Surendhranatha, 2024). Students must also know how to assess their accuracy, reliability, and applicability. Students should learn how to assess the effectiveness of predictive models using metrics such as accuracy, remember, and area under the curve (AUC). These power metrics help you understand how models work, how they can improve, and how to ensure that predictions are reliable.

Furthermore, students need to know something about model verification techniques, such as cross-validation, to ensure that the model is generalized to unseen data. Data visualization is key in supporting corporate experts in understanding complex data and presenting clear and implementable knowledge. AI-powered visualization tools allow users to interact with data in real-time, uncover trends, and generate knowledge that may be overlooked (Leon and Sung, 2025). These tools allow students to convert raw data into meaningful graphics such as diagrams, graphics, dashboards, and more that provide a clear presentation of the data, helping students decide the fastest and most accurate interpretation of tables and power BIs when interpreting the most frequently used business intelligence (BI) platforms (BI) and machine learning characteristics. These platforms allow users to create interactive dashboards and reports showing data trends, key performance indicators (KPIs), and forecasts. For example, students can create dashboards using Tableau or Power BI to pursue sales, customer acquisition, and financial metrics. AI has improved the capabilities of these platforms. Automatic trend recognition and predictive analytics allow students to uncover hidden insights without complex coding or manual analysis (Zhou et al., 2024).

Students can use these findings to inform business decisions. Adapt marketing strategies or optimize product prices. Students will learn Python skills when working with data, performing statistical analysis, and using algorithms for machine learning using libraries such as Pandas, NumPy, and Scikit-Learn. Python also seamlessly integrates with visualization libraries such as Matplotlib, Seaborn, and Plotly, allowing students to create high-quality data visualizations that effectively convey their knowledge. Learning how Python is used for data analysis and visualization allows students to explore large data records, use predictive models, and generate interactive diagrams and graphics that improve the impact on data understanding and business decisions.

Integrating AI in visualization tools is particularly advantageous for students looking at business analytics, as it may go beyond traditional data visualization techniques (Leelavathi & Surendhranatha, 2024). AI algorithms can automatically identify patterns and outliers in data that can be emphasized in visualization for further research. For example, AI-driven features in Tableau or Power BI recognize anomalies in sales data and recognize students of potential issues such as fraud, inventory mismatches, and market shifts. These tools provide the most effective visualization recommendations based on the data type analyzed and help students make more sound decisions about presenting their results. NLP is an AI branch that focuses on the interaction between computers and human languages. It allows machines to understand, interpret, and generate human language (Mu and Zhao, 2024).

Companies can analyze textual data from various sources, including customer feedback, social media, and market reports. Business analysis can use NLP to analyze customer moods, identify market trends, and extract valuable knowledge from unstructured data. By processing large amounts of textual data, the NLP algorithm can identify positive, negative, or neutral feelings that customers express in ratings, research, or social media posts (Yadav, 2025). For example, students can use NLP techniques to analyze and evaluate online customer reviews of products to determine how customers feel about their features, quality, and price. Mood analysis helps businesses understand customer perceptions and make data-driven decisions to improve their products and services. Using NLP for customer feedback, students can also identify new trends and collaborative issues they must address, such as frequent complaints about product features or inquiries about additional features. By analyzing news articles, blogs, and financial reports, the NLP algorithm can extract key topics, identify relevant keywords, and track changes in the market mood over time. In this way, companies can stay up to date through industry development, monitor the activities of their competitors, and predict market changes (Creely, 2024). For example, students can use NLP to analyze messages about a particular industry and identify emerging technologies, regulatory changes, or economic trends that may affect this sector. Using NLP allows students to understand market dynamics better and make better-informed decisions. Students studying NLP can extract valuable information from documents and explore techniques such as entity recognition (NER), tagging, and theme modeling to identify significant findings. For example, students can use NER to extract company names, product expectations, or geographic locations from many financial reports. This process helps businesses quickly identify the most relevant information from large data records, save time, and improve decision-making efficiency. By teaching students how to use AI for predictive modeling, decision analysis, data visualization, and mood analysis, institutions can acquire the skills they need to succeed in a data-controlled business environment. These AI technologies allow students to make more accurate predictions, gain deeper insights from the data, and improve decision-making capabilities (Nguyen et al., 2024).

When the business world relies on AI and machine learning, students who acquire these technologies will have a competitive advantage in the labor market. Machine learning enables predictive modeling and decision analysis, allowing businesses to make data-driven decisions based on historical data and future predictions (Suryanarayana et al., 2024). AI-powered visualization tools such as Tableau, Power BI, and Python allow students to transform raw data into meaningful knowledge and improve their ability to communicate results effectively. Additionally, NLP allows students to analyze textual data, gain insight into customer moods, and track market trends. Together, these AI technologies shape the future of business analytics training and provide students with the skills they need to succeed in an increasingly data-driven, AI-driven business environment.

## Personalized and Adaptive Learning in Management Education

Integrating artificial intelligence (AI) into the educational environment has revolutionized how business education is provided. The ability to process large amounts of data and learn from patterns helps AI educators personalize learning experiences and adaptive, interactive formation, helping them meet the diverse needs of their students. In addition to the various applications of AI in the education sector, personalized learning paths, AI-driven chatbots for student support, and adaptive, AI-based learning platforms, key innovations need to be highlighted. These technologies are intended to create more learning environments for students. Students are aware of their individual needs, which ultimately improves their learning process, improves engagement, and prepares them for the challenges of the modern business world (Onesi-Ozigagun et al., 2024).

Traditional education systems often follow a uniform approach where all students are expected to follow the same curriculum at the same pace, regardless of their learning style or skills. However, this approach may not be effective for students with various needs, strengths, and preferences. AI provides the opportunity to create a tailor-made learning experience that adapts to each student's progress, learning style, and interests, and learns how it suits them. AI can generate personalized learning paths that optimize their chances of success by analyzing data about students' past performances, interactions with course materials, and commitment. For example, if students distinguish between specific subjects, AI systems can accelerate learning by providing more advanced topics and challenging tasks. Suppose students have to struggle in a particular area. In that case, the system can provide additional resources, tutorials, or exercises to capture concepts more effectively. This individualized approach allows students to receive the right tasks and support, improving their commitment and learning outcomes. Personalized learning paths can also consider various factors, including student prior knowledge, learning speed, and learning styles, such as video, reading, interactive exercises, and further improving the general learning experience (Uzumcu & Acilmis, 2024). For example, in the Business Management course, AIs can help student understand marketing, operations, and finance and adapt their curriculum based on knowledge in all fields. Suppose students are showing special interest in finance. In that case, the AI system can suggest related case studies, articles, or videos that provide an opportunity to inform this topic more deeply. This approach improves student proficiency in business concepts and encourages them to explore areas of personal interest. Additionally, personalized learning paths help students build a wide range of skills in different aspects of their business, allowing them to become well-rounded professionals who can navigate business complexity for navigation (Keskar, 2024). These virtual assistants can help you guide students through the course, answer common questions instantly, and help you plan and develop your career. In contrast to traditional student support methods, where many people have to wait for business hours or email responses, AI-powered chatbots offer real-time and 7 days a year. It can address natural language students, answer questions, provide instructions, and provide emotional support when needed. For example, suppose students are unsure about task requirements or the steps required to complete a project. In that case, they can ask their chatbot to clarify (Demartini et al., 2024). Chatbots can quickly provide relevant information, guide students through the process, and ensure they stay on the right track. Additionally, chatbots can help students navigate complex business research or tasks by providing information, tips, or related resources that will help them improve their understanding and do it more efficiently. Economic students often experience uncertainty about their career paths. They may need guidance for the transition from science to the workforce. AI-operated virtual assistants can provide personalized expert advice by analyzing students' academic achievements, interests, and skills (Pawar and Dhumal, 2024).

It can propose potential career options, provide information on different industries, and even provide insight into the skills required for different roles in management, marketing, finance, human resources, and entrepreneurship. Additionally, these chatbots will help you create a CV and prepare for interviews, providing tailor-made support to students throughout the application process. The convenience and immediacy of chatbot support help students overcome obstacles, stay motivated, and make well-informed decisions about their academic journeys and professional efforts. Additionally, chatbots help to reduce the burden on instructors and academic consultants, focus on the more complex needs of students, and ensure that students still receive timely and valuable support (Ellikkal & Rajamohan, 2024). These platforms use AI algorithms to continuously evaluate student performance and adapt content, difficulty, and learning strategies based on individual progress. In contrast to traditional learning platforms that can present a static set of materials to all students, adaptive AI systems create dynamic, personalized learning experiences that develop in real time as student needs change.

For example, an adaptive learning platform can start with a business management course and present basic leadership, strategy, and organizational behavior material. Within students, the system monitors understanding of these concepts and adjusts content to accommodate the level of knowledge. Suppose students have a strong understanding of leadership theory. In that case, the platform can introduce more advanced topics from a strategic decision-making or global business perspective (Portuguez-Castro, 2024). On the other hand, if students must address a particular concept, the platform can provide additional explanations, test scenarios, or practice scenarios to deepen their understanding. This adaptive approach ensures that students can improve their commitment and storage significantly and are not overwhelmed by excessively complex content or material that is too easy. By analyzing data about student interaction with the platform, trainers can gain insight into how students deal with the material, where they stand out, and when additional support is needed (Mu & Zhao, 2024). This data control approach helps trainers make well-developed decisions on how to adapt teaching methods, provide targeted interventions, and ensure that all students receive the support they need to succeed. For example, a platform can present corporate research by companies that present themselves from the corporate perspective, such as Issues of reduced sales or employee commitment. The platform allows students to analyze problems, make decisions, and assess how they respond to changing conditions. Based on student decisions, the system can generate feedback, provide insight into the approach's effectiveness, and lead to more effective solutions. By addressing dynamic, real-world business scenarios, students can learn how to make data-controlled decisions, control complex tasks, and understand the outcomes of actions. These platforms can also provide a safe environment for students to experiment with different strategies and learn from mistakes without learning about the risk of failure in a real business environment. Whether students study Marketing, Finance, Operations, or HR, an adaptive learning system can create a tailor-made experience that reconciles academic and career goals (Rahiman & Kodikal,2024). This level of adaptation improves the learning process by ensuring that students receive content and experiences directly related to their interests and future careers.

An example is the use of AI in business simulations, where students develop the skills needed to experience real business challenges and effectively navigate them. These simulations often contain elements of gamification. In this element, students have tasks to manage virtual companies and solve complex business problems. The AI system dynamically sets the simulations to adapt to student decisions, provide feedback, and reflect the outcome of these decisions. Such simulations can help teach corporate management. It provides a safe environment for students to experiment and learn without facing financial or professional risks in the real world. These platforms analyze student performance and commitment to curating relevant and challenging content to help students stay motivated and committed during their studies (Onesi-Ozigagun et al., 2024). The system can also suggest additional resources such as articles, videos, case studies, and more to help students understand a particular topic better. With the ongoing adaptation of students to study trips, these platforms offer a more flexible and contrasting approach to business education. These innovations make business education more committed, effective, and accessible by providing students with a dynamic, tailor-made learning experience that addresses their unique strengths, interests, and goals. Because AI can track student progress, provide real-time feedback, and simulate real-world business scenarios, AI helps students develop the skills they need to succeed in a rapidly moving, data-controlled business world. While AI is developing, it undoubtedly plays an increasingly central role in designing the future of business education, allowing students to harness their potential and thrive in their careers.

## Challenges and Ethical Considerations in AI Integration

Integrating AI into education has been praised as a game-changer. It offers a personalized learning experience, accessibility, and increased efficiency. However, given the rapid adoption of AI-driven educational equipment, there have been several vital challenges that AI needs to address to achieve its full potential in the education sector (Essien et al., 2024). Most urgent issues include distortions in AI algorithms, data protection and security concerns, and teachers' overcoming AI adoption. These challenges can challenge the effectiveness of AI in education and the ability to create a fair, safe, and productive learning environment. While AI is developing and playing an increasing role in the educational environment, navigating these topics and understanding how to ensure that AI-controlled systems, including students, educators, and institutions, benefit all involved is essential. AI systems are based on a large amount of data to make decisions, and the algorithms that run these systems learn from historical data to predict results, identify patterns, and personalize learning experiences. However, if the data used to train AI models is not biased or representative, AI systems can maintain or tighten existing inequalities. It is mainly used to use AI control tools to assess student progress, provide personalized learning recommendations, and evaluate performance. If these systems are biased, certain groups of students, groups that lead to factors such as breed, gender, socioeconomic status, and disability, can be unfairly disadvantaged, which leads to unequal educational outcomes. It includes collecting data from different students and providing a good presentation of different demographic groups to identify and mitigate all distortions in the data. For example, when using AI systems to recommend learning resources to students, the data for training the system should differ from learning style, cultural background, and previous knowledge. Suppose the system is trained solely with data from a particular demographic group. In that case, there may be no practical recommendations for students of varying backgrounds and learning preferences (Rahiman and Kodikal, 2024).

The algorithm aims to make predictions based on data patterns (Strielkowski et al., 2024). However, if the algorithm design prefers a particular outcome compared to other outcomes, this can lead to biased predictions. For example, algorithms can prescribe a particular type of academic service or learning behavior compared to other priorities, assessing student performance, and leading to biased reviews. Developers must be transparent about how these algorithms are designed and will evaluate them impartially and continuously. An approach to combating distortion is implementing equity-conscious machine learning techniques that explicitly consider the modeling processes' prediction and outcomes' fairness (Pang & Wei, 2025). By integrating fairness into the design of AI algorithms, developers can create fairer and less biased systems. When AI tools record large amounts of personal data from students and process academic achievements, learning behaviors, and interactions with educational platforms, there are concerns about how this data is stored, shared, and used (Gupta et al., 2024). Protecting student privacy and data security is about maintaining trust in AI-powered educational instruments and maintaining compliance with data protection regulations such as the General Data Protection Regulation (GDPR) in Europe and the Family Educational Rights and Privacy Act (FERPA) in the United States. First, there are problems with data collection. The AI system often collects a wide range of data, including sensitive information about academic progress, student behavior, and personal functioning (Wang, 2024). If this data is not protected correctly, it may be accessed or abused by unauthorized parties, which leads to a violation of privacy. Secondly, there is a problem with data exchange. AI-equipped systems can share data across different platforms, create risks related to data usage, and determine who can access it.

In some cases, third-party companies may be involved in developing or operating AI systems. That is, concerns about some students and use for other purposes are used as educational improvements, such as targeted advertising. These measures include encryption of sensitive data, anonymizing student data for anonymizing student data, and strict access controls to confirm that only authorized people can access the data (Zohuri & Mossavar-Rahmani, 2024). Additionally, institutions must determine clear data protection guidelines and control information that informs students and parents about how their data about how they used, stored, and shared. By ensuring that student data is safe and privacy is respected, institutions can promote trust in AI-driven learning tools and ensure that these tools are used ethically and responsibly. Additionally, AI developers must develop data protection regulations and stay up to date to ensure that their systems meet legal requirements. For example, in the European Union, the GDPR provides strict guidelines regarding how personal data is collected, processed, and stored, including requests for express consent from individuals before data is used. Similarly, FERPA regulates the privacy of records in student education in the United States, and institutions must ensure that AI operational systems meet these regulations to avoid legal consequences and protect student rights. By including privacy and security in the design of AI systems, developers can minimize the risks associated with data collection and ensure that the system functions within legal restrictions. AI promises to improve teaching and learning, but many educators are reluctant to integrate AI into educational practices. This resistance can be attributed to various factors, including fear of job change, lack of knowledge of AI technology, concerns about the effectiveness of AI in education, and perceptions that AI tools are too complicated to implement. Overcoming this resistance is essential for effectively integrating AI-controlled tools into the educational environment, allowing faculty to use AI in ways that benefit lessons and students. This training should focus on the technical aspects of AI tools. Educators must understand how AI can personalize learning, support student commitment, and improve lesson effectiveness.

Furthermore, it is necessary to emphasize the possibility that professional development programs may supplement traditional teaching methods of AI through exchange. By teaching that AI is a tool that helps improve lessons and better meet the diverse needs of students, institutions can reduce resistance and promote a more positive attitude towards AI acceptance. Suppose faculty are involved in selecting and implementing AI technology. In that case, they will likely feel wealth through the process and be invested further in success (Jin et al., 2025). Collaboration between faculties, administrators, and AI developers can help ensure that AI systems are interpreted to the specific needs of educators and students. Teachers should be allowed to control AI tools, provide feedback, and suggest improvements to the course. This collaborative approach helps educators become familiar with AI. It ensures that the tools effectively align with users and educational goals. AI tools can automate recurring tasks such as assessments, administrative tasks, and basic student inquiries, allowing faculty to focus more on high-quality tasks such as student mentoring, course design, and commitment. By highlighting how AI reduces workloads and improves efficiency, institutions can reduce fear of job losses and help demonstrate AI's potential benefits for educators and students. Teachers may have valid concerns about AI's suitability for a particular educational context or field, and these concerns should be addressed with open dialogue and ongoing support. By taking a flexible and collaborative approach to AI adoption, institutions can create environments where educators can use AI in ways that respond to educational philosophy and improve students' learning experiences. It is used ethically and effectively. Institutions can create learning environments that benefit all involved by ensuring fairness in AI-driven educational instruments, ensuring student data, and providing educators with the necessary training and support. AI can revolutionize business education by providing personalized learning paths, improving student commitment, and optimizing administrative tasks. However, it must be implemented thoughtfully and responsibly to maximize its potential. With appropriate strategies, AI can improve the educational experience, promote more inclusive learning, and prepare students for future challenges.

## Case Studies and Best Practices

Integrating artificial intelligence (AI) in business schools and management training is revolutionizing how students prepare for the rapidly changing requirements of the global economy. From personalized learning experiences to AI control simulation and predictive analytics, AI tools can help modernize your curriculum and improve educational outcomes. Many institutions worldwide recognize the potential for AI transformation and have implemented innovative strategies to use these technologies to improve student learning, improve operational efficiencies, and promote better commitment to the industry. Additionally, companies are working with universities to design AI-controlled education programs that tailor academic training to real-world business needs and provide students with valuable skills and experiences that are extremely important for their future careers. This cooperation has led to the national development of ART training programs and research initiatives that bridge the gap between science and industry. However, as these AI-based programs are developed, decisive lessons must be created from implementations that can lead future efforts in AI-powered education (Ruiz-Rojas et al., 2024).

An example of this is the use of AI in a personalized learning environment. Many business schools employ learning management systems (LMSs) that are improved by AI algorithms that analyze the performance of individual students and provide personalized content recommendations. These systems pursue ways in which students deal with course materials and adjust based on learning advances. For example, students dealing with a specific concept of financial candidates can present additional resources, exercises, and targeted feedback to improve their understanding (Sarker et al., 2024). This adaptive learning approach provides all students with a learning experience tailored to their needs, improving commitment and retention. In addition to personalized learning, business schools were also used to facilitate a more efficient classification and assessment process. For example, some institutions use AI-based rating systems that automatically evaluate orders, quizzes, and exams, save trainers' time, and provide timely feedback to students. AI can consistently and objectively assess student submissions and help eliminate human error and distortions when classifying. In this way, trainers can focus on giving students deeper, more personalized feedback and celebrating the time they participate in smarter classroom interactions (Sedkaoui and Benaichouba, 2024).

Furthermore, AI tools are used to recognize academic injustice, such as plagiarism, by comparing the vast database of students with the student databases, ensuring that students comply with ethical academic standards. For example, some institutions offer AI-controlled business simulations replicating real business scenarios and allowing students to experiment with decision-making in a risk-free virtual environment (Singh et al., 2025). These simulations cover various business functions, including marketing, finance, operations, and strategy. They can allow students to apply theoretical knowledge to complex, practical problems. AI algorithms within these simulations can make student decisions, assess effectiveness, and provide personalized feedback to help students learn from mistakes and improve their decision-making skills. Business schools that include AI-controlled simulations in their curriculum improve student learning and prepare graduates with the practical skills they need to succeed in a competitive business. AI-powered chatbots and virtual assistants provide students with real-time language for frequently asked questions and use courses to assist with career advice. By automating administrative tasks, these tools save students' and employees' time and ensure students have the information they need when needed. It also helps institutions optimize their business and reduce employee burdens, allowing them to focus on high-level responsibilities such as curriculum development and student commitment (Uzumcu and Acilmis, 2024). As AI becomes an integral part of business strategy, companies are working with universities and business schools to create educational programs that convey the knowledge and skills needed to succeed in the AI control industry. These partnerships often include creating specialized training programs to bridge the gap between academic theory and practical business applications. For example, some universities are working with leading technology companies such as Microsoft, Google, and IBM to create AI-centric management programs that allow students to use AI tools to solve business problems. These partnerships bring industry capabilities into the classroom and ensure students are exposed to the latest progress in AI technology. Working with industry experts, the business school curriculum can develop developments that reflect current labor market requirements and prepare students for the skills needed to move from AI to an increasingly moving world (Wang, 2024).

Additionally, many business schools have established research centers focused on AI, working with companies that allow faculty and students to tackle real-world business issues. These research centers are incubators for innovative AI solutions that can be applied to many industries, from healthcare to fundraising. For example, teachers can work with financial institutions to use AI to improve risk assessment models and develop AI-driven customer segmentation strategies (Sarker et al., 2024). These partnerships provide students with valuable opportunities to address state-ART research and gain practical experience using AI tools and techniques. It also helps to promote a narrower relationship between science and industry. It ensures that business schools remain at the top of AI research and the highest levels. These programs are designed for professionals who want to see how they can be used to improve their understanding of AI and promote innovation within their organization. Through these partnerships, business schools provide unique training for AI topics such as machine learning, data analytics, and AI-driven decision-making, providing the skills needed to control the complexity of an AI-controlled business landscape.

Industry partnerships in executive education allow business schools to keep up with the ever-growing nature of AI, ensuring that programs remain relevant and align with the latest trends and developments. These initiatives allow students to gain real-world experience by working on AI projects and startups (Pawar & Dhumal, 2024). By working with companies, students can gain insight into the challenges and opportunities of AI implementation in various industries that will inform future careers. At the same time, companies benefit from innovative ideas and new perspectives from students and faculty, helping them stay competitive in the rapidly changing AI landscape. An important lesson is ensuring that AI tools are accessible and integrated for all students. AI offers the potential to personalize learning and improve results for many students. However, these tools must not accidentally widen the digital gap. For example, students from disadvantaged backgrounds and those with limited access to technology may face challenges when dealing with AI-powered learning platforms. Therefore, it is essential for institutions that AI tools are designed with inclusiveness in mind and that students are supported by access to various technical capabilities and resources. AI-equipped systems are dynamic and are constantly under development. Therefore, educators must regularly assess how these systems develop in the classroom. It includes gathering feedback from students and trainers, analyzing data on student outcomes, and adapting AI algorithms to ensure that they provide the desired outcome. Institutions that successfully implement AI in their programs understand that these technologies are not static and require continuous improvement to remain effective and relevant. Because AI is ubiquitous in businesses and society, business schools must inform students how to use AI tools and the ethical considerations related to AI use. It includes issues such as algorithm bias, data protection, and the impact of AI on the workforce. By including ethics in AI-focused business programs, institutions can ensure that graduates are students to make responsible decisions about implementing and using AI in the workplace. Business schools use AI tools to personalize learning, optimize management tasks, and provide practical experiences for students through AI simulations. Collaboration in industrial academia has led to the development of AI control programs that provide academic training with real-world business needs and convey the skills needed to succeed in an AI control economy. However, the teachings drawn by these AI-based business training programs emphasize the importance of inclusiveness, ongoing evaluation, and ethical considerations to ensure that AI technology is used effectively and responsibly. While AI is developing, business schools must be agile and innovative, and programs must be adapted to prepare students for the future of business in an AI-powered world.

## CONCLUSION

Artificial intelligence (AI) plays an increasingly transformative role in redesigning management, providing students and institutions with various ways to improve learning experiences, improve lesson effectiveness, and prepare graduates for AI control. In recent years, AI has become a critical tool in business education, providing advanced skills to personalize learning, optimize administrative tasks, accelerate student performance, and simulate complex business scenarios. The rise of AI-driven tools will not only make training more efficient. However, it will also be tailored to individual needs and promote an environment where students and educators can thrive. First, AI enables the development of high-ranking learning experiences that adapt to the special needs of each student. Traditional teaching methods often treat students as homogeneous groups with similar learning styles and functions. Meanwhile, AI can analyze large amounts of student data, including test results, engagement, learning preferences, and more, and provide individual content, resources, and recommendations (Gama & Magistretti, 2025). This personalized approach allows students to move forward at their own pace, reinforce difficult areas, and accelerate learning in prominent areas. Additionally, AI systems provide real-time feedback, which helps students identify and build their strengths. As a result, students can enjoy a more efficient and meaningful learning experience that reflects their specific needs and skills. AI-operated tools allow you to automate and optimize the instructor's process and provide immediate feedback to students through tasks, quizzes, and exam classification. This automated approach saves teachers' time and ensures a more objective and consistent assessment process without human bias. Additionally, AI control tools can assess broader student performance, including behavioral indicators such as participating in discussions and commitments to course content. This comprehensive approach allows for a more accurate and holistic perspective on student performance, providing targeted interventions to enable trainers to compete with students faster and ensure success. Traditional case studies and learning textbooks often do not replicate a real business environment's dynamic and unpredictable nature. However, AI-powered simulations allow students to experiment with decision-making in a risk-free virtual environment. These simulations can mimic various business scenarios, from financial analysis to marketing campaigns to supply chain management, allowing students to use their knowledge and skills in real-world situations. The AI-controlled feedback in these simulations can help students learn from mistakes, improve their decision-making skills, and develop problem-solving strategies. When the business environment is more complex and interconnected, these simulations provide invaluable and practical experiences for students to address challenges at work (Padovano & Cardamone, 2024). For example, AI-powered chatbots can receive routine student inquiries, provide course information, deadlines, and campus services, and assist with career advice. It reduces the administrative burden on faculty and employees, allowing them to focus on smarter interactions with students. AI can also help manage courses, enroll students, and help institutions with data control decisions regarding course planning and resource allocation. By automating time-consuming administrative tasks, AI promotes valuable resources to improve student experiences and facility operations. Institutions that want to integrate AI into their business curriculum have recommendations to help them achieve successful implementation. Many educators have limited experience in AI and are hesitant to use new technologies in their educational practices. The provision of specialized development programs focused on AI training, covering both the technical aspects of AI tools and the educational implications of AI in the classroom, will enable teachers to use AI in lessons effectively. These programs also need to highlight ways AI improves and does not replace traditional teaching methods. Teachers should encourage ways for AI to add to existing approaches. The aim is to clean up the skills and trust educators need to involve AI tools in ways that benefit students. Because AI tools are rooted in the education process, they need to address concerns about algorithm bias, data protection, and accessibility. For example, AI control tools that personalize learning experiences should ensure that all student recommendation data is representative and has no presence. Institutions should assume practices prioritizing equity, transparency, and inclusion, allowing all students to access the benefits of AI-powered education, regardless of background or learning style. Additionally, institutions must take steps to protect student data and ensure that AI systems meet relevant data protection regulations. Institutions can create effective and reliable learning environments that drive AI by prioritizing ethical considerations.

Third, institutions must set clear goals and strategies for integrating AI into their curriculum. AI tools can improve learning in many ways, but their implementation should align with educational philosophy and institutional goals. For example, agencies should consider how AI can support the development of specific skills such as data analysis, problem-solving, and collaboration. AI tools should complement existing teaching methods and provide additional support to students instead of being considered an independent solution. By developing strategic plans for AI integration, institutions can effectively use AI tools to improve their educational experiences and provide measurable results. As the demand for practical skills in the workplace continues to grow, business school students need to equip their students with the practical experience they need to succeed. AI-powered simulations allow students to experiment with real business scenarios and make decisions in a risk-free environment. These simulations help students build skills to solve problems and make decisions, develop strategic thinking, and better understand the complexities of the global business environment. By including AI control simulations in the curriculum, business schools can provide an increasingly immersive and practical learning experience that prepares students to meet modern business challenges. The pace of technological change accelerates, but experts must continuously update their skills to stay competitive in the workforce. The AI-powered platform is well-suited to support lifelong learning by providing personalized learning experiences and adaptive content that fits the learner's career goals.

Executive Education Programs using AI can provide tailor-made training in emerging areas such as data science, AI, and blockchain, ensuring that corporate leaders are ahead of industry trends. The future of AI in management training focuses on upskilling and washing, as AI uses AI to create flexible learning opportunities throughout the professional career. Another trend is the increased use of AI to learn together. While traditional business education often focuses on individual services, AI could enable a more collaborative, peer-driven learning experience. AI tools help students work on projects, exchange knowledge, and receive real-time feedback from their ages and trainers. These tools can promote a more interactive and participatory learning environment. This environment allows students to work together to solve complex business challenges. AI-controlled collaborative platforms can enable students from various geographic locations to connect, exchange ideas, and learn from each other. They can further improve the global scope of business education. AI systems can analyze student data in real time and provide trainers with insight into student progress, commitment, and difficulty. This data control approach allows educators to make more informed decisions about teaching and identify students who need additional support. If AI tools become more demanding, they could also predict student outcomes and problem intrusions, allowing for a more proactive approach to student success. As AI continues to change industries, business school students must prepare for roles that require a combination of business sense and technical knowledge. Through AI-controlled training, students can access various disciplines and learning materials to build cross-functional skills in data science, ethics, and entrepreneurship. Business schools are increasingly offering programs that combine traditional business education with ambitious technology to ensure graduates are equipped to control the complexities of the digital economy. Institutions should prioritize undergraduate training, ethical considerations, and strategic planning to implement successful tools for AI operations in their business curriculum. The future of AI-controlled education is full of exciting opportunities, including expanding lifelong learning, increasing cooperative learning, and increasing the use of predictive analytics. By implementing AI and adapting the curriculum to the needs of the digital economy, business schools can ensure that students are well-prepared for future challenges and opportunities.

## REFERENCES


Adeleye, O. O., Eden, C. A., & Adeniyi, I. S. (2024). Innovative teaching methodologies in the era of artificial intelligence: A review of inclusive educational practices. *World Journal of Advanced Engineering Technology and Sciences, 11*(2), 069-079.

Amdan, M. A. B., Janius, N., & Kasdiah, M. A. H. B. (2024). Concept paper: Efficiency of Artificial Intelligence (AI) tools for STEM education in Malaysia. *International Journal of Science and Research Archive, 12*(2), 553–559. DOI: 10.30574/ijsra.2024.12.2.1273

Clegg, S., & Sarker, S. (2024). Artificial intelligence and management education: A conceptualization of human-machine interaction. *International Journal of Management Education, 22*(3), 101007. DOI: 10.1016/j.ijme.2024.101007

Creely, E. (2024). Exploring the role of generative AI in enhancing language learning: Opportunities and challenges. *International Journal of Changes in Education, 1*(3), 158–167. DOI: 10.47852/bonviewIJCE42022495

Demartini, C. G., Sciascia, L., Bosso, A., & Manuri, F. (2024). Artificial intelligence bringing improvements to adaptive learning in education: A case study. *Sustainability (Basel), 16*(3), 1347. DOI: 10.3390/su16031347

Ellikkal, A., & Rajamohan, S. (2024). *AI-enabled personalized learning: empowering management students for improving engagement and academic performance.* Vilakshan-XIMB Journal of Management.

Essien, A., Bukoye, O. T., O'Dea, X., & Kremantzis, M. (2024). The influence of AI text generators on critical thinking skills in UK business schools. *Studies in Higher Education, 49*(5), 865–882. DOI: 10.1080/03075079.2024.2316881

Gama, F., & Magistretti, S. (2025). Artificial intelligence in innovation management: A review of innovation capabilities and a taxonomy of AI applications. *Journal of Product Innovation Management, 42*(1), 76–111. DOI: 10.1111/jpim.12698

Grájeda, A., Burgos, J., Córdova, P., & Sanjinés, A. (2024). Assessing student-perceived impact of using artificial intelligence tools: Construction of a synthetic index of application in higher education. *Cogent Education, 11*(1), 2287917. DOI: 10.1080/2331186X.2023.2287917

Gupta, P., Mahajan, R., Badhera, U., & Kushwaha, P. S. (2024). Integrating generative AI in management education: A mixed-methods study using social construction of technology theory. *International Journal of Management Education, 22*(3), 101017. DOI: 10.1016/j.ijme.2024.101017

Jin, Y., Yan, L., Echeverria, V., Gašević, D., & Martinez-Maldonado, R. (2025). Generative AI in higher education: A global perspective of institutional adoption policies and guidelines. *Computers and Education: Artificial Intelligence*, *8*, 100348. DOI: 10.1016/j.caeai.2024.100348

Kaggwa, S., Eleogu, T. F., Okonkwo, F., Farayola, O. A., Uwaoma, P. U., & Akinoso, A. (2024). AI in decision making: Transforming business strategies. *International Journal of Innovation and Scientific Research*, *10*(12), 423–444. DOI: 10.51244/IJRSI.2023.1012032

Keskar, A. (2024). Driving operational excellence in manufacturing through generative AI: Transformative approaches for efficiency, innovation, and scalability. *International Journal of Research and Analytical Reviews*, *11*, 245–261.

Leelavathi, R., & Surendhranatha, R. C. (2024). ChatGPT in the classroom: navigating the generative AI wave in management education. *Journal of Research in Innovative Teaching & Learning*, (ahead-of-print).

Leong, K., & Sung, A. (2025). Introducing airsim: An innovative ai-driven feedback generation tool for supporting student learning. *Technology, Knowledge and Learning*, 1-23.

Mu, Q., & Zhao, Y. (2024). Transforming entrepreneurship education in the age of artificial intelligence. *Resources Data Journal*, *3*, 2–20.

Nguyen, A., Kremantzis, M., Essien, A., Petrounias, I., & Hosseini, S. (2024). Enhancing student engagement through artificial intelligence (AI): Understanding the basics, opportunities, and challenges. *Journal of University Teaching & Learning Practice*, *21*(6), 1–13. DOI: 10.53761/caraaq92

Onesi-Ozigagun, O., Ololade, Y. J., Eyo-Udo, N. L., & Ogundipe, D. O. (2024). Revolutionizing education through AI: A comprehensive review of enhancing learning experiences. *International Journal of Applied Research in Social Sciences*, *6*(4), 589–607. DOI: 10.51594/ijarss.v6i4.1011

Padovano, A., & Cardamone, M. (2024). Towards human-AI collaboration in the competency-based curriculum development process: The case of industrial engineering and management education. *Computers and Education: Artificial Intelligence*, *7*, 100256. DOI: 10.1016/j.caeai.2024.100256

Pang, W., & Wei, Z. (2025). Shaping the future of higher education: A technology usage study on generative AI innovations. *Information (Basel)*, *16*(2), 95. DOI: 10.3390/info16020095

Pawar, S., & Dhumal, V. (2024). The role of technology in transforming leadership management practices. *Multidisciplinary Reviews*, *7*(4), 2024066–2024066. DOI: 10.31893/multirev.2024066

Portuguez-Castro, M. (2024). Reimagining the future of business education through educational innovation. *International Journal of Markets and Business Systems*, *5*(2), 192–208. DOI: 10.1504/IJMABS.2024.10069258

Rahiman, H. U., & Kodikal, R. (2024). Revolutionizing education: Artificial intelligence empowered learning in higher education. *Cogent Education*, *11*(1), 2293431. DOI: 10.1080/2331186X.2023.2293431

Ruiz-Rojas, L. I., Salvador-Ullauri, L., & Acosta-Vargas, P. (2024). Collaborative working and critical thinking: Adoption of generative artificial intelligence tools in higher education. *Sustainability (Basel)*, *16*(13), 5367. DOI: 10.3390/su16135367

Sarker, M. S., Khan, F. S., & Roon, S. L. (2024). The Impact of Artificial Intelligence (AI) on Business Operations in Bangladesh.

Sedkaoui, S., & Benaichouba, R. (2024). Generative AI as a transformative force for innovation: A review of opportunities, applications and challenges. *European Journal of Innovation Management*. Advance online publication. DOI: 10.1108/EJIM-02-2024-0129

Singh, E., Vasishta, P., & Singla, A. (2025). AI-enhanced education: Exploring the impact of AI literacy on generation Z's academic performance in Northern India. *Quality Assurance in Education*, *33*(2), 185–202. DOI: 10.1108/QAE-02-2024-0037

Strielkowski, W., Grebennikova, V., Lisovskiy, A., Rakhimova, G., & Vasileva, T. (2024). AI-driven adaptive learning for sustainable educational transformation. *Sustainable Development*.

Suryanarayana, K. S., Kandi, V. P., Pavani, G., Rao, A. S., Rout, S., & Krishna, T. S. R. (2024). Artificial intelligence enhanced digital learning for the sustainability of education management system. *The Journal of High Technology Management Research*, *35*(2), 100495. DOI: 10.1016/j.hitech.2024.100495

Tariq, M. U. (2024). Generative AI in Curriculum Development in Higher Education. In Fields, Z. (Ed.), *Impacts of Generative AI on Creativity in Higher Education* (pp. 227–258). IGI Global., DOI: 10.4018/979-8-3693-2418-9.ch009

Tariq, M. U. (2025). Bridging Cultures and Languages: Innovative Literacy Strategies for Inclusive and Engaged Classrooms. In Tussey, J., & Haas, L. (Eds.), *Supporting Cultural Differences Through Literacy Education* (pp. 257–282). IGI Global Scientific Publishing., DOI: 10.4018/979-8-3693-9271-3.ch010

Tariq, M. U. (2025). AI and the Ethical Crossroads: Navigating Privacy, Personhood, and Autonomy in the Digital Age. In Chakraborty, S. (Ed.), *Human Values, Ethics, and Dignity in the Age of Artificial Intelligence* (pp. 49–72). IGI Global Scientific Publishing., DOI: 10.4018/979-8-3693-9035-1.ch003

Tariq, M. U. (2025). Integrating ICT for Enhanced Organizational Resilience: Strategies and Case Studies. In Carvalho, L., Reis, L., Neves de Almeida Baptista Figueiredo, A., & Russo, N. (Eds.), *Leveraging Technology for Organizational Adaptability* (pp. 59–80). IGI Global Scientific Publishing., DOI: 10.4018/979-8-3693-6045-3.ch004

Tariq, M. U. (2025). Empowering Patients With AI-Ethical Digital Tools for Health Data Management and Decision. In Pesqueira, A., & de Bem Machado, A. (Eds.), *Navigating Privacy, Innovation, and Patient Empowerment Through Ethical Healthcare Technology* (pp. 197–216). IGI Global Scientific Publishing., DOI: 10.4018/979-8-3693-7630-0.ch008

Uzumcu, O., & Acilmis, H. (2024). Do innovative teachers use AI-powered tools more interactively? A study in the context of diffusion of innovation theory. *Technology. Knowledge and Learning*, *29*(2), 1109–1128. DOI: 10.1007/s10758-023-09687-1

Wang, Z. (2024). Artificial intelligence in dance education: Using immersive technologies for teaching dance skills. *Technology in Society*, *77*, 102579. DOI: 10.1016/j.techsoc.2024.102579

Yadav, S. (2025). Leveraging AI to Enhance Teaching and Learning in Education: The Role of Artificial Intelligence in Modernizing Classroom Practices. In *Optimizing Research Techniques and Learning Strategies With Digital Technologies* (pp. 211-238). IGI Global Scientific Publishing.

Zhou, X., Zhang, J., & Chan, C. (2024). Unveiling students' experiences and perceptions of Artificial Intelligence usage in higher education. *Journal of University Teaching & Learning Practice*, *21*(6), 126–145. DOI: 10.53761/xzjprb23

Zohuri, B., & Mossavar-Rahmani, F. (2024). The symbiotic evolution: Artificial intelligence (AI) enhancing human intelligence (HI) an innovative technology collaboration and synergy. *Journal of Material Sciences and Applied Engineering*, *3*(1).

## KEY TERMS AND DEFINITIONS

**AI-Driven Simulations:** Online environments for experiential business decision-making.

**Personalized Learning:** Customized educational experiences based on student requirements.

**Predictive Analytics:** Data analysis to predict student performance trends

# Chapter 6
# From Chalkboards to Chatbots:
## Technological Transition in Management Education

**Durga Madhab Mahapatra**
https://orcid.org/0000-0003-1272-7285
*North-Eastern Hill Univeresity, India*

**Zakir Hossen Shaikh**
https://orcid.org/0000-0003-4733-4166
*Kingdom University, Bahrain*

**Bhabani Shankar Mohanty**
https://orcid.org/0000-0001-9130-6221
*Central University of Tamil Nadu, India*

**Soumendra Kumar Patra**
*Ravenshaw University, India*

## ABSTRACT

*Artificial Intelligence (AI) is driving the evolution of management education, and India has the potential to be the pioneer of this digital transformation. In an era where Digitization and Gen AI are set to transform industries. B-Schools have a crucial role in bridging the skills gap and reshaping the corporate sector. The Gen AI and the sectors like electric vehicles, renewable and climate change are driving the dynamism of management education. The management graduate start-ups are also challenging the conventional way of doing business, and Gen AI will significantly impact traditional job roles will also emerge. With the changing pace of the world today, the change in hiring practices is about building a workforce that is agile,*

DOI: 10.4018/979-8-3373-2150-9.ch006

*diverse, and capable of meeting the needs of a tech-driven world. The curriculum on sustainability, ESG, Circular Economy, which MBA graduates learn the fundamentals for sustainability, social development, Deglobalization, geopolitical diversity, and sensitivities. This paper focuses the how sustainable technology solutions are useful in Education.*

## INTRODUCTION

India is rapidly accelerating toward becoming one of the world's top three economics, thus B-Schools also need to accept that Industry 4.0 demands skills on Data Analytics, AI and Cloud Computing, making technical expertise more valuable for industry needs. Moreover, Industry is more cautious about hiring due to demand uncertainty and rapidly changing business strategies (Adcroft et al., 2005). Thus, MBA Graduates must stay abreast of the latest trends and acquire relevant skills to enhance their employability. Today's dynamic world needs students and a workforce well-equipped to adapt to change. B-Schools are ensuring that students are well-versed in global business concepts and strategies by using international case studies, simultaneously and specialized courses, (Kumar and Sharma, 2020) and cross-cultural management, which allow students to be exposed to different cultures, business practices, and pedagogy. Through this effect which create a synergistic approach to fostering a global mindset. B-Schools must have to focus on nurturing an entrepreneurial spirit rather than simply producing entrepreneurs. This demonstrating it's significant contribution to the startup and economic development of the nation to create "Atmanirbhar Bharat" so that students learn the skills and information they need to help India become more self-sufficient and sustainable, especially in global markets. India is at a pivotal moment. Sustainable development is the only option because of population expansion, urbanization, and climate change.

The market size of Indian educational system was estimated at around $40 billion in 2023, growing at a CAGR of 15 percent, with over 1200 universities, 49,400 colleges and 12600 standalone institutions. India hosts one of the largest higher education ecosystems in the world. There has been significant influx of digitization in learning with online programs and various platforms providing a broad spectrum of courses online. Today, students are increasingly drawn to interdisciplinary programs (Meghwal, 2020) and new age courses that promise quicker skill acquisition and certification. Thus, there is a significant opportunity for institutions to expand their offerings in those Certification/degree courses where students can learn new skills in less durations. From the above analogy, the B-school of India has no exception. Further, the surge in Ed-tech has been transformative and represents a key area ripe for investment and innovation (Ministry of Human Resource Development. 2020).

The Indian Startup ecosystem has poised to escalate India to become the third largest economy in the world, The Start-up Entrepreneurship culture is drawing, the best MBA talent away from the Job market. Industry is cautions about hiring due to demand uncertainly and rapidly changing business strategic (Kumar and Sharma, 2020). B-Schools also boosts of robust infrastructure. The classroom is set in a modern environment that includes video conferencing platforms like Zoom, Cisco, WebEx and Google meet all used for online classes, hybrid meetings and webinars, Leitch and Harrison (1999). Indian B-Schools where AI is not just a subject, but very fabric of learning. The faculty are using the help of AI, refining their teaching methods (Mavin et al., 2004); and course content bused on data driven insights. The AI-powered personalized learning tools that adopt in real-time to each student's progress and learning style. Picture Virtual reality (VR) simulation where students can practice complex business negotiations or Crisis management scenarios with AI providing instant feedback and coaching. Further, AI-assisted career counselling that matches student's skills and aspirations with emerging job markets.

India is the largest democratic nation globally, characterized by a multilingual, multicultural, and multireligious pluralistic society (Nowani, 2020). In a dynamic technological landscape, India possesses a significant possibility to emerge as the global hub for digital talent. Generation Z serves as a catalyst as millennials transition into mid- to senior management positions, while youngsters born between 1997 and 2012 increasingly enter the workforce. Consequently, global economies are transitioning from conventional employment frameworks to part-time or gig economies. Businesses must cultivate a more diverse and inclusive environment to engage the millennial workforce. Technology is driving us at a never before velocity. The skills for the future will need to (a) impart training in critical thinking, (b) relationship building and collaboration, (c) enhancing emotional intelligence and empathy, (d) management and leadership, (e) cognitive flexibility and creating, over and above the vocational skills, need to perform a job. STEM education will help students leap from technology users to innovators. India's working-age population will grow (Palmer et al., 2023). The demographic dividend is expected to transform India into a large pool of global human capital. Working from home gives women a lot more opportunities to work and be a part of the formal workforce as it has opened a whole new set of the roles of women, in tune with blended and flexible (Bhattacharya and Bhattacharya, 2020).

Ratnakaram et al. (2025) and Mohanty et al. (2025) highlight the transformative potential of wearable and AI-enabled smart technologies in the education sector. Their works, published in the volume *Wearable Devices and Smart Technology for Educational Teaching Assistance*, explore the practical applications, benefits, and technical challenges of integrating wearables into teaching and learning environments. These studies provide valuable insights into how such technologies can enhance engagement, personalization, and accessibility in education. As automation, AI, and digital transformation accelerate, demand for cutting-edge skills in AI, machine learning, data analytics, and cybersecurity is surging. Jobs that once required minimal technological literacy now demand at least a basic understanding of digital tools (Patwardhan and Mittal, 2020). Upskilling can no longer be seen as optional – it's a critical strategy for survival in the modern workforce. The need to democratize access to digital education across socio-economic lines is non-negotiable, as India's future (Braddick, 1991). economic growth hinges on this transformation. The rise of the knowledge economy necessitates a shift from repetitive manual labour to roles that require advanced cognitive skills. Critical thinking, problem-solving, and creativity are becoming the cornerstones of tomorrow's workforce. Building a solid foundation in STEM education is no longer an option but a national priority to equip the next generation with the tools to navigate an increasingly tech-driven world.

AI has unique use cases that are available to all big enterprises, making it a valuable ally in this era of digital acceleration. Artificial intelligence (AI) is transforming traditional paradigms in every sector of the economy, including supply chain management, robotics, healthcare, public safety, retail, HR services, financial services, and financial inclusion and governance (Shaikh et al., 2022; Sheela et al., 2024; Selwin et al., 2024; Gupta et al., 2024; Kusuma et al., 2024; Panigrahi, Rashmi Ranjan, et al., 2023 and Sarea, A.et al., 2021). Education has undergone a dramatic change because of advances in artificial intelligence (AI). changed by the shift from traditional teaching approaches to 4.0 and beyond, which increases the adaptability, individualization, and inclusivity of learning. must be adaptable, and the program is specifically designed to help students acquire and maximize their capacity to adjust to Industry 4.0. Inequitable and inclusive education has a long history in India. The National Education Policy (NEP) 2020 was created in accordance with most of the Sustainable Development Goals (SDGs), which call for reforms at all educational levels. Higher education should be prioritized because it increases social mobility, gives people job skills, and empowers them through creativity and critical thinking.

*Figure 1. Aligning of the industry requirements with education*

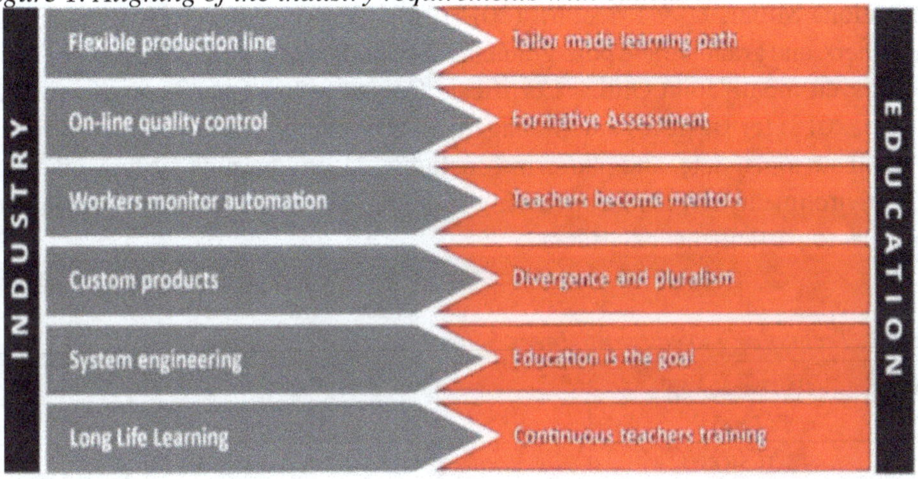


**Source:** *Intelitek, 2018*

## Management Education and Hybrid Model

A hybrid online and offline learning (Satia, 1992) paradigm is emerging globally to optimize student learning capacity. Flipped learning will serve as an institutional technique (Rasche et al., 2013) in which students must hear lectures at home and arrive in classrooms with a foundational understanding of the material to participate in discussions. The nature of cross-cultural exposure results from the heightened utilization of technology in the contemporary business environment. (Puffer, 1993). In the modern digital age, a comprehensive technical orientation is essential in every field of study. Technology has permeated (Dyer and Hurd, 2016) managerial disciplines universally. Social media awareness in marketing, big data analytics, technological innovation, knowledge management, e-commerce, and human resources analytics are all more significant. Moreover, online courseware has been increasingly accepted in recent times. This can consist of two types: recorded videos by in-house teachers or Massive Open Online Courses (MOOCs) from other business schools. MOOCs are accessible at no cost across various disciplines. MOOCs allow (Dehler, 2009) students to enhance their skill set and broaden their post-college prospects. Upgrade, India's leading online higher education brand, announces its foray into vernacular higher education programs through a partnership with Mumbai University, enhancing its degree market footprint. (Anderson, Ellwood, & Coleman, 2017). The institution is introducing two Master of Arts programs in Public Relations & Communications and Journalism, offered in online and mixed learning formats, facilitated by Upgrade. The Fore School of Management solicits applications Millar, J., & Price, M. (2018) from corporate executives, managers, researchers, and graduate and post-graduate students in engineering and management for its seven-month Joint Online Certificate Course in Big Data Analytics (Millar & Price, 2018) for Business and Management. The training is focused on projects. All requisite tools, data, and platforms, including Deep Learning systems, the Hadoop environment, and Kafka streaming technologies essential for mastering data analytics, to participants beforehand.

*Table 1. Technology used by Business Schools during Pandemic time*

| Sl.no | Technology Used | Purpose |
|---|---|---|
| 1 | Zoom | Meetings |
| 2 | TCSION | Enterprise Resume Planning |
| 3 | Exam soft | Examination |
| 4 | eKOSH | Online Assessment |
| 5 | Padlet | Collaboration among students, allows groups to share notes, videos, images, and even post on a common white board. |
| 6 | Cocubes | AI /ML to ensure students do not cheat during exams, |
| 7 | Remote Xs and Mc Graw | Helping students access the best e-content globally with a few clicks, |
| 8 | Deify Box | Features with online, recorded class, assessment, fee collection, |
| 9 | KopyKitab | Using AI/ML to track learning materials, |
| 10 | Oracel's people soft and Anthology | To Automate Administrative Process by maintain a student database, |
| 11 | US-based EBSCO | provided top B-school research data bases |
| 12 | Coursera, Udacing, Edx and IIMBx | learning platforms |
| 13 | DELNET | Research Database |
| 14 | Google Meet, Microsoft Teams and Cisco Webxx, | Video conferencing solutions |

(Source: Authors compilation)

Indian business schools encounter escalating competition nationally and globally. Amidst more than 4,000 business schools nationwide, there exists a perpetual competition for premier students, faculty, and industry collaborations. Furthermore, Indian institutions are progressively competing with international business schools for students inclined to pursue education overseas. Indian business schools must identify strategies to distinguish themselves and maintain competitiveness (Napier et al., 2008). This can be accomplished via curriculum innovation, robust industry collaborations, or an emphasis on specialised fields such as entrepreneurship or rural management. Institutions that establish a distinct identity and provide a unique value proposition will be more effectively positioned to attract elite talent and cultivate a robust reputation in India and internationally. The emergence of digital technologies poses both a challenge and an opportunity for Indian business schools. The growing integration of AI, machine learning, and data analytics in the business sector necessitates educational institutions embed these technologies into curricula. The transition to online learning and digital platforms necessitates substantial investment in infrastructure and technology. Indian business schools have advanced in this domain, with numerous institutions now providing courses on digital transformation and integrating online learning platforms into their curricula. Nonetheless, considerable effort remains necessary to guarantee that students are sufficiently equipped for the digital economy. Currently, students are inclined towards experiential, practical education. This approach is founded on a quest for knowledge that transcends theoretical understanding, integrating practical experiences and projects that enable students to interact directly with the industry. The integration of experiential learning using many methodologies, including case studies, simulations, gaming, and industry-relevant projects. This form of education equips students with both theoretical foundations and practical experience, enhancing the relevance of their learning to real-world business contexts. Although experiential learning is broadly accepted, it must be meticulously crafted to align with the institution's educational objectives and outcomes; otherwise, it may devolve into a mere superficial experience.

**Technology integration and Management education:** The new technology learning such as (i) Artificial Intelligence(AI), (ii) Virtual Reality(VR),(iii) Augmented Reality(AR), (iv) Block chain Technologies,(v) Deep Learning, (vi) Proprietary Algorithms, (vii) Real time Tracking, (viii) Insights and Analytics, (ix) Beat Optimisation, (x) Efficient warehouse Management, (xi)Vehicle allocation and utilisation, (xii)Intuitive 3D Packing(xiii)Measurement of Packages are the new segment in Management Education. Global megatrends, including increasing urbanization, demographic changes, shifts in global economic power, political transformations, and technological advancements, are impacting company operations. Technology, particularly automation and artificial intelligence (AI) as components of Industry 4.0, is reshaping the workplace, the nature of employment, and skill requirements. A substantial decrease in rule- and routine-based employment will occur due to enhanced human-machine interaction and the emergence of adaptive and intelligent technologies. Considering the megatrends that interact with technology disruptions, we have developed a skills framework to comprehend future skill requirements. The learners have also enrolled in courses and specialties in Artificial Intelligence, Data Science, Machine Learning, and Coding during the lockdown. In light of the lockout, business schools are exploring alternatives to conventional methods. Performing evaluations. This entails administering online assessments via an innovative application-oriented and quiz-based question format encompassing scenario-based shooting care inquiries. Moreover, AI-based examinations are implemented to identify individuals before, during, and after the exam through (a) live video feed, (b) facial recognition, (c) impersonation detection, and (d) object detection (Napier et al., 2008).

*Table 2. AI and Management Education*

| Specialisation | Cover up the topics in B-Schools |
|---|---|
| Financial Management | AI can cover up the issues like investment strategies, risk management, issues related to fraud detection. AI algorithms analyse the market trends, the economic indicators, stock price movements and optimise investment portfolios. This can concur through AI-powered chatbots and virtual assistants which provide personalised financial advice to customers, enhancing user experience and engagement. |
| Production and supply chain Management | AI-augmented decision making is transforming manufacturing processes, enabling predictive maintenance, quality control, and supply chain optimisation. Further, AI analyse equipment sensor data to predict potential failures and schedule maintenance proactively, minimising downtime and reducing costs. |
| Marketing Management | AI-driven analytics which also empower businesses to understand consumer behaviour, personalise marketing campaigns, and optimise pricing strategies. AI algorithms analyse customer data from various sources, including social media, online interactions, and purchase history, to identify trends and preferences. Further, AI-powered recommendation systems provide personalised product recommendations, increasing sales and revenue. |
| Health Care | AI-augmented decision making has revolutionised diagnosis, treatment planning, and patient care. |

Source: Compilation by Author

Since the early 1900s, business schools globally have incorporated elements from the sciences, humanities, law, economics, mathematics, and other fields, transforming into application-oriented institutions.

They are institutions that cultivate future leaders, corporate executives, and entrepreneurs. Law schools and medical colleges have influenced the case-driven teaching of business schools, whereas the internship component originated from engineering schools. Technology and design institutions lead in innovation in a rapidly evolving, social media-centric environment (Sharma, 2017). The management students must navigate the significance of agility and adaptation in unexpected scenarios. Moreover, they are unequivocally equipped for the new normal. New training will be required on (a) Business Continuity, (b) Digital Transformation, (c) Building Resilience, and (d) Remote Team Management. They will need to be instructed in a transdisciplinary approach that integrates various disciplines, including Political Science, Science, Technology, and Environmental Studies, into management courses. The fluctuating consumer market exacerbates this situation. Consumer preferences are evolving swiftly, influenced by digital channels and by societal trends. Business models that were effective in the past may no longer be pertinent. Organizations are progressively anticipated to innovate and provide customized experiences; nevertheless, this agility necessitates a workforce proficient in emerging technologies and capable of critical thinking and adaptation to evolving business landscapes. Despite the evident necessity, numerous firms have difficulties in fostering an environment (Albert & Grzeda, 2015) that encourages ongoing learning.

Business schools across the country have similar stories of companies that were not able to either honour their hiring commitments or push joining dates for management graduates. Several business entities recruited more summer interns than normal, with industries fulfilling their commitments, including (a) E-commerce, (b) Ed-Tech, (c) FMCG, (d) Logistics, and (e) Consulting. The greatest reduction in proposals occurred in (a) Manufacturing, (b) Automobile, (c) Banking, and (d) Start-ups (Dayal, 2011). The summer internship project was required to be conducted remotely. The epidemic has necessitated significant behavioural shifts, with meetings transitioning from conference rooms to virtual platforms such as Zoom. Microsoft Teams and Webex. Companies such as Cadbury Silk offer access to their consumer insight application to analyse purchasing behaviour and perspectives on snacking and nutrition. The epidemic has compelled most consumer goods companies to concentrate on their digital and omnichannel strategies. Emerging technologies, like Generative AI, deep learning, blockchain, cryptocurrency, quantum computing, and big data, are radically transforming corporate processes and redefining value generation and management, resulting in the emergence of new efficiencies. The business schools have greater expertise in the uses of AI/ML and other emerging technologies in commerce. Moreover, the leading Indian professionals engaged in "courses" offered by the world's largest edtech platforms, encompassing functional, technological. and behavioural abilities. Artificial intelligence is enhancing the decision-making capabilities of humans. Artificial intelligence appears to be the forthcoming significant advancement across numerous sectors nowadays. In the modern world, businesses across diverse sectors use artificial intelligence as a t ool to meet their goals, be it customer service through organ, an intuitive chatbot or streamlining video production through synthetic voiceovers. Artificial intelligence, while transformative, serves as a facilitator that must be utilised efficiently to attain corporate goals. Companies are employing AI agents to interact with customers, swiftly generate content, analyse transactions, and identify fraud. Despite its numerous problems, the rapidity, personalised content, and targeted recommendations outweigh the disadvantages. AI-driven technologies possess the capacity to improve our existence as both students and professionals. Researchers and developers are consistently enhancing them to replicate human behaviours in activities including as learning and problem-solving. India's advancements in science, technology, and innovation in recent years have been remarkable. India's inclusion in the Global Innovation Index at the 48th position, a significant advancement from 81st in 2015, highlights the nation's potential within the region and its promising future. Today, it is imperative to initiate a national discourse on the promotion of emerging technologies, enabling the country to establish itself as a global leader in this domain while simultaneously selecting the suitable technology to benefit all sectors of the nation. Both talented and unskilled youngsters should be afforded employment opportunities. The nation is achieving unprecedented advancements in robotics, drone manufacturing, and artificial intelligence. To further this trend, it is essential to showcase our achievements globally. However, in light of our country's requirements, it is imperative to implement these technologies in India.

*Table 3. AI and Providers of Management Education*

| Courses | Provided by |
|---|---|
| Foundations: Data, Data, everywhere | Google |
| Leadership skills | IIM Ahmadabad |
| Financial markets | Yale University |
| Supervised machine learning regression and classification | Stansford University and Deep Learning, AI |
| Crash course on Paytm | Google |
| Pro-MBA statistics | IIM Ahmadabad |
| Foundation digital marketing and e-commerce | Google |
| Ask questions to make data, driven decisions | Google |
| Foundations of project management | Google |
| AI for everyone | Deep Learning, AI |

(Source: Authors compilation)

Global collaboration is at a crossroads, (Walck, 2009) necessitating the adaptation of curricula to effectively meet the challenges of the VUCA era. Moreover, they are more adept at embracing changes rapidly and adapting to evolving realities and circumstances. They are also more prepared to explore new job paths and opportunities. In India, prestigious institutions such as the Indian Institutes of Management (IIMs), the) Indian School of Business (ISB), XLRI - Xavier School of Management, and SP Jain Institute of Management and Research (SPJIMR) have attained recognition. These institutions have developed leaders who have risen to the leadership of multinational corporations, influenced public policy, and advanced innovation on both national and global scales. As the world advances, the difficulties facing these institutions become more complex. Business schools must harmonise academic rigour, corporate expectations, and evolving societal needs. As

India rises on the world stage, its business schools must conform to international standards while tackling the unique issues of the Indian market. They must also confront rising technologies, evolving business strategies, and a more integrated global environment (Yawson et al., 2025).

The deregulation of India's in the early 1990s marked a crucial juncture, initiating rapid growth and advancement for Indian business schools. The liberalization of foreign investments, trade, and private firms in India has increased the demand for skilled managers. Business schools were mandated to augment and expand their curriculum to meet the needs of a globalized market. International partnerships may benefit business schools, particularly as entities and governments reinvent themselves and adopt innovative techniques. In an era where AI technology has revolutionized the business landscape, the human element, and organizational culture remain the foremost priorities that B-Schools should address. Tier-2 and Tier-3 cities present a distinctive opportunity for MBA students to collaborate with local entrepreneurs, social enterprises, and community development initiatives. Therefore, SDG-8, which pertains to decent work and economic growth, is attainable only when corporate objectives are aligned with sustainable goals, and B-schools in Tier-2 and Tier-3 cities generate new chances. The Global Employability University Ranking and Survey (GEURS) 2023-24, prepared by the French consultancy Emerging and released in collaboration with Times Higher Education (THE), indicates that graduates who are more socially integrated can improve organizations and thereby enhance their countries economies. These qualities are especially desired in graduates from BRICS countries (Brazil, Russia, India, China, and South Africa), including those pursuing degrees in business engineering and IT. Consequently, premier business schools in India have consistently emphasized the development of soft skills. Additionally, the resolution of issues that management must address in the future will be necessary. Exacerbated by climate change, terrorism, (Perriton & Reynolds, 2018) and other anticipated and unanticipated conditions. Consequently, management graduates will necessitate a broad spectrum of cognitive talents and global awareness. Skills such as effective communication, cooperation, emotional intelligence, and time management are becoming essential for workplace efficiency and productivity (Sandhu, 2020). Therefore, a novel paradigm in management education that is dynamic, inclusive, and responsive to the evolving global scene. B-school graduates must excel in adaptation, self-regulation, and leadership capabilities. Effective personnel management necessitates a profound understanding and implementation of behavioural sciences, encompassing psychology and sociology (Shukla, 2020). Anthropology and neurology enable managers and leaders to construct, sustain, and implement high-performance teams. The organizations want proficient professionals possessing technical and administrative expertise who can effectuate transformations in areas such as Singh, Network Security, Gaming, e-commerce, and dating applications by overseeing the complete robotic process (Upasana, 2023). Curriculum Innovation: In the contemporary, rapidly changing, technology align with industry requirements. Although conventional disciplines such as finance, marketing, and human resources are essential, business schools must also incorporate courses in emerging fields like artificial intelligence (AI), blockchain, and data analytics (Sridharan & Iyengar, 2020). Indian business schools have swiftly adjusted to these transformations. IIM Bangalore has launched specialised programs) in data science and business analytics, highlighting the increasing demand for these competencies in the corporate sector. Likewise, the Symbiosis Institute of Business Management (SIBM) in Pune and the T.A. Pai Management Institute (TAPMI) in Manipal have established formidable reputations for their emphasis on entrepreneurship and innovation, offering programs aimed at assisting students in launching new ventures or expanding existing enterprises. Alongside introducing new courses, business schools must reevaluate their educational delivery methods. (Vardhan, 2020) Digital learning platforms, hybrid educational models, and experiential opportunities such as internships and live projects have become integral elements of contemporary business education. Institutions such as ISB have led this transition by providing flexible, modular programs that enable (Yawson et al., 2025, para. 4) students to reconcile their academic pursuits with professional obligations. Integrating theory and practice is crucial for equipping students with a comprehensive education that prepares them for the intricacies of the business environment. Faculty members actively involved in research introduce contemporary insights and advancements into the classroom, ensuring that students acquire fundamental knowledge while being exposed to innovative concepts. Research constitutes an essential element of a thriving business school.

## Green Generation and Role of Management Education

The roles such as business analyst of ecological sustainability, transport analysis manager of energy control, manager of regulation framework which leading towards green generation. Tech and digital startups as well as large counselling firms are looking for talents with the right set of knowledge, skill and attitude to manage these businesses. That are built on AI or ML based technologies. The market also needs managers who can develop and manage AI enabled products and services and use of ML and analysis at its cost. The New role of manager is now finfluencers who can use public social ride platforms offering advice and sharing personal experiences about money and investment in stocks. The views carrying with budgeting, investing property buying, Crypto currency advice and financial trend tracking. Further, by leveraging digital channels, companies can directly target their customers, partners and influencers. To connect with customers and social media platforms, virtual events, e-commerce alliances, online listing and digital partnerships can be performed by new age managers. The Generation Z refers to the people born between 1990 and 2010. Compared to permanent Jobs, Gigs have more flexibility and opportunity for self-development. Gig workers have an amount of out money. As they work for a variety of institutions, they also create a better connection with people. With the rise of the digital age, Gen Z has become one mobile with the freedom to work from anywhere. This is regarded as a major reason for the rise of the gig economy, which facilitates a more excellent work-life balance, making one's schedule and the freedom to focus on personal interests. (Thaper, 2023). The growing influence of AI has processed industries to integrate this transformative technology into their operators. Across the globe today, Sustainability, Sustainable development, and integration of The MBA Syllabus with the UN's Sustainable Development Goals (SDGs) have become a reality. The most esteemed business schools uphold robust affiliations with the industry. These connections are essential for multiple reasons. Initially, they offer students opportunities for internships, live projects, and executive education, which are crucial for acquiring practical, hands-on experience. Secondly, industry partnerships frequently result in collaborative research initiatives, enabling faculty and students to address authentic business challenges. Third, robust industry connections align the school's curriculum with the demands of the corporate sector. In India, business schools have established robust affiliations with prominent companies across various sectors, both domestically and globally. These collaborations not only augment the educational experience for students but also bolster the school's placement statistics, a vital component of its overall success. The Digital Acceleration report indicates that AI has emerged as a primary catalyst for technology investment in global organizations. The management of service requests is the predominant use of AI/ML due to the straightforward nature of formulating Standard Operating Procedures (SOPs) for such tickets. The SOP, utilizing natural language processing (NLP) for interpretation and classification models and Robotic Process Automation (RPA), can facilitate the automatic resolution of these tickets, provided that authentication is unnecessary. Sometimes, OpsBots (Chatbots) may be an alternative to self-service portals. Chatbots additionally provide the benefit of assisting visually impaired individuals. (Wan Lee, Becker, & Nobre, 2012).

**Green skills and Management education:** Business leaders around the globe have started recognizing green skills as the cornerstone of transformative change. Management education will be seeking greater policy coordination, social dialogue and collaboration with a varied set of stakeholders to develop green skills among graduates (Kumar, 2015). Thus, Business schools to adopt swiftly to nurture a new breed of leaders equipped with green skills which seamlessly inter-twine business acumen with a deep-seated commitment to sustainability. As far as green curriculums concerned, Institutions could establish specialized centres for sustainability research, offer courses on green technologies and practices and encourage student – led community initiatives that address local environmental issues. Thus, AI and green skills, India demonstrates considerable potential such as renewable energy technologies and climate- friendly innovations. As Industries adopt new ESG frameworks, MBA in sustainable management is a futurist course and will continue to grow. Further, in addition to offering general management courses, the curriculum stands out in management education by offering specialized courses on systems thinking, social entrepreneurship, externalities, life (Kulkarni, 2020)) cycle management, stakeholder management and public policy. Further, technology has penetrated this area because the entire ESG reporting process has become automated and dependent on Artificial Intelligence and Machine Learning. (Sridevi, 2021) AI wave will change everything from the (Jain, 2024) way classes are connected to how students must prepare themselves for a new world where corporate board rooms and shop floors will be guided by AI. (Krishan, 2016) Every company, whether small or large is capturing vast amounts of data, Analytics has become central to all initiatives that companies are undertaking. In an era where Digitization and Gen AI are poised to reshape the corporate sector, (Agrawal, 2021) B-Schools have a crucial role to play in bridging the skills gap. The Traditional B-School curricula may not always align with Industry demands. Thus, Industry 4.0 demands skill in data analytics, AI and cloud computing, making technical expertise more valuable.

## Repositioning B-School and Harnessing AI

Research is about innovation and mapping the domain to a faculty's research interests. It also includes management practice insight; a collection of Journal articles picked from any post of the world and translated for managers and business leaders worldwide. Further, the use of virtual reality (VR) as a "game changer in accurately predicting sales for new product launches. The "WISE Tech Project" like the "Y Combinator model" in the US, is another interesting aspect, revolving around a technology Start-up accelerator. Further, Indian B-School graduates who are not just Job seekers but Job Creators in the AI Economy. However, Indian B-Schools will be transformed by AI which redefine the new management education and skill which will shape the global business leaders of tomorrow.

B-School graduates bring energy, Curiosity, and ambition, focusing more on their potential rather than their initial experience. (Amitabh, 2020) The AI based internships and - Al- online live projects are key to forming sustainable and ESG partnership between sustainable Start-ups and Indian B-school graduates, B-Schools are also under significant pressure to stay updated. The type of projects and assignments that B-schools assign to students have Gen AI and chat GPT support. (Batley, 1990) The Intense B-school environment that requires a high level of involvement and coordination between faculty and Student's perspective. Thus, Edtech platforms play an important role) in managing participant enrolment. Baton, (Annurag, 2023) They are responsible for managing a team of counsellors, with technology integration approach. The Revision of Curricula is important and experiential learning which will address the issues like. Edtech platforms are a quality alternative for resume strapped B-Schools to either train their faculty or more relevantly, strike partnerships with top universities with leveraging AI technologies (Agrawal, 2021).

*Table 4. EdTech Companies and Collaboration with B-Schools.*

| EdTech | B-Schools |
|---|---|
| COURSERA | IIT Roorkee, IIM Ahmadabad, SP Jain Instate of Management and Research |
| UPGRAD | BIMTECH, IIT Bombay, 11M Kozhikode. |
| NULEARN | IIM Raipur. |
| GREAT LEARNING | People's Education Society, IIT Bombay. |
| EMERITUS | Indian School of Business, IIM Lucknow, IIM Kozhikode, IIM Calcutta, IIM Indore. |
| SIMPLILEARN | IIM Kanpur, IIT Roorkee. |
| EDTECH | B-schools |
| EDUREKA | IMT Ghaziabad, IIT Ghauhati, IIT Kanpur, NTF Raurkela, Wrangle |
| TALENTEDGE | XLRI, IIM Raipur, IIM Lucknow, MICA, IIT Delhi, IIM Shillong. |

(Source Business Today, 13th October 2024, p.94)

Undoubtly, Technology has disrupted in B-schools also; with the rise of large language to models and Gen AI that are becoming increasingly powerful in assisting students with learning. Thus, B-schools teaching methods has also change tremendously through orientation towards topics which classes are engaging before professors of B-schools. The professor was guide them through practical use cases and applications. This is one way in which technology has disrupted management education (Das, 2024). B-Schools today are increasingly focused on expertise in platforms like AWS and Azure, hiring cloud Architects and Develops Professionals and specialists who can manage and optimize SaaS-based solution.

**Accreditations and AI Earn:** The Accreditation in management education (Hindwan, 2020) refers to business schools certified by three major bodies', (a) the Association to Advance Collegiate Schools of Business (AACSB); (b) The Association of MBAs (AMBA) and EFMD Quality Improvement System (EQUIS). (Debroy, 2020) The B schools have the potential to lead the way in work-life balance, and to build an ecosystem that enables B-school have the potential to lead the way in work life balance and to build an ecosystem that enables B-schools graduates to overcome bias in corporate leadership. B-schools are embracing with AI, ML and

Analytics the technologic like IIM Ahmadabad introduced new courses on AI and Marketing (Bhaskar & Gupta, 2024). AI and HRM, Algorithm and Marketing and leading Digital transformation. Further, in 2020-21 year, it also launched " Brig Data Centre for Data Sciences" and Artificial Intelligence (AI) in 2021-22. Further, IIM Lucknow offers elective options like Data Analysis, Social Media Analytics and Supply Chain Analytics. IIM Indore has also added Analytics within different areas in 2020-21 year including HR Analytics, Marketing and Analytics and Digital Marketing etc. Some skills that B-schools can equip students with more strongly are management and development. Both the term such as: VUCA (volatility, Uncertainty, Complexity and Ambiguity) and BANI (Brittle, Anxious, Non. Liner and Incomprehensible) which create a buzz word apart from AI. Baton, The increasing use of Al and GenAI has had a multifaceted influence and has significantly shaped how management Education is delivered and experienced, with, Advanced e-learning platforms and tools increasingly offering unprecedented flexibility and accessibility; students can now access lectures, study materials and interactive resources from virtually anywhere, enabling more personalized and a self-paced learning. AI has significantly changed the mental models: however, Industry 5.0 emphasis the convergence of human skills with (Chusniyah & Supriyanto, 2025) management and technology. Thus, maintaining the reputation and quality of education at IIMs involves ongoing adoption to the challenges presented by the immersing role of technology, especially the growing prominence & AI and GenAI. B-Schools have realigned their curriculum to the new and emerging phase of industrialization, Industry 5.0 which requires humans working alongside advanced tech and AI powered devices to boost the effectiveness of workplace processes. (Singh & Praneeta, 2025). As tech rises more, AI led e-learning solution are expected to assist faculty members in bridging the knowledge gap between their lectures and generating low storage student materials and other lesions in digital format. The AI- powered algorithms can gather data on student behaviour, such as how long they spent on certain tasks and how they interact with learning and reading materials. AI can help educators create customized lesson plans and assessment that align with each student's unique strengths and weaknesses (Singh, 2025).

## Industry 4.0 and Skill Development

Industry 4.0, which is defined by modern technology and integrated systems, requires a workforce with specialized skills to succeed. This encompasses both soft skills like problem-solving and flexibility as well as technical talents like robotics, artificial intelligence, and data analytics. Companies and educational institutions are funding reskilling and upskilling initiatives that equip people for the demands of the digital economy to close the skills gap.

Closing the skills gap has become a top goal in Industry 4.0, and programs like WISE (Work Integrated Skill Based Higher Education) are setting the foundation for a workforce prepared for the future. WISE significantly contributes to the development of a workforce prepared for this by employing these tactics. By emphasizing upskilling programs for industry occupations, it equips people with the technical and soft skills needed to prosper in a digitally driven economy. The skill shortages can be successfully addressing this challenge include employability skills, flexible learning pathways, industry-academia partnership in skill development, and—above all—technology integration in learning. The emergence of Industry 4.0 ensures interesting and productive training experiences by utilizing state-of-the-art simulation technologies, virtual labs, and AI-driven learning platforms.

*Figure 2. Collaborative Strategies for Addressing Industry 4.0 Skill Shortages*

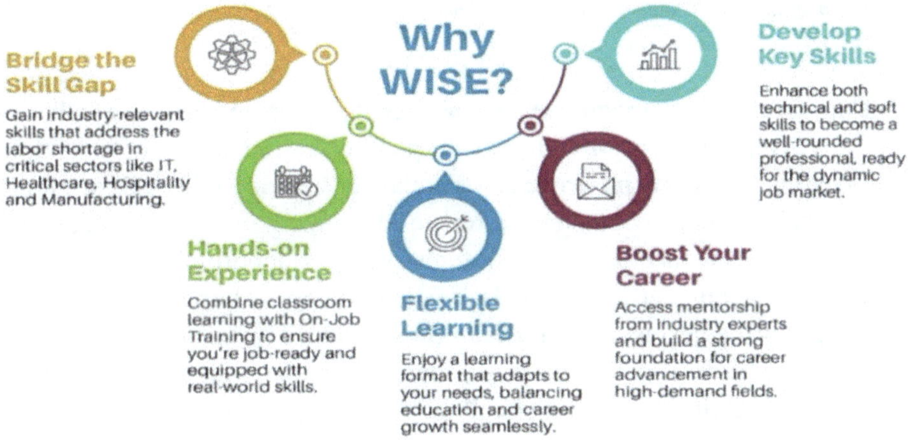


**Source:** *https://www.msu.edu.in/blog/bridging-the-skills-gap-in-industry-4.0:-a-collaborative-approach-with-msu-wise*

## Aligning Higher Education with SDGs

The significance of artificial intelligence (AI) in accomplishing the Sustainable Development Goal of Quality Education (SDG 4) is not only advantageous, but also essential in a world where technology is taking over.

*Figure 3. Technology Ecosystems and the SDGs*

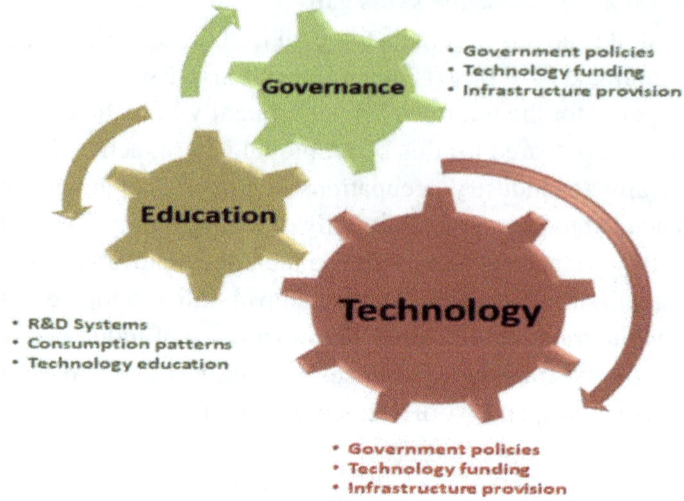


**Source:** *https://www.gdrc.org/techtran/sdg/index.html*

The opportunity to democratize and enhance the reach and quality of education lies within our digital grasp. through resource pooling and the sharing of technologies and applications created to increase each stakeholder's productivity and contribution to the SDGs, technology ecosystems promote economic growth. These ecosystems facilitate the maintenance of current systems and offer opportunities in previously unanticipated domains and use cases. An efficient strategy to hasten the achievement of the SDGs and targets is to establish an ecosystem for technologies that support them. This can be done in several ways, such as creating a foundational platform or technology, creating a network of collaborators: Supporting user and developer communities and Providing rewards for involvement.

## How Does Education Connect to Other SDGs?

Higher education graduates are more employable and make, on average, 54% more than those who have only completed senior secondary school, according to the Economic Co-operation and Development (OECD). Interdisciplinary and multidisciplinary educational systems provide multitalented individuals capable of conducting research and coming up with creative answers to global problems and reaching Sustainable Development in real life.

*Table 5. SDGs are related to Education*

| SDGs linked to education | Solution to Global Challenges | Achievement of Sustainable development in Practicality |
|---|---|---|
| **SDG1:** People are better protected against poverty by a university-inclusive education. | **SDG7:** Clean and reasonably priced energy. | **SDG9:** Private enterprises must work together to develop innovative solutions and start-ups. |
| **SDG2:** Improves hunger prevention. | **SDG11:** Sustainable cities and communities | **SDG12:** Our production and consumption patterns must be drastically altered. |
| **SDG3:** Health and well-being are enhanced by improved education. | **SDG13:** Examining the effects of climate change and global warming on the environment and economy. | **SDG15:** Value-Based Education (VBE) will assist our country attain "Life on Land" by fostering a sense of responsibility among its residents toward themselves, society, and the environment. |
| **SDG5:** Gender equality is promoted via improved education. | | |
| **SDG8:** Better gives people respectable employment, which stimulates economic expansion. | | |
| **SDG10:** It primarily aids in the reduction of inequality. | | |

**Source:** https://pwonlyias.com/editorial-analysis/higher-education-in-india/

## CONCLUSION

The technology capabilities will address real-world problems beyond repetitive and routine tasks. As major corporations such as Amazon, Apple, Google, and Microsoft endeavour to integrate artificial intelligence into their offerings, other firms are diligently advancing their intelligent technologies and services. Artificial intelligence firms are beginning to provide a comprehensive service to their clients by employing sub-technologies such as machine learning, deep learning, edge computing, and business intelligence as their primary business strategy. Artificial intelligence amalgamates diverse data sources, extensive datasets, data security, practical applications, predictive analytics, and cloud operations. Since the inception of AI technology, the world has undergone significant transformations. The future is expected to be more advanced and tailored through artificial intelligence. Most brands aiming to integrate artificial intelligence into their strategies have yet to fully exploit its potential. Conversely, several organizations utilize augmented and virtual realities primarily to improve marketability rather than to demonstrate their true potential. A distinctive aspect of business and content digitization is providing a comprehensive array of services by a single company, enabling client enterprises to operate seamlessly without concerns. These services encompass the study and development of Blockchain, Artificial Intelligence, Cloud Computing, Automation, Data Analytics projects, and other new technologies. This is where start-ups can innovate and build advanced technological solutions that can enhance any or all the five segments in the ed-tech industry. In recent years, artificial intelligence (AI) and digital technologies have revolutionized industries worldwide, particularly in the field of education. Management studies, specifically, have experienced a significant shift in their methodologies. The era of relying solely on classroom lectures for learning has ended. Today, students are anticipated to engage with real-world challenges, collaborate with industry professionals, and remain informed about the latest technological advancements.

## REFERENCES


Abey, J., Velmurugan, R., & Shaikh, Z. H. (2025). Analyzing the Performance of a Deep Learning-Based Model for Stock Market Trend Prediction. In Hamdan, R. K. (Ed.), *Sustainable Data Management. Studies in Big Data* (Vol. 170). Springer., DOI: 10.1007/978-3-031-83915-3_59

Adcroft, A., Dhaliwal, S., & Willis, R. (2005). Insatiable demand or academic supply: The intellectual context of entrepreneurship education. *European Business Review, 17*(6), 518–531. DOI: 10.1108/09555340510630554

Agrawal, A. (2021, November 14th). Has the Pandemic made business education less relevant? *Business Today (Norwich)*, **•••**, 102.

Al Astal, A. Y. M., Shaikh, Z. H., Ali, S. A., & Ratnakaram, S. (2025). Factors that Influence the Effectiveness of AIS Implementation in SMEs in Jordan. In Hamdan, R. K. (Ed.), *Sustainable Data Management. Studies in Big Data* (Vol. 171). Springer., DOI: 10.1007/978-3-031-83911-5_5

Albert, S., & Grzeda, M. (2015). Reflection in Strategic Management Education. *Journal of Management Education, 39*(5), 650–669. DOI: 10.1177/1052562914564872

Amitabh, B. (2020, September 10). *NEP: Ambitious targets set for education sector.* The Deccan Chronicle, p. 10.

Anderson, L., Ellwood, P., & Coleman, C. (2017). The impactful academic: Relational management education as an intervention for impact. *British Journal of Management, 28*(1), 14–28. DOI: 10.1111/1467-8551.12202

Batley, T. (1990). Management Education for Professional Engineers. *Journal of European Industrial Training, 14*(7). Advance online publication. DOI: 10.1108/03090599010135168

Baton, A. (2023) Management Education in a VUCA world, Business World, 16th December 2023, P.6.

Bhaskar, P., & Gupta, P. K. K. (2024). Delving into educators' perspectives on ChatGPT in management education: A qualitative exploration. *Interactive Technology and Smart Education, 21*(4), 645–671. DOI: 10.1108/ITSE-08-2023-0169

Bhattacharya, R., & Bhattacharya, S. (2020, September 20). *A room not for her own.* The Economic Times, p. 12.

Bhattacharyya, R. (2020, November 14). *FMCG adds new campuses to hiring list.* The Economic Times, p. 1.

Braddick, W. A. G. (1991). European Management Education: Internationalization and Harmonization. *Industry and Higher Education, 5*(3), 138–142. DOI: 10.1177/095042229100500303

Chusniyah, A., Makruf, I., & Supriyanto, . (2025). Two decades of sustainable development studies in higher education management: A bibliometric analysis. *International Journal of Sustainability in Higher Education, 26*(3), 614–632. DOI: 10.1108/IJSHE-11-2023-0546

Das, H. (2024). Adopting to a new era. *Business Today (Norwich), 13*(October), 98–99.

Dayal, I. (2011). Globalizing Management Education. *Global Business Review, 12*(3), 473–478. DOI: 10.1177/097215091101200309

Debroy, B. (2020, September 10). *The NEP reboot.* The Indian Express, p. 11.

Dehler, G. E. (2009). Prospects and possibilities of critical management education: Critical beings and a pedagogy of critical action. *Management Learning, 40*(1), 31–49. DOI: 10.1177/1350507608099312

Dyer, S. L., & Hurd, F. (2016). "What's going on?" Developing reflexivity in the management classroom: From surface to deep learning and everything in between. *Academy of Management Learning & Education, 15*(2), 287–303. DOI: 10.5465/amle.2014.0104

Gupta, S., Srivastava, R., Shaikh, Z. H., & Irfan, M. (2024). Revolutionizing Rural Finance:Exploring the Impact of FinTech on Financial Inclusion in India. In Irfan, M., Muhammad, K., Naifar, N., & Khan, M. A. (Eds.), *Applications of Block Chain technology and Artificial Intelligence. Financial Mathematics and Fintech.* Springer., DOI: 10.1007/978-3-031-47324-1_3

Hibbert, P. (2012). Approaching reflexivity through reflection: Issues for critical management education. *Journal of Management Education, 37*(6), 803–827. DOI: 10.1177/1052562912467757

Hindwan, S. (2020, December 13). *New challenges to education during pandemic.* The Pioneer, p. 3. https://intelitek.com/2018/06/06/intelitek-releases-white-paper-on-changing-education-systems-to-prepare-students-for-the-demands-of-modern-society-and-the-industrial-workspace/

Jain, N. (2024, October 13th). Harnessing the Power of AI. *Business Today (Norwich),* •••, 76–77.

Krishan, R. G. (2016, February 19). *Boosting industry-academia linkages*. Business Standard, p. 8.

Kulkarni, V. (2020, October 29). *Apprenticeship: Win-win solutions*. The Economic Times (ET Newsmakers), p. 3.

Kumar, C. R. (2015, December 1). *Five steps to revitalise India's higher education system*. The Economic Times.

Kumar, S. (2020, September 10). *Higher education more corporatized and profit-driven*. The Morning India.

Kumar, S., & Sharma, A. (2020, September 21). *Regional universities and challenges before new education policy*. The Daily Guardian, p. 5.

Kusuma, K., Sheela, P., Panigrahi, R. R., & Shaikh, Z. H. (2024). Blockchain Technology and Islamic Finance: A Decade of Growth Trends. In Irfan, M., Kadry, S., Sharif, M., & Khan, H. (Eds.), *Fintech Applications in Islamic Finance: AI, Machine Learning, and Blockchain Techniques* (pp. 59–79). IGI Global., DOI: 10.4018/979-8-3693-1038-0.ch004

Lee, W. J., Becker, K. and Nobre, H. (2012), Impact of culture on online management education, Cross Cultural Management: An International Journal, Vol. 19 No. 3, pp. 399-420. https://doi.org/DOI: 10.1108/13527601211247116

Leitch, C. M., & Harrison, R. T. (1999). A process model for entrepreneurship education and development. *International Journal of Entrepreneurial Behaviour & Research*, *5*(3), 83–109. DOI: 10.1108/13552559910284065

Mavin, S., Bryans, P., & Waring, T. (2004). Unlearning gender blindness: New directions in management education. *Management Decision*, *42*(3/4), 565–578. DOI: 10.1108/00251740410522287

Meghwal, A. R. (2020, August 31). *On education, looking ahead*. The Indian Express, p. 7.

Millar, J., & Price, M. (2018). Imagining management education: A critique of the contribution of the United Nations PRME to critical reflexivity and rethinking management education. *Management Learning*, *49*(3), 346–362. DOI: 10.1177/1350507618759828

Ministry of Human Resource Development. (2020). *India report on digital education – June 2020*. Government of India.

Ministry of Information and Broadcasting. (2020). *India 2020*. Government of India.

Mohanty, B. S., Shaikh, Z. H., Behera, A. R., Imran, M., & Begum, S. (2025). A Progressive Direction for Startup India: Milestones and Trends from 2016 to 2023. In Hamdan, R. K. (Ed.), *Sustainable Data Management. Studies in Big Data* (Vol. 171). Springer., DOI: 10.1007/978-3-031-83911-5_34

Mohanty, B. S., Shaikh, Z. H., Mahapatra, D. M., Ratnakaranm, S., & Manikeswari, D. (2025). Wearable technologies in education: Advantages, limitations, and technical difficulties. In *Wearable devices and smart technology for educational teaching assistance* (pp. 309–330). IGI Global Scientific Publishing.

Morgan, S. D., & Stewart, A. C. (2019). Teams in Management Education. *Journal of Management Education*, *43*(5), 573–582. DOI: 10.1177/1052562919864377

Napier, N. K., Harvey, M., & Usui, K. (2008). Management Education in Emerging Economies: The Impossible Dream? *Journal of Management Education*, *32*(6), 792–819. DOI: 10.1177/1052562908319994

Nowani, D. (2020, September 25). *Old education policy*. The Indian Express, p. 6.

Palmer, N. J., Davies, J., & Viney, C. (2023). *Growth Patterns of Business and Management Doctorates Around the World, Business and Management Doctorates World-Wide: Developing the Next Generation*. Emerald Publishing Limited., DOI: 10.1108/9781789734997

Palmer, N. J., Davies, J., & Viney, C. (2023). *The Business School Doctoral Experience, Business and Management Doctorates World-Wide: Developing the Next Generation*. Emerald Publishing Limited., DOI: 10.1108/9781789734997

Panigrahi, R. R., Dash, M., Shaikh, Z. H., & Irfan, M. (2023). Review of Machine Learning Techniques in the Supply Chain Management of Indian Industry: A Future Research Agenda. In Irfan, M., Elhoseny, M., Kassim, S., & Metawa, N. (Eds.), *Advanced Machine Learning Algorithms for Complex Financial Applications* (pp. 199–219). IGI Global., DOI: 10.4018/978-1-6684-4483-2.ch013

Patwardhan, B., & Mittal, P. (2020, September 10). *An academic bank of credit will transform Indian education*. The Hindustan Times, p. 11.

Perriton, L., & Reynolds, M. (2018). Critical Management Education in challenging times. *Management Learning*, *49*(5), 521–536. DOI: 10.1177/1350507618795090

Puffer, S. M. (1993). The Booming Business of Management Education in Russia. *Journal of Management Development*, *12*(5), 46–59. DOI: 10.1108/02621719310038962

Rajput, J. S. (2020, August 27). *Education makes the man*. The Pioneer, p. 8.

Rasche, A., Gilbert, D. U., & Schedel, I. (2013). Cross-disciplinary ethics education in MBA programs: Rhetoric or reality? *Academy of Management Learning & Education*, *12*(1), 71–85. DOI: 10.5465/amle.2011.0016a

Ratnakaram, S. P. K., Manikeswari, D., Shaikh, Z. H., & Mahapatra, D. M. **Mohanty, B. S.**, & Soni, A. (2025). Wearables and AI-smart technologies: Transforming the education sphere. In Wearable devices and smart technology for educational teaching assistance (pp. 27-52). IGI Global Scientific Publishing.

Sandhu, V. (2020, December 4). *Ad Council report has a message for celebs, education sector*. Business Standard, p. 14.

Sarea, A., Subramanian, S., Alareeni, B., Shaikh, Z. H., Hawaldar, I. T., & Elshaker, A. H. (2021). Financial Disclosures by Using Machine Learning Analysis. In Alareeni, B., Hamdan, A., & Elgedawy, I. (Eds.), *The Importance of New Technologies and Entrepreneurship in Business Development: In The Context of Economic Diversity in Developing Countries. ICBT 2020. Lecture Notes in Networks and Systems* (Vol. 194). Springer., DOI: 10.1007/978-3-030-69221-6_5

Satia, J. K. (1992). Reshaping Management Education. *Vikalpa*, *17*(4), 25–28. DOI: 10.1177/0256090919920405

Selwin, S., Saseendran, H., Vemavarapu, K. R., Shaikh, I., Shaikh, Z. H., & Harris, S. B. (2024). AI-Driven Employee Engagement: Transforming Banking Workforce Dynamics Using the BEULA Model. In Awwad, B. (Ed.), *The AI Revolution: Driving Business Innovation and Research. Studies in Systems, Decision and Control* (Vol. 525). Springer., DOI: 10.1007/978-3-031-54383-8_32

Shaikh, Z., Irfan, M., Sarea, A., & Panigrahi, R. R. (2024). *The Emergence of Islamic Fintech and Bahrain: Prospect for Global Financial Sectors* (Vol. 503). Springer., DOI: 10.1007/978-3-031-43490-7_52

Shaikh, Z. H., Irfan, M., Nomran, N. M., & Lawin, M. L. (2024). The Effect of Strategic Partnership on Innovation and Business: Performance of the Fintech Industry in Bahrain. In Irfan, M., Kadry, S., Sharif, M., & Khan, H. (Eds.), *Fintech Applications in Islamic Finance: AI, Machine Learning, and Blockchain Techniques* (pp. 236–254). IGI Global., DOI: 10.4018/979-8-3693-1038-0.ch016

Shaikh, Z. H., Irfan, M., Nomran, N. M., & Ratnakaram, S. P. (2024). Unlocking the Potential of AI for Efficient Governance: Innovative Approaches of Bahrain. In Irfan, M., Elmogy, M., Gupta, S., Khalifa, F., & Dias, R. (Eds.), *AI-Driven Decentralized Finance and the Future of Finance* (pp. 115–142). IGI Global Scientific Publishing., DOI: 10.4018/979-8-3693-6321-8.ch005

Shaikh, Z. H., Irfan, M., Nomran, N. M., Ratnakaram, S. P., Abey, J., & Anto, M. L. (2025). Measuring Vital Sign: A Case Study of India's Emerging Wearable Technology (EzeCheck) for Mass Screening and Health Monitoring. In Ul Rehman, S. (Ed.), *Wearable Devices and Smart Technology for Educational Teaching Assistance* (pp. 285–308). IGI Global Scientific Publishing., DOI: 10.4018/979-8-3693-7817-5.ch011

Shaikh, Z. H., Irfan, M., Vemavarapu, K. R., Sadayan, S., Hawaldar, I. T., & Rehman, S. U. (2024). Assessing the Effectiveness of Learning Outcomes: In Achieving Quality Education at Higher Learning Institutions in Bahrain. In Naim, A., Saklani, A., Khan, S., & Malik, P. (Eds.), *Evaluating Global Accreditation Standards for Higher Education* (pp. 50–65). IGI Global Scientific Publishing., DOI: 10.4018/979-8-3693-1698-6.ch004

Shaikh, Z. H., Sarea, A., & Irfan, M. (2022). *Islamic Banking Strategies in the World of Fintech: Success Story of Bahrain* (Vol. 423). Springer., DOI: 10.1007/978-3-030-93464-4_10

Sharma, R. R. (2017). A Competency Model for Management Education for Sustainability. *Vision (Basel)*, *21*(2), x–xv. DOI: 10.1177/0972262917700970

Sheela, P., Kusuma, K., Panigrahi, R. R., & Shaikh, Z. H. (2024). Fintech and Islamic Banking: A Systematic View and Future Research Agenda. In Irfan, M., Kadry, S., Sharif, M., & Khan, H. (Eds.), *Fintech Applications in Islamic Finance: AI, Machine Learning, and Blockchain Techniques* (pp. 1–23). IGI Global., DOI: 10.4018/979-8-3693-1038-0.ch001

Shukla, B. (2020, December 2). *HEIs have their task cut out.* The Pioneer, p. 9.

Singh, J. (2025) The Trust challenge in the Age to AI, IT NEXT January - February 2024, Pp:8-9.

Singh, J., & Praneeta (2025) Balancing fresh talent with Experienced experts is key to AI success, CIOs Leader, March 2025, Pp. 28-31.

Soni, A., Shaikh, Z. H., Alhejair, A., Dora, N., Gulati, N., & Saseendran, H. (2025). AI in Expanded HR Ecosystems: Mapping Research Trajectories and Future Prospective. In Hamdan, R. K. (Ed.), *Sustainable Data Management. Studies in Big Data* (Vol. 171). Springer., DOI: 10.1007/978-3-031-83911-5_41

Sridevi, K. B. (2021). Filling the quality gaps for a futuristic management education. *Journal of Economic and Administrative Sciences*, *37*(4), 393–400. DOI: 10.1108/JEAS-09-2018-0097

Sridharan, S., & Iyengar, S. (2020, November 16). *Gig work & India's Gen-Z challenge: Melding this subset of millennials to the workforce.* Business Line, p. 13.

Thaper, N. (2023, July 9th). Good B-school Builds credibility. *Business Today (Norwich)*, •••, 106–107.

Upasana (2023) AI: Harbinger of unprecedented wave of Automation", Business world, 16th December 2023, Pp 110-111.

Vardhan, S. (2020, August 29). *Hits and misses of NEP 2020 and its impact on legal education*. The Daily Guardian, p. 8.

Walck, C. (2009). Integrating Sustainability Into Management Education: A Dean's Perspective. *Journal of Management Education*, *33*(3), 384–390. DOI: 10.1177/1052562908323091

Yawson, R. M., Johnson-Kanda, I., & Yarney, L. (2025), Participant journaling as a data collection method in management education research, Qualitative Research Journal, Vol. ahead-of-print No. ahead-of-print. https://doi.org/DOI: 10.1108/QRJ-01-2025-0021

# Chapter 7
# Leveraging AI to Create Personalized Learning Experiences in Management Education

**Indranil Mutsuddi**
https://orcid.org/0000-0002-4202-8744
*JIS University, India*

## ABSTRACT

*The integration of Artificial Intelligence (AI) technologies is rapidly advancing across all sectors of business, including higher education. Management education is gradually undergoing significant changes due to the effective adoption of AI-driven applications, which have made curricula more evidence- and data-based, experiential, and immersive, thereby enhancing student learning through increased engagement and personalization. Building on this premise, this chapter aims to explore and analyze the impact of AI-driven technologies on expanding and improving the scope of personalized learning experiences for management students. It serves as a valuable reference for management experts, faculty members, researchers, and policymakers to reshape and transform contemporary management education, in order to enrich management learning and development practices and program curricula.*

## INTRODUCTION

Artificial Intelligence (AI) is revolutionizing management education by enhancing both the learning process and administrative operations. AI-driven tools customize learning experiences by tailoring content to the individual needs of each

DOI: 10.4018/979-8-3373-2150-9.ch007

student, better preparing them for future challenges. Beyond improving educational outcomes, AI streamlines administrative tasks such as grading, scheduling, and resource management, enabling educators to focus more on teaching and engaging with students. AI also bridges the gap between theory and practice, offering innovative ways to transform experiential learning and case study methods. The advancement of AI-powered natural language processing (ANLP) tools has enhanced case-based learning, allowing students to engage with complex scenarios in a more interactive and dynamic manner, improving their ability to apply theoretical knowledge to real-world contexts (Clegg & Sarkar, 2024). AI tools like ChatGPT have demonstrated their effectiveness in supporting active learning, fostering critical thinking, and stimulating creativity among management students and researchers. By incorporating ChatGPT into teaching strategies, educators can foster more active, critical, and creative learning environments, adapting to diverse learning styles for a more personalized and engaging experience. AI is progressively reshaping management education by transforming both how students learn and how institutions deliver instruction. It enables the personalization of educational content to suit the unique needs and preferences of each student. AI algorithms, by analyzing student data and performance, can offer tailored recommendations for study materials, exercises, and learning paths, helping students progress at their own pace and focus on areas that need improvement. Drawing on this understanding and a comprehensive review of the literature, this chapter aims to develop a theoretical perspective on the growing significance of AI in reshaping management education, particularly by facilitating personalized and enriched learning experiences for students, researchers, and faculty members.

## REVIEW OF LITERATURE

Management education (ME) is uniquely positioned to provide key insights into the future integration and adoption of technology aimed at enhancing and scaling the learner experience, given its focus on encouraging innovation and experimentation in teaching and learning. Artificial intelligence (AI) is one such technology that offers the potential to create more personalized and responsive learning experiences (Fellenz et al., 2022). This is a growing demand among learners that business schools often struggle to fulfill, primarily due to large student populations and limited resources. Integrating AI tools like ChatGPT into management education has the potential to create a more dynamic learning environment, encouraging greater engagement, problem-solving, and innovation (Leelavathi & Surendhranatha, 2024). As industries increasingly shift toward an AI-driven landscape, exploring the advantages of adopting such technologies is becoming ever more critical. Educators can leverage AI to offer diverse teaching strategies that better address the needs of different learners. Advanced language models like ChatGPT, with their ability to process large datasets and generate human-like text, have the potential to transform industries such as customer service, content creation, and communication (Geraldi et al., 2024). Despite its promise, this technology also presents challenges, including concerns over misinformation, ethical responsibility, unintentional content duplication, and privacy risks.

ChatGPT offers considerable opportunities to enhance learning, particularly in areas like coding and problem-solving. However, it also has limitations, such as restricted access to data sources and the potential for generating misinformation. It is crucial for students to understand both the capabilities and limitations of ChatGPT to maximize its effectiveness in their educational journey. Rapid advancements in machine learning research have accelerated the development of language generation models (Dwivedi et al., 2021), driving innovations in technologies like AI-driven tools for content creation and digital media production, including scriptwriting and content development(Hu, 2023). AI's ability to swiftly gather, process, and analyze data to provide near real-time insights has the potential to significantly improve decision-making for educational leaders in management studies, enabling evidence-based choices (Wang, 2021). However, this reliance on AI for decision-making may conflict with ethical principles based on human values and moral judgments.

Furthermore, research indicates that entrepreneurship education requires more advanced pedagogical approaches that focus on diagnosing, predicting, intervening, preventing, and recommending strategies tailored to specific entrepreneurial content and processes while maintaining alignment with entrepreneurial pedagogy (Chen et al., 2024). Machine learning can also help reduce the workload of educators and improve the accuracy of assessments. Generative AI tools are reshaping multiple sectors, including healthcare, and understanding their impact is vital to realizing their full potential. (Gupta et al., 2024) demonstrated how these tools can be thoughtfully integrated into research and practice, with the potential to transform healthcare. Their study provides evidence-based guidance for practitioners and policymakers on how to adopt this technology effectively, while addressing regulatory and ethical concerns. Educators still face uncertainty regarding how to leverage AI for pedagogical benefits on a larger scale and how it can impact teaching and learning in higher education.

AI's natural language processing (NLP) capabilities have a significant impact on various sectors of management, offering diverse use cases. NLP is a branch of AI focused on enabling computers to interact with human language, helping them understand, analyze, and generate text or speech (Rana, 2023). This subfield combines computational techniques with linguistic models to enhance human-computer communication. NLP finds applications across industries such as investment (sentiment analysis), customer relationship management (via chatbots), retail and operations (decision support systems), legal services, architecture, and transportation, among others (Chowdhary, 2020).

The core techniques in NLP include statistical modeling, machine learning, and deep learning. These methods contribute to the development of algorithms that can process and interpret natural language. In recent years, large language models (LLMs)—a form of NLP technology—have become increasingly prominent, highlighting their growing role in revolutionizing tasks that require understanding and generating human language.

In terms of personalized learning, the study by (Liu & Yushchik, 2024) demonstrated a significant improvement in the knowledge levels of students who participated in personalized AI-enhanced learning. Similarly, (Chen & Perez, 2023) explored the role of AI in personalizing learning and enhancing assessments. Another study by (Zheng et al., 2024) suggested that the proposed approach could substantially improve collaborative knowledge building, cognitive engagement, socially shared regulation behaviors, and group performance. Engaging with AI-driven technology has also been shown to enhance language communication skills (Polakova & Klimova, 2024) and improve its perceived effectiveness in second language acquisition at the university level—an important aspect of personalized learning in today's management education.

Furthermore, some authors have investigated the integration of self-determination theory (SDT) principles into management education, focusing on enhancing student motivation, engagement, and academic performance (AP). The findings indicate that the AIPL model effectively boosts student interest and improves academic performance (Ellikkal & Rajamohan, 2024). A variety of AI tools and platforms are available online, designed specifically to personalize the learning experience for management students. AI-powered tutors and interactive learning environments provide individualized support, fostering deeper engagement with the material. The diverse capabilities of AI enable educators to create more effective and inclusive learning experiences (*AI Tools and Platforms for Personalized Learning*, 2025).

AI holds the potential to transform education by offering personalized learning experiences tailored to the unique strengths and needs of each student. The compilation of AI tools and platforms is based on an analysis of their features, including criteria such as free access, personalization capabilities, and their suitability for educational use (Riapina, 2024). AI-powered personalized learning systems adjust educational content to match individual student needs, boosting both engagement and academic performance. Furthermore, AI promotes fairness by minimizing biases in admissions and grading processes and providing accessibility features for students (Ahmed et al., 2024).

Additionally, AI helps streamline administrative tasks through automation, allowing institutions to expand their educational offerings to a diverse, global student body. By integrating AI into smart education systems, it becomes possible to identify and adapt to various learning styles, leading to better student engagement and improved outcomes. Using advanced AI algorithms, educational platforms can analyze students' behaviors, preferences, and performance data to customize content and teaching approaches according to each student's learning style (Yamijala et al., 2024). This adaptive approach not only creates a more inclusive learning environment but also enhances the overall effectiveness of educational delivery.

The integration of AI in education is increasingly recognized as a powerful tool for improving learning outcomes and teaching methods, ultimately reshaping the educational landscape (Dubey, 2024). AI leverages advanced algorithms and data analysis to personalize content, pacing, and teaching strategies, ensuring that each student's needs are met, improving engagement, and minimizing disruptions. Additionally, automated assessment tools provide immediate feedback, freeing up educators to focus on more interactive teaching (Elshazly, 2024).

The above review of literature had presented a comprehensive analysis of the changing paradigms in management as well as higher education brought in by the introduction of AI technologies which had opened a sea of opportunities for learning and development and academic excellence. While considering personalized learning perspectives, the review had indicated that there is a scope of further research and discussions on the role of AI-enabled technologies to facilitate personalized learning of students and research scholars – which infact is the primary objective of this book chapter.

## AI IN MANAGEMENT EDUCATION

Management studies have undergone a paradigm shift with the incorporation of AI-driven technologies. AI has the potential to tackle some of the most significant challenges in management education, transform teaching and learning methods, and fast-track progress toward SDG 4, which aims to ensure universal access to quality education and lifelong learning opportunities. AI is playing an increasingly vital role in society, thanks to its ability to analyze vast amounts of data and recognize patterns. It is being utilized across various applications, from automating administrative tasks to personalizing learning experiences and forecasting academic trends. For instance, machine learning algorithms are being used to examine academic and behavioral data of management students, helping to identify performance trends, enhance instructional quality, optimize business school schedules, and facilitate better communication between management institutions and potential industry recruiters. Table 1 elaborates the hallmarks of the application of AI in management education.

*Table 1. Application of AI in Management Education (Source: Authors)*

| Sl. No. | Application of AI in Management Education | Features |
|---|---|---|
| 1 | Academic Big Data Analytics | The role of AI-powered analysis of academic big data is to process and interpret extensive educational data, revealing patterns, trends, and actionable insights. This capability enhances decision-making across various domains, such as student performance, curriculum design, resource management, and personalized learning. In the context of management education, it can identify performance trends and predict behavioral patterns among students, enabling educators to offer tailored and timely feedback. Additionally, it supports predictive analytics for academic outcomes, streamlines administrative processes, and enhances overall educational strategies and student engagement. AI can efficiently analyze extensive datasets to reveal key insights into management education. By identifying patterns, trends, and correlations in student performance, engagement, and learning outcomes, AI helps inform improvements in curriculum development, teaching approaches, and student support structures. |
| 2 | Personalized Curriculum Delivery | AI enables personalized curriculum delivery by tailoring it to the unique needs of each management student. Given the diverse backgrounds of management students, this becomes particularly important for management educators & faculty members. Machine learning algorithms assess individual performance and learning preferences, offering customized recommendations for activities and educational resources that best meet their specific needs. |
| 3 | Automation of administrative tasks | AI can automate tasks such as grading, scheduling, and report generation, while also supporting the continuous evaluation of management students |
| 4 | Facilitating Creative Endeavours | AI enhances the practical application of management theories by providing a more efficient means of translating theoretical concepts into real-world practices. AI-driven tools have the potential to transform experiential learning and case study approaches, fostering greater creativity and innovation among both students and faculty members. |
| 5 | Real-time Automated Tutoring Support | AI-powered tutoring applications offer interactive, real-time support to management students which is especially helpful for learning technical subjects like Operations Research, Digital Marketing, Business Statistics, Advanced Financial management etc. By leveraging natural language processing and machine learning algorithms, these systems can comprehend student inquiries and deliver precise answers, assisting with assignments, problem-solving, and grasping key concepts. |
| 6 | Conduct of Smart Classes | AI tools can enrich the management learning experience through immersive virtual environments and business simulations. Virtual and smart classrooms facilitate remote as well as hybrid learning, allowing students and instructors to interact seamlessly across distances. Business Simulations create realistic settings where students can apply management theories and make decisions, offering hands-on experience without the risk of real-world consequences. |

continued on following page

*Table 1. Continued*

| Sl. No. | Application of AI in Management Education | Features |
|---|---|---|
| 7 | Personalized Evaluation | AI can create personalized learning evaluations that adjust in real-time based on a student's progress. This approach ensures students are engaged at the right level of difficulty while providing constructive feedback, helping them evaluate their comprehension of key concepts and identify areas for further growth. |
| 8 | AI-enabled Collaborative Learning | AI-driven collaboration platforms improve interaction and cooperation among management students. By offering tools for document sharing, project coordination, and joint problem-solving, these platforms increase student involvement and foster a collaborative, community-driven learning environment. |
| 9 | AI-enabled Research | AI can assist in management research by processing large datasets, predicting/ detecting patterns, and making efficient forecasts. This enables research scholars in management and managers to make more informed decisions, enhance efficiency, and boost productivity. AI algorithms can support researchers by facilitating the exploration of innovative ideas, identifying emerging patterns, and synthesizing insights from large volumes of scholarly content. |
| 10 | Innovation | AI can drive management innovation by automating tasks, analyzing data, and forecasting future trends. This allows management researchers and students to gain valuable insights into new products and services more efficiently, leading to more informed decisions about resource allocation. AI algorithms can assess market trends and consumer behaviors to guide the strategic direction of product development. By predicting potential challenges, AI helps identify and address risks early in the product development process. Additionally, AI optimizes resource allocation by pinpointing the most promising projects and refining timelines and budgets. AI plays a key role in streamlining workflows, forecasting trends, personalizing customer experiences, and fostering innovation. The integration of AI in innovation management is not just a passing trend—it represents a transformative shift, ushering in next-generation, AI-powered innovation processes and stages. |

**Source:** Author(s)

## PERSONALIZED LEARNING IN MANAGEMENT

Personalized learning in management education is an approach that customizes learning materials to match students' individual interests, needs, and learning preferences. It empowers students to progress at their own pace and select topics that align with their goals. This tailored approach ensures learners access the content they need to develop the right skills at the most opportune moments. Ultimately, it bridges the gap between students' career aspirations and organizational objectives, fostering success for both individuals and the organization. In personalized learning, each student receives a customized "learning plan" tailored to their unique learning style, existing knowledge, skills, and interests. This contrasts with the traditional "one size fits all" approach commonly seen in many management institutions.

Personalized learning enables management educators to offer tailored educational experiences that align with each learner's needs, helping them absorb information more efficiently and comprehensively. This context-driven approach focuses on relevance, fostering engagement and enhancing the effectiveness of workplace learning programs. Implementing personalized learning in student development creates more engaging and effective learning experiences, allowing management institutions to better respond to shifting academic and industry demands while preserving their competitive advantage in a changing landscape.

***Hallmarks of Personalized Learning in Management:*** The essential hallmarks or attributes of personalized learning in management are as follows (Table 2):

*Table 2. Hallmarks of Personalized Learning (Source: Authors)*

| Sl. No. | Features of Personalized Learning | Features |
|---|---|---|
| 1 | Learner Profiling | A key element of personalized learning is the development of individual learner profiles, which capture essential details about each learner, such as their learning history, preferences, goals, backgrounds and relevant academic performance evaluations. These profiles provide the necessary insights to effectively support management students throughout their learning journeys. |
| 2 | Customized Learning Plans | Individual learning paths lie at the heart of personalized learning. This approach allows faculty teams to evaluate learners' current skill levels and offer a customized roadmap that outlines the learning activities and milestones they will follow to achieve their goals. By developing role-based learning programs, management students can reach proficiency more quickly, aligning with both institutional objectives and industry demands. Personalized learning emphasizes adapting instruction to each student's pace, promoting long-term progress. Thanks to learning management systems, this process has become more efficient, enabling educators to create courses, assess students, and design tailored learning paths. |
| 3 | Competency Development | In personalized learning, the emphasis moves from requiring all learners to reach the same milestones simultaneously to enabling individual progress based on competency models. Management institutions must conduct regular assessments to determine when students have mastered a particular task or learning stage and are ready to move forward. This approach allows learners to advance at their own pace, ensuring they don't feel overwhelmed by new information before fully understanding the concepts. |
| 4 | Learning Flexibility | Flexible learning environments are essential to personalized learning. Whether the learning takes place online or in person, management students should have the opportunity to engage with academic content in comfortable, less formal settings compared to traditional classroom set-ups. Such environments help minimize distractions and reduce stress, giving learners the freedom to take charge of their learning experience |

continued on following page

*Table 2. Continued*

| Sl. No. | Features of Personalized Learning | Features |
|---|---|---|
| 5 | Evidence & case based instruction | A fundamental element of personalized learning in management is grounding instruction in data, evidence, and case-based findings. Insights from screenings, evaluations, presentations, seminars and learning assessments should be used to identify areas requiring more attention or less focus, allowing for continuous adjustments to each learner's journey. This data-driven approach eliminates ambiguity and reduces redundancy, resulting in a more efficient and effective learning experience. |
| 6 | Learner ownership in the learning process | Management learners should be given the flexibility to learn in ways that align with their unique needs and interests. While assessments remain important, they function more as tools to guide the learning process rather than strict measures of its outcomes. Management students at personal levels should be encouraged to have well defined learning goals and objectives. Personalized learning includes opportunities for learning beyond the classroom, such as real-world experiences in the community or digital learning platforms. |
| 7 | Student-led interdisciplinary approach | Management education in its very essence should be characterized by student-led interdisciplinary flavour which would enable them to get embedded with the broader perspective of understanding concepts regarding management practices and business strategies |

**Source:** Author(s)

Personalized learning centers on linking a learner's prior knowledge, experiences, and skills to training materials that integrate their existing understanding with new information. By drawing on data from a learner's past experiences and connecting it to new concepts, personalized learning deepens understanding, boosts engagement, and enhances knowledge retention. Ultimately, it makes the learning process more effective.

In management studies, personalized learning should encourage a collaborative relationship between faculty and students, with students actively participating in decision-making. In this model, both faculty and management students co-create the curriculum and assessments. Faculty provide a variety of learning options, while students choose methods that best meet their needs. In this context, management faculty act as knowledge facilitators and mentors, designing strategies tailored to individual learners. Students, in turn, select topics that align with their interests and preferred ways of demonstrating their knowledge.

## ROLE OF AI IN PERSONALIZED LEARNING IN MANAGEMENT

AI is pivotal in facilitating personalized learning by processing large volumes of data to assess each student's strengths, weaknesses, learning styles, and preferences. AI-powered adaptive learning platforms are engineered to dynamically adjust the difficulty of tasks based on a student's real-time performance. Traditional education models often assume that all students learn at the same pace and in the same way, but this isn't accurate. Every student has a distinct learning style, speed, and level of comprehension. AI-driven adaptive learning systems are transforming education by personalizing the learning process, enabling students to progress at their own pace and in a manner that suits their individual needs. These systems analyze student performance data and deliver tailored feedback, ultimately improving learning outcomes and boosting student engagement.

## AI-Enabled Adaptive Learning

AI-powered adaptive learning represents a transformative educational method that utilizes Artificial Intelligence in Education (AIED) to customize the learning experience for each student. By leveraging data analytics and machine learning algorithms, this approach evaluates students' strengths, weaknesses, and learning patterns. Based on these insights, the system dynamically adjusts content, pace, and difficulty to match the learner's needs and abilities in real-time.

A significant advantage of AI-driven adaptive learning is its ability to tailor the learning journey for each student, personalizing content, pacing, and complexity according to their unique strengths and challenges. By analyzing vast amounts of data, AI algorithms determine the most effective teaching methods for individual learners. This personalized approach enables students to focus on areas where they need the most support, reinforcing their understanding and improving long-term retention of knowledge.

AI-adaptive learning technologies provide educators with real-time insights into student performance, allowing them to track individual and group progress more effectively. These tools help educators identify learning gaps and adjust their strategies accordingly, ensuring timely interventions for students who may be struggling. The AI-driven system also optimizes the allocation of resources, ensuring students receive targeted support where it is needed most. This data-driven approach empowers educators to make informed decisions, enhancing the overall efficiency and effectiveness of the teaching process.

A key benefit of AI in personalized learning is its ability to create adaptive learning environments. AI-powered platforms assess each student's unique learning patterns and strengths, delivering customized content and exercises that are specifically suited to their needs. Through the use of AI and machine learning (ML), adaptive learning personalizes the educational experience, boosting student engagement, academic performance, and overall well-being.

Traditional classroom models often assume all students learn at the same pace and in the same manner, but this is far from reality. Each student has a distinct learning style, pace, and level of comprehension. AI-powered adaptive learning systems are revolutionizing education by allowing students to progress at their own speed and in ways that align with their individual learning preferences. These systems continuously analyze student performance data and provide personalized feedback, fostering improved learning outcomes and increased engagement. AI-powered adaptive learning has transformative potential in education, delivering personalized and efficient learning experiences (Fig 1).

*Figure 1. Essential features of AI-enabled Adaptive Learning*

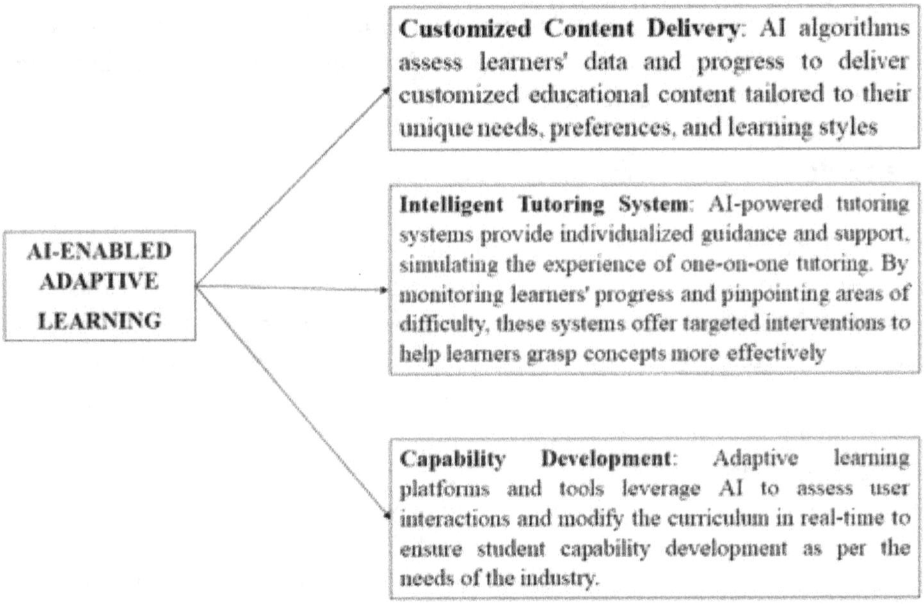


*(Source: Author)*

By dynamically adjusting content speed and complexity to match a student's proficiency level, AI enables a tailored learning experience that supports effective achievement of goals. AI-driven adaptive learning is integrated into Learning Experience Platforms (LXP), Learning Management Systems (LMS), Talent Management Systems (TMS), and other eLearning tools, addressing various educational challenges, including custom LMS development. A key advantage of AI and adaptive learning is enhanced accessibility. Technology-driven solutions help remove educational barriers, giving students access to high-quality learning materials, no matter their location or background. For instance, students in remote areas can engage with online courses and resources, while those with disabilities can take advantage of assistive technologies that support their learning needs.

Moreover, AI-powered adaptive learning ensures sustained student engagement throughout the learning process. Each student embarks on a personalized learning journey designed to enhance their skills and competencies. Faculty members have access to detailed performance metrics, which provide valuable insights into students' progress, strengths, and areas for improvement. This data-driven approach significantly enhances the ability to deliver a more customized and impactful learning experience.

By continuously monitoring student progress and performance, adaptive learning platforms can identify where students need additional support or more challenging tasks. This real-time feedback and personalized content delivery foster a more engaging and effective learning environment. Additionally, adaptive learning benefits educators by offering insights into students' learning behaviors, enabling them to refine their teaching strategies for improved outcomes.

## AI-enabled Virtual & Augmented Reality

Virtual and augmented reality technologies have the potential to create immersive learning experiences that deeply engage students and facilitate a stronger understanding through interaction with 3D objects. AI-powered VR and AR learning combines artificial intelligence (AI) with virtual reality (VR) and augmented reality (AR), transforming education by personalizing learning, creating immersive environments, and delivering real-time feedback.

Augmented reality (AR) enhances the physical world by overlaying digital content, offering interactive, hands-on learning experiences. Meanwhile, virtual reality (VR) creates fully immersive simulations, allowing students to explore and engage with complex concepts in a virtual space. AI further personalizes the experience by adapting content to meet each student's needs and providing instant feedback, which helps guide their progress.

These technologies allow students to visualize intricate ideas, explore new environments, and practice real-world skills—such as performing surgeries or engineering tasks—in a risk-free, controlled setting. At the same time, advancements in Natural Language Processing (NLP) and computer vision are enabling AI to better understand and respond to the unique needs of individual management students.

Furthermore, AR/VR technologies play a crucial role in designing dynamic and interactive learning experiences. For management students, these technologies allow for simulations and practical exercises that enable them to tackle complex concepts and develop critical thinking skills. AI enhances this by customizing the educational content and activities to the individual learner. For example, an AI-driven learning system can monitor a student's progress and provide additional support when needed, or design personalized learning paths based on their goals and interests.

This personalized approach also promotes inclusivity by adapting coursework for students with disabilities or those in remote locations. The integration of VR, AR, and AI in eLearning is transforming education by offering more engaging, immersive, and individualized learning experiences that enable collaboration among students from diverse backgrounds and locations. Example: EdX employs adaptive learning techniques to personalize content for each learner and offer tailored course recommendations. By utilizing AI, EdX enhances the learning experience. Additionally, many of its courses incorporate AR/VR elements to create immersive learning environments, particularly in fields such as management, architecture, engineering, and healthcare.

## Use of AI-Enabled Chatbots

Conversational AI is a technology that allows computers to communicate with humans using natural language. In the field of management education, conversational AI can deliver real-time feedback and assistance to students, enhancing their learning outcomes. Chatbots powered by conversational AI can respond to management student inquiries, offer feedback on assignments, and guide students through complex course materials. Chatbots can assist management students in quickly accessing course information by directing them to key details. This helps reduce the workload for instructional staff, as the chatbot becomes the initial point of contact for inquiries related to due dates, assignment details, homework resources, and more. These chatbots can also be tailored to cater to the specific needs of various learners and educational settings.

Generative AI represents a groundbreaking advancement in AI technologies, particularly in the realm of AI agents and chatbots. Unlike traditional bots, generative AI can craft new, context-sensitive responses, enabling more fluid and natural interactions. This leap in AI capabilities makes it especially valuable for modern educational environments, where nuanced, intelligent communication is essential. AI-driven chatbots powered by generative AI can also function as virtual teaching assistants, offering personalized support to both students and instructors.

Streebo, renowned for its expertise in digital transformation and artificial intelligence, has applied its cutting-edge chatbot technology to the education sector. These sophisticated chatbots leverage leading AI frameworks such as GPT on Microsoft Azure, IBM Watson, AWS SageMaker, and Google PaLM, specifically tailored to meet the unique needs of educational institutions. With advanced natural language processing (NLP) capabilities from platforms like IBM Watson, Google DialogFlow, Amazon Lex, and Microsoft Azure's CLU, these chatbots are designed to understand and respond to educational inquiries in a way that feels both intuitive and conversational. Trained on vast, education-focused datasets, they provide accurate, context-aware responses, greatly enhancing the learning experience while streamlining educator-student interactions.

*Figure 2. Queries made for AI-enabled Chatbots*

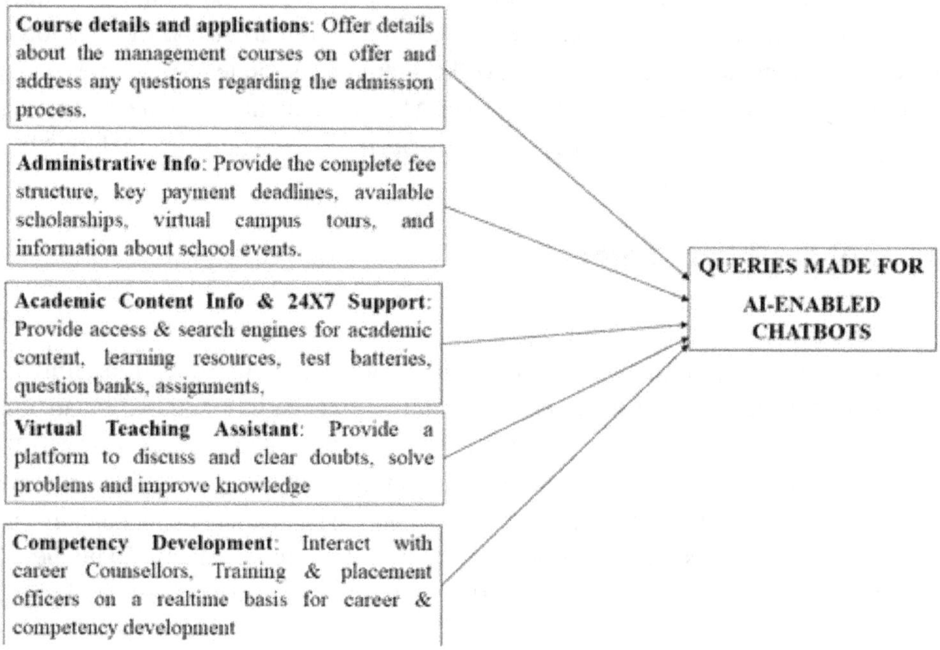


*(Source: Author)*

Figure 2 illustrates the diverse queries which could be made to AI-enabled chatbots. Of these the features of virtual tutoring tools and 24X7 virtual student support tools have immense importance for disseminating essential information and knowledge to students.

***Virtual Tutoring Tools*:** One of the most valuable uses of AI in management education is AI-powered, automated (virtual) tutoring tools. These AI-driven tools can teach management students through a series of conversational messages, similar to a typical chat, but structured like a lecture. These systems can quiz students, ask questions, and assess their progress. Instead of waiting for a teacher's response, students can directly message an educational AI chatbot and receive immediate, personalized support with instruction and continuous assessment. Here the AI-chabot intervenes by evaluating each student's comprehension level and delivers the next portion of the lecture based on their progress. As data is continuously gathered, the

the application can pinpoint areas where students need improvement and recommend additional practice on those skills to help boost student performance.

***24 X 7 Virtual Student Support Tools***: AI-driven chatbots and virtual assistants do more than just answer simple queries or give weather forecasts. They can actively manage a student's personal tasks by organizing their calendar, sending reminders, and helping with other responsibilities. Haptik's AI-enabled chabot capabilities allow the application to deliver personalized assistance to students, addressing their specific concerns, offering support, and supplying the necessary information pertaining to complete various academic processes in the institution. Quizbot, an AI-powered chatbot, can conduct quizzes and assess student performance. It can automatically generate quizzes, provide real-time feedback on incorrect answers, adjust to different difficulty levels, and incorporate gamification elements to boost student engagement.

## AI-driven Cognitive Tutoring Tools

AI-powered cognitive tutoring systems have the potential to revolutionize the way learners receive academic support. These systems engage students in interactive problem-solving activities, adapting to their responses and providing immediate, personalized feedback. By simulating the experience of one-on-one tutoring, they offer continuous guidance and support. Utilizing well-established instructional strategies, cognitive tutoring systems deliver customized assistance that enhances students' understanding of concepts and promotes the development of critical thinking skills.

For instance, IBM Watson Tutor uses AI to provide personalized tutoring and academic support. Watson understands natural language queries, delivering contextually appropriate and detailed responses tailored to each student's needs. Similarly, Coursera's AI analyzes students' interests, past course completions, and learning goals to recommend courses and resources that align with their personal objectives.

One of the major advantages of AI in education is its ability to provide a more targeted and personalized approach to teaching. Traditional classroom settings often struggle to accommodate the diverse learning needs of all students. In contrast, AI enables students to learn complex concepts at their own pace, ensuring that they can fully grasp material before moving forward. The adaptability of AI algorithms ensures that students receive customized instruction tailored to their level of understanding, which leads to better retention and improved academic outcomes.

## AI-enabled Dynamic Content Delivery

AI can personalize educational content for each student, adjusting in real-time according to their progress and individual learning styles. AI-powered learning systems present this content in various formats, such as videos, interactive simulations, or text-based materials, catering to diverse learning preferences. Dynamic content optimization further enhances the learning experience by making real-time adjustments to course parameters, including content quality, teaching methods, and case examples. This ensures students receive an optimal learning experience, customized to their abilities and skill development needs. Additionally, AI-driven content distribution systems create personalized learning journeys based on detailed analysis and tailored learning paths, which include targeted activities to enhance engagement, assessments aligned with personal goals, and supplementary resources to reinforce learning.

## AI-enabled Learning Management Systems

AI-enabled Learning Management Systems (LMS) have transformed how students engage with course content and assessments. By leveraging sophisticated AI algorithms to analyze student performance data, these systems (example: Edmingle) offer valuable insights. Using machine learning, AI-driven LMS can suggest tailored learning resources, identify areas where students require further practice, and monitor progress over time. This results in a more personalized and effective learning journey for students. AI-powered Learning Management Systems (LMS) leverages artificial intelligence to tailor educational experiences and enhance the delivery of content. In contrast to traditional LMS platforms that primarily focus on course organization and delivery, an AI-powered LMS has revolutionized modern learning and development. It offers intelligent features and algorithms that personalize the learning journey with tailored recommendations, provide adaptive learning experiences based on feedback and past training, and collect data-driven insights on training progress and engagement. By automating tasks such as progress tracking and assessment, AI-powered LMSs enable organizations to save both time and resources, streamlining administrative processes and improving efficiency. The essential features (Table 3) of AI-enabled LMS include those of:

*Table 3. Hallmarks of AI-enabled LMS*

| Sl. No. | Features of AI-enabled LMS | Features |
|---|---|---|
| 1 | Adaptive Learning capabilities | The adaptive learning feature of an AI-powered LMS allows the system to adjust content and training pace in real-time, delivering targeted interventions and personalized feedback to maximize engagement and mastery. By customizing the learning experience, it improves outcomes, supports individualized learning paths, and creates a more engaging and effective educational journey. |
| 2 | Smart Recommendations | Smart recommendations offer tailored content suggestions based on the learner's strengths, preferences, and areas for growth. |
| 3 | Data Analytics (Learning & development) | AI-driven learning & development analytics monitor and analyze student data to deliver valuable insights into learners' behavior and progress. Analytics experts & faculty can leverage this data to enhance the learning experience, assess student performance and evaluate student industry readiness, and make more informed decisions regarding academic content development depending upon feedback drawn from analytics. AI detects patterns and trends in student learning data, enabling Business Schools to take proactive actions rather than reacting after the fact. |
| 4 | Gamification | Gamification reimagines traditional course delivery, making it more engaging and enjoyable by adding elements like animation, storytelling, and friendly competition. AI-driven quiz generators automatically create multiple-choice questions from any given text or data. Incorporating these interactive quizzes into your courses helps maintain learner engagement while evaluating their comprehension and knowledge. |
| 5 | Academic Performance Management | AI-driven grading and feedback systems lighten the burden on management faculty by automatically evaluating assessments according to set performance evaluation criteria as per University norms. This technology provides management students with accurate and timely feedback, improving their overall learning process. |
| 6 | Automated Academic Administration | AI-driven LMS platforms enable organizations to automate time-consuming administrative tasks, freeing up valuable resources. These systems can generate performance reports, track student participation and engagement, monitor involvement in experiential activities, and automate notifications, among other tasks. |

**Source:** Authors

## AI-Enabled Automated Assessment

AI-driven automated assessments offer immediate feedback and customized support, enabling timely interventions that accelerate progress toward learning goals. By powering intelligent tutoring systems and learning assistants, AI enhances multimodal learning by adjusting materials, difficulty levels, and practice exercises to meet the unique needs of each student. Additionally, AI enables the creation of adaptive, dynamic assessments that adjust in real time based on a student's performance, providing a personalized learning experience tailored to individual abilities. AI-powered grading tools can evaluate both written and spoken responses effectively. Natural Language Processing (NLP) models assess written content, while speech and linguistic analysis evaluate spoken answers. This automation not only saves educators time but also ensures grading is consistent, objective, and free from bias. AI assessment tools can identify areas where students need additional support, adjusting difficulty levels as required to maintain an engaging and effective learning experience.

AI-powered bots also offer interactive role-play simulations, providing students with realistic, immersive assessment scenarios that mirror potential real-world situations in their future careers. Moreover, AI can perform statistical and psychometric analyses, offering detailed insights into both student performance and the quality of assessments. With the help of data visualizations and result interpretations, educators can identify strengths, weaknesses, and areas for improvement, enabling data-driven decisions about curriculum design, teaching strategies, and assessment methods.

### AI-Enabled Communication Skill Development

Developing effective communication skills is an essential requirement for management students especially as a part of their personality and soft skill development perspective. Learning a business (corporate) language can be difficult, but AI tools have made it more accessible and engaging. AI technologies are now being used to create interactive language learning experiences. These tools can simulate real-life conversations, analyze student pronunciation, and adjust lessons based on individual progress. By harnessing AI, students can practice and refine their language skills in an immersive, dynamic setting, boosting their fluency and confidence.

## CHALLENGES & ETHICAL ISSUES

While AI offers numerous benefits and applications in management education, challenges and ethical concerns surrounding its increasing use persist. Safeguarding user privacy and upholding the highest security standards are essential to ensure compliance and prevent cyber incidents in the digital environment.

- ***Catering Biasness:*** AI applications are programmed on data from particular subject areas, which can create limitations in the dataset and affect the machine learning model's analysis. Additionally, algorithm design may unintentionally introduce biases from developers, potentially distorting results in favor of or against specific groups of learners. Monitoring AI systems for biases that could disadvantage certain student groups is a significant challenge, potentially limiting the widespread use of AI in management education. Educators must regularly update and audit AI algorithms to ensure fairness. Proactively addressing bias is essential to fostering an equitable learning environment.

- ***Transparency & Data Privacy Issues:*** Management educators should clearly explain to students how AI tools function and how their data is utilized. Transparency in these areas fosters trust and encourages responsible use. Offering insights into the AI decision-making process can help demystify the technology and promote informed, thoughtful usage. Analyzing learner data and sharing it with third parties requires compliance with regional, national, and international regulations. With growing global concerns about data privacy and rapid technological advancements, regulations are constantly evolving, making it challenging for data-driven organizations to remain compliant.
- ***Statutory Compliance Management:*** Maintaining the highest standards of statutory compliance and transparency as desired by regulations prescribed by UGC, AICTE, NAAC, NBA etc is crucial for data-driven operations related to administrative management in higher education sector. While responsible development and automated compliance checks can streamline the process, human oversight remains essential to ensure the ethical use of AI-powered solutions with concerns for data leakage and misuse remain issues of concern for management education institutions.
- ***Quality Management:*** AI-generated content can be inconsistent and inaccurate, potentially reinforcing biases present in the student data. AI systems are only as effective as the content they provide. Ensuring that the educational material delivered by AI tools is accurate, current, and aligned with the curriculum presents a major challenge. Additionally, there is a risk of homogenization, where AI may prioritize standardized content over diverse perspectives and critical thinking. Educators must actively curate and monitor the content used by AI systems to uphold the quality of education.
- ***Over dependence on Technology:*** As AI becomes increasingly embedded in higher education (management) education, there is a concern that both students and educators may become overly reliant on technology. This dependence could hinder critical thinking and problem-solving abilities, as students might lean too heavily on AI for answers and solutions. Moreover, technological failures or limitations could interrupt the learning process. It is crucial to ensure that AI enhances rather than replaces traditional educational approaches, enabling students to cultivate a diverse set of skills.
- ***Changes in Assessment System:*** The growing use of AI has prompted institutions to shift from traditional assessment methods toward more holistic evaluation approaches that prioritize authenticity and lifelong learning. While this transition enhances assessment quality, it also places a greater burden on faculty, necessitating increased communication with staff and students, the

adoption of diverse assessment strategies, and the thorough documentation of results, among other responsibilities.

- ***Human Resistance:*** Some educators and trainers in management studies may resist adopting AI due to fears of job displacement, a lack of understanding about the technology, or doubts regarding its effectiveness. Furthermore, faculty members may also require proper training to integrate AI tools into their teaching learning perspectives and methods effectively. Without sufficient professional development, the full potential of AI to enhance education may remain untapped.

## ROADMAP AHEAD: SCOPE OF FURTHER STUDIES

Integrating AI into management and other higher education fields is a complex and time-intensive process, but its potential advantages are considerable. Management institutions must ensure that faculty members are equipped with the necessary tools and knowledge to incorporate AI into their teaching practices. At the same time, there is a growing need to develop AI literacy programs for students to encourage critical thinking and responsible technology use. In this regard, think tanks within management institutions should promote a collaborative, interdisciplinary approach to education, where AI is seamlessly integrated to enhance learning while maintaining equity, inclusivity, and ethical standards. However, human expectations and perceptions of AI often diverge from reality. Given the complexity of human thought, attitudes, biases, and the tendency toward irrational decision-making, this is not surprising. While these biases and cognitive distortions help individuals navigate the world, they can also shape how people interact with AI. As a result, individuals may fail to recognize the opportunities AI presents or may not fully grasp the risks involved.

Based on the extensive literature review and discussions in this chapter, researchers, academicians, and management education experts must develop a comprehensive strategic plan to foster the effective integration of AI-enabled applications into traditional management education. Researchers can also explore the issues raised in this discussion to identify unexplored areas and uncover opportunities for emerging AI technologies to enhance management education, making it more effective and better aligned with industry needs for students.

## CONCLUSION

This chapter has explored how artificial intelligence (AI) is rapidly transforming management education by enhancing engagement, driving data-based decision-making, and offering immersive experiential learning opportunities for business school students. It has analyzed the role of AI-driven technologies in supporting personalized learning, using a variety of practical examples and illustrations. The insights presented in this chapter will be highly valuable for practitioners and management think tanks involved in curriculum development in management education. Additionally, it aims to inspire management faculty and researchers to not only embrace AI technologies to reshape management education but also to encourage the integration of these immersive and analytical tools to drive transformation in management students, making them more prepared for the industry.

## REFERENCES


Ahmed, Y., Ahmed, T., Raza, A., & Jan, I. (2024). *Harnessing AI for Personalized Learning*. Equity, and Administrative Efficiency in Transnational Higher Education., DOI: 10.4018/979-8-3693-7016-2.ch009

*AI Tools and Platforms for Personalized Learning*. (2025). (pp. 25–60)., DOI: 10.4018/979-8-3693-3474-4.ch003

Chen, J. J., & Perez, C. (2023). Enhancing Assessment and Personalized Learning Through Artificial Intelligence. *Childhood Education*, *99*(6), 72–79. DOI: 10.1080/00094056.2023.2282903

Chen, L., Ifenthaler, D., Yau, J. Y.-K., & Sun, W. (2024). Artificial intelligence in entrepreneurship education: A scoping review. *Education + Training*, *66*(6), 589–608. DOI: 10.1108/ET-05-2023-0169

Chowdhary, K. R. (2020). Natural Language Processing. In *Fundamentals of Artificial Intelligence* (pp. 603–649). Springer India., DOI: 10.1007/978-81-322-3972-7_19

Clegg, S., & Sarkar, S. (2024). Artificial intelligence and management education: A conceptualization of human-machine interaction. *International Journal of Management Education*, *22*(3), 101007. DOI: 10.1016/j.ijme.2024.101007

Dubey, P. K. (2024). *Personalized Learning and Pedagogy*., DOI: 10.4018/979-8-3693-6130-6.ch004

Dwivedi, Y. K., Ismagilova, E., Hughes, D. L., Carlson, J., Filieri, R., Jacobson, J., Jain, V., Karjaluoto, H., Kefi, H., Krishen, A. S., Kumar, V., Rahman, M. M., Raman, R., Rauschnabel, P. A., Rowley, J., Salo, J., Tran, G. A., & Wang, Y. (2021). Setting the future of digital and social media marketing research: Perspectives and research propositions. *International Journal of Information Management*, *59*, 102168. DOI: 10.1016/j.ijinfomgt.2020.102168

Ellikkal, A., & Rajamohan, S. (2024). AI-enabled personalized learning: Empowering management students for improving engagement and academic performance. *Vilakshan - XIMB. Journal of Management*. Advance online publication. DOI: 10.1108/XJM-02-2024-0023

Elshazly, E. (2024). *Promoting Accessibility and Personalizing Learning Experiences Through AI*., DOI: 10.4018/979-8-3693-5538-1.ch005

Fellenz, M. R., Hoidn, S., & Brady, M. (2022). *The Future of Management Education*. Routledge., DOI: 10.4324/9781003095903

Geraldi, J., Locatelli, G., Dei, G., Söderlund, J., & Clegg, S. (2024). AI for Management and Organization Research: Examples and Reflections from Project Studies. *Project Management Journal*, *55*(4), 339–351. DOI: 10.1177/87569728241266938

Gupta, P., Mahajan, R., Badhera, U., & Kushwaha, P. S. (2024). Integrating generative AI in management education: A mixed-methods study using social construction of technology theory. *International Journal of Management Education*, *22*(3), 101017. DOI: 10.1016/j.ijme.2024.101017

Hu, K. (2023). *ChatGPT Sets Record for Fastest-Growing User Base*. Https://Www.Reuters.Com/Technology/Chatgpt-Sets-Record-Fastest-Growinguser-Base-Analyst-Note-2023-02-01/

Leelavathi, R., & Surendhranatha, R. C. (2024). ChatGPT in the classroom: navigating the generative AI wave in management education. *Journal of Research in Innovative Teaching & Learning*. DOI: 10.1108/JRIT-01-2024-0017

Liu, Z., & Yushchik, E. (2024). Exploring the prospects of using artificial intelligence in education. *Cogent Education*, *11*(1), 2353464. Advance online publication. DOI: 10.1080/2331186X.2024.2353464

Polakova, P., & Klimova, B. (2024). Implementation of AI-driven technology into education – a pilot study on the use of chatbots in foreign language learning. *Cogent Education*, *11*(1), 2355385. Advance online publication. DOI: 10.1080/2331186X.2024.2355385

Rana, S. (2023). AI and GPT for Management Scholars and Practitioners: Guidelines and Implications. *FIIB Business Review*, *12*(1), 7–9. DOI: 10.1177/23197145231161408

Riapina, N. (2024). *Unleashing the Potential of Every Child*., DOI: 10.4018/979-8-3693-1022-9.ch002

Wang, Y. (2021). Artificial intelligence in educational leadership: A symbiotic role of human-artificial intelligence decision-making. *Journal of Educational Administration*, *59*(3), 256–270. DOI: 10.1108/JEA-10-2020-0216

Yamijala, S. M. S., Chodisetty, R. S. C. M., Chakravorty, C., & Sai, K. P. (2024). *AI-Powered Learning Revolutionizing Smart Education With Personalized Learning Styles*., DOI: 10.4018/979-8-3693-8151-9.ch007

Zheng, L., Fan, Y., Gao, L., Huang, Z., Chen, B., & Long, M. (2024). Using AI-empowered assessments and personalized recommendations to promote online collaborative learning performance. *Journal of Research on Technology in Education*, •••, 1–27. DOI: 10.1080/15391523.2024.2304066

# Chapter 8
# Revolutionising Business and Management Education With Generative AI

**Shyam Sunder Agrawal**
https://orcid.org/0009-0004-3648-0584
*Lovely Professional University, India*

**Amanjot Singh Syan**
*Canadore Stanford International College, Canada*

## ABSTRACT

*Business education is integrating Generative AI (GAI) so as to transform the conventional teaching model by enhancing learning experiences, promoting innovation, and improving decision-making. This study deals with curriculum design enhancement, personalized learning, and the nurture of essential skills such as problem-solving and strategic thinking with the help of GAI tools. However, despite the emergence of GAI provided the direct application, effectiveness, and scalability in business education but for better understanding a gap still found. A systematic literature review using the PRISMA framework was conducted from 2014 to 2025, identifying studies on GAI application in business schools. Findings reveal that GAI provides personalized learning, assists real-time decision-making, and scales up curriculum delivery. However, challenges like faculty preparedness, ethical concerns, and integration issues remain. The study emphasizes the need for curriculum redesign, faculty capacity building, and the ethical use of AI.*

DOI: 10.4018/979-8-3373-2150-9.ch008

# 1. INTRODUCTION

## 1.1 Background of the Study

Artificial Intelligence (AI) has been transformed the education sector by improving learning experiences, automating administrative tasks, and enhancing research capabilities. AI applications in education evolved in 1960s, with early expert systems providing personalized tutoring (Rane, 2023). Over time, advancements in machine learning and natural language processing (NLP) have enabled AI-driven tools such as intelligent tutoring systems, automated grading software, and predictive analytics platforms (Vujović, 2024).

Nowadays, AI plays a critical role in higher education, including business and management studies. Universities worldwide use AI to analyze student performance, detect learning patterns, and provide adaptive learning experiences. According to a report by HolonIQ, the global AI-in-education market is expected to reach $20 billion by 2027, driven by increasing demand for personalized learning and data-driven decision-making in academics (Nguyen & Truong, 2025). However, most AI applications in education have historically focused on automation rather than content creation or interactive engagement, leading to a gap that Generative AI (GAI) aims to fill (Mittal et al., 2024).

## 1.2 Emergence of Generative AI (GAI) in Business and Management Studies

Generative AI, a branch of artificial intelligence that creates new content based on large datasets, has rapidly gained traction in education. Unlike traditional AI models that analyze and classify information, GAI can generate human-like text, images, code, and even business insights. This shift from analytical AI to creative AI presents new opportunities for business and management education (Linkon et al., 2024).

The rise of Generative AI can be attributed to breakthroughs in deep learning, particularly transformer-based architectures such as OpenAI's GPT (Generative Pre-trained Transformer) models and Google's Gemini (formerly Bard). According to a McKinsey report (2023), Generative AI could automate up to 60% of business-related tasks, including market analysis, strategy development, and financial forecasting, all of which are key components of business education (Marr, 2024).

In business schools, GAI is being integrated into learning in multiple ways (Mudrinić & Šoda, 2024):

- Case Study Generation: AI can create dynamic and updated case studies tailored to specific industries, making traditional case-based learning more relevant.
- Business Simulations: Generative AI allows students to run simulations of market conditions, test business strategies, and analyze financial risks in real time.
- Content Summarization & Report Generation: GAI can assist in summarizing academic papers, generating business reports, and providing concise industry insights.
- Interactive Tutoring & Feedback: AI-driven chatbots and virtual tutors provide instant explanations and feedback on business concepts, reducing faculty workload and enhancing student engagement.

Both the Harvard Business School and the Institut Europeen d'Administration des Affaires (INSEAD) have already used a few AI tools that can be used to enhance the learning process. Nevertheless, the GAI provides solutions to society along with challenges to adopt difficult, such as those related to the accuracy of such interventions, their ethics, and potential bias (Kohnke et al. 2023).

## 1.3 Research Objectives and Significance

The research seeks to critically examine the role of Generative AI in management and business studies by highlighting its practical uses, advantages, and limitations (Markouh et al., 2024). The research responds to the following main objectives in particular:

- Analyze the adoption of Generative AI in business education, focusing on its impact on curriculum, interactive learning, and assessment.
- Evaluate the effectiveness of AI-driven tools in enhancing student engagement, critical thinking, and decision-making skills.
- Investigate challenges in implementing Generative AI, including faculty concerns, ethical dilemmas, and infrastructural barriers.
- Recommend strategies for the ethical and effective integration of AI in business education to support faculty and student success.

The significance of this research lies in its potential to bridge the gap between emerging AI technologies and educational practices. While studies have examined AI in general education, there is limited research focusing on its impact specifically within business and management programs. Given the increasing reliance on AI in corporate environments, equipping future business leaders with AI literacy is essential (George, 2023).

This study will contribute to the ongoing discourse on digital transformation in education, offering insights that can guide business schools, educators, and policymakers in adopting AI responsibly (Cronin, 2024). By understanding both the potential and limitations of GAI, institutions can make informed decisions on integrating AI-driven learning models that enhance student outcomes while maintaining academic integrity.

## 1.4 Research Gap

Although AI is becoming more common in education, there is still a significant gap in understanding how Generative AI (GAI) specifically impacts business and management education. Most existing research regarding GAI focuses on traditional AI applications like automation, data analytics, and predictive modelling and does not speculate on the creative or interactive functionalities of GAI (Bell & Bell, 2023). There seems to be limited research on the role that GAI could play in redefining curriculum design, enabling personalized learning, and helping students with the development of such critical business skills as strategic thinking, problem-solving, and decision-making. While GAI holds promise for enhancing student engagement and faculty-student interaction, the extent to which it has been effective in these areas is uncertain (Elbourn, 2024). An under-explored area of concern is the approach to ethical considerations-in-planning concerning GAI use in education, which includes issues of plagiarism and bias, as well as the will and capability of faculty and institutions to integrate the technology (George, 2023). Further, there are limited studies concerning the scalability and sustained effects of GAI tools applied in business schools. This research intends to bridge those gaps by analyzing GAI adoption, its effectiveness on business education, and the big issues faced by educators and institutions in its implementation. The intention is to frame practical recommendations for the integration of GAI into business education in a responsible and impactful manner. The gaps identified will be presented in Table 1 along with their justification (Holmström & Carroll, 2024).

*Table 1. Identified Research Gaps*

| Research Focus | Identified Gap | Justification for Bridging the Gap | Citations |
|---|---|---|---|
| Integration of GAI in Business Education | Lack of structured frameworks for incorporating GAI into business school curricula and pedagogical strategies. | Developing clear guidelines will help educators effectively integrate GAI into teaching methodologies, ensuring alignment with learning objectives. | (Kshetri et al., 2023), (Malhotra, 2024) |
| GAI's Role in Skill Development | Limited empirical evidence on how GAI fosters critical skills like creativity, strategic thinking, and decision-making in management education. | Understanding GAI's impact on skill development can help design AI-enhanced learning experiences tailored to business students' needs. | (Kadaruddin, 2023), (Lee et al., 2024) |
| Student Engagement and Learning Outcomes | Unclear impact of GAI-driven personalized learning and adaptive content on student motivation, comprehension, and performance. | Assessing student responses to GAI-generated materials will determine its effectiveness in improving engagement and retention. | (Portuguez-Castro & Marchena Sekli, 2025), (Ratten & Jones, 2023) |
| Faculty Readiness and AI Adoption Challenges | Lack of faculty training and resistance to adopting GAI due to limited awareness, skill gaps, and concerns about academic integrity. | Addressing faculty concerns through targeted training programs will ensure smooth integration and maximize the potential of GAI in education. | (Sandhu et al., 2024), (Owoseni et al., 2024) |
| Ethical and Bias Concerns in GAI | Insufficient research on ethical dilemmas such as AI-generated misinformation and biases in training data and their implications for business decision-making. | Establishing ethical guidelines will ensure responsible AI use, mitigating risks of misinformation and biased decision-making in management education. | (Singh et al., 2024), (Hacker et al., 2023) |
| Scalability and Long-Term Impact | Limited insights into the scalability of GAI-driven education models in diverse institutional settings and across different business disciplines. | Understanding long-term impacts will help business schools make informed decisions about AI adoption and investment. | (AlAli & Wardat, 2024), (Matthew et al., 2023) |
| Industry-Academic Collaboration for GAI Implementation | There is a lack of collaboration between academia and industry to create real-world AI-driven business simulations and case studies. | Stronger industry partnerships will enhance the relevance of AI-driven learning experiences and better prepare students for evolving business landscapes. | (Saeger et al., 2024), (Yelamarthi et al., 2024) |

**Source:** Author's preparation

## 2. REVIEW OF LITERATURE

### 2.1 Understanding Generative AI: What It Is and How It Works

Generative AI (GAI) is one of the advanced forms of artificial intelligence. It creates new content such as text, images, music, videos, and even software code. While traditional AI works with data analysis and processing by applying predefined rules, GAI, instead, is capable of generating outputs from zero that are similar to human creativity and thinking (Sedkaoui & Benaichouba, 2024). This makes it a good tool for various industries, including business education, where it is being used to augment learning experiences, automate content creation, and enhance decision-making competencies (Owoseni et al., 2024).

Generative AI primarily uses deep learning techniques, usually transformer architecture, such as the Generative Pre-trained Transformer (GPT). Such models are trained on huge volumes of data, where they are learning patterns and structural information of language, images, or even any type of data (Nyoko & Hanafiah, 2024). Because of this ability, it can provide very meaningful and contextual output based on user input. Some of these tools, for example, include OpenAI's ChatGPT, Google's Gemini, and Midjourney, which are employed in text and image generation, while GitHub Copilot assists in writing and debugging code (Kadaruddin, 2023).

The core functionalities of Generative AI are set to create a paradigm shift in educational and corporate areas. Natural Language Processing (NLP) enables engaging in human-like conversations, summarizing reports, and translating languages (George, 2023). It also constructs high-quality images and videos from mere word descriptions that can assist in marketing and design. In terms of business analytics, Generative AI automates and generates reports based on data processing, with insights beneficial for students and professionals to make decisions. It's also clear that AI-driven chatbots and virtual assistants would improve learning by addressing student queries instantaneously (Chakraborty et al., 2023). These things make GAI a key part of business education, focusing on problem-solving, smart thinking, and real-life use.

### 2.1 The Evolution of AI in Higher Education

The integration of AI has been gradual; first was the simple automation tools of learning until advanced AI-enhanced learning environments developed (Al-Smadi, 2023). In the early 2000s, universities primarily relied on digital platforms such as Learning Management Systems (LMS) like Blackboard and Moodle to digitize and upload course materials and automate some administrative tasks (Khan et al., 2024). These systems were the basis for online e-assessment to offer wide accessibility for students around the world. The next phase in aligned progress was that AI cemented its place in personalized learning. During the 21st century, learning technologies were adaptive, beginning with platforms like Coursera, Knewton, and Duolingo (Malhotra, 2024). These systems aligned course content with personalized learning styles based on collective feedback. Intelligent tutoring systems evolved, providing students with real-time feedback and pipeline guidance, after which tools for AI plagiarism detection, led by Turnitin, found great adoption in academic institutions (Matthew et al., 2023).

AI has changed the present situation of education due to the ease and automation that comes with Generative AI. AI today is no longer a mere assistive technology for administering and assessment; it has become an active participant in the teaching and learning processes (Mittal et al., 2024). AI chatbots or virtual assistants can tutor students on a one-on-one basis through the questioning of complicated concepts and general assistance in following through with course materials. AI-generated case studies and simulation technology offer students a hands-on learning experience in virtually practicing financial modelling, marking strategies, and business negotiations. AI analytics enables teachers to gain insights into student performance to implement timely interventions and make learning more data-driven (Rane, 2023).

The shift toward AI application in learning is increasingly driven by the job requirements of digital skills. Since businesses today make decisions with the help of artificial intelligence, students must learn to use such tools for data analysis, problem-solving, and strategic planning (Rane, 2023). Therefore, integrating Generative AI into higher education is not merely an improvement over traditional methods of learning but a fundamental change necessary to prepare students for the future of work (Yelamarthi et al., 2024).

## 2.2 The Role of Generative AI in Business Education

Business education, in particular, stands to gain significantly from the Generative AI application. Business students need to develop skills in decision-making, critical thinking, and data analysis that AI can help with. The integration of AI-powered tools in the learning program will offer business schools an opportunity to enhance the overall learning experience by making it much more engaging, practical, and efficient (Matos et al., 2024).

Generative AI impacts curriculum design on a broad level; it assists professors in developing updated case studies, assignments, and other course materials that are coherent with present industry trends. Instead of traditional textbooks that might become outdated quickly, professors could be using AI to create real-time business situations and data-driven insights (Marr, 2024). In this way, students will receive the most relevant and applicable knowledge to prepare for the rapidly changing business landscape (Lee et al., 2024).

Generative AI can also help make lessons more interactive and engaging. AI simulations and virtual worlds let students try business strategies in a realistic setting (Matos et al., 2024). For example, finance students may trade stocks in an AI simulation, while marketing students may look at consumer behaviour through AI-generated data modelling. These AI chatbots function as 24/7 e-tutors, responding to questions and clarifying complex business concepts. Such tools greatly enhance experiential learning, allowing students to transpose theoretical knowledge to real-world situations (Nyoko & Hanafiah, 2024).

Another major benefit of AI for business education entails furthering decision-making skills using data analytics. It can process huge amounts of business data, prepare reports, and produce insights that help students with predictive analytics and financial-modelling education. For instance, AI is useful for studying stock market trends, checking investment risks, and reviewing a company's financial health. Using such tools, students learn to analyze data in developing evidence-based business decisions as opposed to instinctive ones (Rane, 2023).

The emergence of Generative AI is fast transforming the assessment and feedback mechanisms in business education. AI-based grading systems instantly provide grading of student assignments, which means quick feedback and recommendations for improvements. Consequently, this saves teaching time, and students are granted continuous and personalized learning assistance. AI system-driven analytics can also trace patterns in student performance, Allowing professors to identify struggling students early and provide the right support (Asad & Ajaz, 2024).

AI also helps students outside the classroom get ready for the job market through career guidance and skill development. AI-enabled platforms identify students' strengths and career interests and suggest relevant courses, certifications, and job opportunities (Bell & Bell, 2023). Resume-building AI helps students optimize their CVs, and AI-based interview simulators allow practice scenarios that enhance their job readiness. In this day and age, with businesses intensely working on AI-powered decision-making tools, students equipped with AI applications will have an edge over others in the job market (Cronin, 2024).

## 2.3 Challenges and Ethical Considerations

Despite its potential, the integration of Generative AI into business education comes with several challenges. One of the primary concerns is academic integrity. Since AI can generate essays, reports, and even code, there is a risk that students might misuse these tools to complete assignments without putting in the necessary effort. Universities must establish clear guidelines on AI usage, ensuring that students use it as a learning aid rather than a shortcut to completing work (Elbourn, 2024).

Another group of challenges is bias and fairness in AI-generated content. AI models are trained on existing datasets, which can come with some language, gender representation, and cultural bias. Due to these inaccurate models of business case studies and insights created by AI, such learning outcomes can be flawed when it comes to reflection (Akbar et al., 2024). Thus, these teachers must be aware of limitations and focus on making AI-generated content inclusive, diverse, and accurate. (George, 2023).

The need for faculty training and resistance from faculty also comes into existence. In the first instance, some of the educators feel that AI would result in the disappearance of the usual means of educating students; in other instances, Those unfamiliar with effectively using AI in their courses may also struggle with resistance and adapting to the changes, business schools need to actively venture into investment within the faculty training program geared toward understanding these students on what benefits AI can yield and how it can be used for ethical ends and efficiency (Holmström & Carroll, 2024).

## 2.4 The Future of Generative AI in Business Education

Generative AI is not just a passing trend; it is a transformative force that is reshaping business education. AI-integrated curriculum design, interactive learning, data-driven decision-making, and transitioning into careers would offer richer experiences in learning for business schools (Akpan et al., 2025). Equally vital to whatever advantages AI introduction to education has, its effectiveness therein is determined by the degree of responsibility with which it is executed. For universities, this means finding a balance between the benefits of technology and any ethical concerns it may raise. This way, AI-powered learning stays effective and efficient while maintaining academic honesty (Kohnke et al., 2023). The future of business education, AI-based innovation, and personalized learning experiences that create links between them; therefore, AI will be becoming 'the business brain' as organizations lean into it for decision-making. Business schools must prepare students to navigate this AI-driven world with critical thinking, ethical awareness, and practical skills (Linkon et al., 2024).

## 2.5 Comparison of Traditional and AI-Driven Pedagogical Models

The advancement of artificial intelligence (AI) within business education is revolutionizing traditional pedagogy into AI-driven, adaptive learning environments. The traditional business school pedagogy has been based on prescribed curricula, case studies, and teacher-guided learning. Generative AI (GAI), though, is revolutionizing business education through real-time simulations, automated feedback, and one-on-one learning experiences (Markouh et al., 2024).

A McKinsey report of 2024 identifies that AI-based education platforms enhance student engagement by 45% and decrease faculty workload by 30%, making it possible for business schools to extend quality education to the world. In the meantime, a Harvard Business Review study (2023) established that AI-facilitated decision simulations boost strategic thinking abilities by 60% compared to conventional classroom-based case study discussions (Matthew et al., 2023).

Table 2 below provides a data-backed comparison of traditional vs. AI-driven business education models:

*Table 2. Comparison of traditional vs. AI-driven business education model*

| Aspect | Traditional Business Education Model | AI-Driven Business Education Model | Citations |
|---|---|---|---|
| Content Delivery | Static, textbook-based curriculum, revised every few years. | AI-generated, real-time course materials adapting to market trends (e.g., ChatGPT, Bard). | Owoseni et al., 2024 |
| Student Engagement | Lecture-based, passive learning, limited interactivity. | AI-driven interactive tools and personalized learning experiences. Studies show a 50% increase in engagement (HolonIQ, 2023). | Rane et al., 2024 |
| Assessment Methods | Manual grading, standardized exams, time-intensive evaluation. | AI-automated grading with real-time feedback reduces faculty workload by 30% (EdTech Review, 2024). | Sandhu et al., 2024 |
| Faculty Role | Primary knowledge provider, structured curriculum with minimal flexibility. | AI-assisted facilitator, enabling real-time course updates and student-specific recommendations. | Vecchiarini & Somia, 2023 |
| Decision-Making Simulations | Case study-based, static business scenarios. | AI-powered real-time business simulations using live financial data (e.g., Wharton AI Lab). | Jayasinghe, 2024 |
| Industry Relevance | Theoretical models with outdated examples and limited real-world application. | AI-driven business case studies with current market data, improve employability by 40% (World Economic Forum, 2024). | Hacker et al., 2023 |

continued on following page

*Table 2. Continued*

| Aspect | Traditional Business Education Model | AI-Driven Business Education Model | Citations |
|---|---|---|---|
| Scalability | Limited to faculty availability and classroom size. | AI-powered online education, scalable to global learners with personalized curricula. | Markouh et al., 2024 |
| Corporate Training & Job Readiness | Standard MBA coursework with outdated job market trends. | AI-powered career guidance and AI-driven resume optimization tools (LinkedIn AI). | Asad & Ajaz, 2024 |
| Data-Driven Learning | One-size-fits-all syllabus, limited personalization. | Adaptive learning paths based on AI analytics; 75% of students perform better in AI-driven environments (McKinsey, 2024). | Al-Smadi, 2023, Daniel et al., 2025 |
| Collaboration & Communication | Classroom-based discussions, manual research collaboration. | AI-assisted discussion forums, virtual tutors, and multilingual AI-powered learning tools (MIT AI Education, 2023). | Portuguez-Castro & Marchena Sekli, 2025 |
| Ethical & Integrity Concerns | Plagiarism detection through traditional tools like Turnitin. | AI-generated content raises new risks of plagiarism, requiring advanced AI-integrity frameworks (IEEE AI in Education Report, 2023). | Saeger et al., 2024 |

Source: Self -created

## 2.6 GAI and Learning Outcomes

Generative AI is transforming business and management education by enabling highly personalized, interactive, and adaptive learning experiences that go beyond traditional classroom boundaries for both faculty and students (Wijayati et al., 2024). Using large language models and generative technologies, educators have designed dynamic case studies, simulated real-world business scenarios, and created intelligent tutoring systems that cater to individual learning styles and paces (Ooi et al., 2025). This has positive as well as negative effects both because every coin has two faces. This revolution not only enhances engagement but also sharpens critical thinking, creativity, and decision-making skills among students (Mangaiyarkarasi et al., 2025). Learning outcomes in this AI-enhanced environment include improved problem-solving abilities, deeper conceptual understanding, data literacy, and readiness for digital-age challenges (Khan et al., 2025). As a result, graduates are better equipped with the analytical and strategic competencies needed for the evolving landscape of global business (Lim & Lee, 2024).

## 2.7 Conceptual Framework

The shift from Traditional Business Education to AI-based business Education can be explained by three levels of AI adoption. At the Traditional Business Education level (Low AI, Low Personalization), instruction is mostly teacher-centered, with a fixed syllabus, fixed case studies, and manual grading (Saeger et al., 2024). This approach is based on standardized teaching practices with little technological intervention. Proceeding to the AI-Augmented Business Education level (Medium AI, Moderate Personalization), AI starts enhanced learning through AI-created content, automated evaluations, and business simulations. AI-driven career insights and engagement tools personalize learning, making it more interactive and dynamic (Al-Smadi, 2023). Lastly, at the AI-based business Education level (High AI, High Personalization), AI is seamlessly embedded within the curriculum, building adaptive learning experiences, real-time business simulations, and AI-based decision labs. AI-based assessments offer immediate feedback, and simulations relevant to the industry prepare students for actual business situations (Matthew et al., 2023).

*Figure 1. Level of AI Adoption*

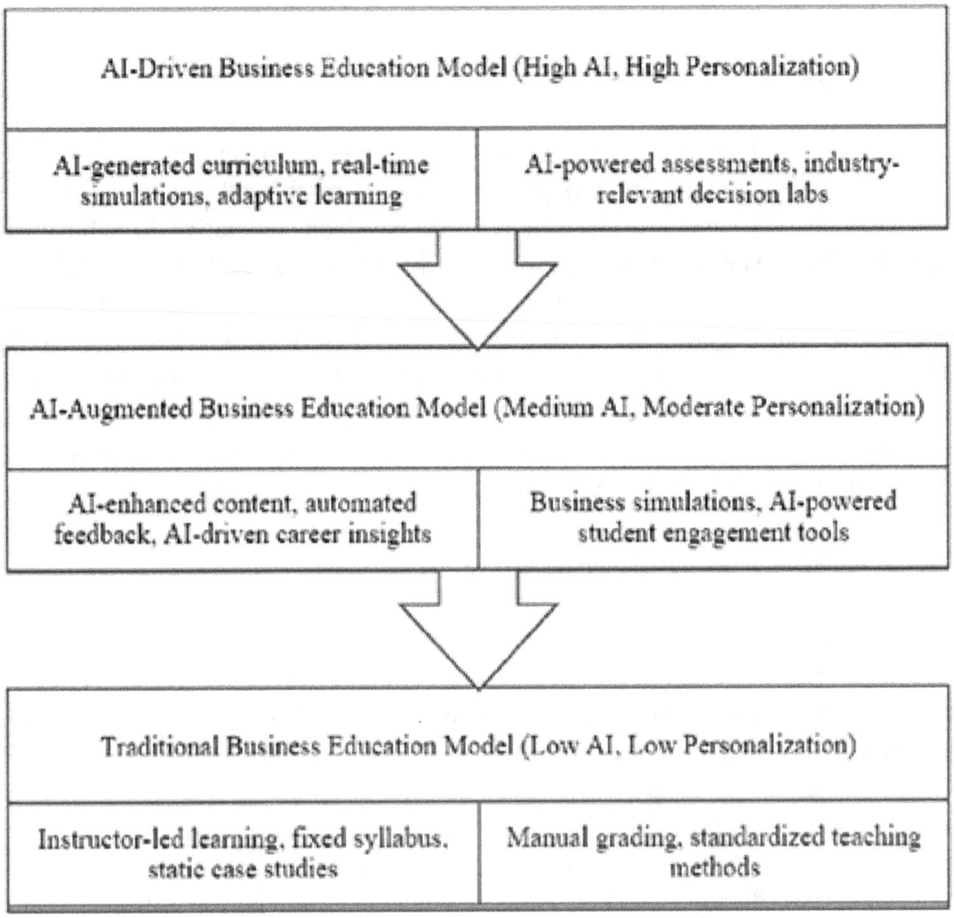


*Source: Author's Creation*

## 3. RESEARCH METHODOLOGY

The study used the PRISMA (Preferred Reporting Items for Systematic Reviews and Meta-Analyses) framework in conducting a systematic literature review on how generative artificial intelligence is integrated into business and management education. PRISMA also provided a systematic, transparent, and replicable approach to identifying screening and analyzing relevant studies (Al-Zubidy & Carver, 2019). The methodology was divided into four key aspects; they include identification of studies, inclusion and exclusion criteria, eligibility assessment, and data extraction & analysis. It supports selection criteria for including high-quality relevant studies, typically published during the period 2014 to 2025, selected to signify a timeframe capturing some recent advancements made in AI-driven education (Lee et al., 2024).

## 3.1 Identification of Studies

A broad search within different academic databases, including Scopus, Web of Science, IEEE Xplore, and Google Scholar, was performed to extract relevant literature. The search intended to summarize research on Generative AI in business education, AI-driven teaching approaches and schooling procedures, and AI's impact on course planning and student participation. Some of the keywords included: "Generative AI in Business Management," OR "AI-driven business learning," AND "adaptive AI-based learning," AND "AI-powered pedagogy in Management." The results of the initial search were 2350 articles published within the period 2014-2025, implying several empirical studies, systematic reviews, case studies, and theoretical papers, and Boolean operators were applied for the search strategy.

## 3.2 Inclusion and Exclusion Criteria

The dataset was refined through inclusion and exclusion criteria set in place to further ensure the relevance and quality of the studies selected. Included were those studies that were either published in a peer-reviewed journal or conference proceedings, concerned with AI-driven education in business and management studies, or provided empirical or theoretical insights about how AI contributes to curriculum design, learning outcomes, or student engagement. Excluded were papers in the following classes: those published before 2014; those centered around AI applications not within education, such as AI in healthcare or engineering; those that were not in English; those appearing to be duplicate entries across databases; and those that presented no empirical evidence or theoretical depth. A full 1120 articles were removed in adherence to these criteria, with 1230 papers left for further scrutiny.

*Table 3. Inclusion and Exclusion Criteria*

| Criteria | Inclusion | Exclusion |
|---|---|---|
| Publication Type | Peer-reviewed journal articles, conference proceedings | Non-peer-reviewed sources, book chapters, white papers, unpublished work |
| Time Frame | 2014-2025 | Studies published before 2014 |
| Language | English | Non-English papers |
| Subject Area | AI-driven education in business and management | AI applications in unrelated domains (e.g., healthcare, engineering) |

continued on following page

*Table 3. Continued*

| Criteria | Inclusion | Exclusion |
|---|---|---|
| Empirical/Theoretical Basis | Studies with strong theoretical framework, empirical evidence, case studies | Opinion pieces, articles lacking empirical findings |
| Duplication | Unique articles across databases | Duplicates identified across sources |

Source: Author's Creation

## 3.3 Eligibility Assessment

A manual review of the abstracts, methodology sections, and conclusions of the remaining 1,230 papers was conducted to assess their relevance to the research objectives. The focus was on studies that provided quantitative and qualitative evidence on the integration of GAI in business education, its impact on student learning, faculty adoption challenges, and ethical considerations. Preference was given to studies published in high-impact journals from publishers such as Elsevier, Springer, Wiley, and IEEE. Studies that did not offer considerable insights into AI's role in business education were excluded, resulting in a final dataset of 41 articles that were deemed eligible for detailed data extraction and analysis. Figure 2 provided more clarity about the eligibility of articles for this study:

*Figure 2. PRISMA Flow diagram*

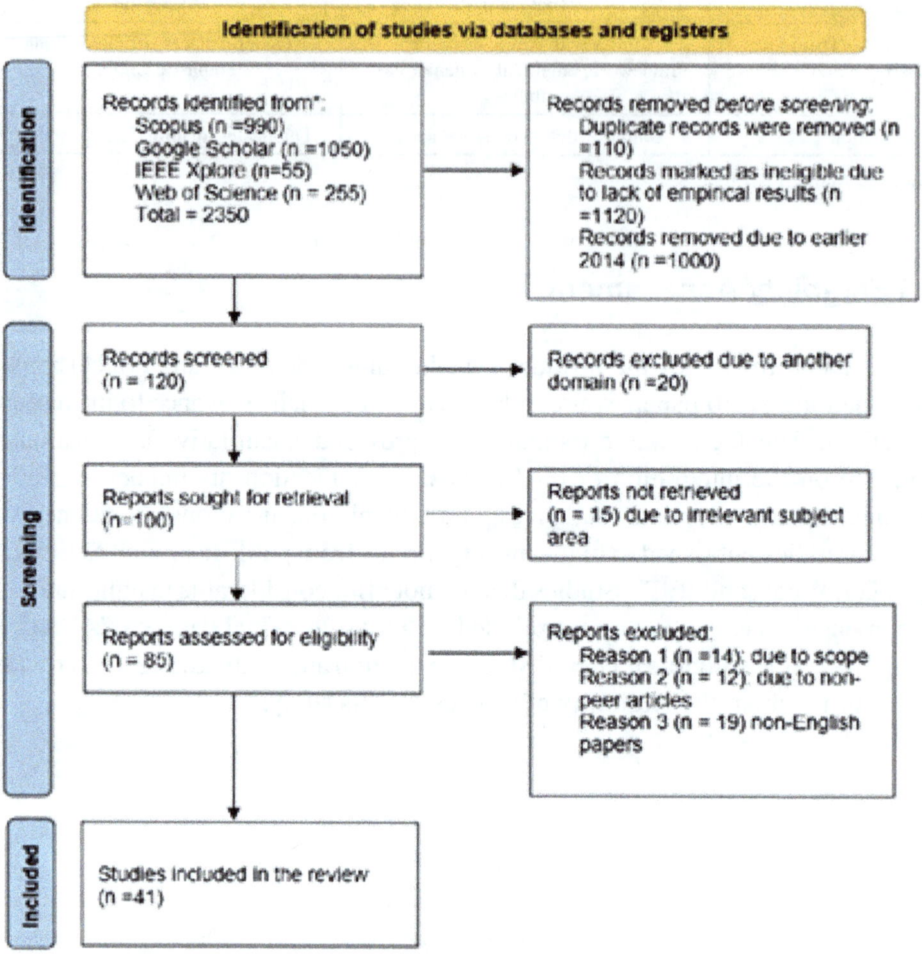


## 3.4 Data Extraction and Analysis

The selected 41 articles were analyzed using a structured data extraction process. A data extraction sheet was developed to systematically record key details, including study title, author(s), year of publication, journal or conference source, AI models examined (e.g., GPT-4, Gemini, Llama), key findings, challenges identified, and recommendations for future research. The combination of quantitative and qualitative analysis techniques was used to synthesize findings (Malhotra, 2024). For studies that had statistical data, AI adoption trends, improvement in learning outcomes, and faculty-student perceptions were collected and processed for comparison across multiple data sets. This systematic review provided a sound, data-driven basis for assessing GAI's effectiveness, challenges, and prospects in business and management education. After going through a PRISMA-based methodology, the outcomes of this research were scientifically robust and practically relevant for educators, regulators, and institutions involved in integrating AI into business learning environments (Ed-Dafali et al., 2025).

## 4. FINDINGS OF THE STUDY

It has been established that GAI has made very great changes in business education where it is significantly used for the design of curricula and instructional deliveries. AI tools have made it possible for courses to be easy, understandable, data-driven, and interactive instead of the traditional static courses (Kenthapadi et al., 2023). This allows teachers to be adaptive and personalize the learning experiences of different students. It has made possible decision-making simulations in real time and case-based learning that have made business education practical through interaction between students with realistic AI-generated business scenarios covering real-life issues that are competency towards industry challenges (Jayasinghe, 2024). Automating assessments and feedback has also improved effectiveness by giving instant AI-generated student evaluations that show the areas that need improvement (Benmamoun, 2024). The no. of studies published related to our topic from 2014 to 2025 which has been given below in Figure 3;

*Figure 3. Studies published from 2014 to 2025*

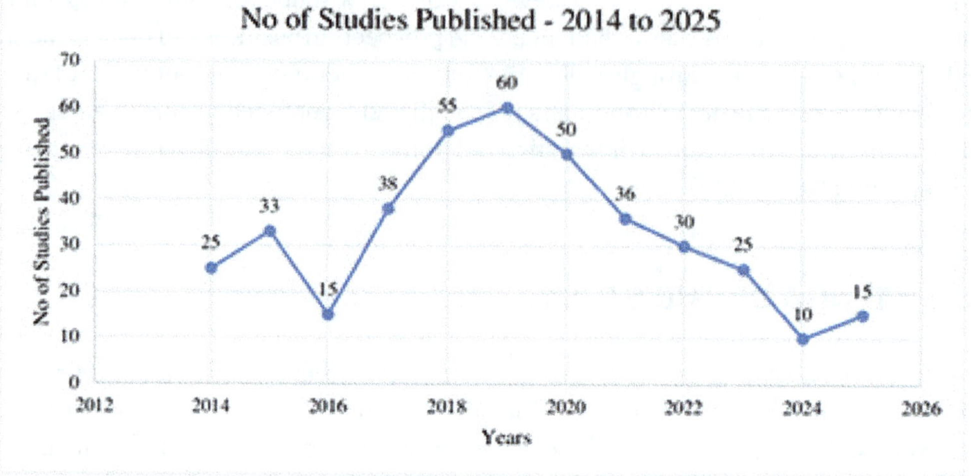


*Source: Self-created*

Another significant finding of the study relates to the influence of Generative AI in developing such competencies as problem-solving, critical thinking, creativity, and innovation. Sometimes, these AI tools help students deal with business problems using data, which has certainly improved their strategic decision-making ability (Adedoyin & Christiansen, 2024). Further, AI-based business simulations have developed leadership and strategic thinking as students gain practical exposure to realistic business environments (Aydın & Karaarslan, 2023). AI also helped bring students from different fields together, allowing them to collaborate and work as a team on AI projects.

Although some advancements were noted, the study also mentioned various hindrances and ethical concerns regarding the use of AI in business education by teaching (Budhwar et al., 2023). It came up with the faculty resistance and preparedness challenges because most of the educators were lacking the required AI training and almost reluctant to include AI in their teaching methods. Bias occurrence in AI-generated content, issues about academic integrity, and danger to personal data privacy are just some of the ethical concerns mentioned as hindrances. Further, adopting AI in education was slow because it required a lot of money for technology and teacher training (Alhusban et al., 2025). The need for clear regulatory frameworks and improvement in the AI literacy level among educators was cited to ensure responsible and effective application of AI in academia (Ed-Dafali et al., 2025).

The findings revealed that Generative AI' has created a significant impact on business education, making learning more individualized, interactive, and skills-oriented. But despite its vast advantages, the strategies should also consider addressing ethical issues and challenges in execution. Moving forward, business schools must give attention to training their faculty, ethical use of AI in the classroom, and policy regulations to fully realize the promise of AI-driven education (Gupta et al., 2024).

## 5. IMPLICATIONS OF THE STUDY

GAI, with rapid advancements towards business and management education, has far-ranging implications and may require changes in curriculum design, faculty orientation, institutional policies, and student readiness. AI has now evolved into a virtual disruptor of how business schools operate, educate, and prepare students for the future situations (Holmström & Carroll, 2024).

### 5.1 Curriculum Redesign for AI-Driven Education

Incorporation of AI across most formal and informal avenues of teaching within business education creates one of the greatest challenges in reconfiguring business curricula for AI-sustained methods. Traditional textbooks and case studies led by teachers should move ways towards real-time AI-generated business simulations, adaptive learning experiences, and industry AI applications (Kohnke et al., 2023). The current observation requires some shift from non-AI-based to AI-based learning modules, where students would be taught business analytics by AI, decision models, and market forecasting tools. For example, leading institutions such as Harvard, MIT, and INSEAD have initiated the utilization of AI-driven learning methods by blending case studies and simulation in strategic management and financial forecasting classes (Kshetri et al., 2023). Personalized learning paths are possible on AI-driven platforms, whereby lesson content is tailored by student performance and learning style, thus attaining their attention and the effectiveness of the learning process (Marr, 2024).

### 5.2 Faculty Training and Professional Development Programs

The successful integration of AI requires that faculty members receive proper training to help them develop a thorough understanding and streamline their use of AI tools. Many educators in business schools are still unaware of AI-based coaching models, and such unfamiliarity gives rise to either resistance or ineffective implementation. Hence, institutions must put in place some form of professional development for teachers to provide them with literacy about AI, data analytics skills, and strategies to integrate AI into the curriculum (Mittal et al., 2024). The training comprises hands-on workshops, AI boot camps, and other forms of continuous learning, which will allow faculty to remain updated about the trends in AI. Most importantly, AI should not replace faculty but enhance and empower them as facilitators of learning. Faculty would thus be enabled to mentor and generate discussion, critical thinking, and ethical decision-making using AI-powered teaching assistants instead of spending unnecessary time on administrative tasks like grading and content development (Pattanayak, 2021).

## 5.3 Institutional Policies for Ethical AI Use

AI is becoming part of academic business education, which now demands the formulation and implementation of ethical policies regarding AI educational use. In this respect, the use of AI-generated content raises issues regarding academic integrity, biases in AI models, privacy of data, and intellectual property rights (Samala et al., 2024). The demand is always urgent as it calls for guidelines on AI-aided assignment work, plagiarism detection, and how to use AI responsibly in college course work. These two institutions, namely universities and business schools, should implement AI ethics committees to guarantee that the learning tools are transparent and unbiased, as well as according to valid academic integrity standards. In addition, AI would only serve as an assistant tool but never replaces critical thinking and independent analysis since skill in problem-solving is not overdeveloped by students relying on automated solutions forever (Ryzhko et al., 2024).

## 5.4 Preparing Students for AI-Powered Business Environments

The application of AI in education goes beyond the academic setting and onto the terrain of AI-driven workplaces, wherein data-driven decision-making and AI-assisted strategies have evolved into standard business practices (Benmamoun, 2024). Business schools have to make sure that their graduates understand how to partner with AI, interpret insights generated using AI, and use AI as a tool for business innovation (Amankwah-Amoah et al., 2024). Increasingly, companies are hiring employees to incorporate AI into their financial modeling, marketing analytics, supply chain optimization, and strategic planning. Hence, business education will increasingly work to integrate AI-driven business labs, interdisciplinary AI training, and project work with real-life AI implications for hands-on learning. The emphasis on soft skills such as ethical decision-making, adaptability, and collaboration will give students an upper hand in effectively operating in an AI-enabled business landscape (Marr, 2024).

## 6. FUTURE DIRECTIONS AND RECOMMENDATIONS

Chakraborty et al. (2023) recommend that, as AI influences business education, one must close the research gaps, strategically plan for the future, enhance cooperation among academia and industry, and lay down policy frameworks for the responsible adoption of AI. Institutions need to play a more active role in integrating AI into business education while keeping ethics and skill development at the center of this transformation.

### 6.1 Bridging the Research Gap Through Empirical Studies

Although AI is generally acknowledged for its disruptive potential on business education, little extensive empirical research has been undertaken on its long-term effects (Kshetri et al., 2023). Existing studies tend to focus on AI primarily as a means of instructional delivery; however, much deeper empirical work is needed to assess its role in the areas of skill development, enhancement of critical thinking, and ethical implications. In the future, longitudinal studies will need to assess the impact of AI on student employability and career progression (Hacker et al., 2023). While recent developments, including AI-based grading systems and the use of virtual teaching assistants, have shown promise in enhancing student engagement and efficiency, their long-term effects have yet to be explored in more depth (Linkon et al., 2024).

### 6.2 Long-Term Strategies for AI Integration in Business Education

Business schools need to develop a systematic, long-term method for integrating AI into their curricula instead of just depending on an experimental approach. AI must be seen not as an adjunct but as an integral part of business education. Leading institutions design programs by embedding AI fluency in their foundation knowledge, applications within the business environment, and ethical issues (Kohnke et al., 2023) within the curriculum and beyond-the-classroom experiences. It will also be important to have AI-driven experiential learning models, such as real-time business simulations and decision-making frameworks, as standard parts of all MBA and executive education programs. In addition, schools should invest more rapidly in developing AI-powered learning management systems (LMS) for personalized learning experiences and offering real-time feedback through the students. Ensure faculty training and continuing professional development programs for the readiness of educators in effectively employing AI in classrooms (Owoseni et al., 2024).

## 6.3 Enhancing Collaboration Between Academia and Industry

Such collaborations can provide a way for students to practice using AI-based business analytics, predictive modeling, and decision-making tools. Programs like MIT Sloan's AI for Business Strategy and IESE Business School's AI for Executives focus on training students to work with AI in business (Rane, 2023). In addition, use of AI case studies and projects co-developed with multinational corporations will ensure the applicability of theoretical studies in AI to practical business use by students. Also, industry partnerships would assist in bridging the gap by ensuring student-audience conformity so they would be trained according to industry requirements to easily fit into jobs in an AI-driven business setting (Nyoko & Hanafiah, 2024).

## 6.4 Policy Recommendations for Responsible AI Adoption

As the adoption of AI in education deepens, a legal framework should be devised to ensure ethical AI use, protect data privacy, and maintain academic integrity. The institutions must enforce policies to ban AI bias and minimize the risk of dependence on AI for assessments and decision-making (Samala et al., 2024). AI ethics committees should be formed at universities devoted to controlling the use of AI in learning and research so that it is governed by institutional values and educational goals. Included within this is the establishment of programs to promote AI literacy among students and faculty in raising their awareness of the potential and limitations of AI, along with the associated ethical concerns (Sedkaoui & Benaichouba, 2024).

# 7. CONCLUSION

This systematic literature review, conducted following the PRISMA framework, synthesized findings from 41 studies to evaluate the impact of Generative AI (GAI) in transforming business education. The analysis revealed that AI has fundamentally changed the learning landscape by facilitating personalized education, automating assessments, and integrating real-world simulations into coursework (Vujović, 2024). Unlike traditional static learning models, AI-driven approaches have introduced dynamic, interactive, and data-driven learning experiences that align closely with industry demands. Students now have access to AI-powered decision labs, adaptive teaching methodologies, and automated feedback mechanisms that enhance engagement and learning efficiency (Markouh et al., 2024). Additionally, AI has supported skill development in areas such as critical thinking, problem-solving, and strategic decision-making, equipping learners with the competencies required to navigate an AI-driven business environment. However, the study also unexplored significant challenges, including faculty resistance to AI adoption, concerns about bias in AI-generated content, and difficulties in integrating AI within existing educational infrastructures (Jayasinghe, 2024). These findings underscore the need for structured AI adoption strategies to maximize its benefits while mitigating associated risks.

The place where business education is growing may be the most fitting GAI environment to influence learning and its future, employing disciplines of advanced analytics, machine learning algorithms, and intelligent tutoring systems. Leading institutions took the first steps toward incorporating applications of AI into the learning process, which, in turn, works toward fostering AI fluency in students and faculty alike (Cronin, 2024). On the other hand, ethical concerns warrant priority since data privacy, academic integrity, and fairness of outputs generated through AI must be controlled. Faculty training programs and AI literacy initiatives must be ramped up to equip educators with the capabilities to effectively use AI tools in teaching (Kadaruddin, 2023). Furthermore, academic institutions and industry should work together to align AI-driven education with relevant industry concerns. Strong industry partnerships would enable the creation of case studies with AI, internships, and experiential learning projects that give students first-hand exposure to AI in business decision-making. Such collaborative ventures will be significant in preparing the future generation of professionals for thriving in AI-enhanced workplaces (Aydın & Karaarslan, 2023).

In order to maximize the possible benefits of GAI in business education, more empirical evidence needs to be collected that assesses the long-term effects on student learning outcomes and employability. Extended research should deal with how AI moulds critical thinking, leadership skills, and ethical decision-making in scenarios related to business. Institutions should also develop sound strategies for the responsible and ethical use of AI in education to ensure that AI-driven tools are used along with rather than instead of traditional pedagogical methods. With a strategic and balanced approach to AI adoption (George, 2023), business schools can create an innovative education model that focuses on advanced technology and excellent ethics. This will not only improve business education but also ensure that the graduates are well schooled to negotiate and lead within a world economy increasingly dependent on AI technologies (Sandhu et al., 2024).

## REFERENCES

Adedoyin, F. F., & Christiansen, B. (Eds.). (2024). *Generative AI and Multifactor Productivity in Business*. IGI Global. DOI: 10.4018/979-8-3693-1198-1

Akbar, K., Nyika, F. D., & Mbonye, V. (2024). Revolutionizing Creative Education: The Role of Generative AI in Enhancing Innovation and Learning in Higher Education. In *Impacts of Generative AI on Creativity in Higher Education* (pp. 307-330). IGI Global.

Akpan, I. J., Razavi, R., & Akpan, A. A. (2025). Evolutionary Trends in Decision Sciences Education Research from Simulation and Games to Big Data Analytics and Generative Artificial Intelligence. *Big Data*, big.2024.0128. DOI: 10.1089/big.2024.0128 PMID: 40019821

Al-Smadi, M. (2023). ChatGPT and beyond: The generative AI revolution in education. *arXiv preprint arXiv:2311.15198.*

Al-Zubidy, A., & Carver, J. C. (2019). Identification and prioritization of SLR search tool requirements: An SLR and a survey. *Empirical Software Engineering*, *24*(1), 139–169. DOI: 10.1007/s10664-018-9626-5

AlAli, R., & Wardat, Y. (2024). Opportunities and challenges of integrating generative artificial intelligence in education. *International Journal of Religion*, *5*(7), 784–793. DOI: 10.61707/8y29gv34

Alhusban, M. I., Alshurafat, H., & Khatatbeh, I. N. (2025). Exploring professional perspectives on integrating generative artificial intelligence into corporate learning and development: An organizational change perspective. *Development and Learning in Organizations*, *39*(2), 21–24. DOI: 10.1108/DLO-05-2024-0131

Amankwah-Amoah, J., Abdalla, S., Mogaji, E., Elbanna, A., & Dwivedi, Y. K. (2024). The impending disruption of creative industries by generative AI: Opportunities, challenges, and research agenda. *International Journal of Information Management*, *79*, 102759. DOI: 10.1016/j.ijinfomgt.2024.102759

Asad, M. M., & Ajaz, A. (2024). Impact of ChatGPT and generative AI on lifelong learning and upskilling learners in higher education: Unveiling the challenges and opportunities globally. *The International Journal of Information and Learning Technology*, *41*(5), 507–523. DOI: 10.1108/IJILT-06-2024-0103

Aydın, Ö., & Karaarslan, E. (2023). Is ChatGPT leading generative AI? What is beyond expectations? *Academic Platform Journal of Engineering and Smart Systems*, *11*(3), 118–134. DOI: 10.21541/apjess.1293702

Bell, R., & Bell, H. (2023). Entrepreneurship education in the era of generative artificial intelligence. *Entrepreneurship Education*, *6*(3), 229–244. DOI: 10.1007/s41959-023-00099-x

Benmamoun, M. (2024). Reinventing international business education: Integrating the power of generative AI. *AIB Insights*, *24*(1), 1–7.

Budhwar, P., Chowdhury, S., Wood, G., Aguinis, H., Bamber, G. J., Beltran, J. R., Boselie, P., Lee Cooke, F., Decker, S., DeNisi, A., Dey, P. K., Guest, D., Knoblich, A. J., Malik, A., Paauwe, J., Papagiannidis, S., Patel, C., Pereira, V., Ren, S., & Varma, A. (2023). Human resource management in the age of generative artificial intelligence: Perspectives and research directions on ChatGPT. *Human Resource Management Journal*, *33*(3), 606–659. DOI: 10.1111/1748-8583.12524

Chakraborty, U., Roy, S., & Kumar, S. (2023). *Rise of Generative AI and ChatGPT: Understand how Generative AI and ChatGPT are transforming and reshaping the business world (English Edition)*. BPB Publications.

Cronin, I. (2024). *Understanding Generative AI Business Applications*. Springer Nature. DOI: 10.1007/979-8-8688-0282-9

Daniel, K., Msambwa, M. M., & Wen, Z. (2025). Can Generative AI Revolutionise Academic Skills Development in Higher Education? A Systematic Literature Review. *European Journal of Education*, *60*(1), e70036. DOI: 10.1111/ejed.70036

Ed-Dafali, S., Adardour, Z., Derj, A., Bami, A., & Hussainey, K. (2025). A PRISMA-Based Systematic Review on Economic, Social, and Governance Practices: Insights and Research Agenda. *Business Strategy and the Environment*, *34*(2), 1896–1916. DOI: 10.1002/bse.4069

Elbourn, S. (2024). The Impact of Generative AI on Student Churn and the Future of Formal Education. *arXiv preprint arXiv:2412.00605*.

George, A. S. (2023). The potential of generative AI to reform graduate education. *Partners Universal International Research Journal*, *2*(4), 36–50.

Gupta, P., Mahajan, R., Badhera, U., & Kushwaha, P. S. (2024). Integrating generative AI in management education: A mixed-methods study using social construction of technology theory. *International Journal of Management Education*, *22*(3), 101017. DOI: 10.1016/j.ijme.2024.101017

Hacker, P., Engel, A., & Mauer, M. (2023, June). Regulating ChatGPT and other large generative AI models. In *Proceedings of the 2023 ACM conference on fairness, accountability, and transparency* (pp. 1112-1123). DOI: 10.1145/3593013.3594067

Holmström, J., & Carroll, N. (2024). How organizations can innovate with generative AI. *Business Horizons*. Advance online publication. DOI: 10.1016/j.bushor.2024.02.010

Jayasinghe, S. (2024). Harnessing generative AI for self-directed learning: Perspectives from top management. *Development and Learning in Organizations*.

Kadaruddin, K. (2023). Empowering education through Generative AI: Innovative instructional strategies for tomorrow's learners. *International Journal of Business, Law, and Education*, *4*(2), 618–625. DOI: 10.56442/ijble.v4i2.215

Kenthapadi, K., Lakkaraju, H., & Rajani, N. (2023, August). Generative ai meets responsible ai: Practical challenges and opportunities. In *Proceedings of the 29th ACM SIGKDD conference on knowledge discovery and data mining* (pp. 5805-5806). DOI: 10.1145/3580305.3599557

Khan, H., Chetan, V., Hukkeri, S. V., & Neelima, M. (2025). Future of Productivity Management: The Role of Generative AI. In *Generative AI for Business Analytics and Strategic Decision Making in Service Industry* (pp. 89–112). IGI Global Scientific Publishing. DOI: 10.4018/979-8-3693-7026-1.ch004

Khan, N., Khan, Z., Koubaa, A., Khan, M. K., & Salleh, R. B. (2024). Global insights and the impact of generative AI-ChatGPT on multidisciplinary: A systematic review and bibliometric analysis. *Connection Science*, *36*(1), 2353630. DOI: 10.1080/09540091.2024.2353630

Kohnke, L., Moorhouse, B. L., & Zou, D. (2023). Exploring generative artificial intelligence preparedness among university language instructors: A case study. *Computers and Education: Artificial Intelligence*, *5*, 100156. DOI: 10.1016/j.caeai.2023.100156

Kshetri, N., & Hughes, L. (2023). "So what if ChatGPT wrote it?" Multidisciplinary perspectives on opportunities, challenges and implications of generative conversational AI for research, practice and policy. *International Journal of Information Management*, *71*, 102642. DOI: 10.1016/j.ijinfomgt.2023.102642

Lee, K., Datta, S., Paek, H., Rastegar-Mojarad, M., Huang, L. C., He, L., . . . Wang, X. (2024). AID-SLR: A Generative Artificial Intelligence-Driven Automated System for Systematic Literature Review. medRxiv, 2024-07. DOI: 10.1101/2024.07.03.24309897

Lim, S. C. J., & Lee, M. F. (2024). Rethinking education in the era of artificial intelligence (AI): Towards future workforce competitiveness and business success. In *Emerging Technologies in Business: Innovation Strategies for Competitive Advantage* (pp. 151–166). Springer Nature Singapore. DOI: 10.1007/978-981-97-2211-2_7

Linkon, A. A., Shaima, M., Sarker, M. S. U., Badruddowza, B., Nabi, N., Rana, M. N. U., & Chowdhury, F. R. (2024). Advancements and applications of generative artificial intelligence and large language models on business management: A comprehensive review. *Journal of Computer Science and Technology Studies*, *6*(1), 225–232. DOI: 10.32996/jcsts.2024.6.1.26

Malhotra, P. (2024). The rise of passive investing: A systematic literature review applying PRISMA framework. *Journal of Capital Markets Studies*, *8*(1), 95–125. DOI: 10.1108/JCMS-12-2023-0046

Mangaiyarkarasi, T., Catherine, S., & Kalaiselvi, K. (2025). Adapting to Generation AI: Navigating the Future of Business and Technology. In *Navigating Data Science in the Age of AI: Exploring Possibilities of Generative Intelligence* (pp. 13-33). Emerald Publishing Limited.

Markouh, O., Adadi, A., & Berrada, M. (2024, May). Towards a Blockchain Generative AI Driven Education: An Exploratory Study. In *2024 4th International Conference on Innovative Research in Applied Science, Engineering and Technology (IRASET)* (pp. 1-9). IEEE.

Marr, B. (2024). *Generative AI in practice: 100+ amazing ways generative artificial intelligence is Changing Business and Society*. John Wiley & Sons.

Matos, E. J., Bertoncini, A. L. C., Ames, M. C. F. D. C., & Serafim, M. C. (2024). The (lack of) ethics at generative AI in Business Management education and research. *RAM. Revista de Administração Mackenzie*, *25*(6), eRAMD240061. DOI: 10.1590/1678-6971/eramd240061

Matthew, U. O., Bakare, K. M., Ebong, G. N., Ndukwu, C. C., & Nwanakwaugwu, A. C.Ugochukwu Okwudili MatthewKafayat Motomori BakareGodwin Nse EbongCharles Chukwuebuka NdukwuAndrew Chinonso Nwanakwaugwu. (2023). Generative Artificial Intelligence (AI) Educational Pedagogy Development: Conversational AI with User-Centric ChatGPT4. *Journal of Trends in Computer Science and Smart Technology*, *5*(4), 401–418. DOI: 10.36548/jtcsst.2023.4.003

Mittal, U., Sai, S., Chamola, V., & Sangwan, D. (2024). A comprehensive review on generative ai for education. *IEEE Access : Practical Innovations, Open Solutions*, *12*, 142733–142759. DOI: 10.1109/ACCESS.2024.3468368

Mudrinić, D., & Šoda, I. (2024, November). The Rise of Generative Artificial Intelligence in Business. In *2024 IEEE 17th International Scientific Conference on Informatics (Informatics)* (pp. 493-498). IEEE. DOI: 10.1109/Informatics62280.2024.10900880

Nguyen, T. N., & Truong, H. T. (2025). Trends and emerging themes in the effects of generative artificial intelligence in education: A systematic review. *Eurasia Journal of Mathematics, Science and Technology Education, 21*(4), em2613. DOI: 10.29333/ejmste/16124

Nyoko, A. E., & Hanafiah, M. H. (2024, May). A Systematic Literature Review on Entrepreneurial Intention: PRISMA Method. In *Proceedings of the International Conference on Economic Management, Accounting and Tourism (ICEMAT 2023)* (pp. 254-273). Springer Nature. DOI: 10.2991/978-94-6463-411-2_21

Ooi, K. B., Tan, G. W. H., Al-Emran, M., Al-Sharafi, M. A., Capatina, A., Chakraborty, A., Dwivedi, Y. K., Huang, T.-L., Kar, A. K., Lee, V.-H., Loh, X.-M., Micu, A., Mikalef, P., Mogaji, E., Pandey, N., Raman, R., Rana, N. P., Sarker, P., Sharma, A., & Wong, L. W. (2025). The potential of generative artificial intelligence across disciplines: Perspectives and future directions. *Journal of Computer Information Systems, 65*(1), 76–107. DOI: 10.1080/08874417.2023.2261010

Owoseni, A., Kolade, O., & Egbetokun, A. (2024). Generative AI and Its Implications for Higher Education Students and Educators. In *Generative AI in Higher Education: Innovation Strategies for Teaching and Learning* (pp. 1–25). Springer Nature Switzerland. DOI: 10.1007/978-3-031-60179-8_1

Owoseni, A., Kolade, O., & Egbetokun, A. (2024). *Generative AI in Higher Education*. Springer Books. DOI: 10.1007/978-3-031-60179-8

Pattanayak, S. (2021). Leveraging Generative AI for Enhanced Market Analysis: A New Paradigm for Business Consulting. *International Journal of All Research Education and Scientific Methods, 9*(9), 2456–2469.

Portuguez-Castro, M., & Marchena Sekli, G. (2025). Empowering educators: A multi-case study investigating the transformative integration of generative AI tools for teaching in business education. *Journal of Education for Business, 100*(4), 1–11. DOI: 10.1080/08832323.2025.2470731

Rane, N. (2023). ChatGPT and similar generative artificial intelligence (AI) for smart industry: role, challenges and opportunities for industry 4.0, industry 5.0 and society 5.0. *Challenges and Opportunities for Industry, 4*.

Rane, N. (2023). Role and challenges of ChatGPT and similar generative artificial intelligence in business management. *Available at SSRN* 4603227. DOI: 10.2139/ssrn.4603227

Rane, N., Choudhary, S., & Rane, J. (2024). Gemini or ChatGPT? Capability, performance, and selection of cutting-edge generative artificial intelligence (AI) in business management. *Capability, Performance, and Selection of Cutting-Edge Generative Artificial Intelligence (AI) in Business Management (February 19, 2024).*

Ratten, V., & Jones, P. (2023). Generative artificial intelligence (ChatGPT): Implications for management educators. *International Journal of Management Education, 21*(3), 100857. DOI: 10.1016/j.ijme.2023.100857

Ryzhko, O., Krainikova, T., Vodolazka, S., & Sokolova, K. (2024). Generative AI changes the book publishing industry: Reengineering of business processes. *Communicatio Socialis,* •••, 255–271.

Saeger, K. J., Finley, L. R., & Wickam, M. J. (2024). The AI revolution: Awareness of and readiness for AI-based digital tools and technologies in business education. *The Journal of Research In Business Education, 64*(1).

Samala, A. D., Rawas, S., Wang, T., Reed, J. M., Kim, J., Howard, N. J., & Ertz, M. (2024). Unveiling the landscape of generative artificial intelligence in education: A comprehensive taxonomy of applications, challenges, and future prospects. *Education and Information Technologies,* •••, 1–40.

Sandhu, R., Channi, H. K., Ghai, D., Cheema, G. S., & Kaur, M. (2024). An introduction to generative AI tools for education 2030. *Integrating generative AI in education to achieve sustainable development goals*, 1-28.

Sedkaoui, S., & Benaichouba, R. (2024). Generative AI as a transformative force for innovation: A review of opportunities, applications and challenges. *European Journal of Innovation Management.* Advance online publication. DOI: 10.1108/EJIM-02-2024-0129

Singh, N., Chaudhary, V., Singh, N., Soni, N., & Kapoor, A. (2024). Transforming Business with Generative AI: Research, Innovation, Market Deployment and Future Shifts in Business Models. *arXiv preprint arXiv:2411.14437.*

Vecchiarini, M., & Somia, T. (2023). Redefining entrepreneurship education in the age of artificial intelligence: An explorative analysis. *International Journal of Management Education, 21*(3), 100879. DOI: 10.1016/j.ijme.2023.100879

Vujović, D. (2024). Generative AI: Riding the new general purpose technology storm. *Ekonomika preduzeća, 72*(1-2), 125-136.

Wijayati, T., Hayatie, M. N., & Safitri, Y. D. (2024). Enhancing Business Communication Skills in Vocational Education: A Generative Ai Approach for Personalized Learning. *Frontier Management Science*, *1*(2), 53–60. DOI: 10.53893/fms.v1i2.270

Yelamarthi, K., Dandu, R., Rao, M., Yanambaka, V. P., & Mahajan, S. (2024). Exploring the potential of generative AI in shaping engineering education: Opportunities and challenges. *Journal of Engineering Education Transformations*, *37*(2), 439–445. DOI: 10.16920/jeet/2024/v37is2/24072

# Chapter 9
# Machine Learning vs. Traditional Models:
## A Comparative Analysis of LSTM and ARIMA for Stock Prediction With Management Education Applications

**K. Priya**
https://orcid.org/0000-0002-9491-1600
*SRM Institute of Science and Technology, India*

**Premkumar Balaraman**
https://orcid.org/0000-0003-1188-326X
*SRM Institute of Science and Technology, India*

**C. Sundar**
*SRM Institute of Science and Technology, India*

## ABSTRACT

*This study presents a comparative analysis of Long Short-Term Memory (LSTM) versus Auto-Regressive Integrated Moving Average (ARIMA) models for stock price prediction in the Indian automobile sector. Using ten-year historical data (2014-2024) from five leading companies—Tata Motors, TVS Motors, Ashok Leyland, Bajaj Motors, and Mahindra & Mahindra—the research evaluates predictive performance through MAPE, RMSE, and MAE metrics. LSTM demonstrated forecasting accuracy with 84-87% error reduction compared to traditional ARIMA models, effectively capturing non-linear market dynamic and long-term dependencies. The methodology incorporates data preprocessing and normalization techniques. Results reveal*

DOI: 10.4018/979-8-3373-2150-9.ch009

*LSTM's enhanced capability in modeling volatile financial time series, with MAPE values consistently below 2% across all tested companies. This research contributes significantly to management education by demonstrating practical applications of AI-driven financial analytics, enabling experiential learning in predictive modeling, algorithmic trading, and data-driven investment strategies.*

## 1. INTRODUCTION

The stock market, which is seen as a measure of the health of the economy, is a dynamic and complicated setting which has continued to fascinate investors, educators and researchers. The stock market is difficult enough to predict prices without taking into account the interaction of political, economic, market-driven, and societal factors. Stock movement is highly linear and non-linear and thus extracting meaningful patterns is hard, which requires sophisticated computational methods (Eapen, 2019). The correct forecasting of the stock prices is not only critical to the success of investors wishing to maximize their returns, but it is also a crucial pedagogical example in management training- to help the learners in comprehending risk, data analysis, and decision-making in situations of uncertainty.

Considering the sheer amount of wealth that is traded in the global equity markets, prediction errors can have major financial implications, even when they are not that large. Hence, practitioners and future business leaders need to develop resilient AI-driven models. With the development of financial technologies, the introduction of machine learning models into educational programs will allow students to learn practical knowledge and technical literacy in the field of predictive analytics. A good example of such exploration can be found in the Indian automobile industry- which contributes about 7.1 percent to the GDP of India and almost 50 percent to the manufacturing GDP. With the development of this industry towards electric mobility, IoT integration, sustainable manufacturing, and so on, it offers a perfect setting in terms of implementing AI models in the industry learning environment and management.

In previous literature, it has been shown that stock price prediction can be done using a number of statistical methods including linear regression, the random walk theory, and Auto-Regressive Integrated Moving Averages (ARIMA). Nevertheless, such traditional models do not always work when it comes to complex, non-linear dynamics of financial markets. The advent of such a high-profile subfield of artificial intelligence as machine learning (ML) has provided researchers and educators with tools that can be used to find hidden patterns and improve the accuracy of predictions. Neural networks and deep learning algorithms are ML models that not only enhance the performance of forecasting but also can be used as an educational tool in the management curriculum. They allow students to work with real-world data, model decision-making situations, and solve business problems using AI-based analytics in such areas as finance, healthcare, sports and manufacturing. Here, the stock market can be an irresistible learning sandbox to learn through experience in AI and data-driven strategic thinking.

## 1.1 Algorithmic Trading

The fact that algorithmic trading has become more rapidly developed in the last few decades can be explained by a number of converging factors, such as the blistering pace of machine learning method development, increasing data processing capacity, and the explosive growth of data storage infrastructure. With financial markets becoming more competitive, the complexity of algorithmic trading strategies has grown, especially between market players that are able to use automation to trade over those adhering to manual systems. Such a change highlights the need to investigate the role of different machine learning algorithms in managing the difficulties of algorithmic trading.

In addition to its practical implications to hedge funds and institutional investors, the study of AI-based trading systems is of profound value in management education. It exposes learners to interdisciplinary skills that are a combination of finance, data science, and computational thinking. Incorporating such practical AI applications into the business school curriculum, students will have a chance to get first-hand experience in model building, back testing, and data-driven decision-making, which are essential skills of future financial analysts, investment strategists, and technology-based managers. Besides, the study will contribute to the theoretical foundations of machine learning as an essential field with a wide scope of application to various industries, including operations, logistics, marketing, and strategic planning.

## 1.2 Machine Learning in the Stock Market

The stock market is a vibrant marketplace where equity instruments are traded and proper price forecasting is very crucial in the determination of investment activities and profitability within the various sectors. Analysts and researchers have since the inception of formal trading systems come up with a spectrum of methodologies to forecast the price behavior, such as fundamental analysis, technical analysis, and computational models. The approaches have been used in the formulation of investment strategies though at times they give divergent insights. Improving the accuracy of predictions is one of the priorities of financial institutions and market players aimed at outperforming the benchmarks.

In this regard, machine learning (ML) or specifically deep learning has become a revolution in stock price forecasting. The paper will specifically concentrate on the relative usefulness of ML methods like Long Short-Term Memory (LSTM) networks that are outstanding at recognizing multifaceted, non-linear connections in financial time series information. Whereas the common algorithms such as random forests and support vector machines have been extensively investigated, deep learning models have become a favorite due to their ability to learn adaptively and recognize patterns better despite the fact that they are computationally demanding.

Such models present an important chance to the educators and learners of management programs to work with real financial data and use the AI-driven tools to imitate the behavior of the market. This exploration revolves around neural networks such as feedforward and backpropagation networks where data preprocessing forms a major pillar of model building. This paper will examine the historical stock data of five well-known Indian car companies namely TVS Motors, Ashok Leyland, Tata Motors, Bajaj Motors and Mahindra & Mahindra through performance measures, Mean Absolute Percentage Error (MAPE), Mean Absolute Error (MAE) and Root Mean Square Error (RMSE). This does not only allow effective empirical validation but also data-driven learning in financial analytics education.

## 2. REVIEW OF LITERATURE

As computer technologies evolved, the techniques of predictive modeling advanced, especially artificial neural networks (Paluch, 2023), which are aimed at stimulating the human brain cognitive processes. Of these, the recurrent neural networks (RNNs) have proved to be very powerful in sequential data processing like audio, language and time-series financial data (Hochreiter & Schmidhuber, 1997). One of the major advances in this field is the Long Short-Term Memory (LSTM) model that overcomes the limitations of the RNN like vanishing gradient and has been useful in financial predictions (Li, 2018).

Stock price forecasting has been highlighted in various papers especially in regards to the choice of investors. As pointed out by Shah (2023), proper forecasting is important in maximizing buy/sell strategy and minimizing exposure to risk. Kanthimathi (2023) argued about the increasing use of artificial intelligence (AI) in stock prediction, stating that machine learning (ML) algorithms are capable of properly analyzing large data sets and identifying positive or negative trends. The most common traditional time series technique remains the univariate forecasting techniques, especially ARIMA. According to Mashadihasanli, differencing methods in ARIMA models can be used to transform non-stationary data to stationary forms so that it can be more predictive. Dong et al. (2017) have tested the ARIMA models on financial data of Yahoo Finance and proved their effectiveness in short-term forecasting.

Conversely, recent works have been done on how ML algorithms particularly LSTM perform better than classical statistical models in modeling nonlinear market dynamics. Rezaei and Faaljou (2021) also noted that LSTM networks do not apply so many assumptions regarding data distribution and provide more accurate results in terms of predictions. Bathla (2020) also confirmed that deep learning models, when evaluated with the help of such evaluation measures as MAPE, outperform support vector regression models in any case.

Notably, these innovations present excellent new opportunities to teach management through real-time market analytics, ML model interpretation, and financial forecasting activities in business schools. This enriches experiential learning and makes students ready to work with unstable datasets, develop predictive models, and implement the AI tools in the areas of strategic finance and investment.

Paliwal and Sharma (2022) focus on the use of the evolutionary algorithm in neural network architecture and hyperparameter optimization and note the complexity of the model design and the accuracy needed to obtain high predictive performance. These improvements do not just improve the detection of more general market trends but also improve the predictability of the forecasts, which is essential both to the practitioners and the educators that wish to model the real world market behavior in the classroom.

In the study by Verma et al. (2023), a comparative study of LSTM and RNN models was carried out, which showed that LSTM model results were more predictive, and the forecasts were much closer to the real values of the stocks. This is why it is necessary to choose neural architectures that are adapted to specifics of financial data. To supplement this, Yifei Zhang (2023) used data of Indian market, e.g. historical open, close, high, low prices, and transaction volumes, to evaluate the predictive ability of deep learning models. When LSTM was compared to the classical econometric methods such as Vector Auto-Regression (VAR) and Support Vector Machines (SVM), LSTM model performed better than both of the alternatives, showing that it is effective in modeling complex, non-linear relationships which exist in the financial time series.

Zhang (2024) further expanded on this investigation and considered the CSI 300 Index during a turbulent phase of post-COVID-19. The study used Mean Absolute Error (MAE) and Root Mean Squared Error (RMSE) as error metrics to determine the accuracy of the model that used ARIMA and LSTM models. Although LSTM initially lagged in the ability to respond to sudden changes in the market, it performed better than ARIMA in the predictive accuracy. The findings are suggestive that

LSTM models may be rather robust yet they may require domain specific features or more comprehensive datasets in order to achieve full potential.

These observations have great implications on management education whereby incorporating such comparative studies in the curriculum design would allow students to examine trade-offs between traditional and AI-driven models. By actively working with the algorithms and the real-life data, the learners will gain more advanced skills in strategic forecasting, model testing, and machine learning applications to the finance domain.

Ahammad (2024) stated that in some cases, ARIMA performs better than LSTM in stock price prediction, especially showing more accuracy in Root Mean Square Error (RMSE) and Mean Absolute Error (MAE). This implies that traditional time series models could be used in providing reliable predictions in a stable market. In contrast, Hum et al. (2022) discovered that a single-layered LSTM model with a similar number of hidden neurons, about 50, fitted and also made more accurate predictions than the multi-layered ones, which is why the architecture of a neural network is also crucial in the performance of a model.

Abe (2020) went even further and created a model that would allow predicting several parameters of the stock simultaneously, exploiting the ability of LSTM to learn the interconnectedness of financial indicators. Although in the past Recurrent Neural Networks (RNNs) were preferred to process sequential data, they had problems with long-term dependencies because of gradient vanishing. Sethia (2019) has overcome this limitation by explaining that LSTM networks, such as forget, update, and output gates, are effective in handling both short-term and long-term memory and thus they are very applicable to complex time-series data.

A comparison between ARIMA and LSTM shows the merits and weaknesses of each of them. ARIMA is quite adequate in estimating linear trends and seasonality although it can perform poorly when faced with high volatility or when there is structural break in the series (Wang, 2024). LSTM models, in their turn, are better at capturing the non-linear relationships and are better at working with long-term dependencies and can outperform ARIMA in the dynamic and turbulent markets. These observations indicate that none of the models is always more effective than the other; rather, the effectiveness of models depends on the characteristics of data and the purpose of forecasting.

This comparison of two models is of great educational importance in management learning. By introducing the students to statistical as well as AI-based methods of forecasting, it is possible to familiarize them with methodological trade-offs, critical model criticism, and practical analysis of real-life data. As far as practical implications are concerned, this research will be helpful in the creation of intelligent stock forecasting systems that aid in autonomous trading and investment decision making. With the incorporation of models such as ARIMA and LSTM, these systems will be able to traverse the complexities of the market in a better manner, aid in risk tracking, and have an edge in predictive decision making when financial environments are rapidly changing.

The broad aim of this study is to examine the relative usefulness of intelligent forecasting models in the financial markets and find out ways of improving their accuracy and usefulness in practice. The research is expected to add to the theoretical basis and the pedagogical embedding of AI and machine learning in management training with the focus on finance.

## 3. RESEARCH METHODOLOGY

### 3.1 Research Gap

Although impressive progress has been made in time series, modeling and machine learning, the ability to predict the stock market remains very challenging because of the volatile and multifactorial nature of financial systems. Market patterns are easily thrown off course by political instability, macroeconomic changes, and unforeseeable events in society, making the job of proper forecasting a difficult one. The critical weaknesses of the existing literature are identified: the absence of the comparative analysis between classical statistical models and sophisticated machine learning methods, inadequate inclusion of various data characteristics, poor interpretability of the model, and low practical applicability to sector-specific environments.

One of the largest gaps is the poor management of the temporal dependencies and non-linear trends in long term stock data. Although some researches have employed conventional approaches such as ARIMA and simple ML models to forecast the general market, they fail to perform well in high volatility markets like the Indian automobile industry. The currently existing models cannot provide solutions to such crucial problems as the vanishing gradient issue in deep learning, overfitting the models on noisy data, and lacking domain-specific optimizing approaches.

The automotive industry, which is a major pillar of the Indian economy and contributes about 7.1 percent to the national gross domestic product and 35 percent to manufacturing gross domestic product, offers a great test bench of financial forecasting models. The recent changes in the industry, such as the emergence of electric vehicles, the adoption of the IoT, and the changing demands of the consumers have only added to the complexity of market forces. The present study reveals the necessity of creating more accurate and smarter forecasting models that not only enhance the accuracy of predictions but also can be used as pedagogical tools in management education because such models will allow students to develop critical skills of working with real financial data and thinking algorithmically in the practical setting.

## 3.2 Problem Statement

The problem of creating a working and predictable model of stock price remains a complex issue, and it is even more problematic in such a high-volatility sector like the Indian automotive market. The main challenges are the successful representation of long term temporal dependencies in price changes, dealing with volatility peculiarities of the sector, handling massive amounts of historical data, and producing sufficiently accurate predictions despite market uncertainty and unforeseeable economic shocks.

In order to overcome these difficulties, this study applies two of the most popular models, the Auto-Regressive Integrated Moving Average (ARIMA) and the Long Short-Term Memory (LSTM) networks. Although ARIMA is a long-established statistical model that works well when the linear trend is sought, LSTM, a deep learning architecture, has the advantage of remembering and learning the long-term patterns in complex and nonlinear data. The paper uses these models to historical stock data of five large Indian automobile companies: Ashok Leyland, Bajaj Motors, TVS Motors, Tata Motors and Mahindra & Mahindra, on a ten-year data set between 2014-2024.

The fundamental goal of the proposed research is to compare the ARIMA and LSTM on the basis of predictive performance, which is quantified as accuracy metrics of RMSE, MAE, and MAPE. As the empirical findings reveal, LSTM is much more effective as compared to ARIMA, with the rates of prediction error reduction observed being between 84 and 87 percent. Also, the study examines the impact of the differences in training epochs on the performance of LSTM models, which also contributes to the optimization of deep learning in financial forecasting.

In addition to its research significance, the work is also educative in its ability to demonstrate the possibility of incorporating AI and ML tools in the management curriculum. The study encourages learning by doing and acquiring the skills of making data-driven decisions in the courses of finance and analytics by exposing students to real-life datasets and algorithmic modeling practices.

The use of quantitative interpretation of predictive models provides an extensive perspective through which stock price trends may be examined, especially in comparison to more general time-series and neural network methods. Time series analysis is one of the most basic instruments of interpreting such data and helps in making strategic decisions in various fields including finance, economics, and environmental science. By the use of trend analysis, seasonal decomposition, and forecasting, analysts are able to detect the long-term trends, seasonal variations and isolate the irregular variations in the sequential data.

In financial analytics, such methods can be especially applied to understanding how stocks move, where the movement is driven by many micro- and macroeconomic factors. ARIMA and LSTM forecasting techniques have become popular methods because of their corresponding advantages, namely, the ability to model linear trends and seasonality, and an ability to model nonlinear relationships and long-term dependencies, respectively. Support Vector Machines (SVM), Seasonal ARIMA (SARIMA), Recurrent Neural Networks (RNN) and Random Forests (RF) are other methods commonly used in financial forecasting among others. All these have a unique contribution to the market behavior prediction and understanding.

In the given study, two models, namely, ARIMA and LSTM, are considered to determine their efficiency in predicting the stock prices of the chosen companies within the Nifty Auto index: TVS Motors, Ashok Leyland, Tata Motors, Bajaj Motors, and Mahindra and Mahindra. These firms, whose compound annual growth rates (CAGR) have been above 7 per cent in the last 10 years, constitute a healthy slice of the Indian automobile industry. The research will use these models in analysis of historical data in order to produce synthetic predictive data that will be plotted visually to provide holistic information on price trends. Not only does this method contribute to the empirical knowledge of market behavior, but it also helps management students learn more by allowing real-time use of forecasting methods to analyze sector-specific data.

*Figure 1. Representing the LSTM Methodology*

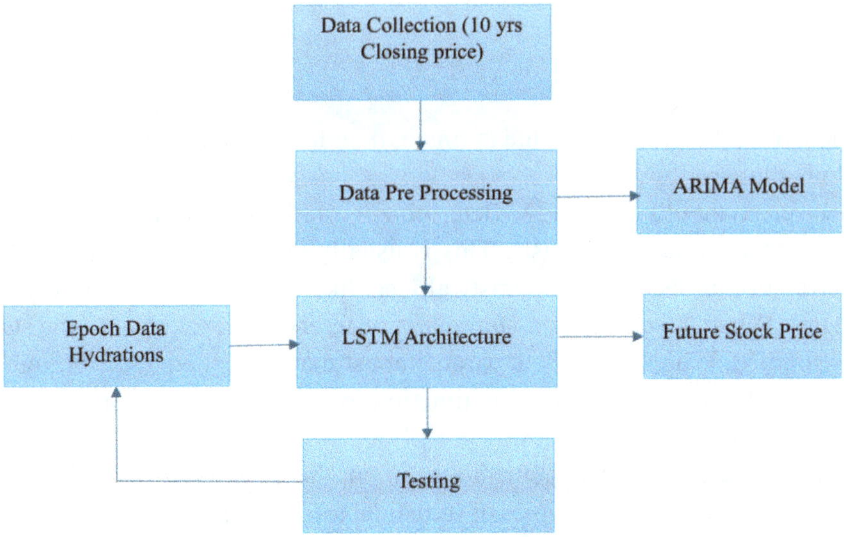

Experimental data used in the study includes real historical stock prices that were acquired in the CMIE Prowess IQ database. The data used entails daily trading data- opening price, closing price, high, low and trading volume of the five major Indian automobile companies: TVS Motors, Ashok Leyland, Tata Motors, Bajaj Motors and Mahindra and Mahindra. The data is ten years covering May 2, 2014 to April 30, 2024, which provides a complete time series to carry out a sound analysis.

The forecasting models were implemented in the Python language within the Jupyter Notebook on a windows 11 platform. The libraries used to process the data, analyse, and visualize it are Pandas, NumPy, and Matplotlib. These open-source tools are used on large scale in industry and academia and thus they are best suited to be incorporated into management education. With the help of these tools, this research shows that the real-life financial analytics processes can be simulated in a classroom to provide students with practical knowledge of AI-based forecasting, data manipulation, and visualization.

ARIMA:

Auto-Regressive Integrated Moving Average (ARIMA) model is a traditional Stochastic time series model mostly applied in forecasting future values using past observations. It is comprised of three important parts, namely Autoregressive (AR) (connect the current value to its earlier values); Integrated (I) (differencing the data to render it stationary); and Moving Average (MA) (model the relationship between an observation and the residual errors of a moving average model of lagged values).

ARIMA models are characterized by three parameters p, d and q that indicate the number of autoregressive terms, number of differencing operations required to render the series stationary and number of lagged forecast errors respectively. The simple formulation of the ARIMA is as:

$$Y_t = a + b_1 Y_{\{t-1\}} + e_t \tag{3.1}$$

Where $Y_t$ is the predicted value at time *t*, *a* and *b* are model coefficients, and $e_t$ represents the error term.

Time series should be tested to determine its stationarity to make sure that the model produces reliable forecasts. This is usually done using graphical analysis, Autocorrelation plots and also statistical tests like the Augmented Dickey-Fuller (ADF) test. When the data is non-stationary, differences are taken until the stationarity is attained. When confirmed, parameter estimation is then done through such methods as Maximum Likelihood Estimation to optimize the performance of the model and identify the anomalies.

Within the setting of management education, the knowledge of ARIMA offers learners the fundamental principles of statistical forecasting. It provides the student with the capability of analyzing the market trends and volatility through rigorous quantitative methods and this makes it a great tool in the course of study in analytics-based decision making and financial modeling.

LSTM:

The Long Short-Term Memory (LSTM) model is an extended type of the Recurrent Neural Network (RNN) specifically created to accept sequential data and to address the weaknesses of the RNN in the ability to capture long-range dependencies. The main issue with conventional RNNs is the vanishing gradient problem in which the gradients decrease through the backpropagation process, and thus the model fails to remember and learn about the distant past input. LSTM resolves this problem by the distinctive design of the cell structure that includes a self-loop connection and a cell state with a specific role of memory pathway to store information over long time periods.

The LSTM networks are designed according to three different gates namely, the forget gate, input gate and the output gate. The forget gate decides what information in the previous cell state to forget and the input gate decides what information in the new state to add. Output gate allows or prevents exposure of the current cell state to the output. Such gating mechanism can make LSTM selectively update, retain or discard information and the network can remember longer sequences and effectively handle temporal dependencies in non-linear, noisy time series data- like stock prices.

Mathematically, it is based on the model that employs the activation functions (sigmoid and tanh) on each gate to control the flow of data. The input is measured, weighted and combined with the previous states to make predictions at each time step. This renders LSTM especially applicable in situations in which the past patterns play a dominant role in predicting the future.

Within the scope of stock price prediction, LSTM has the power due to its capability to capture the non-linear relationship and learn based on a large amount of data in the past. Educational perspective Going by an educational perspective, the introduction of LSTM models in management and business analytics programs will increase the knowledge of students in the field of deep learning, time series modeling and their practical utility in financial decisions. It prepares the students with the skills needed to apply the AI-based predictive models to the real-life investment and strategy situations.

*Figure 2. LSTM Framework*

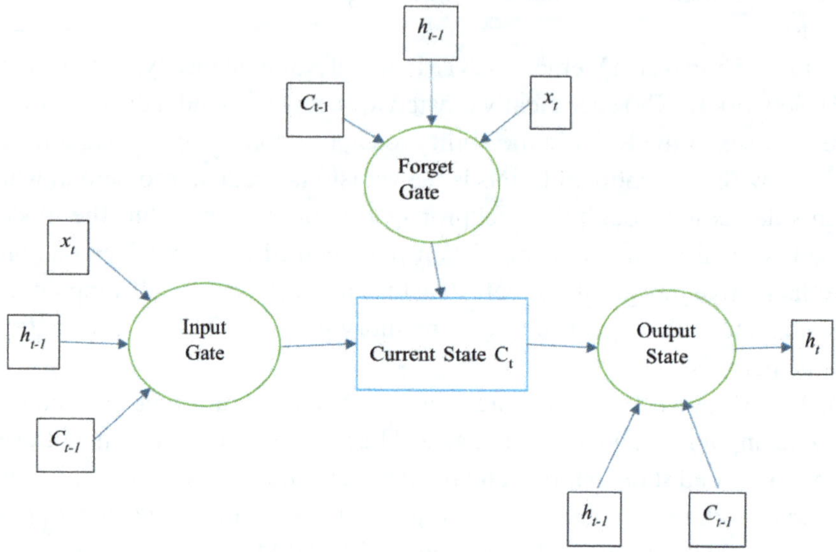


The architecture of a Long Short-Term Memory (LSTM) cell is shown in figure 3.2 and the sequential flow of information through the gates. The input layer is used with a sigmoid non-linearity, which measures the pertinence of new incoming data. This defines the retention or discarding of a certain input. At the same time, a tanh activation layer produces a candidate cell state vector *Ct*, which is suggested to be concatenated to the existing memory of the cell.

$$C_t = f_t \cdot C_{\{t-1\}} + i_t \cdot \widehat{\{C\}}_t \tag{3.2}$$

Where calculations of $i_t$ & $\hat{C}_t$

$$i_t = \sigma(\ W_i \cdot [h_{\{t-1\}}, x_t] + b_i) \tag{3.3}$$

$$\widehat{\{C\}}_t = \backslash tanh\ (\ W_c \cdot [h_{\{t-1\}}, x_t] + b_c) \tag{3.4}$$

The output gate controls the number of current neural unit states that are filtered, and the number of filtered controlling unit states is shown in equation 3. 5 and 3.6

$$o_t = \sigma(\ W_o \cdot [h_{\{t-1\}}, x_t] + b_o) \tag{3.5}$$

$$h_t = o_t \cdot \tanh(C_t) \tag{3.6}$$

This process enables the LSTM cell to store pertinent past information and reject noise, which is especially useful in such fields as stock price forecasting where trends, reversals and outliers are present.

To students and researchers in management education, the knowledge of this framework helps in the practical learning of data science, especially in the fields of financial analytics and algorithmic trading. By visualizing and executing LSTM cell operations, learners will understand the way AI-based systems work with time-dependent data, which is in between theoretical knowledge on AI and practical financial decision-making.

## LSTM: Training and Evaluation

Among the main advantages of the Long Short-Term Memory (LSTM) networks, it is possible to note that they are able to remember and learn sequences of data in contrast to classic Recurrent Neural Networks (RNNs). The LSTM nodes have a memory cell which holds pertinent information between time steps. The top cell in the LSTM structure acts like a direct data conveyance path, in and out of time, allowing long-term memory storage. These memory cells operate in parallel and are steered by gate mechanisms determining what information to remember or revise or forget, and this lets the model dynamically adapt to rich input sequences such as financial time series.

An important terminology in training an LSTM model is epoch; this is defined as a single pass through the entire training dataset. As deep learning algorithms are based on gradient descent optimization, the model has to be trained on the data several times to optimize weights and increase the accuracy of predictions. The number of epochs needed is a factor of the size and complexity of the data set and volatility of the data being modeled. Noisy and unpredictable financial data, e.g. stock prices, may need a lot more epochs.

RMSE =

$$\sqrt{\frac{\sum_{i=1}^{n}(y_i - \hat{y}_i)^2}{n}} \tag{3.7}$$

n is the number of observations, $y_i$ is the observed value, $\hat{y}_i$ is the predicted value

Mean absolute percentage error finds the accuracy of the forecast method by estimating the percentage difference between actual and predicted values.

$$MAPE = \frac{1}{n}\sum_{i=1}^{N}\left[\frac{yi - \widehat{yi}}{yi}\right] \tag{3.8}$$

n is the number of observations, $y_i$ is the observed value, $\hat{y}_i$ is the predicted value

Mean Absolute errors find the magnitude of errors between actual and predicted values.

MAE=

$$\frac{1}{n}\sum_{i=1}^{n}(y_i - \hat{y}_i) \tag{3.9}$$

Where $y_i$ is the original time series $\widehat{yi}$ is the predicted time series computed from the model.

MAPE estimates the size of the error computed as the relative average of the error.

The effectiveness of the Model is performed by calculating a 15-day forecast of the closing price and compared with actual closing prices. The forecasted price exhibit similar to the original price.

## Data Pre-processing, Training, and Evaluation Strategy

Preprocessing of data is a very important stage in improving the performance and reliability of the neural network models especially in a volatile environment like the stock market. As it is emphasised by Huang et al. (2021), preprocessing can substantially enhance the accuracy of the model, as it is shown in the case of hydrological and geomorphological data, which is also similar to the problems of financial forecasting. The very nature of the stock market, which is unstable and is prone to many outside factors, requires strict data preparation to guarantee validity and applicability of the model.

LSTM and ARIMA models are trained and tested in this research on a wide-range historical stock data. The data consists of the ten-year data on the daily stock prices, namely opening, closing, high, low and volume. To facilitate strong forecasting, the data is split into training set (70%) which is spanned by May 2, 2014 to April 29, 2022, and a test set (30%) which is spanned by May 2, 2022 to April 30, 2024. This split will provide that model evaluation is done on unseen data, and an unbiased evaluation of the prediction performance is made.

In LSTM, preprocessing entails normalization of input features to make the variables of similar magnitude. The scaled data is then transformed into pairs of input and output with the input being a sliding window of past historical prices and the output being the future price of the stock. This allows the model to be able to learn temporal dependencies over several sequences. In the case of ARIMA, the preprocessing involves application of differencing to make the process stationary, and estimation of the parameters of the autoregressive and moving average parts of the model, e.g. by means of maximum likelihood estimation or least squares.

Most importantly, this modeling framework resembles real-life data analytics workflows in AI-based financial analytics. Educationally, the use of such real-world preprocessing, model training and testing techniques can provide students with a chance to learn applied data science through experience. It assists learners to develop expertise in some of the most important fields, including feature engineering, time series analysis, and predictive model evaluation. The fact that the real historical market data can be used also allows the students to mimic the decisions made by investors, further strengthening the importance of the machine learning models in modern financial strategy.

It is interesting to note that only the closing prices on a daily basis are being taken out of the data set to make final predictions because they are the ones that are usually the most decisive when it comes to the stock buying and selling decisions made by the investors.

## 4. RESULTS AND ANALYSIS

### 4.1 Training

The training set of this work consists of daily closing stock prices of five leading companies in the Indian automobile market, which covers 2471 trading days. The companies identified are TVS Motors, Ashok Leyland, Tata Motors, Bajaj Motors, and Mahindra & Mahindra. The price ranges observed during the training period are as follows: TVS Motors (91.9 to 2,151.4), Ashok Leyland (23.5 to 171.5), Tata Motors (99.3 to 413.5), Bajaj Motors (2,049.4 to 9,144.9) and Mahindra & Mahindra (1,001.75 to 1,921.35).

To set up the data to train the models successfully, all the stock price values were normalized, an ordinary preprocessing feature that scales numeric values to a common range, usually 0 and 1. This makes sure that no single stock will have disproportionate effect on learning process because of varying magnitudes of price. In the current research, min-max normalization is employed based on the following expression:

$$x\ norm = (x - x\ min) / (x\ max - x\ min) \quad (4.1)$$

where x norm represents the normalized value

x min and x max - minimum and maximum values in the training dataset.

This normalization process improves the work of machine learning models, especially LSTM, as it normalizes all the inputs to the same level. Educationally, application and knowledge of data normalization are core elements in machine learning course work. It strengthens the skills of students in using real-world data, pre-processing data to neural networks, and model converging stability during training.

The forecasting models were implemented experimentally in a Python programming language on a Windows 11 platform in the Jupyter Notebook environment. Some of the important Python libraries used in the project are Pandas to do data manipulation, NumPy to do numerical work and Matplotlib to visualize. These applications are popular in industry and academia and thus are appropriate to teach in a data science and business analytics curriculum.

The processed data after normalization was fed to the LSTM model with a sliding window of 100 time steps which allowed the model to learn the past patterns to predict the price of the stock 10 days in advance. After the generation of the predictions, the inverse transformation was used to denormalize the results so that the predicted stock values could be put back to the original scale.

The dataset was trained with three epoch configurations, 25, 50 and 100 epochs to evaluate the learning behavior of the model. This enabled the comparative analysis of the effect of the length of training on the accuracy of the prediction and the tendency of overfitting. The experimental design is not only useful to optimize the model performance, but also has a pedagogical value of training models iteratively, tuning hyperparameters and effect of computation learning cycles in practice.

When applied to management education, the experience of students with these tools and configurations can help them to perform practical AI modeling, test various training environments, and analyze the results through the prism of business strategy.

*Figure 3. Visualization of Historical prices– TATA Motors*

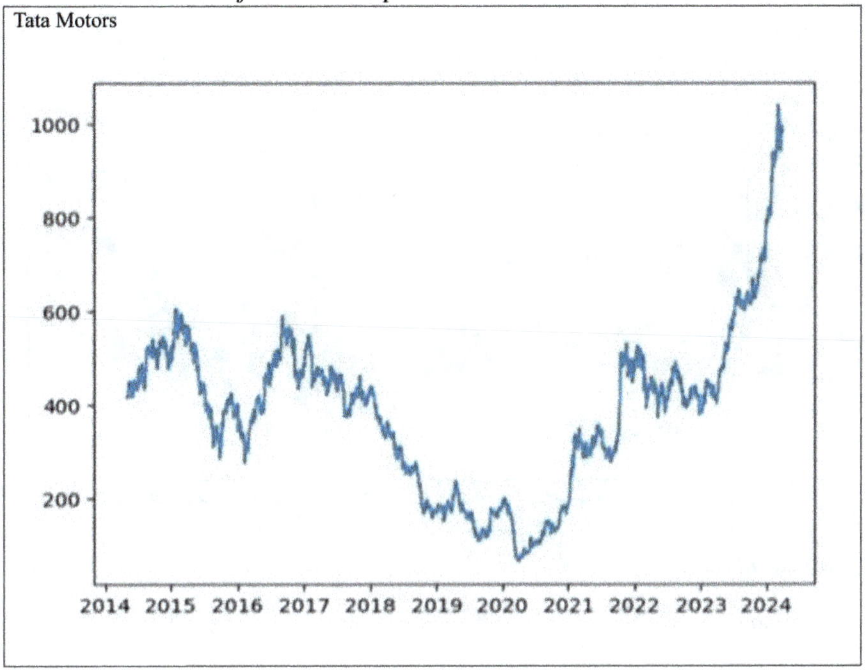

*Figure 4. Visualization of Historical prices– TVS Motors, Mahindra and Mahindra*

TVS Motors

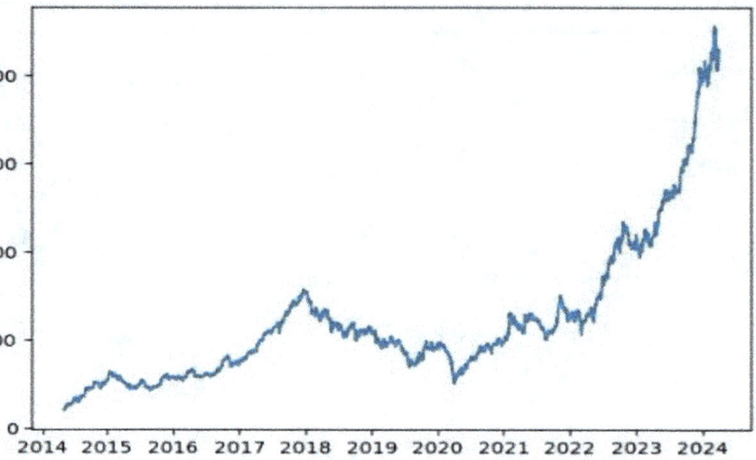


Mahindra & Mahindra

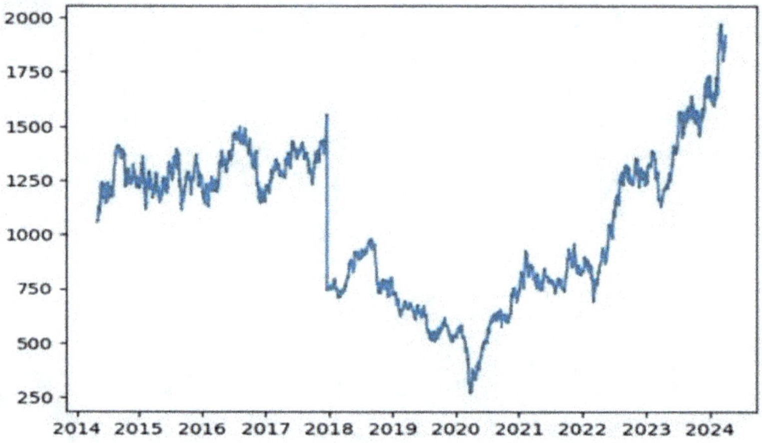

*Figure 5. Visualization of Historical prices– Ashok Leyland, Bajaj Motors*

As

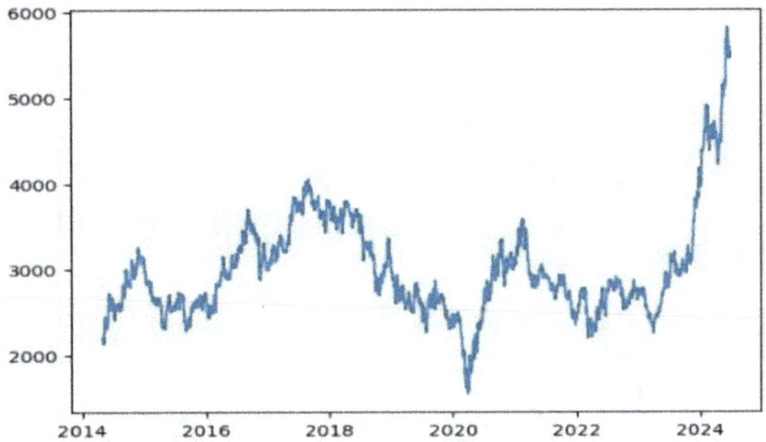


Bajaj Motors

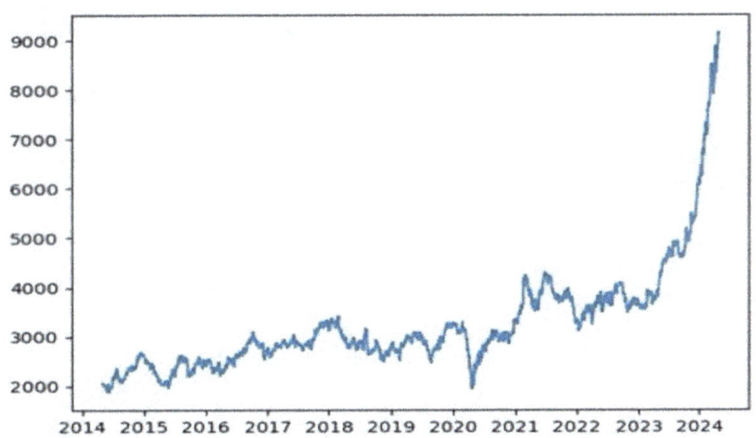


Figure 3 to Figure 5 shows the historical stock prices. The blue color line indicates the closing stock prices of the selected automobile stocks within the time interval from May 2014 to April 2024. The closing prices overall direction is upward despite several irregularities.

*Figure 6. Prediction using LSTM – TATA Motors*

Tata Motors

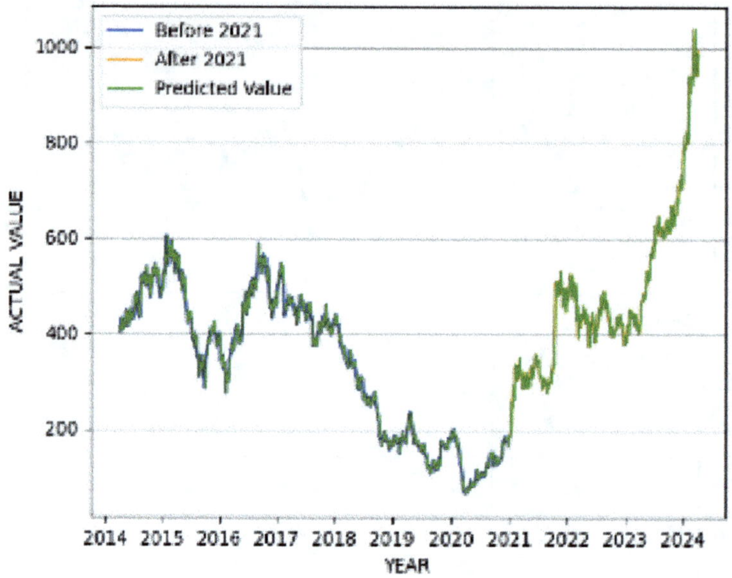

*Figure 7. Prediction using LSTM – TVS Motors, Mahindra and Mahindra*

TVS Motors

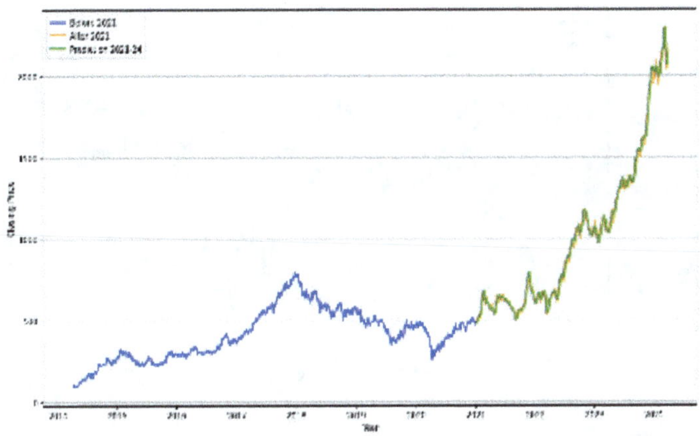

Mahindra & Mahindra

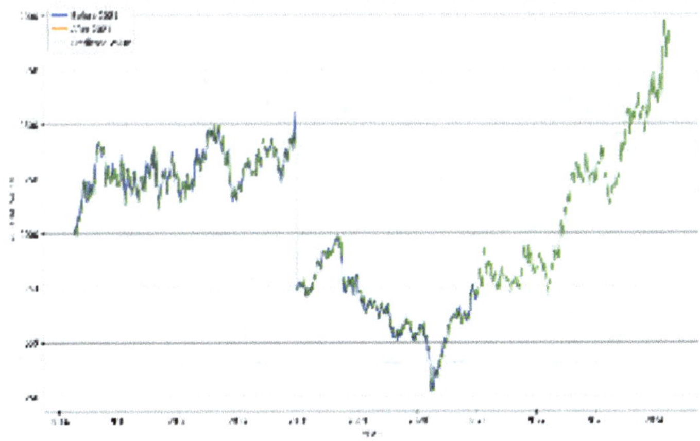

*Figure 8. Prediction using LSTM– Ashok Leyland, Bajaj Motors*

Ashok Leyland

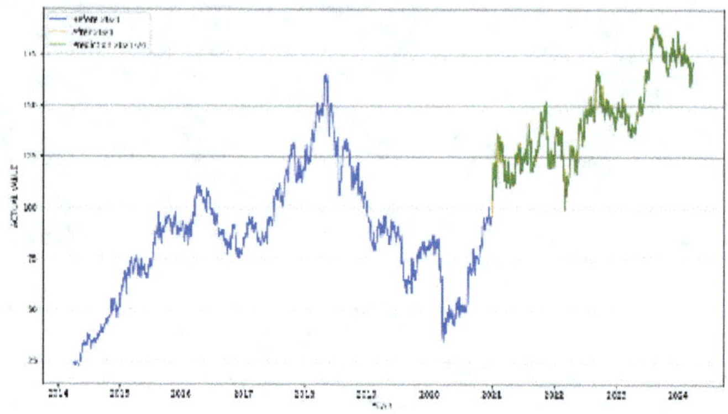

Bajaj Motors

Figure 6 to Figure 8 depicts the results of LSTM model in stock price prediction. The model was trained using 100 epochs and the trained model was used to make predictions on test data LSTM can make predictions of non-linear and highly variable price movement with decent accuracy of prediction. The study established that the accuracy of the neural network models must exceed 95 percent.

Based on the above figures 6 to 8, the blue line shows the actual closing price, the yellow line is the prediction in training data, and the green line is the prediction in test data.

The plotted prediction values depict that there is a close match between the output of the LSTM model and the actual closing prices. During the training, the estimated price curve is very close to the actual historical price curve and thus shows that the model can learn and reproduce underlying patterns in the data. More to the point, such alignment is carried through to the test stage that implies that the model is not merely effective in fitting the training data, but is also effective in generalizing to unseen data with a high level of accuracy.

This uniformity on training and testing performance confirms the strength and reliability of the model to predict. LSTM model was able to capture both the positive and negative price trends including volatile moments, like the V-shaped market recovery in 2020 after the COVID-19 pandemic. This shows the ability of the model to predict the stock prices under a very dynamic and noisy market condition.

It is important to note that the model did not show signs of overfitting since its accuracy was consistent across the various datasets. The model was trained by 100 epochs and it achieved the best results, offered a better precision of the forecasting without compromising the generalization capacity. These results confirm the effectiveness of the LSTM networks as feasible methods of stock price prediction.

Academically, this kind of empirical evidence will be used to stress the significance of introducing AI-based predictive modeling into the finance and analytics curricula. The students are able to gain applied skills in deep learning and understanding real-life uses of deep learning in financial forecasting by experimenting with model training, tuning and validation- this improves their technical and strategic decision-making abilities.

*Figure 9. Prediction using ARIMA – TATA Motors*

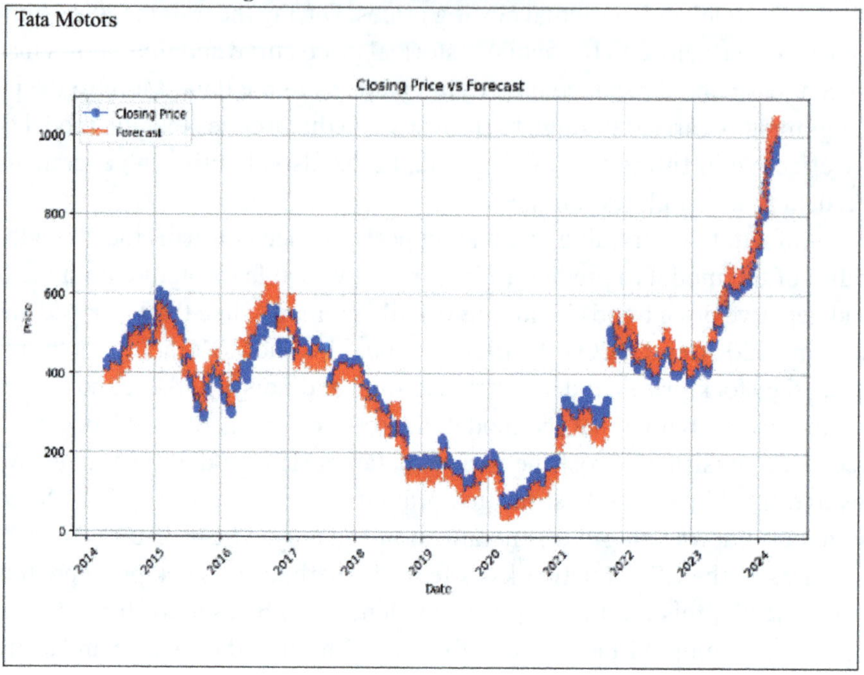

*Figure 10. Prediction using ARIMA – TVS Motors, Mahindra and Mahindra*

TVS Motors

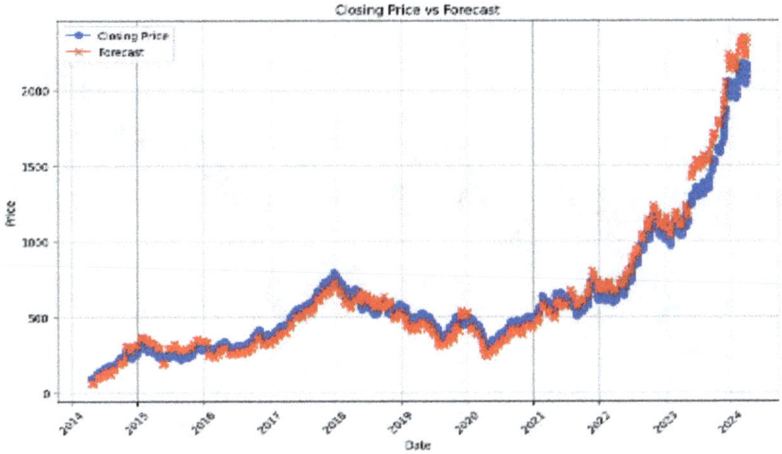


Mahindra & Mahindra

*Figure 11. Prediction using ARIMA – Ashok Leyland, Bajaj Motors*

Ashok Leyland

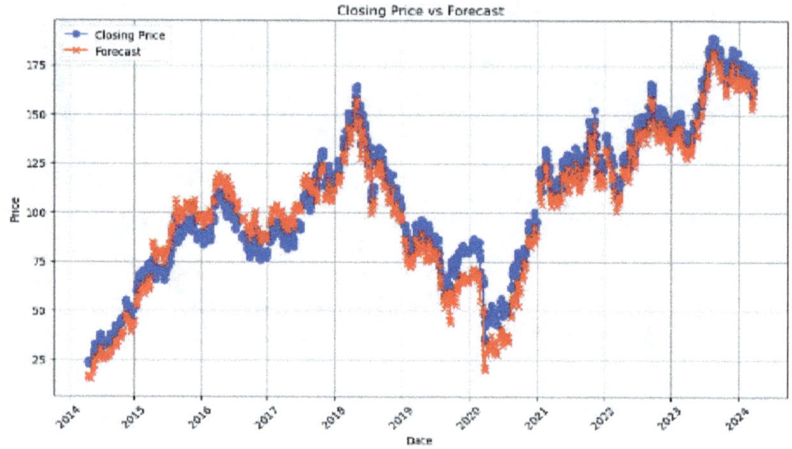


Bajaj Motors

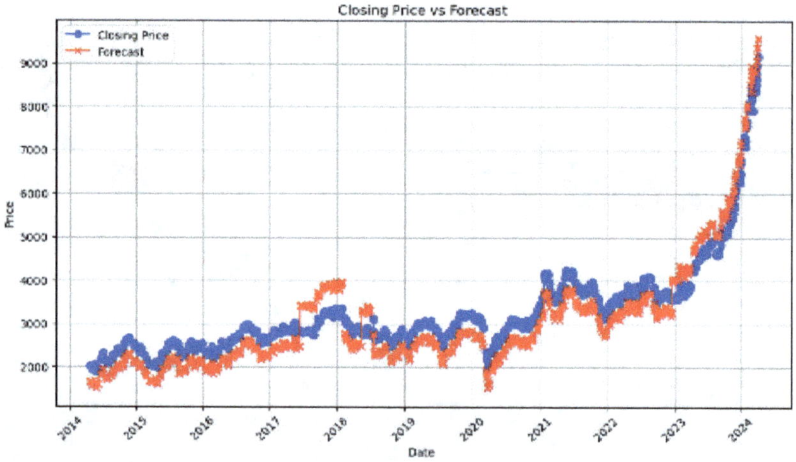


The findings obtained using the ARIMA model show that the stock price data attained stationarity when first-order differencing was used and thus, the ARIMA (1,1,1) model was chosen. The blue line in the visual output indicates the actual closing prices whereas the red line indicates the forecasted values. Despite showing adequate predictive accuracy, there is a visible difference between the actual and the predicted curves which shows that the ARIMA model was not accurate enough to capture sudden variations and non-linear dynamics in the data.

Nevertheless, the ARIMA model can be said to be somewhat consistent during its training and testing period as it is able to generalize patterns on the basis of linear dependencies and short-term autocorrelations. Nevertheless, in comparison to the LSTM model, ARIMA is inferior in terms of following the complex dynamics of stock prices and especially when the volatility is high.

The LSTM model, in its turn, demonstrates significantly better correspondence to actual closing prices, which proves the robustness of the model in representing complex and non-linear relationships and long-term dependencies. Although the ARIMA model is effective in modeling trend and seasonal time series, its inabilities to model quick changes and multifactorial effects are well witnessed in stock market prediction.

This comparative analysis is a learning opportunity to students and practitioners in the field of management education. It brings out the advantages and limitations of classical statistical models such as ARIMA over contemporary AI models such as LSTM. By including these practical assessments in business analytics or financial modeling classes, it is possible to improve theoretical knowledge and provide students with practical skills in choosing and implementing the proper tools of forecasting in practice (See Table 1).

The metric values are calculated using the PYTHON STATS package.

*Table 1. Summary of results for LSTM & ARIMA model*

| COMPANY NAME | LSTM | | | ARIMA | | |
|---|---|---|---|---|---|---|
| | MAPE | RMSE | MAE | MAPE | RMSE | MAE |
| Ashok Leyland | 1.87% | 1.92 | 1.74 | 2.35% | 2.12 | 2.02 |
| Bajaj Motors | 1.53% | 1.43 | 1.78 | 3.18% | 3.02 | 3.21 |
| Mahindra & Mahindra | 1.41% | 1.84 | 1.68 | 3.62% | 3.01 | 2.85 |
| Tata Motors | 1.79% | 1.48 | 1.26 | 3.03% | 2.85 | 2.77 |
| TVS Motors | 1.32% | 2.03 | 2.74 | 2.75% | 2.57 | 2.92 |

Source: Compiled by Author(s).

The comparative study of both LSTM and ARIMA models shows that LSTM performs better in all the main evaluation criteria such as Mean Absolute Percentage Error (MAPE) and Root Mean Square Error (RMSE) compared to ARIMA. The benefit of LSTM is that it can be used to model nonlinear relationships and long-term dependencies in time series data. This gives it specific advantage in predicting the stock price trends of automobile companies whose trends can be particularly affected by complex market and economic forces.

By comparison, although ARIMA is a useful method of modelling linear and stationary time series, its usefulness is constrained in settings that are highly volatile, seasonal and subject to exogenous shocks, which are typical in real world financial markets. The results of this research show that LSTM had the MAPE values which were around 50 percent lower than ARIMA, which proves that LSTM is more accurate in terms of prediction.

The study adds to the current discussion on the effectiveness of the AI and deep learning models in financial prediction. With big data analytics and AI still transforming decision-making in any industry, the applicability of such models is no longer confined to research but also applies to the financial sphere.

Educationally, this comparative assessment will be a strong instructional tool to students of management. It enables experiential learning because the learners can experiment, analyze and compare classical statistical methods and more complex machine learning models over real-world market data. Incorporating these analyses into management curricula increases the students' awareness of how to choose the right model, how to analyze the performance of the model, and how to consider the strategic effects of algorithmic decision support in a financial setting.

## 5. CONCLUSION

Stock price prediction is a topic of strategic concern to equity traders, individual investors, and portfolio managers. Nevertheless, its volatile, nonlinear and noisy nature continues to pose a problem to accurate and consistent prediction. There are many factors involved in influencing the behavior of stock prices, such as technical indicators, macroeconomic indicators, and market sentiment that make prediction even harder. This paper examines the use of the Long Short-Term Memory (LSTM) neural networks in forecasting stock prices of some automobile companies: Ashok Leyland, Bajaj Motors, Mahindra & Mahindra, Tata Motors, and TVS Motors. Through a comparative study with the conventional ARIMA model, the study indicates the better performance of LSTM, especially in the modeling long dependencies and non-linear patterns. The MAPE-based assessment proves that the LSTM model provides better forecasts than the ARIMA model on the sample companies.

One of the valuable insights of the research is that data preprocessing and variable engineering allow increasing the accuracy of the models. The methodology applied here is simple to modify to larger market indices that exhibit similar behavioral characteristics, therefore, providing a replicable model to financial analysts and investors.

Practically, the LSTM-based model proposed can be an effective decision-support tool due to its ability to help investors make more informed decisions to buy or sell. This research strengthens the position of introducing financial modeling based on

AI into management education, as a skill that can be essential to learners in terms of data-driven decision-making in the field of finance. To be able to improve the results in future research, it is possible to apply more sophisticated deep learning models with unstructured data sources that include financial news, market reports, and macroeconomic variables (inflation, political stability, or global events). These types of hybrid models promise to provide even stronger stock price forecasts using a combination of financial and sentiment and contextual intelligence.

The conclusions of the study have significant practical implications on a wide variety of stakeholders in the financial and investment ecosystem. The work is an effective demonstration of the fact that modern machine learning algorithms like Long Short-Term Memory (LSTM) can actually do much better than more classical statistical models like ARIMA in predicting stock prices, especially when it comes to highly volatile and nonlinear data as is the case with the automotive industry. To financial analysts and institutional investors, the introduction of LSTM models in their analysis platforms increases the precision in technical forecasting, thus, aids in more knowledgeable investment decisions. The predictive analytics can help automobile companies not only to decipher the investor sentiment and market behavior but also to guide internal strategic processes like pricing, production planning and marketing decisions based on the future stock market trends.

Regulatory bodies like Securities and Exchange Board of India (SEBI) can seek the help of the learning gleaned by the machine learning-based forecasting to track the efficiency and transparency of equity markets. The behavior of the algorithmic models is helpful in the development of regulatory systems to control the automated trading system and reduce the risk of market manipulation.

This comparative study between LSTM and ARIMA is also another contribution to the growing literature in the financial time series forecasting. It highlights the fact that one should select context-sensitive forecasting methods depending on the nature of the data as well as the purposes of the prediction. To the academic community, the research presents opportunities to investigate hybrid prediction models and use external variables as well as apply the research to other high-impact areas.

## 5.1 Implications for Management Education

The application of AI and machine learning algorithms like LSTM and ARIMA in forecasting the stock market has great pedagogical contribution to management education. The current research will offer a practical guideline to show how predictive analytics can improve data-driven financial decision-making so that students can understand how machine learning is used in practice in investment strategy and risk evaluation. Investigating the history of the Indian automotive market and evaluating the error metrics of sector-specific volatility, the research contributes to the establishment of a greater insight into the sphere of model choice, performance comparison, and strategic planning. These insights prepare future managers, analysts, and business leaders with important analytical and technical skills needed in the current AI-based financial environment. Moreover, the inclusion of such empirical studies in management programs facilitates experiential learning, so that the learners can connect the theoretical frameworks with the practice of machine learning in finance.

## REFERENCES


Abe, M., & Nakagawa, K. (2020, May). Cross-sectional stock price prediction using deep learning for actual investment management. In *Proceedings of the 2020 Asia Service Sciences and Software Engineering Conference* (pp. 9–15). DOI: 10.1145/3399871.3399889

Ahammad, I., Sarkar, W. A., Meem, F. A., Ferdus, J., Ahmed, M. K., Rahman, M. R., ... & Islam, M. S. (2024). Advancing stock market predictions with time series analysis including LSTM and ARIMA. *Cloud Computing and Data Science*, 226–241.

Bathla, G. (2020, November). Stock price prediction using LSTM and SVR. In *2020 Sixth International Conference on Parallel, Distributed and Grid Computing (PDGC)* (pp. 211–214). IEEE. DOI: 10.1109/PDGC50313.2020.9315800

Bhandari, H. N., Rimal, B., Pokhrel, N. R., Rimal, R., Dahal, K. R., & Khatri, R. K. (2022). Predicting stock market index using LSTM. *Machine Learning with Applications*, *9*, 100320. DOI: 10.1016/j.mlwa.2022.100320

Computation, N. (2016). Long short-term memory. *Neural Computation*, *9*, 1735–1780. PMID: 9377276

Ding, G., & Qin, L. (2020). Study on the prediction of stock price based on the associated network model of LSTM. *International Journal of Machine Learning and Cybernetics*, *11*(6), 1307–1317. DOI: 10.1007/s13042-019-01041-1

Eapen, J., Bein, D., & Verma, A. (2019, January). Novel deep learning model with CNN and bi-directional LSTM for improved stock market index prediction. In *2019 IEEE 9th Annual Computing and Communication Workshop and Conference (CCWC)* (pp. 264–270). IEEE. DOI: 10.1109/CCWC.2019.8666592

Gao, T., & Chai, Y. (2018). Improving stock closing price prediction using recurrent neural network and technical indicators. *Neural Computation*, *30*(10), 2833–2854. DOI: 10.1162/neco_a_01124 PMID: 30148707

Ghosh, P., Neufeld, A., & Sahoo, J. K. (2022). Forecasting directional movements of stock prices for intraday trading using LSTM and random forests. *Finance Research Letters*, *46*, 102280. DOI: 10.1016/j.frl.2021.102280

Ho, M. K., Darman, H., & Musa, S. (2021, July). Stock price prediction using ARIMA, neural network and LSTM models. In *Journal of Physics: Conference Series* (Vol. 1988, No. 1, p. 012041). IOP Publishing. DOI: 10.1088/1742-6596/1988/1/012041

Hochreiter, S., & Schmidhuber, J. (1997). Long short-term memory. *Neural Computation, 9*(8), 1735–1780. DOI: 10.1162/neco.1997.9.8.1735 PMID: 9377276

Kaushik, M., & Giri, A. K. (2020). Forecasting foreign exchange rate: A multivariate comparative analysis between traditional econometric, contemporary machine learning & deep learning techniques. *arXiv preprint*, arXiv:2002.10247. https://arxiv.org/abs/2002.10247

Mehtab, S., & Sen, J. (2020, November). Stock price prediction using CNN and LSTM-based deep learning models. In *2020 International Conference on Decision Aid Sciences and Application (DASA)* (pp. 447–453). IEEE. DOI: 10.1109/DASA51403.2020.9317207

Moghar, A., & Hamiche, M. (2020). Stock market prediction using LSTM recurrent neural network. *Procedia Computer Science, 170*, 1168–1173. DOI: 10.1016/j.procs.2020.03.049

Paliwal, S., & Sharma, S. (2022). Stock prediction using neural networks and evolution algorithm. [IJRASET]. *International Journal for Research in Applied Science and Engineering Technology, 10*(4), 661–671. DOI: 10.22214/ijraset.2022.41331

Paluch, M., & Jackowska-Strumiłło, L. (2018). Hybrid models combining technical and fractal analysis with ANN for short-term prediction of close values on the Warsaw Stock Exchange. *Applied Sciences (Basel, Switzerland), 8*(12), 2473. DOI: 10.3390/app8122473

Samarawickrama, A. J. P., & Fernando, T. G. I. (2017, December). A recurrent neural network approach in predicting daily stock prices: An application to the Sri Lankan stock market. In *2017 IEEE International Conference on Industrial and Information Systems (ICIIS)* (pp. 1–6). IEEE. DOI: 10.1109/ICIINFS.2017.8300345

Singh, A., Bhardwaj, G., Srivastava, A. P., Bindra, A., & Chaudhary, P. (2022, April). Application of neural network to technical analysis of stock market prediction. In *2022 3rd International Conference on Intelligent Engineering and Management (ICIEM)* (pp. 302–306). IEEE. DOI: 10.1109/ICIEM54221.2022.9853162

Sundermeyer, M., Schlüter, R., & Ney, H. (2012, September). LSTM neural networks for language modeling. *Interspeech, 2012*, 194–197.

Vijh, M., Chandola, D., Tikkiwal, V. A., & Kumar, A. (2020). Stock closing price prediction using machine learning techniques. *Procedia Computer Science, 167*, 599–606. DOI: 10.1016/j.procs.2020.03.326

Chapter 10

# Enhancing Data Analytics and Forecasting Education Through Machine Learning Algorithms


**Subramanian R. Siva**
*SRM Institute of Science and Technology, India*

**R. Kennady**
*Rajalakshmi Institute of Technology, India*

**T. Venketbabu**
https://orcid.org/0000-0002-0488-9332
*Vel Tech Rangarajan Dr. Sagunthala R&D Institute of Science and Technology, India*

**R. Saranya**
*Panimalar Engineering College, India*

**P. Rashmi**
*Velammal Engineering College, India*

**Baby P. Vinitha**
*Vel Tech Multi Tech Dr. Rangarajan Dr. Sakunthala Engineering College, India*

**Gracious L. A. Anto**
https://orcid.org/0000-0003-2386-9182
*R.M.K. College of Engineering and Technology, India*


## ABSTRACT


*The chapter explores the transformative role of machine learning in enhancing the teaching and learning of data analytics and forecasting. It highlights how ML supports adaptive, personalized, and efficient educational practices, enabling students to develop skills essential for the modern data-driven landscape. The chapter discusses curriculum integration, hands-on strategies, and the relevance of ML*



DOI: 10.4018/979-8-3373-2150-9.ch010

*algorithms in analytical modeling and forecasting techniques. Emphasis is placed on project-based learning, and overcoming pedagogical challenges such as algorithm complexity, skill gaps, and resource constraints. Through innovative methods including gamification, interdisciplinary approaches, and AI-assisted learning tools, the chapter demonstrates how educators can equip students with both theoretical and practical competencies. The chapter concludes by identifying future opportunities in ML education, including global accessibility, academic-industry collaboration, and the need for inclusive, scalable, and adaptive learning environments in shaping data science professionals.*

## 1. INTRODUCTION

### 1.1 Overview of Data Analytics and Forecasting

In the data-driven world of today, data analytics and forecasting have become an inseparable part of virtually all areas, including business and finance, healthcare, education, and public administration. With the capacity to derive actionable intelligence out of data, organizations can make informed decisions, optimize operations, and strategically plan in the future. Data analytics is a method of data analysis that is done systematically through computation. It entails the analysis of vast and complicated data to identify unknown patterns, correlations, trends and anomalies that can be used in decision-making. The essence of this is to convert raw information to useful information. This is normally done through data collection, data cleaning, data integration, data exploration and data interpretation. As the amount, speed and the type of data are growing, sophisticated methods and tools of analysis are being embraced to achieve more insights. Organizations in different industries are using data analytics to improve their processes and have a competitive advantage. Fraud detection, credit risk, customer segmentation, and portfolio are also some of the applications of analytics in the finance industry. In healthcare, it can be used in the optimization of patient care, accuracy of diagnosis, and resource allocation. Analytics helps the retailers to know more about the consumer behavior, how to manage the inventory, and how to customize the marketing campaigns. Data analytics is an important aspect in the technology sector especially in terms of product development, user experience and optimization of the system.

Forecasting on the other hand is a process of making predictions about future based on past results, statistical models and machine learning algorithms. It forms a major element of strategic planning and risk management. Organizations will be in a position to make proactive decisions as opposed to reactive ones by being able to predict the future trends and events. There are such areas where forecasting is used as demand planning, financial predictions, sales forecasting, weather forecasting and economic modeling. The forecasting techniques range between qualitative techniques, which are based on expert opinion and market research, and quantitative techniques, which are based on time series analysis, regression models and machine learning. Artificial intelligence (AI) and machine learning (ML) are becoming more common in modern forecasting because they allow working with complicated data more precisely and faster. The techniques are able to detect complex patterns and non linear relationships that would have been missed by the conventional models. Forecasting in business strategy assists in the determination of realistic objectives, allocation of resources, and the possible risks and opportunities. As an example, a company can better manage its inventory by predicting customer demand and prevent stockouts and over-stocking. Government agencies in policy making rely on forecasting to make predictions on economic indicators, unemployment rates and health trends in the population hence coming up with effective intervention programs. Increasing significance of data analytics and forecasting may also be observed in the scientific research, as they assist in hypothesis testing, experimental design, and innovation. As an example, in climate science, the data of different sensors and satellites are used to predict weather conditions and simulate how climate change will affect it. As so many data are created by digital platforms, sensors, and IoT devices, the existing data analysis and forecasting techniques cannot be applied. Such torrent of data requires more advanced methods capable of processing large data. As a result, machine learning has become one of the potent complements to the conventional analytical approach. The ML algorithms are able to learn based on data and adjust to new circumstances and better their predictions as time goes by. In addition to that, predictive analytics, which is a subfield of data analytics, refers to the combination of statistical methods and machine learning to predict events in the future by using extremely precise forecasts. This has helped companies to predict their customers need, identify possible failures in their systems and maximize their performance. In short, data analytics and forecasting play a critical role in making organizations succeed in such a dynamic and intricate environment. These fields of knowledge can be used to streamline operations, minimize risks, and innovate, as they allow interpreting huge volumes of information and understanding what will happen in the future. This is because as the technology keeps advancing, they will even become more central in influencing the future of decision-making across various sectors and fields.

## 1.2 Machine Learning in Education

Machine Learning (ML) has greatly changed education, introducing useful tools to make learning and teaching better. Nowadays, using ML is becoming common in schools worldwide as they focus on improving learning with new and flexible methods (Alenezi, H. S., & Faisal, M. H. 2020). Because of such advanced algorithms, systems can analyse data, recognize patterns and decide on the best actions with little help from people, improving and customizing the educational experience. Machine learning is very useful in education because it supports adaptive learning. These systems monitor student progress as they work and change the lessons and teaching speed to fit each person's learning. Because of this, each student gets help in their weaknesses and can move ahead quickly in their strengths. This style of teaching helps students understand the subject and remains interesting for them (Luan, H., & Tsai, C. C. 2021). ML can also be applied to graduate and assess student work. The usual way of grading takes a lot of time and can be biased. Still, machine learning algorithms can assess assignments, quizzes and written essays. Use of automation in grading allows teachers to work less and spend more time with students. Many educational institutions now rely on predictive analytics which is an important ML tool, to keep track of students' progress and predict their future achievements. With the help of historical information, these models can recognize students who may not do well or leave school and prompt early help(Jalil et al., 2019). After identifying the needs, teachers and administrators can help these students by offering tutoring, changing the way topics are taught or including parents in the process. Machine learning is important in making it easier to teach data science, forecasting and computer programming. Due to ML, students can get feedback immediately, use simulations and solve problems in a way that lets them relate their school knowledge to real life. Through this method, students learn more about the concepts and get ready for jobs in data-focused fields. In addition, ML is changing the way administrative work is done in schools and universities. ML applications help in managing classes, finding out about any unusual cases in attendance and making better choices about students. This improves the way the school runs, helping both the teachers and students. AI and ML used in education encourage students to learn about data. Because of their experience with AI tools, they learn how to use data analytics, think critically and solve problems using technology. This helps students learn and also gain the important skills needed today (Luan, H., & Tsai, C. C. 2021). Besides, students get familiar with the ethics and challenges of using AI technologies in the right way. All in all, machine learning is playing a major role in education by providing tools that make learning more personal, efficient and predictable. Using machine learning, teachers can improve their teaching, and administrators can make their jobs easier which benefits everyone involved. When more schools use and develop these technologies, learning will probably become easier to understand, more welcoming and driven by data (Tiwari, R. 2023).

### 1.3 Purpose and Scope of the Chapter

This chapter discusses how the application of machine learning in the education process can contribute to the improvement of the teaching and learning of data analytics and forecasting. It describes the use of ML in enhancing the delivery of education, its effectiveness and relevance to the market. The chapter discusses the different teaching techniques using ML, problems that may be encountered when implementing ML in data analytics courses, and possible improvements. Further, the chapter explores the evaluation methods of students, integration of theory and practice, and the accomplishment of skill deficits through programmatic approaches. This chapter seeks to be useful to the growing market for data analytics professionals by offering practical methods of teaching how to apply machine learning to data analysis and forecasting.

## 2. MACHINE LEARNING ALGORITHMS OVERVIEW

### 2.1 Machine Learning

Machine learning can be described as a subfield of artificial intelligence that involves the use of algorithms to give a system the ability to improve its performance from data and information without being programmed. ML models work with large datasets, analyse and find patterns, as well as learn from their previous experiences (Prabha et al., 2024). The three forms of machine learning include:

*Figure 1. Machine Learning Algorithms Overview*

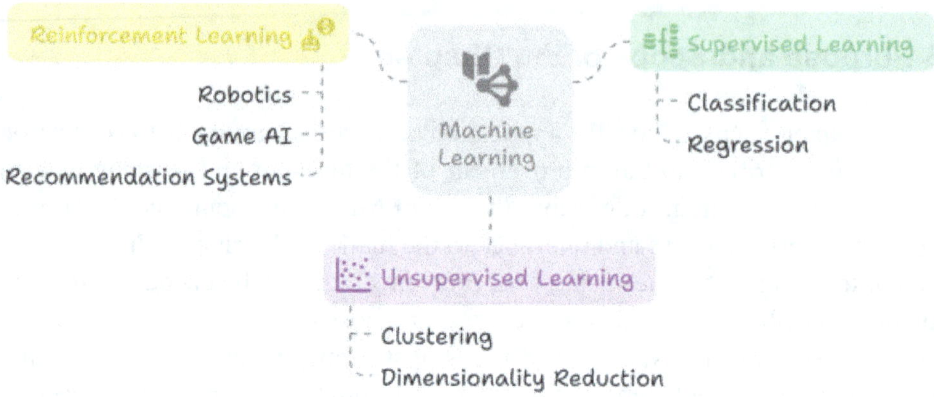


1. Supervised Learning – This is characterized by training of an algorithm with the help of labelled data in which both the input and output are defined. Some of the most common use of SVM are the classification problems such as the email spam detection and the regression problems such as the stock market prediction. Some of the examples include linear regression, decision trees, and even neural networks, among others.
2. Unsupervised learning – is used with data that have no labels and aims at finding the patterns and associations. Some of the common examples of tasks are clustering such as customer clustering and dimensionality reduction such as principal component analysis. They are k-means clustering and hierarchical clustering (Munir, H et al., 2022).
3. Reinforcement Learning – A form of learning that deals with teaching agents to make decisions that are sequential in nature through an environment in which they are rewarded or penalized. It is used in robotics, game artificial intelligence and in recommendation systems. It consists of two algorithms namely Q-learning and Deep Q networks (Sreelakshmi et al., 2024).

## 2.2 Relevance of ML Algorithms in Data Analytics and Forecasting

Machine learning is used in analytics and forecasting as it helps in the automation of several processes and increases the range of precision. One of the most important components of PA, whereby the results of past events are used to produce expected results, is ML algorithms. For instance, while developing a classification model, they can predict fraudulent transactions, while using clustering they can group customers, and using a regression model they can predict future sales performance. In forecasting, time-series models used in association with the help of ML give the business and researchers an idea about the future trends with the help of history. For example, Autoregressive Integrated Moving Average (ARIMA) models are used in financial forecasting and Long Short-Term Memory (LSTM) are used in the field of sequence forecasting such as weather and demand forecasting (Lakumarapu et al 2024).

### 2.2.1 Common Algorithms Used in Data Analytics and Forecasting

For time data analysis and forecasting, several methods and approaches are available in machine learning.

1. Linear Regression – This is a basic yet effective form of supervised learning algorithm for the prediction of continuous type of variables such as sales or price.
2. Decision Trees – A tree-based model, which is used in classification as well as in regression models, used in customer segmentation, credit risk assessment.
3. k-Nearest Neighbors (k-NN) – An algorithm that is based on the distance measurement used in recommendation systems and anomaly detection.
4. Random Trees – An ensemble learning method that is made up of many different decisions trees that is usually applied in identification of frauds or risk assessment.
5. Neural Networks – A type of artificial intelligence used in solving complex problems for patterns recognition in big data sets. CNN is used in image recognition while RNN and LSTM are used in sequential data such as speech recognition and stock price prediction.
6. XGBoost (Extreme Gradient Boosting) – A boosting algorithm used in structured data problems and is often used in models that win the competitions.

*Figure 2. Common Algorithms in Data Analytics and Forecasting*

These algorithms present efficient, precise, and computerized work methods for businessmen, educators, and researchers. When applied to the educational system, the integration of the ML-based analytics and forecasting models will help students to obtain the practical experience in the field, which is essential for the further work as data scientists (Subha et al., 2024).

## 3. TEACHING DATA ANALYTICS USING MACHINE LEARNING

### 3.1 Curriculum Design and Integration

Thus, the inclusion of machine learning into curricula in data analytics is crucial to ensuring students are ready to comprehend and apply such programs to solve problems they encounter in practice. Most of the traditional taught courses in big data analytics cover statistical tools and techniques, data visualization, and simple programming. However, the new generation curricula in the era of big data and AI requires the use of ML-based analytics in the development of competencies in aspects like predictive modeling, pattern recognition and automation (Hilbert et al., 2021).

To this end, the universities and other learning institutions establish a combined program encompassing data science, business analytics and computer science. A well-structured curriculum typically includes:

- Fundamental Concepts: Introduction to data analytics, statistics, and probability theory.

- Introduction to Machine Learning: Types of Machine Learning such as Supervised and Unsupervised learning, Model assessment and performance measure.
- Practical Implementation: Familiarity with the working of Python and R at a professional level by using various machine learning libraries including Scikit-learn, TensorFlow, and XGBoost.
- Applications: A number of case applications includes but not limited to Customer analytics-where predictions are made for customers buying behaviours, fraud detection and Sentiment analysis.
- Machine Learning Applications: Capstone Projects which are intended to be the solution of real-life problems by using the concepts of machine learning for analysis (Ambhika et al., 2024).

The combination of theory and practice in terms of the ratio is another significant factor that needs to be considered in the learning process. The theoretical preparations of the course are modules in mathematical theories of ML, which is followed by practical modules that focus on coding exercises, simulations, datasets, or models.

## 3.2 Practical Approaches for Teaching

Thus, the ML education should be based on the principles of experiential learning. Instructors should give more emphasis on practical experience rather than on the conceptual explanations. Some key teaching strategies include:

*Figure 3. ML Education Strategies Pyramid*

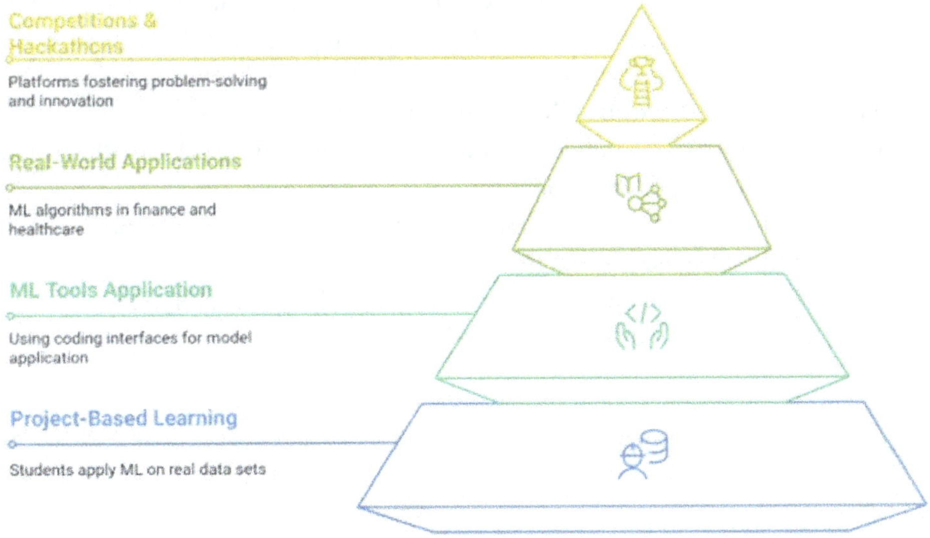

1. Project-Based Learning – makes the students use ML techniques on actual data sets like customer profiling, machinery health monitoring, or recommendation engine.
2. Real-World Applications – It involves the use of finance, healthcare, and marketing datasets whereby students can see how the use of ML algorithms enhances the business.
3. Competitions and Hackathons – Encouraging participation in platforms like online platform or university ML competitions fosters problem-solving skills and innovation.

## 3.3 Challenges and Strategies

The process of teaching data analytics based on ML has the following challenges:

- Advanced Level of ML Algorithms – This is an area that students find a bit challenging especially on issues such as gradient descent, deep learning architectures and feature engineering.
- Diverse Learning Paces – Some of the students may have prior knowledge in programming while others have no coding knowledge at all.
- Bridging the Gap Between Theory and Practice – There is a difference between learning the basic concepts of Machine Learning, and applying such concepts in practice (Aswini et al., 2024).

Strategies to Overcome These Challenges:

- Goal-oriented learning – The sequence of learning should be from basic models such as linear regression to more complex models such as neural networks.
- Interactive Visualizations – It is equally important to ensure that the students learn the concepts by applying them on tools such as TensorFlow Playground or Shapley values for explainability.
- Fostering Collaboration – It makes the use of group assignments and peer learning to make them learn from other people's experiences while also enhancing their knowledge of the operations of ML-based analytics.

# 4. TEACHING FORECASTING WITH MACHINE LEARNING

## 4.1 Forecasting Models and Techniques

Prediction is an important part of data analysis that helps in anticipating future trends from past data collected. In the past, forecasting was accomplished using statistical techniques such as ARIMA and Exponential Smoothing; however, today, it incorporates various elements of ML.

Some of the most common ML algorithms used in forecasting are as follows:

- ARIMA – A conventional method of time series forecasting based on statistical analysis.
- LSTM (Long Short-Term Memory) – This is a deep learning model that is particularly useful for sequential data and thus, it is useful in predicting the stock market and energy consumption.
- SARIMA (Seasonal ARIMA) – It is a variation of ARIMA that incorporates seasonal factors into the model.

Thus, understanding how these models are structured and when they should be used will assist learners in creating effective and efficient forecast models.

## 4.2 Curriculum Strategies for Forecasting

In order to teach forecasting with the help of ML, a curriculum has to be defined that covers both the more traditional statistical methods and the modern methods based on ML. A well-designed syllabus includes:

1. Their measures – Concepts like stationarity, autocorrelation, or moving averages.
2. Before introducing the use of machine learning–based models, it is preferable to teach students about ARIMA and exponential smoothing, which are more conventional forecasting techniques.
3. Feature Engineering for Forecasting – Techniques for feature creation from time-series data including the process of developing trends and seizing periodicity.
4. Time Series Analysis – Training models such as LSTM, XGBoost, and Facebook Prophet for the purpose of forecasting time series.
5. Model Evaluation – It refers to evaluation or testing of the model using statistical equations like RMSE (Root Mean Square Error), MAPE (Mean Absolute Percentage Error) etc. and cross-validation techniques.

6. Industry Applications – Examples of supply chain forecasting, the application of the technique in financial market prediction, and the use of the technique in demand forecasting in the retail sector.

To enhance the interaction with the material, the focus should be placed on the practical application of Python and R. The use of actual time-series data lets the students apply and fine-tune different forecasting models for the best results.

## 4.3 Hands-on Learning and Case Studies

In order to teach forecasting, students have to employ the use of ML on real-world data. Some of the suggested practical activities are as follows:

- Stock Market Prediction – using the historical data on the stock price and using it to train ML models in order to predict stock movements.
- Sales Forecasting – Using data of the retail sales for developing demand forecasting models for the purpose of inventory.
- Power Usage Forecasting – predicting the electricity usage based on the previously recorded values.
- Climate and Weather Forecasting – Using ML, so that one can be able to predict changes in temperatures and other extreme weather conditions.

Incorporating case studies helps the students to understand how the concept of ML-based forecasting is applied in various fields. For instance, in finance, forecasting models assist in determining the best portfolio and the risks associated with the portfolio while in supply chain management, they help in inventory and logistics.

## 4.4 Overcoming Challenges in Teaching Forecasting

There are some issues that are associated with forecasting using ML and they are as follows:

Non-stationary Data – Most of the temporal data sets in practice are non-stationary since they contain trends and seasonality which cannot be trained directly with ML models. Result – Precision – Several advanced forecast models like LSTMs entail the use of a lot of computational resources and time to train. Interpreting Forecasting Outputs – This is one of the major challenges faced by students in that they are unable to understand model prediction and uncertainty estimation.

Solutions to These Challenges:

Begin with Simple Models – It is better to train the audience on ARIMA before moving to more complex ML models for a good foundation. Cloud-Based Platforms –can be used in training of complex models. Visual Explanations – Encourage students to plot time-series trends and residual errors to better understand forecasting performance. In this way, teachers can give their students a solid theoretical background as well as show them how to apply it in practice with the help of the chosen ML models. To teach data analytics and forecasting using machine learning, an approach that integrates theory with practice is used so that the students can be exposed to both theoretical and practical aspects. Through the integration of ML-based techniques in curriculum, the students will be in a position to solve real-world data challenges.

## 5. STUDENT ASSESSMENT AND EVALUATION IN ML-BASED ANALYTICS AND FORECASTING

As educators, being able to assess students' understanding of the concepts covered is an important goal in delivering effective lectures and tutorials. It should be noted that assessment of the learning in ML should cover both theoretical knowledge and practical skills. A well-rounded assessment strategy includes Quizzes and Exams: Testing students on ML concepts, algorithms, and mathematical foundations. Questions can be simple multiple-choice to deriving the equations of ML. Practical Assignments: Students use different ML models to process datasets, assess models' performance, and make conclusions. These assignments assess their capacity of applying the algorithms in a practical manner. Code Reviews: This way it is possible to evaluate the quality, the efficiency and the readability of the code provided by the students and guarantee that they adhere to the best practices. Introducing theoretical and practical methods guarantees that students understand not only the theory of applying ML techniques but also the practical way of applying them.

### 5.1 Project-Based Evaluation

This is because project-based learning is one of the most effective approaches to teach ML since it enables the students to practice what they are taught. The following are the ways of assessing students through projects:

- Individual Projects: Students select their own dataset and build up an ML model and then assess the results and report them. Group Projects: These are effective in that they bring together a group of people with the aim of solving problems. It allows the students to work on more complex datasets and create more complete ML applications. Peer assessment: Students assess each other's works, which enhances the critical thinking skills among the students.

- Examples of ML project topics for assessment: Predicting customer churn in a telecom company. Forecasting: Using the time series analysis on stock price. Sentiment analysis of social media posts. Recommender systems for e-commerce platforms. Using real-life examples, teachers assist students in enhancing problem-solving abilities that are relevant in professional positions(Kumar, A., & Gupta, D. 2021).

## 5.2 Challenges in Assessment

1. Balancing Theory and Practical Skills

It is not uncommon to find a student who is good at theory but poor at coding or a student who is good at coding but has no mathematical skills. Solution: Assigning theoretical and practical allows for a balance between the two aspects. Teaching coding is made easier by ensuring the students are given numerous coding problems with solutions.

2. Academic Integrity in Machine Learning Coursework

Since there are open-source ML models and solutions available on the internet, plagiarism is a major issue. Solution: Using programs such as plagiarism check (for instance check plagiarism detection system for programming assignments). To ensure that the work of the students is their own, the students should write a report or present an explanation of the code.

3. Evaluating Complex ML Models

Some of the models take long to train and use a lot of resources hence making their assessment challenging. Solution: Providing the students with the opportunity to train the models in cloud-based ML environments. Promoting the idea of students to pay more attention to explainability of the model rather than its accuracy.

In the following, there are some general requirements that should be met by a well-designed assessment framework in ML education: The two most important things to assess are knowledge and performance. Engage the learners in real-life activities through project-based approach. Increase the effectiveness of learning outcomes to use peer review and collaboration. There are ways that can be adopted in the prevention of plagiarism and the fight against dishonesty in academic work. This way, by using diverse assessment means, teachers can guarantee that the students comprehend the material in terms of analytics and forecasting and can apply the notion of ML in practice.

## 6. CHALLENGES IN TEACHING MACHINE LEARNING FOR ANALYTICS AND FORECASTING

It is not easy to teach machine learning for data analytics and forecasting in the following ways. These challenges vary from student preparedness and deficiencies in knowledge and skills, algorithms' difficulty, and restrictions in the use of resources. These are some of the problems that require attention in order to develop the best learning environment.

### 6.1 Student Readiness and Skill Gaps

One of the most significant issues in teaching students of ML is that they have different academic backgrounds, and while some of them are good in mathematics, statistics, and programming, others are not. These are the key skills that every student needs to possess in order to grasp the essence of ML algorithms, but, as it was mentioned earlier, the students often encounter difficulties with them.

#### 6.1.1 Common Skill Gaps

Computer Science: ML involves implementation of algorithms in computer science such as optimization algorithms, object-oriented concepts, etc. This is because it seems that many students have poor background knowledge in the above listed areas thus they find it very hard to understand concepts such as the gradient descent technique, optimization and probabilistic model. Programming Skills: In order to implement ML models, one needs to have the programming knowledge of languages. Students who are new to programming may find it challenging to code models, solve errors that occur during coding, and learn to use tools. Data Handling and Preprocessing: Most students do not have exposure to data cleaning, feature engineering, or data exploration, which are very important when constructing an ML model.

### 6.1.2 Strategies to Bridge Skill Gaps

Pre-course preparatory modules: It is useful to offer the basic courses in Python programming, statistics, and linear algebra before starting the main course in ML.

Gradual revelation of concepts and ideas that allows learners to grasp relatively simple models such as linear regression before proceeding to deep learning.

Interactive Lectures and Practical Sessions: Engaging active learning strategies such that the students work with real datasets

Grouping: Grouping and pairing students can be effective in helping the students learn from each other and to enhance learning of areas that they lack as compared to their counterparts.

## 6.2 Complexity of Machine Learning Algorithms

The different forms of ML algorithms include simple models like regression models and complex models such as artificial neural networks. There are times when the basic understanding of mathematics, the design of an algorithm or how it can be implemented becomes challenging to many students.

### 6.2.1 Challenges Related to Algorithm Complexity

Mathematical Aptitude versus Coding Skills: It is possible for a learner to grasp the theoretical concepts of a certain ML model but lack the ability to code it or, on the other hand, be a good coder but lack the mathematical understanding of the model. Hyperparameter Tuning and Model Optimization: Sometimes there is a need to fine-tune the models, select hyperparameters, and assess model performance that may be done so by experience. Interpreting Model Results: To a certain extent, many students fail to understand why a model predicts in a certain way (decision trees versus neural networks).

### 6.2.2 Strategies to Simplify Learning

1. Use Visualizations: Graphical explanations such as decision trees, neural networks assist the students in comprehending abstract concepts in ML.
2. Begin with simple models: Begin with the linear regression model and then the decision tree before going to complex models such as deep learning.
3. Real-world examples: Presenting how ML is implemented in finance, healthcare, marketing, and forecasting makes it easier for the students to understand the real-world application of the concept.

## 6.3 Resource Limitations

In teaching, ML entails commodity, computation power, large dataset, and tool, which are scarce in many institutions due to financial constraints.

### 6.3.1 Common Resource Challenges

Accessibility to GPUs and Cloud Computing: the training of such models demands computational power that may be expensive for most learners or institutions. Data Quality: The data used in training ML models should be of high quality, which might not be available in the public domain. Software and Licensing Costs: Some of the tools and platforms used in ML are paid, this may be costly to students and institution.

### 6.3.2 Strategies to Overcome Resource Limitations

1. Free and Open sources: Use free platform to test the ML models.
2. Datasets: Kaggle, UCI Machine Learning Repository, Dataset Search are few websites from where students can get datasets for their projects.
3. Industry and Research Institutions: Working with industry and other research institutions to access data and computational resources of the private sector.

Nonetheless, with the right approach, such as strategic curating of the curriculum, breaking down of complex concepts, and use of existing resources, it is possible to make the teaching of ML easier. Thus, today's educators can address student's weaknesses; make complex algorithms more comprehensible; and overcome the lack of resources to help students build analytical and forecasting capabilities based on ML.

## 7. INNOVATIVE APPROACHES IN TEACHING ML FOR DATA ANALYTICS AND FORECASTING

With the ever-growing influence of ML in several sectors, it is crucial for educators to come up with new methods of teaching this subject in data analytics and forecasting. Lecturing has become an ineffective approach to educate students and help them understand the concepts of ML in the current generation. Thus, such elements as the interactive learning methods, interdisciplinary approaches and the use of the new technologies are defining the new way of ML education.

## 7.1 Interactive Learning Methods

As earlier noted, the best way of teaching ML is through active and experiential learning. To enhance learning comprehension, retaining, and practical application of knowledge, it is advisable to include games, simulations, and collaboration in the learning process.

### 7.1.1 Gamification in ML Learning

As an application of games rules, that involves introducing characteristics of games into learning activities for example points, badges, competitions, and trials.

- ML Coding Challenges: Most of the ML platforms such as Kaggle, Data Camp, and Hacker Rank provide students a chance to solve coding challenges on Machine Learning and compete with their peers. ML-Based Games: Some educators also design mini-games in which the students train models on games such as chess or image recognition games.
- Simulations and Interactive Platforms: It is imperative that students get a feel of how the ML models work and this can be achieved with simulations. Virtual Labs- Some of the useful tools which provide the environment for coding and running ML models without the need for a complex setup. Interactive environments to learn with Machine: Students can understand how an ML model is constructed and how it changes over time with the help of platforms.
- Collaborative Learning and Peer-to-Peer Teaching: Teamwork is also very important in the learning process of ML where students are allowed to work in groups, code together and share knowledge. Pair programming: As much as coding the ML models, students should be forced to work in pairs so that they can discuss the models and solve the problems together. ML Study Groups: Formation of the groups among the students enables them to share with others and revise the content learned in the course.

## 7.2 Integration with Other Disciplines

It is advisable to combine machine learning with computer science, statistics, and domain knowledge to make learning more realistic.

- Interdisciplinary ML Education: Computer Science and ML: Integrating teaching of ML with software engineering makes it easier for students to implement the models in a given application. Probability& Hypothesis testing:

Probability, hypothesis testing and Bayesian methods are valuable, as they help students understand the result of ML algorithms.

- Domain-Specific ML Applications: Finance: Explaining to the students how these ML models can be used in predicting stock prices, identifying fraud, and managing investments. The four areas of application are Healthcare: applying machine learning for analyzing images, for predicting diseases and creating personalized treatments.
- Marketing: Applying ML for customer segmentation, recommendation systems, and sentiment analysis. This way, students will understand how it works in practice by connecting ML with examples from the industry.

### 7.2.1 Future Trends in ML Education

Due to the dynamic nature of ML, the educators have to adapt to new trends and technologies in the society.

- Deep Learning and Reinforcement Learning: Deep Learning (DL): As a result of the neural networks, students need to be familiar with CNNs (for image recognition), RNNs (for sequential data), and transformers (for NLP tasks)( Ansari, G et al., 2021). Reinforcement Learning (RL) This approach involves training the students how the RL models work such as training an agent to play games like AlphaGo in order to enable them understand AI decision making.
- AI-Driven Personalized Learning Tools: Adaptive learning systems in education are used to deliver content based on the performance of the students. Automated ML Tutors: These assist in the assessment of the performance of the students and offer feedback on the ML assignments. Chatbots for ML Learning: There are many tools like AI driven Question and Answer bots that help students in debugging the code and getting to learn about the concepts of ML.
- Virtual and Augmented Reality in ML Education: Virtual Reality (VR): Some institutions apply VR where students see the ML models virtually. Augmented Reality (AR): Augmented reality-based Machine Learning makes it possible for students to engage with real-world data in a more real-life manner. Such approaches present creative and interactive learning environment that differs from the conventional teaching methods.

These include gamification, interactive simulations, interdisciplinary integration, and the application of innovative AI tools to the learning process that become beneficial to ML students. Thus, using such an approach and employing technology in the learning process, educators can not only teach the students about ML but also prepare them to use this knowledge to solve analytics and forecasting problems.

## 8. FUTURE DIRECTIONS AND OPPORTUNITIES

Since the emergence of machine learning (ML), it has been adopted across many industries, and the same is true for education. The future advancements in the field of ML for education will be marked by enhancing technology, closer industry-academia relations, and increased availability of learning resources across the world. These factors will define how students acquire understanding of ML, use it in practice, and progress to data analysis and prediction professions.

### 8.1 Evolution of ML Tools for Education

Another trend affecting the ML education is the increased use of the teaching assistants and AI-based learning applications. These are helpful in improving the ways through which students engage with the ML concepts and build their skills.

AI-Powered Teaching Assistants: AI-based assistants like chatbots and virtual tutoring assist the students in debugging the code along with helping them understand the concepts of ML and also there is an option of feedback on the assignments. AI tutors can monitor the performance of the students as well as recommend the best learning strategies depending on the student's level.

Personalized Learning through AI: The adaptive learning systems change the content depending on the performance of the learners so that learners will be able to progress through the course at their own rate. AI can also learn from a student's previous errors and provide recommended exercises to enhance the understanding of areas of challenge. There are benefits of automating grading in assignments and projects in the field of ML, which can assist the instructors in enhancing the learning process. These tools also ease the load of the educators while improving the level of student interaction and understanding of the ML concepts.

### 8.2 Academic and Industry Connection

Since the use of ML has extended in the various fields, universities should incorporate it into their teaching curriculum. Industry partnerships are also beneficial to the students in that they offer practical experience and the kind of skills that most employers are looking for in the job market.

### 8.2.1 Industry-Academia Collaborations

Universities can work with the industries to design their course programs in such a way that the training offered is useful in the business, healthcare, financial, and other industries. Some of the companies that offer academic partnership which enables students get acquainted with industrial level ML tools and cloud computing platforms. Industry guest lectures and mentorship help the students to see the current trends and issues in the field of ML.

### 8.2.2 Internships and Project-Based Learning

Software engineering, businesses, finance, and healthcare industries provide students with opportunities to develop ML projects based on real-life cases. Capstone projects where students create end to end solutions are effective in this regard of closing the gap between theory and practice. The incorporation of industry-based projects in the curriculum of the educational institutions can help in the creation of professional and competent ML experts.

## 8.3 Global Trends in Data Analytics Education

As the market for data scientists and ML engineers grows, educational institutions globally are introducing new methods of teaching and making new tools available for learning ML.

Growing Global Demand for ML and Data Analytics Professionals: The World Economic Forum also expect the data science and AI jobs to be some of the most prevalent job opportunities in the next decade. Several governments worldwide, as well as universities, are putting their efforts in setting up centres of Artificial Intelligence, machine learning boot camps and specialisation programs in ML degrees to prepare the workforce. Online platforms are now providing equal opportunities to the people across the globe to gain knowledge in the field of ML, DA, and forecasting.

Remote Learning and Global Accessibility: Online Platform provide exposure of Massive Open Online Courses that the student from any part of the world can seek ML from premiere schools. Students are able to learn in virtual and hybrid classrooms which makes them to learn from different parts of the world. There are now low-code and no-code tools for ML such as Online learning and worldwide availability of materials for ML allow people from different backgrounds to obtain the necessary knowledge for data-oriented professions.

The future of ML education will be in the form of intelligent tutoring systems, adaptive learning, enhanced partnership between the academia and industry, and access to education for students across the globe. With the current increase in demand for ML experts, more education systems need to be put in place to ensure that students are trained to fit analytics and forecasting fields. Subsequently, ML education can assist in the pursuit of closing this gap through the use of technology, involving real-world applications, and through creating global learning experiences for students to prepare the next generation of data professionals.

## 9. CONCLUSION

All in all, it may be said that the ML algorithms are assuming a very critical role in improving the education of data analysis and forecasting. By incorporating ML into classrooms, teachers are able to expose students to exciting and engaging ways of learning that will enable them to learn how to manipulate big data and make predictions, thus enabling them to solve real life problems. The characteristic of Machine Learning makes it possible for a student to be able to learn at his or her own pace and style. It not only aids the learners in understanding the theories in the course but also enables them in developing their skills in using data, developing models, and making decisions. Thus, it can be concluded that the further development of using ML in teaching methods is critical for further progress in this aspect. This means that as technology advances, so does the technological equipment that is available to teachers. With the help of deep learning and reinforcement learning, educators will be able to enhance the level of their strategies in teaching and make learning more effective. The significance of carrying out research and development in the teaching techniques cannot be overemphasized, given that the field of data science and analytics is ever evolving. There are some of the prospects and avenues for research in ML education for analytics as follows: One of the main issues is to make the educational platforms usable by all students, and to give them the same chances regardless of their status and previous experience in using the technologies. Moreover, there is a need to investigate how various teaching approaches, including game-based learning or group learning, can be applied in conjunction with ML in the learning process to improve students' interest and understanding. These are some of the challenges that create great potential for the further development, where educators and researchers will be able to work together to define the direction for the development of data analytics education.

## REFERENCES


Alenezi, H. S., & Faisal, M. H. (2020). Utilizing crowdsourcing and machine learning in education: Literature review. *Education and Information Technologies*, *25*(4), 2971–2986. DOI: 10.1007/s10639-020-10102-w

Ambhika, C., Gayathri, S., Anish, T. P., & Sheena, B. G. (2024, August). Enhancing Predictive Modeling in High Dimensional Data Using Hybrid Feature Selection. In *2024 5th International Conference on Electronics and Sustainable Communication Systems (ICESC)* (pp. 873-879). IEEE. DOI: 10.1109/ICESC60852.2024.10690153

Ansari, G., Gupta, S., & Singhal, N. (2021). Natural Language Processing in Online Reviews. In *Natural Language Processing for Global and Local Business* (pp. 40–64). IGI Global Scientific Publishing. DOI: 10.4018/978-1-7998-4240-8.ch003

Aswini, J., Sudha, K., Ganesh, G., Subramanian, S., & Ghinea, G. (2024). AI-powered parallel computing architecture and its applications. In *The convergence of self-sustaining systems with AI and IoT* (pp. 23–39). IGI Global. DOI: 10.4018/979-8-3693-1702-0.ch002

Hilbert, S., Coors, S., Kraus, E., Bischl, B., Lindl, A., Frei, M., Wild, J., Krauss, S., Goretzko, D., & Stachl, C. (2021). Machine learning for the educational sciences. *Review of Education*, *9*(3), e3310. DOI: 10.1002/rev3.3310

Jalil, N. A., Hwang, H. J., & Dawi, N. M. (2019, July). Machines learning trends, perspectives and prospects in education sector. In *Proceedings of the 3rd International Conference on Education and Multimedia Technology* (pp. 201-205). DOI: 10.1145/3345120.3345147

Kumar, A., & Gupta, D. (2021). Sentiment analysis as a restricted NLP problem. In *Natural language processing for global and local business* (pp. 65–96). IGI Global. DOI: 10.4018/978-1-7998-4240-8.ch004

Lakumarapu, S., Nithyanandhan, R., Bhargavi, V. S., Anish, T. P., & Nalini, M. (2024, August). Machine Learning Approaches for Liver Disease Prediction: A Comparative Analysis. In *2024 5th International Conference on Electronics and Sustainable Communication Systems (ICESC)* (pp. 159-164). IEEE. DOI: 10.1109/ICESC60852.2024.10689974

Luan, H., & Tsai, C. C. (2021). A review of using machine learning approaches for precision education. *Journal of Educational Technology & Society*, *24*(1), 250–266.



Luan, H., & Tsai, C. C. (2021). A review of using machine learning approaches for precision education. *Journal of Educational Technology & Society*, *24*(1), 250–266.

Munir, H., Vogel, B., & Jacobsson, A. (2022). Artificial intelligence and machine learning approaches in digital education: A systematic revision. *Information (Basel)*, *13*(4), 203. DOI: 10.3390/info13040203

Prabha, D., Subramanian, R. S., Dinesh, M. G., & Girija, P. (2024). Sustainable Farming Through AI-Enabled Precision Agriculture. In *Artificial Intelligence for Precision Agriculture* (pp. 159–182). Auerbach Publications. DOI: 10.1201/9781003504900-8

Sreelakshmi, S., Babu, A. A., Lakshmipriya, C., Gracious, L. A., Nalini, M., & Subramanian, R. S. (2024, October). Enhancing Intrusion Detection Systems with Machine Learning. In *2024 2nd International Conference on Self Sustainable Artificial Intelligence Systems (ICSSAS)* (pp. 557-564). IEEE. DOI: 10.1109/ICSSAS64001.2024.10760341

Subha, S., Balakrishnan, C., & Anish, T. P. (2024, August). Optimizing Machine Learning Algorithms for Heart Disease Prediction in Healthcare: A Comparative Study. In 2024 5th International Conference on Electronics and Sustainable Communication Systems (ICESC) (pp. 866-872). IEEE. DOI: 10.1109/ICESC60852.2024.10689877

Tiwari, R. (2023). The integration of AI and machine learning in education and its potential to personalize and improve student learning experiences. *International Journal of Scientific Research in Engineering and Management*, *7*(2). Advance online publication. DOI: 10.55041/IJSREM17645

# Chapter 11
# Machine Learning and Management Education:
## A Pathway to Sustainability

**Tanya Chouhan**
https://orcid.org/0000-0002-2644-7033
*Galgotias College of Engineering and Technology, India*

**Avinash Chopra**
https://orcid.org/0000-0003-0273-0800
*SRM Institute of Science and Technology, India*

## ABSTRACT

*This paper examines the integration of Artificial Intelligence (AI) and Machine Learning (ML) in management education, enhancing learning methodologies while aligning with sustainable development goals (SDG) 4, 9, and 12 promoting sustainability-driven educational practices and innovation. Data has been collected by use of semi-structured interviews with 60 participants by using thematic analysis to find essential patterns in gathered datasets. Individual learning requirements and their corresponding educational outcomes receive enhanced benefit from AI-powered adaptive education which increases inclusion levels. The combination of sustainable projects with artificial intelligence technology helps students develop data-oriented solution techniques which they use to solve real-life challenges linked to SDG 12. The emerged need for ethical guidelines has been addressed for both privacy risks for data and automatic decision-making bias problems. Academic partnerships between higher education and industry entities became vital because they enabled both innovation and hands-on training.*

DOI: 10.4018/979-8-3373-2150-9.ch011

## 1. INTRODUCTION

Sustainability, a strategic priority globally, is reimagining the training of future managers to ensure ethical and effective decision-making in complex environments (Böhm et al., 2022; McPhail et al., 2024). This pressing issue across the globe is making the educatioinal system to possess relevant skills to address these problems (Glavič, 2020; Miao & Nduneseokwu, 2024). Within this notion, the integration of machine learning (ML) into management education has paved a transformative pathway to achieving the Sustainable Development Goals (SDGs). ML, equipped with the ability to analyze large datasets and detect complex patterns, empowers innovative solutions for sustainability-related problems.

Within educational settings, ML supports the personalization of learning experiences, enhances administrative processes, and augments data-driven decision-making (Alsbou & Alsaraireh, 2024). These submissions not only improve learning outcomes but also support sustainable educational practices by curtailing waste, energy consumption, and inefficiencies. Research indicates that game-based education proves effective as an instructive method to deliver sustainability management instruction. Educational games that imitate real-life situations allow students to apply their decision-making abilities and risk-management skills in safe virtual settings which results in better sustainability competencies (Jääskä et al., 2021; Novaes, 2025).

Using experimental learning methods within the educational framework improve both students' engagement and educational performance (Salinas-Navarro, Palma-Mendoza, et al., 2024). Furthermore, as higher education undergoes rapid digital transformation, the role of ML becomes even more critical. Universities and business schools are leveraging ML not only to digitize content but also to monitor learning analytics, measure carbon footprints of digital platforms, and evaluate the social impact of educational technologies (Khan et al., 2025; Zou et al., 2024). However, the sustainable integration of these technologies requires careful alignment with pedagogical values and ethical guidelines.

Despite growing interest, existing research lacks an integrative framework that explains how ML can simultaneously enhance management education and foster sustainability outcomes (Kioupi & Voulvoulis, 2019; Li et al., 2023; Warburton, 2003). Prior studies often focus on either ML in education or sustainability in isolation, with limited intersectional analysis. There is also a paucity of empirical research on how ML-driven pedagogy impacts students' sustainability mindset, behavioral change, and long-term competencies in responsible leadership. While individual strands of literature explore either the role of AI/ML in education or sustainability in management education, there is a lack of integrated studies that explore ML as a pedagogical and operational tool for embedding sustainability into management education (Abdulmuhsin et al., 2025; Viera Trevisan et al., 2024). Moreover, empirical evidence on how ML-driven interventions influence sustainability mindsets, competencies, or organizational change in educational institutions remains scarce.

Furthermore, the digital transformation of higher education necessitates sustainable management practices. Educational institutions that implement new technologies need to evaluate both environmental and social consequences that result from their transformations. Researchers indicate a rising interest in sustainable management during digital transformation since sustainability needs incorporated into education technology development (Abad-Segura et al., 2020).

The convergence between machine learning and management education provides sustainability opportunities through enhanced educational practices, superior sustainability assessment, and innovative educational techniques. Education institutions must integrate machine learning because it stands essential to training students to solve future sustainability problems. This study aims to bridge that gap by exploring the convergence between machine learning and management education as a holistic strategy to promote sustainable development. Specifically, it investigates how ML can support curriculum innovation, sustainability assessment, and transformative learning models in business schools, ultimately preparing students to become sustainability-focused leaders of the future.

## 2. LITERATURE REVIEW

### 2.1. Historical Overview of Technological Advancements in Education

The integration of digital technologies in education has undeniably revolutionized teaching and learning processes worldwide. However, this technological progress has also exacerbated the global digital divide, particularly between developed and developing regions. The post-2021 period saw an unprecedented surge in educational technology (EdTech) adoption driven by the COVID-19 pandemic, significantly accelerating the use of hybrid and remote learning models (Alrefaee et al., 2025; Laifa et al., 2024). A significant number of educational institutions in low- and middle-income countries continue to face challenges such as limited internet infrastructure, inadequate access to digital devices, and insufficient digital literacy among teachers and students (UNESCO, 2023). Education underwent major expansion during the twentieth century because of technological progress. Electronic technology significantly benefited education upon the introduction of film radio and television through its innovative educational practices along with student engagement methods (Schindler et al., 2017). Students experienced fundamental educational development through computers because these devices granted them unlimited access to information alongside innovative educational frameworks (Gikas & Grant, 2013).

The Industrial Revolution 4.0 (IR 4.0) unites AI and communication platforms to generate educational progress and educational obstacles for learning institutions. Contemporary situations demand the evaluation of traditional educational methods because they need to adjust to the modern technological environment (Kinshuk et al., 2016). The successful adoption of advanced technologies such as AI and ML in education relies not only on infrastructure but also on robust policy frameworks and institutional readiness. Across the globe, governments and educational bodies are introducing strategic initiatives to embrace Education 4.0. For instance, India's National Education Policy (NEP) 2020 explicitly supports the integration of AI, machine learning, and data science into higher education curricula to foster innovation and employability. Emerging technologies such as virtual reality (VR), the metaverse, and immersive environments are being explored as next-generation educational tools, enhancing experiential learning (Kayyali, 2024; Kozinets, 2023). Learning Analytics and Adaptive Learning Systems have become pivotal components of Education 4.0, allowing institutions to dynamically tailor learning content. The European Union's Digital Education Action Plan (2021–2027) emphasizes enhancing digital literacy, investing in digital infrastructure, and promoting open educational resources (European Commission, 2021). The provision of contemporary technologies enables better teaching-learning experiences through their delivery of state-of-the-art educational tools as well as technological platforms that serve both teachers and learners (Haleem et al., 2022a).

For instance, during the COVID-19 pandemic, while students in high-income countries transitioned to hybrid or fully online models with relative ease, millions of learners in sub-Saharan Africa, South Asia, and parts of Latin America experienced prolonged learning disruptions due to technological limitations (OECD, 2022). This divide poses a major threat to the inclusivity goal of SDG 4, which emphasizes equal access to quality education. Bridging this gap is imperative for any technology-led management education initiative to be truly sustainable and globally impactful.

## 2.2. Role of AI and ML in Management Education

As sustainability becomes central to business strategies worldwide, management education must go beyond traditional knowledge delivery and focus on equipping students with practical competencies aligned with the SDGs. AI and ML have accelerated changes shaping the educational environment for enhancing instructional processes and student learning. This amalgamation enables administrative support with the help of adaptive learning systems for detecting learning styles automatically (Ezzaim et al., 2024). These educational technologies deliver strong outcomes to facilitate academic success. AI technologies help university administrators to automate procedures and improve their decision-making abilities in facing educational growth (Haleem et al., 2022b; Wang, 2021). Recent frameworks map AI/ML applications directly to AACSB and other accreditation learning standards, fostering competency-driven education (Zhang & Patel, 2022). AI-enabled mentorship systems and virtual career counselors are increasingly used in business schools to offer real-time guidance and skill recommendations.

Recent empirical studies illustrate how leading business schools are already leveraging AI and ML to enhance curriculum delivery, decision-making, and personalized learning pathways. For example, Harvard Business School has incorporated machine learning into its executive education modules through simulations that analyze stakeholder behavior and sustainability trade-offs (Harvard Online, 2022). Similarly, INSEAD uses AI-powered learning analytics to track learner engagement and tailor content in its digital strategy and operations courses. In India, IIM Bangalore launched AI-based learning platforms to support case-based pedagogy during the pandemic, which allowed faculty to dynamically adjust teaching strategies based on real-time student feedback (IIMB Case Centre, 2023). AI and ML act as educational transformational technologies because they create platforms that meet student needs better and accelerate teaching delivery times (Mishra, 2024). Case-based and experiential learning modules embedded with AI simulations have demonstrated improved learning retention and strategic thinking skills (Salinas-Navarro, Vilalta-Perdomo, et al., 2024). Agarwal (2023) explained how education changes teaching practices while implementing smart educational systems through AI integration. Scholars increasingly advocate for curriculum revisions that include ethics of algorithmic decision-making, transparency, and bias mitigation. AI education technology will achieve full implementation once data privacy concerns and AI system complexity problems are resolved to handle present difficulties (Chan, 2023; Luan et al., 2020). Educational acceptance of AI and ML stands at a high level as institutions seek to create personalized effective educational systems that need active research development (Strielkowski et al., 2025). These initiatives help close the skills gap and ensure future managers are not only tech-savvy but also ethically competent in deploying AI for inclusive and sustainable growth.

## 2.3. AI and ML in Management Education Led to Sustainability

AI-driven education promotes personalized, flexible, and sustainable learning experiences through adaptive systems (Strielkowski et al., 2025). AI/ML technologies enable educational fields to develop permanent educational systems through individualized learning programs that benefit from these capabilities. Through adaptive learning tools, AI supports sustainable development because it offers flexible educational programs that education systems can access conveniently (Isaeva et al., 2025). AI/ML technology operates on educational platforms by processing extensive educational data to discover individual student traits for developing curriculum suggestions and tailored long-term educational programs (López-Meneses et al., 2025). The deployment of personal learning AI technologies depends on effective privacy protection measures as well as bias elimination strategies and sufficient educator training standards.

Data-driven instruction enhances learning outcomes and teaching quality (Angeioplastis et al., 2025). A transformative change happened in education when data-driven instructional strategies were adopted because they utilize analytics data for better educational outcomes and teaching operational choices. Data-approach evaluation tools allow teachers to create personalized teaching strategies for different student learning needs resulting in both cognitive development and social-emotional growth at the beginning of language and literacy acquisition (Tafrihah et al., 2024). Educational strategies that use data to transform course operations while creating tutoring systems prove effective at improving student achievement numbers (Ateş, 2025). Through data-driven methods in educational mathematics, the establishment of learning spaces becomes possible leading to enhanced educational quality within accessible platforms for students (Isaeva et al., 2025). Academic success along with future student development emerges from data-based educational approaches used in person-centered educational delivery.

AI/ML support SDG 4 by improving educational access, personalization, and equity. The application of AI together with ML delivers essential educational improvements alongside broader inclusivity in business studies for achieving quality education. AI technology boosts educational practices by addressing individual learning requirements and helping educators with their teaching activities to establish a fair and inclusive education system (Yadav, 2025). The implementation of EdTech frameworks in education strives to achieve accessibility for all students by enhancing test performance primarily among members of minority groups and distant learners (Costan et al., 2021; Strielkowski et al., 2025). Despite implementation hurdles, AI represents a transformative educational system that develops modern teaching practices that fulfill the range of student learning demands thus aiding SDG 4 (Strielkowski et al., 2025; Yadav, 2025).

Educational institutions should implement joint education-industry practices for innovation as part of SDG 9. SDG 9 aligns with management education through industry-academia innovation partnerships (Arya et al., 2025). A strong research and business technology application platform emerges from industry-academia integration to promote both quality research and technological business applications thus driving organizational innovation and growth (S. C. et al., 2025). The innovation field recognizes University-industry collaborations (UIC) as primary tools that move information between academic and industrial domains to satisfy the changing needs of educational and industrial groups. Strategic alignment between these collaborations improves their success while cognitive expertise together with trust-based relationships and operational compatibility function as essential elements for successful partnerships (Dwivedi & Sharma, 2025).

These education-industry cooperative practices support both SDG 9 and sustainable development's main goal by teaching students how to interact with and contribute innovations to their industries. The alignment of educational institutions enables them to support effectively the sustainable development and innovative industrial practice establishment. SDG 12 promotes responsible consumption and production as core learning in management education (Novaes, 2025). Higher education institutions should maintain their essential duty to incorporate sustainability principles into educational programs because these programs provide leadership training needed for solving worldwide challenges. Educational professionals choose to prioritize environmental SDG elements above other fundamental social economic and governance aspects primarily because the SDG targets are complex. According to Greenland (2023) the implementation of all central aspects represents essential elements in achieving complete environmental management education. The implementation of AI vehicles in educational pursuit results in superior student learning outcomes by providing actual sustainability practice through interactive educational methods. The combination of hands-on learning approaches and arts and crafts activities in instruction demonstrates effective performance for teaching students about their SDG 12 contributions. Participation in cost-related sustainability projects enables students to gain a comprehensive about responsible consumption and production behaviors (Delacroix 2023). Students gain better comprehension about SDGs particularly SDG 12 through actively participating in service-based learning initiatives which concentrate on 2030 Agenda values.

The implementation of SDG 12 within management education through AI-based projects and new educational strategies helps students develop abilities to support sustainable development. Higher education institutions can effectively support the SDGs through sustained learning programs that handle aspects from environmental protection to social development and economic stability.

*Table 1. Review of Literature*

| Author(s) & Year | Focus Area | Methodology | Key Findings | Relevance to Study |
|---|---|---|---|---|
| Li (2023) | Historical Tech Advancements | Historical Review | Printing press revolutionized access to education. | Shows the foundational role of tech in educational expansion. |
| Ghory (2021) | ICT & Computers | Thematic Analysis | ICT transformed teaching and learning methods. | Bridges traditional and digital learning environments. |
| Gunana (2022) | Modern EdTech Tools | Literature Review | Tech tools enhance both teaching delivery and student access. | Supports tech-integration relevance in current education. |
| Essa (2023) | AI in Learning Systems | Empirical Study | Adaptive systems improve outcomes via personalized learning. | Validates AI's role in learner-centric education. |
| Chatterjee (2020) | AI in Administration | Case Analysis | AI automates tasks and supports decision-making. | Ties AI to sustainable institutional processes. |
| Maghsudi (2021) | AI & Predictive Analytics | Quantitative Study | Predictive modeling supports student performance tracking. | Links ML to personalized education design. |
| Artyukhov (2024) | SDG 4 - Quality Education | Policy Review | AI improves inclusivity and accessibility in education. | Aligns AI deployment with SDG 4 targets. |
| Costa (2023) | EdTech Accessibility | Impact Evaluation | Enhances equity for marginalized or remote learners. | Supports inclusive education policy framing. |
| Almaida (2023) | SDG 9 - Industry Collaboration | Case Synthesis | University-industry linkages boost innovation and research. | Shows how management education links to innovation infrastructure. |
| Delacroix (2023) | SDG 12 - Sustainability Practice | Experimental Study | Project-based learning instills responsible consumption values. | Promotes hands-on sustainability education. |
| Abimbola (2024) | AI Ethics | Ethical Framework Review | Bias, transparency, and fairness are critical in AI application. | Addresses the ethical dimension of tech in education. |
| Dolo (2024) | Infrastructure Gaps | Mixed Methods | Limited digital resources hinder effective AI implementation in schools. | Frames accessibility and infrastructure as barriers to tech adoption. |

Source: Author's own

## 2.4. Ethical and Practical Challenges

The education sector implements AI/ML while facing numerous ethical problems that need proper management for fair education implementation. The main issue arises from algorithmic bias which tends to reinforce current social inequalities unless proper intervention is applied. Frameworks such as the UNESCO Recommendation on the Ethics of AI (2021) and the EU's Ethics Guidelines emphasize fairness, inclusivity, and transparency. Educational institutions must integrate these global principles to ensure that AI systems serve learners equitably and uphold student autonomy. AI systems should maintain transparency with accountability because it remains crucial to prevent biases when ensuring fairness in educational outcomes (Memarian & Doleck, 2023).

Educational data privacy together with security concerns emerges as critical challenges because AI systems analyze huge student data collections. Protecting student data requires strong policies which must be implemented to maintain privacy standards (Brown & Klein, 2020; Reidenberg & Schaub, 2018). The use of AI technologies introduces ethical questions about their influence on the way AI tools shift the traditional teacher-student interaction. Additionally, recent studies highlight that many educators face a digital trust gap, expressing uncertainty toward AI-generated feedback and job displacement concerns. These challenges necessitate faculty training programs, co-governance of AI tools, and transparent algorithmic design to build confidence and capacity (Startari, 2025). The learning potential of AI exists through personalization but teachers should maintain a primary role in education because these tools need to supplement human interaction for students to engage socially (Reiss 2021, Abimbola et. Al 2024, & Johnson et. Al 2023). Al 2024 & Johnson et. Al 2023).

Education ethics regarding AI implementation must preserve student autonomy together with their capacity to make decisions independently Furthermore, algorithmic bias often stems from data training sets that fail to represent diverse geographies, languages, and socio-economic contexts, which risks marginalizing non-Western and rural learners. AI models must be co-developed with diverse stakeholder input to ensure fairness in representation and output (Haleem et al., 2022a; Trajkovski, 2024). A multidisciplinary group should establish complete ethical frameworks and standards that instruct responsible AI utilization within educational environments (Fu & Weng, 2024; Nguyen et al., 2023). Through purposeful engagement with these ethical elements' stakeholders achieve the beneficial elements of AI in education and protect from adverse effects to create equitable and inclusive learning capabilities (Díaz-Rodríguez et al., 2023; Nguyen et al., 2023). Several practical obstacles exist which include insufficient educational hardware and insufficient training for instructors.

Education faces substantial obstacles because of insufficient infrastructure together with insufficient trainer preparation among different educational settings. In response, initiatives like the World Bank's EdTech Hub, UNICEF's Giga Project, and Africa's Digital Schools Network aim to bridge infrastructure gaps through scalable, culturally adaptive, and affordable solutions. Sustainable AI deployment must align with such global efforts to ensure educational equity and long-term access. Online STEM teaching meets significant barriers because of broken digital infrastructure and insufficient digital know-how among both students and teachers making education delivery ineffective. Inclusive education faces significant problems due to training inadequate for teachers as well as limited adapted infrastructure which negatively affects students' academic success and their social-emotional development (Reicher, 2010). Developing economies encounter two main obstacles to Education 4.0 implementation which stem from not having adequate training resources together with insufficient technological resources (Akinradewo et al., 2025; Costan et al., 2021). The student community needs extensive instructor training and improved school facilities to establish an environment that enables proper educational services in all learning institutions.

## 3. METHODOLOGY

### 3.1. Research Design

A qualitative method guided the research investigation of AI and ML technologies in management education. The leading research target revolved around gathering genuine stories from students and teaching staff together with administration personnel in educational institutions about their use of these technologies. Data collection for this research involved using classroom observation and semi-structured interviews as main methodologies.

### 3.2. Data Collection Methods

#### 3.2.1. Semi-Structured Interviews

Three respondent groups consisting of students and educators and educational administrators participated in semi-structured interview sessions. Research included interviews with 60 participants who were divided between the mentioned groups (Table 2).

*Table 2. List of interviewees*

| Respondents | Number |
|---|---|
| Students | 20 |
| Educators | 20 |
| Educational Administrators | 20 |

Source: **Author's own**

### 3.2.2. Interview Process is given below in Table 3.

*Table 3. Format of the interview process*

| Format | The interviews followed individual sessions of 45 minutes duration. |
|---|---|
| Question type | The interview questions remained open-ended to permit natural viewpoints from interviewees. |
| Key focus Area | The interview focused on three main aspects: AI personalized education, ethical AI problems and sustainability initiatives in educational practice. |
| Objective | The objectives of this study include examining AI and ML technological effects on schooling while analysing newly emerged sustainability initiatives and AI-based tool ethical complications. |
| Data Collection approach | The approach for collecting data involved permitting participants to submit personal anecdotes and practical examples which created more detailed qualitative information. |
| Outcome | Diverse collection methods enabled researchers to identify key patterns about educational advantages and drawbacks as well as ethical and implementation challenges of integrating AI and ML in educational systems. |

Source: **Author's own**

## 3.3. Data Analysis

The graphical representation of AI and ML effects on management education displays five sections using a pie chart. The AI/ML Technologies segment stands as the biggest component at 25% which demonstrates the core importance of these technologies in educational development during modern times. These technologies form the foundation through which organizations execute automation and perform data-based choices and predictive analytical operations in educational settings.

The 60% of the chart features three equal sections that show Personalized Learning followed by Sustainability in Education (SDG 12) then Industry Collaboration (SDG 9). The learning environment benefits from AI since it offers individualized educational activities that deliver assessment tests which adjust to student abilities and instant performance feedback. The focus of Sustainable Education on education institutions involves AI applications to manage resources effectively and reduce waste as well as promote responsible consumption practices. Industry Collaboration represents AI's functions to build academic-business partnerships which create functional learning programs and creates spaces for innovative work.

Ethical Considerations encompasses 15% of the scope and examines the issues that AI presents like data privacy problems along with biased decision systems and necessary proper AI management for education.

The comprehensive chart represents a fair overview of AI and ML's transformative power on the education of management that combines digital progress with responsible application methods (see Figure 1).

*Figure 1. Impact of AI & ML on Management Education*

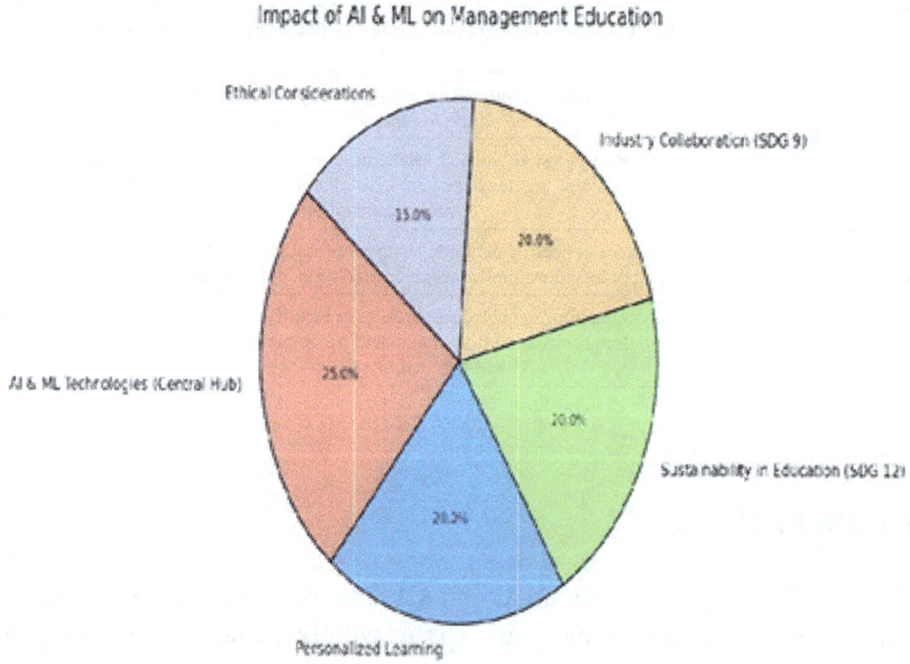

## 3.4. Findings

The research analysis through thematic methods discovered main themes about AI and ML applications in management education. Personalized Learning became the primary finding throughout the study because AI tools provided individualized learning routes which helped students with adaptive testing and immediate feedback improving their educational experiences. AI-Assisted Teaching Strategies enabled instructors to use analytics-driven by AI to create personalized learning materials and automated processes for administrative work as well as deliver customized assistance for students. AI-powered tools were used for Green Management purposes to maximize sustainability projects and business resource efficiency and environmental preservation in studies.

*Table 4. Emerging themes from the interview*

| Variables | Theme Identified | Explanation |
|---|---|---|
| Learning Experience | Personalized learning | AI-driven tools enabled customized learning paths, adaptive assessments, and real-time feedback, enhancing student engagement and comprehension. |
| Teaching Strategies | AI-Assisted | Educators used AI-driven analytics to tailor lessons, automate administrative tasks, and provide targeted support. |
| Sustainability Initiatives | AI for green management | AI-powered tools facilitated sustainability-focused projects, such as optimizing resource usage and promoting eco-friendly business strategies. |
| Ethical Concern | Data Privacy issues | Concerns emerged about the security of student data, potential misuse, and algorithmic bias in decision-making. |
| Implementation challenges | Technological Barriers | Limited access to AI infrastructure, lack of training for educators, and resistance to technology integration posed challenges. |

**Source:** Author's own

Major ethical challenges emerged owing to student data protection privacy issues as well as algorithmic bias and poor protection of students' information systems in academic decision-making AI applications. Implementation challenges were common among most organizations due to technological barriers that involved limited access to AI infrastructure and poor training of teachers along with technological user resistance (see Figure 2).

*Figure 2. Participants Perspective on AI in Management Education*

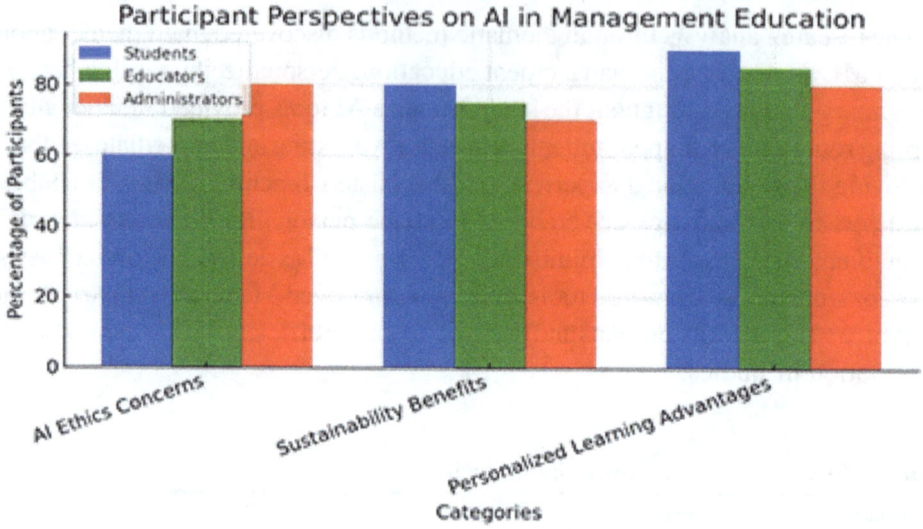


All interviews revealed how Artificial Intelligence transforms the educational landscape in business institutions. Students indicated their positive attitude toward AI-based personalized learning because this system adapted education to match their individual study speed and understanding levels. The academic community viewed AI teaching technology as an effective system that conducts administrative activities and generates personalized learning plans for learners. AI inclusion was an administrative action to promote organizational effectiveness and sustainability based on institutional guidance. Organizations often conveyed their concern for the security of AI systems in addition to their scepticism about non-bias AI processes and digital access hurdles which prompted them to demand ethics guidance and policy development.

The research results reveal that AI and ML bring considerable advancements in management learning by stimulating custom-based training along with environmental project support and optimization of school activities. Implementation barriers along with ethical considerations hinder full integration of AI. Managers face barriers while adopting AI technologies due to the need to ensure proper deployment of these technologies.

*Figure 3. Advantages to Management education through AI/ML*

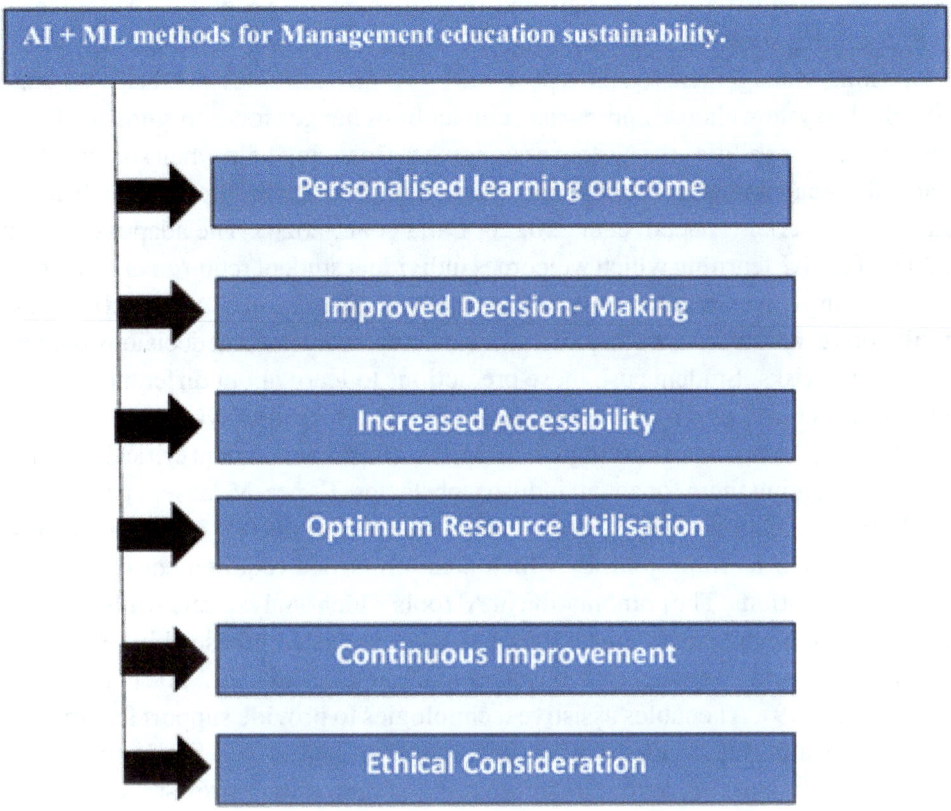


*Source: Author's Own*

## 4. DISCUSSION

Management training systems clasp a critical position in building future organizational leaders and decision-makers. As organizations transforms its operations in response to technological changes in conjunction with environmental needs and global developments, hence management instruction needs to change accordingly (Angeioplastis et al., 2025; Costan et al., 2021). Management education demonstrates sustainability when it supports prolonged beneficial educational experiences which directly match current industry needs. Management education benefits greatly from AI and ML through personalized education delivery to students. Education systems that use traditional classrooms serve students using standardized teaching approaches that do not fulfil distinct educational requirements. Assets from adaptive learning systems process student results with their activities to deliver personalized educational content and testing materials and recommendation programs (Akinradewo et al., 2025; Kinshuk et al., 2016).

Learning Management Systems powered by AI provide assessments for students that help the system choose appropriate curriculum changes for each student. Due to its analytical capabilities the system assigns extra financing help when students find financial management hard but shows marketing aptitude by providing advanced marketing material (Haleem et al., 2022b; Laifa et al., 2024). The adaptive system enables effective learning which welcomes individual student requirements to boost understanding and maintain memory retention. The application of AI-based business simulations gives students a chance to address actual management decisions without facing actual risks. Students use these predictions to learn about different business strategy consequences through ML-based outcome forecasting systems. An experiential learning environment through this approach improves student critical thinking along with training them for actual industry obstacles (López-Meneses et al., 2025).

AI-powered data analytic systems enable students to decode intricate business data during their learning journey which is an important requirement for modern managerial positions. The combination of AI tools which analyze data while spotting patterns enables students to create data-based decisions and these abilities remain vital for success in contemporary business markets (Jääskä et al., 2021; Kioupi & Voulvoulis, 2019). AI enables assistive technologies to provide support for students who have disabilities. Students who are visually impaired and hearing impaired can take part in learning activities through the combination of text-to-speech and speech-to-text applications. Prediction functions as well as smart predictive tools through AI help students with disabilities effectively study educational materials (Reidenberg & Schaub, 2018; Salinas-Navarro, Palma-Mendoza, et al., 2024; Tafrihah et al., 2024).

AI-powered online education platforms provide flexible management education options to students. IT-driven educational platforms assist working students through adaptable and interactive material delivery systems which adapt to their work schedules. The ability to learn at any age represents a central aspect of sustainable education because of system flexibility.

Development programs in education encounter obstacles because of how education budgets are used up in terms of teaching personnel allocation and space accommodations along with monetary limitations. AI and ML systems maximize the use of resources which leads to educational sustainability (Miao & Nduneseokwu, 2024; Yadav, 2025).

AI administrative systems speed up the management workflow by handling scheduling and assessment and student data analysis tasks. The implementation of automated grading systems frees instructors to provide guidance and interactive teaching because they reduce teacher workload (Díaz-Rodríguez et al., 2023). AI scheduling systems institutions optimize how they distribute classrooms and teachers effectively thus maximizing their resource efficiency.

Through predictive analytical methods based on AI institutions gain improved student enrolment projection abilities that guide resource distribution and academies of study design output. The system safeguards institutions against wasting money on empty courses while maintaining courses that support industry requirements. Among the criteria of sustainable management education stands the need for outstanding adaptability to retain its value. The combination of AI and ML allows educational institutions to achieve curriculum enhancements through the evaluation of student feedback as well as learning patterns from both students and industry trends.

The contributions of AI and ML to sustaining management education need evaluation regarding ethical matters. There are important matters concerning data privacy and algorithmic bias and digital divide distribution that need proper supervision (Abad-Segura et al., 2020; Akinradewo et al., 2025). Schools need to create strong data protection rules which will protect student information from security threats. AI algorithms need to prevent discrimination through the use of algorithmic decision-making processes built on diverse fundamental data sets.

Higher education institutions need to invest in cost-effective AI-developed learning solutions and give students and faculty proper training regarding technology effectiveness. The long-term sustainability requires complete accessibility for everyone to receive AI-powered education.

*Table 5. AI/ML contributions to SDG 4, 9, and 12.*

| Sustainable Development Goal (SDG) | How AI/ML Contribute |
|---|---|
| SDG 4 – Quality Education | - Enhances learning by tailoring lessons to individual students' needs.<br>- Makes education more inclusive with tools like language translation and accessibility features for students with disabilities.<br>- Helps educators track student progress and identify learning gaps early for better support. |
| SDG 9 – Industry, Innovation, and Infrastructure | - Bridges the gap between universities and industries by integrating real-world applications into education.<br>- Supports research and innovation by providing advanced data analysis and predictive insights.<br>- Automates routine tasks in educational institutions, improving efficiency and resource allocation. |
| SDG 12 – Responsible Consumption and Production | - Encourages sustainable practices in education by optimizing energy use and reducing waste.<br>- Helps businesses and students develop environmentally friendly strategies through data-driven insights.<br>- Provides interactive learning experiences to teach responsible resource management and ethical decision-making. |

**Source:** Author's own

The table reveals AI and ML skills that help to achieve SDGs 4, 9 and 12 through educational developments and industry partnership.

Future leaders graduating from management educational systems inhibiting passion to transform others and creating innovative practices will lead to effective and sustainable business progress. The alignment between the SDGs with management education creates graduates who deliver substantial contributions to global progress towards sustainable development and inclusiveness alongside technological innovation.

## 5. IMPLICATIONS

The current research builds upon current theories regarding educational technology by proving that AI and ML not only augment personalized learning but also incorporate sustainability concepts in line with SDGs 4, 9, and 12. The results theoretically fill the gap between sustainable education models and technological innovation, showing how adaptive systems powered by AI promote data-driven problem-solving competencies crucial for sustainable development. The study adds to collaboration theories by highlighting the contribution of university-industry alliances toward co-creation of knowledge and experiential learning in practices that make management education more relevant and sustainable. The research provides theoretical basis for integrating ethical issues into AI-driven education, deepening debates about algorithmic bias and ethical technology adoption within educational contexts.

Learning institutions must invest in adaptive learning systems facilitated by AI and ML that adapt curricula to the specific needs of every student to enhance learning outcomes and engagement towards sustainable objectives. Universities and management programs are encouraged to foster partnerships with industry to co-develop curricula and provide hands-on training that connects theoretical knowledge with real-world sustainable business practices. Policymakers and curriculum designers need to integrate AI-driven methodologies and sustainability content to prepare students for future managerial roles that emphasize responsible decision-making and innovation for sustainable development. Institutions must establish ethical frameworks and governance policies to mitigate risks such as algorithmic bias, ensuring fairness, transparency, and inclusivity in AI-based educational interventions. Training faculty members on AI and ML tools and their sustainable applications is critical to maximize the benefits of these technologies in delivering effective management education.

## 6. LIMITATIONS AND RECOMMENDATIONS FOR FUTURE RESEARCH

This study has several limitations that provide opportunities for future research. Firstly, the qualitative design, while rich in insights, limits the generalizability of the findings across different educational contexts and geographical regions. Future research could adopt a mixed-methods or large-scale quantitative approach to validate and extend the current findings. Additionally, the focus on AI and ML implementation within management education institutions may not fully capture the nuances of other disciplines or levels of education, suggesting that further studies could explore the impact of these technologies in diverse academic fields or vocational training programs. Another limitation is the relatively small sample size of 60 participants, which may not represent the broader population of educators, students, and administrators involved in AI-driven education.

Subsequent studies must also explore the long-term implications of AI and ML adoption on student learning achievements and professional success, and how these technologies impact institutional sustainability practices after some time. There is a need to explore the ethical concerns in depth, including measures to address algorithmic bias and provide equitable access to AI-enacted educational materials. In addition, examining the potential role of new technologies, including augmented reality and blockchain, in supporting AI and ML for sustainable education may offer interesting insights. In total, future research might be directed toward creating holistic frameworks that support the responsible and sustainable implementation of AI and ML in education to enhance their beneficial contributions to learners and society.

## 7. CONCLUSION

The findings of the study have qualitatively examined how AI and ML is transforming management educational system which is enhancing personalized learning, promoting sustainability and leading towards achievement of SDGs. The integration of these technologies in our educational system will cater diverse student requirements, thus supporting SDG 4 which presses on providing quality education through inclusive and targeted approaches. Tools powered by AI-technology helps educators in detecting individual learning challenges and helps in creating tailored solutions fostering active student engagement and problem-solving. By integrating sustainability-focused projects into the curriculum, students gain real-world competencies that contribute to SDG 12. Industry-academia collaborations are crucial for bridging theoretical learning with practical applications. This collaboration exposes students to use real-life cases assisted by AI/ML enabling them to provide innovative and reliable solutions that support SDG 9.

However, the ethical implementation of AI is critical. This is unearthed through the qualitative analysis of the previous research findings which emphasizes the importance of addressing data privacy, algorithmic bias, and accountability. Institutions must establish pure ethical guidelines and integrate AI education to guarantee responsible use and substitute decision-making skills. Continuous specialized growth for professors is also essential. Educators need to stay updated with developing AI tools and pedagogies to maximize their impact while upholding ethical and sustainable goals in education.

## REFERENCES

Abad-Segura, E., González-Zamar, M.-D., Infante-Moro, J. C., & Ruipérez García, G. (2020). Sustainable Management of Digital Transformation in Higher Education: Global Research Trends. *Sustainability (Basel)*, *12*(5), 2107. DOI: 10.3390/su12052107

Abdulmuhsin, A. A., Alkhwaldi, A. F., Dbesan, A. H., & Tarhini, A. (2025). *Empirical insights on organisational sustainability: Exploring the influence of communities of practice and associated technologies*. Sustainability Accounting, Management and Policy Journal., DOI: 10.1108/SAMPJ-02-2024-0155

Akinradewo, O., Hafez, M., Aliu, J., Oke, A., Aigbavboa, C., & Adekunle, S. (2025). Barriers to the Adoption of Augmented Reality Technologies for Education and Training in the Built Environment: A Developing Country Context. *Technologies*, *13*(2), 62. DOI: 10.3390/technologies13020062

Alrefaee, S., Khan, M., & Alrefaee, Y. M. H. A. (2025). *A Bibliometric Analysis of Online Education Research in India (2014-2024): Trends, Patterns, and Future Directions*. In Review. DOI: 10.21203/rs.3.rs-5830161/v2

Alsbou, M. K. K., & Alsaraireh, R. A. I. (2024). Data-Driven Decision-Making in Education: Leveraging AI for School Improvement. *2024 International Conference on Knowledge Engineering and Communication Systems (ICKECS)*, 1–6. DOI: 10.1109/ICKECS61492.2024.10616616

Angeioplastis, A., Aliprantis, J., Konstantakis, M., & Tsimpiris, A. (2025). Predicting Student Performance and Enhancing Learning Outcomes: A Data-Driven Approach Using Educational Data Mining Techniques. *Computers*, *14*(3), 83. DOI: 10.3390/computers14030083

Arya, V., Saraf, A., Chichkanov, N., Papa, A., & Romano, M. (2025). AI-enhanced competency transfer hubs: A conceptual framework for university-industry engagement and knowledge sharing. *The Journal of Technology Transfer*. Advance online publication. DOI: 10.1007/s10961-025-10233-7

Ateş, H. (2025). Integrating augmented reality into intelligent tutoring systems to enhance science education outcomes. *Education and Information Technologies*, *30*(4), 4435–4470. DOI: 10.1007/s10639-024-12970-y

Böhm, S., Carrington, M., Cornelius, N., De Bruin, B., Greenwood, M., Hassan, L., Jain, T., Karam, C., Kourula, A., Romani, L., Riaz, S., & Shaw, D. (2022). Ethics at the Centre of Global and Local Challenges: Thoughts on the Future of Business Ethics. *Journal of Business Ethics*, *180*(3), 835–861. DOI: 10.1007/s10551-022-05239-2 PMID: 36212626

Brown, M., & Klein, C. (2020). Whose Data? Which Rights? Whose Power? A Policy Discourse Analysis of Student Privacy Policy Documents. *The Journal of Higher Education*, *91*(7), 1149–1178. DOI: 10.1080/00221546.2020.1770045

Chan, C. K. Y. (2023). A comprehensive AI policy education framework for university teaching and learning. *International Journal of Educational Technology in Higher Education*, *20*(1), 38. DOI: 10.1186/s41239-023-00408-3

Costan, E., Gonzales, G., Gonzales, R., Enriquez, L., Costan, F., Suladay, D., Atibing, N. M., Aro, J. L., Evangelista, S. S., Maturan, F., Selerio, E.Jr, & Ocampo, L. (2021). Education 4.0 in Developing Economies: A Systematic Literature Review of Implementation Barriers and Future Research Agenda. *Sustainability (Basel)*, *13*(22), 12763. DOI: 10.3390/su132212763

Díaz-Rodríguez, N., Del Ser, J., Coeckelbergh, M., López De Prado, M., Herrera-Viedma, E., & Herrera, F. (2023). Connecting the dots in trustworthy Artificial Intelligence: From AI principles, ethics, and key requirements to responsible AI systems and regulation. *Information Fusion*, *99*, 101896. DOI: 10.1016/j.inffus.2023.101896

Dwivedi, P. P., & Sharma, D. K. (2025). Performance measures of sustainable development goals using SWI MCDM methods: A case of the Indian states. *International Transactions in Operational Research*, itor.13609. DOI: 10.1111/itor.13609

Ezzaim, A., Dahbi, A., Aqqal, A., & Haidine, A. (2024). AI-based learning style detection in adaptive learning systems: A systematic literature review. *Journal of Computers in Education*. Advance online publication. DOI: 10.1007/s40692-024-00328-9

Fu, Y., & Weng, Z. (2024). Navigating the ethical terrain of AI in education: A systematic review on framing responsible human-centered AI practices. *Computers and Education: Artificial Intelligence*, *7*, 100306. DOI: 10.1016/j.caeai.2024.100306

Gikas, J., & Grant, M. M. (2013). Mobile computing devices in higher education: Student perspectives on learning with cellphones, smartphones & social media. *The Internet and Higher Education*, *19*, 18–26. DOI: 10.1016/j.iheduc.2013.06.002

Glavič, P. (2020). Identifying Key Issues of Education for Sustainable Development. *Sustainability (Basel)*, *12*(16), 6500. DOI: 10.3390/su12166500

Haleem, A., Javaid, M., Qadri, M. A., & Suman, R. (2022a). Understanding the role of digital technologies in education: A review. *Sustainable Operations and Computers, 3*, 275–285. DOI: 10.1016/j.susoc.2022.05.004

Haleem, A., Javaid, M., Qadri, M. A., & Suman, R. (2022b). Understanding the role of digital technologies in education: A review. *Sustainable Operations and Computers, 3*, 275–285. DOI: 10.1016/j.susoc.2022.05.004

Isaeva, R., Karasartova, N., Dznunusnalieva, K., Mirzoeva, K., & Mokliuk, M. (2025). ENHANCING LEARNING EFFECTIVENESS THROUGH ADAPTIVE LEARNING PLATFORMS AND EMERGING COMPUTER TECHNOLOGIES IN EDUCATION. *Jurnal Ilmiah Ilmu Terapan Universitas Jambi, 9*(1), 144–160. DOI: 10.22437/jiituj.v9i1.37967

Jääskä, E., Aaltonen, K., & Kujala, J. (2021). Game-Based Learning in Project Sustainability Management Education. *Sustainability (Basel), 13*(15), 8204. DOI: 10.3390/su13158204

Kayyali, M. (2024). Immersive Technologies: Virtual and Augmented Reality in Higher Education. In Braman, J., Brown, A., & Richards, M. J. (Eds.), (pp. 99–114). Advances in Educational Technologies and Instructional Design. IGI Global., DOI: 10.4018/979-8-3693-1310-7.ch007

Khan, S., Mazhar, T., Shahzad, T., Khan, M. A., Rehman, A. U., Saeed, M. M., & Hamam, H. (2025). Harnessing AI for sustainable higher education: Ethical considerations, operational efficiency, and future directions. *Discover Sustainability, 6*(1), 23. DOI: 10.1007/s43621-025-00809-6

Kinshuk, C., Chen, N.-S., Cheng, I.-L., & Chew, S. W. (2016). Evolution Is not enough: Revolutionizing Current Learning Environments to Smart Learning Environments. *International Journal of Artificial Intelligence in Education, 26*(2), 561–581. DOI: 10.1007/s40593-016-0108-x

Kioupi, V., & Voulvoulis, N. (2019). Education for Sustainable Development: A Systemic Framework for Connecting the SDGs to Educational Outcomes. *Sustainability (Basel), 11*(21), 6104. DOI: 10.3390/su11216104

Kozinets, R. V. (2023). Immersive netnography: A novel method for service experience research in virtual reality, augmented reality and metaverse contexts. *Journal of Service Management, 34*(1), 100–125. DOI: 10.1108/JOSM-12-2021-0481

Laifa, M., Akhrouf, S., Mohdeb, D., & Belazzoug, M. (2024). Satisfaction of students and teachers with blended learning during COVID-19 pandemic: An Algerian case study. *International Journal of Learning Technology*, *19*(3), 273–297. DOI: 10.1504/IJLT.2024.142509

Li, F., Yigitcanlar, T., Nepal, M., Nguyen, K., & Dur, F. (2023). Machine learning and remote sensing integration for leveraging urban sustainability: A review and framework. *Sustainable Cities and Society*, *96*, 104653. DOI: 10.1016/j.scs.2023.104653

López-Meneses, E., Mellado-Moreno, P. C., Gallardo Herrerías, C., & Pelícano-Piris, N. (2025). Educational Data Mining and Predictive Modeling in the Age of Artificial Intelligence: An In-Depth Analysis of Research Dynamics. *Computers*, *14*(2), 68. DOI: 10.3390/computers14020068

Luan, H., Geczy, P., Lai, H., Gobert, J., Yang, S. J. H., Ogata, H., Baltes, J., Guerra, R., Li, P., & Tsai, C.-C. (2020). Challenges and Future Directions of Big Data and Artificial Intelligence in Education. *Frontiers in Psychology*, *11*, 580820. DOI: 10.3389/fpsyg.2020.580820 PMID: 33192896

McPhail, K., Kafouros, M., McKiernan, P., & Cornelius, N. (2024). Reimagining Business and Management as a Force for Good. *British Journal of Management*, *35*(3), 1099–1112. DOI: 10.1111/1467-8551.12846

Memarian, B., & Doleck, T. (2023). Fairness, Accountability, Transparency, and Ethics (FATE) in Artificial Intelligence (AI) and higher education: A systematic review. *Computers and Education: Artificial Intelligence*, *5*, 100152. DOI: 10.1016/j.caeai.2023.100152

Miao, Q., & Nduneseokwu, C. (2024). Advancing Environmental Leadership: Education, Development, and Training. In Q. Miao & C. Nduneseokwu, *Environmental Leadership in a VUCA Era* (pp. 467–538). Springer Nature Singapore. DOI: 10.1007/978-981-96-0324-4_10

Mishra, P. (2024). Revolutionizing Education With AI and ML. In Reddy, C. (Ed.), *M. Ouaissa, M. Ouaissa, H. Lamaazi, M. El Hamlaoui, & K. K* (pp. 53–94). Advances in Educational Technologies and Instructional Design. IGI Global., DOI: 10.4018/979-8-3693-8151-9.ch003

Nguyen, A., Ngo, H. N., Hong, Y., Dang, B., & Nguyen, B.-P. T. (2023). Ethical principles for artificial intelligence in education. *Education and Information Technologies*, *28*(4), 4221–4241. DOI: 10.1007/s10639-022-11316-w PMID: 36254344

Novaes, A. L. (2025). Enhancing sustainability education in higher education through simulation-based learning: Integrating sustainable development goals. *International Journal of Sustainability in Higher Education*. Advance online publication. DOI: 10.1108/IJSHE-08-2024-0571

Reicher, H. (2010). Building inclusive education on social and emotional learning: Challenges and perspectives – a review. *International Journal of Inclusive Education, 14*(3), 213–246. DOI: 10.1080/13603110802504218

Reidenberg, J. R., & Schaub, F. (2018). Achieving big data privacy in education. *Theory and Research in Education, 16*(3), 263–279. DOI: 10.1177/1477878518805308

S. C. V., V. P., A., & Vidhyapriya, P. (2025). Enhancing R&D Success in Entrepreneurship Education With Industry: Academia Collaboration and Simulation Tools. In A. N. Masouras, S. Anastasiadou, G. A. Deirmentzoglou, H. Ph. Sophocleous, & E. E. Anastasopoulou (Eds.), *Integrating Simulation Tools Into Entrepreneurship Education* (pp. 213–238). IGI Global. DOI: 10.4018/979-8-3693-9040-5.ch011

Salinas-Navarro, D. E., Palma-Mendoza, J. A., & Vilalta-Perdomo, E. (2024). Integrating Circular Supply Chains into Experiential Learning: Enhancing Learning Experiences in Higher Education. *Sustainability (Basel), 16*(23), 10789. DOI: 10.3390/su162310789

Salinas-Navarro, D. E., Vilalta-Perdomo, E., Michel-Villarreal, R., & Montesinos, L. (2024). Designing experiential learning activities with generative artificial intelligence tools for authentic assessment. *Interactive Technology and Smart Education, 21*(4), 708–734. DOI: 10.1108/ITSE-12-2023-0236

Schindler, L. A., Burkholder, G. J., Morad, O. A., & Marsh, C. (2017). Computer-based technology and student engagement: A critical review of the literature. *International Journal of Educational Technology in Higher Education, 14*(1), 25. DOI: 10.1186/s41239-017-0063-0

Startari, A. V. (2025). AI, Tell me your protocol: The Intersection of Technology and Humanity in the Era of Big Data. SSRN *Electronic Journal*. DOI: 10.2139/ssrn.5260083

Strielkowski, W., Grebennikova, V., Lisovskiy, A., Rakhimova, G., & Vasileva, T. (2025). AI -driven adaptive learning for sustainable educational transformation. *Sustainable Development (Bradford), 33*(2), 1921–1947. DOI: 10.1002/sd.3221

Tafrihah, U., Utanto, Y., & Pristiwati, R. (2024). Optimizing Digital Literacy Integration in Early Childhood Education: A Case Study of Tarbiyatul Athfal Bulumanis Kidul Kindergarten. *Golden Age: Jurnal Ilmiah Tumbuh Kembang Anak Usia Dini*, *9*(4), 757–770. DOI: 10.14421/jga.2024.94-14

Trajkovski, G. (2024). Bridging the public administration-AI divide: A skills perspective. *Public Administration and Development*, *44*(5), 412–426. DOI: 10.1002/pad.2061

Viera Trevisan, L., Leal Filho, W., & Ávila Pedrozo, E. (2024). Transformative organisational learning for sustainability in higher education: A literature review and an international multi-case study. *Journal of Cleaner Production*, *447*, 141634. DOI: 10.1016/j.jclepro.2024.141634

Wang, Y. (2021). Artificial intelligence in educational leadership: A symbiotic role of human-artificial intelligence decision-making. *Journal of Educational Administration*, *59*(3), 256–270. DOI: 10.1108/JEA-10-2020-0216

Warburton, K. (2003). Deep learning and education for sustainability. *International Journal of Sustainability in Higher Education*, *4*(1), 44–56. DOI: 10.1108/14676370310455332

Yadav, S. (2025). Leveraging AI to Enhance Teaching and Learning in Education: The Role of Artificial Intelligence in Modernizing Classroom Practices. In Basha, J. S., Alade, T. O., Al Khazimi, M. O. A., Vasudevan, R., & Khan, J. B. (Eds.), *Optimizing Research Techniques and Learning Strategies With Digital Technologies* (pp. 211–238). IGI Global., DOI: 10.4018/979-8-3693-7863-2.ch008

Zou, Y., Zhong, N., Chen, Z., & Zhao, W. (2024). Bridging digitalization and sustainability in universities: A Chinese green university initiative in the digital era. *Journal of Cleaner Production*, *469*, 143181. DOI: 10.1016/j.jclepro.2024.143181

Chapter 12

# AI-Driven Business Systems: Pioneering Innovation and Transformation

**Vandana Dubey**
https://orcid.org/0000-0002-0523-1540
*Sagar Institute of Research and Technology, India*

**Kavita Patel**
https://orcid.org/0000-0001-5939-1278
*Ashoka Institute of Technology and Management, India*

**Shikha Singh**
https://orcid.org/0000-0002-3704-7131
*Amity School of Engineering and Technology, Amity University, India*

**Tasneem Jahan**
*Sagar Institute of Research and Technology, India*

**Priti Kumari**
https://orcid.org/0000-0002-5809-2804
*Ashoka Institute of Technology and Management, India*

**Sonam Dubey**
https://orcid.org/0009-0000-1349-7819
*Sagar Institute of Research and Technology, India*

## ABSTRACT

*Artificial Intelligence (AI) is changing how businesses work by automating tasks, improving decision-making, and making operations more efficient. This chapter explains AI's role in business, including key technologies like machine learning, natural language processing, deep learning, and computer vision. AI helps companies analyze large amounts of data, optimize supply chains, manage customer relationships, and improve human resources. However, AI adoption also brings challenges like data privacy issues, algorithmic bias, and cybersecurity risks. Businesses must ensure ethical AI use with proper regulations and security measures. This chapter discusses real-world applications in finance, healthcare, retail, and manufacturing,*

DOI: 10.4018/979-8-3373-2150-9.ch012

*showing how AI improves efficiency and customer satisfaction. Emerging AI trends like generative AI and explainable AI will shape the future of business. Companies that embrace AI-driven innovation will gain a competitive edge. This chapter provides insights into AI's benefits, challenges, and future impact on industries.*

## INTRODUCTION

Artificial Intelligence (AI) is transforming business operations across the world. AI refers to computer systems that can simulate human intelligence, including learning from data, recognizing patterns, making decisions, and improving over time (Russell & Norvig, 2021). Businesses are adopting AI to automate processes, enhance customer interactions, and make better strategic decisions. With the ability to process vast amounts of data quickly, AI helps organizations gain insights that were previously impossible using traditional methods (Davenport & Ronanki, 2018). AI is being used in various business applications. One major area is automation, where AI-driven software performs repetitive tasks, such as processing transactions, managing supply chains, and handling customer service inquiries (Brynjolfsson & McAfee, 2017). Another crucial area is predictive analytics, where AI models analyse past data to predict future trends, helping businesses make proactive decisions. Additionally, AI enhances customer experience through chatbots, virtual assistants, and recommendation systems that personalize services based on user preferences (Brock & Von Wangenheim, 2019).

The integration of AI with business systems is improving efficiency and reducing operational costs. Companies are leveraging machine learning (ML) to optimize inventory, detect fraud, and automate financial reporting (Chui, Manyika & Miremadi, 2018). In marketing, AI-powered tools analyse consumer behaviour to target advertisements more effectively. In healthcare, AI assists in diagnosing diseases and recommending treatments, while in banking, AI-driven fraud detection systems help prevent cybercrime (Jordan & Mitchell, 2015). While AI brings numerous benefits, its adoption also presents challenges. Businesses must address ethical concerns, including data privacy, bias in AI models, and the impact of automation on employment (Binns, 2018). Furthermore, organizations need to invest in training employees and upgrading their technological infrastructure to successfully integrate AI into their operations.

Innovation in AI is revolutionizing industries by enabling businesses to operate more efficiently and competitively. AI-driven innovation involves using intelligent systems to develop new products, services, and business models that drive growth and enhance customer satisfaction (Taddy, 2019). Companies that invest in AI innovation gain a competitive advantage by improving speed, accuracy, and scalability in their operations. One of the major benefits of AI innovation is enhanced decision-making. Traditional decision-making relies on human intuition and historical data, which can be limited. AI-powered systems analyse real-time data, identify patterns, and provide data-driven insights that help businesses make better decisions (McKinsey Global Institute, 2020). For example, financial institutions use AI to assess credit risk and detect fraudulent transactions, reducing losses and improving customer trust.

AI is also driving personalization in business. E-commerce platforms like Amazon and streaming services like Netflix use AI algorithms to recommend products and content based on user preferences (Gentsch, 2019). This personalization improves customer engagement and increases sales. Similarly, AI-driven chatbots and virtual assistants, such as Siri and Alexa, enhance customer service by providing instant responses to queries and automating support tasks. Another significant impact of AI innovation is process optimization. AI helps companies streamline their workflows, reduce waste, and improve productivity. In manufacturing, AI-powered robots perform complex assembly tasks with high precision. In logistics, AI optimizes delivery routes, reducing fuel consumption and improving efficiency (Manyika et al., 2017).

However, AI innovation also poses challenges. The rapid development of AI technologies requires businesses to continuously adapt and upskill their workforce. Additionally, ethical concerns related to AI bias and decision-making transparency need to be addressed to ensure responsible AI use. Companies must implement governance frameworks to monitor AI systems and ensure compliance with regulations. This chapter provides a detailed exploration of AI-driven business systems and their growing impact on various industries. It aims to analyse how artificial intelligence is transforming business operations by automating processes, enhancing decision-making, and improving efficiency across multiple sectors. The chapter also emphasizes the significance of AI-driven innovation, examining both its advantages and the challenges organizations face when implementing AI technologies. By presenting real-world applications, the discussion highlights how AI is being utilized in industries such as finance, healthcare, retail, and logistics, demonstrating its practical benefits and potential for future growth. Additionally, ethical and regulatory considerations, including concerns over data privacy, algorithmic bias, and responsible AI usage, are addressed to ensure a balanced perspective on AI adoption in business. The chapter also explores emerging trends and future developments in AI, offering insights into how technological advancements will continue to shape business strategies.

The discussion extends to various AI applications in business management, marketing, finance, supply chain, and customer service. By offering an in-depth examination of these areas, the chapter helps businesses understand the opportunities and challenges associated with AI integration. A structured approach is followed to ensure clarity and logical flow, beginning with an introduction that outlines the role and importance of AI in business. The foundational concepts of AI, including machine learning, deep learning, and natural language processing, are explained to provide a technical understanding of AI systems. AI-driven innovations in business processes are explored, focusing on automation, predictive analytics, and personalization. The chapter also examines ethical and regulatory challenges, followed by case studies demonstrating AI success across industries. The final sections discuss future trends and provide recommendations for businesses looking to leverage AI effectively. This approach ensures that readers gain a comprehensive understanding of AI's role in modern business systems and how organizations can adopt AI strategies for long-term success.

This chapter aims to provide a comprehensive understanding of how artificial intelligence is transforming modern business systems. It examines the integration of AI technologies into core business functions, highlights innovations in automation and data analytics, and discusses the ethical and regulatory challenges associated with AI adoption. The chapter also presents real-world applications across key industries and evaluates the potential of emerging AI tools in shaping future business strategies. By exploring these dimensions, the objective of this chapter is to equip readers with insights into the opportunities, implications, and strategic considerations of AI-driven business transformation.

## BACKGROUND

### Foundations of Artificial Intelligence in Business Systems

Artificial Intelligence has become an essential part of modern business operations, helping organizations improve efficiency, automate tasks, and make better decisions. Across various industries, AI-driven technologies are transforming traditional business models by enabling automation, predictive analysis, and enhanced customer interactions. Companies are using AI to streamline workflows, extract meaningful insights from data, and offer personalized experiences to customers.

AI-powered business systems rely on advanced technologies such as Machine Learning (ML), Natural Language Processing (NLP), and Deep Learning (DL) to analyse vast amounts of information and generate precise predictions. Machine Learning helps businesses automate processes like fraud detection, recommendation systems, and risk assessment by allowing computers to learn from past data. Natural Language Processing is widely used in virtual assistants, chatbots, and sentiment analysis, enabling businesses to interact with customers more naturally. Deep Learning, a more advanced subset of ML, is responsible for complex tasks such as image recognition, speech processing, and autonomous decision-making.

Over time, AI has evolved significantly and is now deeply integrated into industries like finance, healthcare, retail, and logistics. In banking, AI improves security and fraud detection, while in healthcare, it enhances diagnostics and personalized treatments. In retail, AI-driven recommendation engines suggest products to customers, improving sales and engagement. In supply chain management, AI optimizes inventory levels and demand forecasting, reducing operational inefficiencies.

When comparing AI-driven business models with traditional ones, the advantages of AI become evident. Traditional businesses rely on manual processes, which are often time-consuming and prone to human errors. In contrast, AI-driven systems automate repetitive tasks, analyse data in real-time, and improve decision-making accuracy. By leveraging AI, companies can enhance productivity, reduce costs, and remain competitive in an increasingly digital world. Understanding AI's role in business is essential for organizations looking to harness its full potential and drive innovation.

## Key AI Technologies (Machine Learning, NLP, Deep Learning, etc.)

AI encompasses several core technologies that enable businesses to automate processes and make data-driven decisions. One of the most significant AI technologies is Machine Learning (ML), which allows computers to learn patterns from historical data and make predictions without explicit programming (Kelleher, 2019). ML is widely used in fraud detection, demand forecasting, recommendation systems, and customer segmentation. Businesses use ML algorithms to analyse consumer behaviour, optimize pricing strategies, and enhance operational efficiency.

Another essential AI technology is Natural Language Processing (NLP), which enables machines to understand and interpret human language. NLP is used in virtual assistants, chatbots, voice recognition systems, and sentiment analysis (Cambria et al., 2017). Companies leverage NLP to automate customer interactions, improve response times, and analyse customer feedback from social media and reviews. AI-powered chatbots, for example, help businesses provide instant support to customers, reducing the need for human intervention and enhancing user experience.

Deep Learning (DL), a subset of Machine Learning, utilizes artificial neural networks to process complex patterns in large datasets. It is particularly effective in image and speech recognition, natural language processing, and medical diagnostics (Schmidhuber, 2015). Deep Learning enables businesses to develop advanced AI applications such as facial recognition, autonomous vehicles, and AI-driven medical diagnosis. Companies in healthcare, finance, and e-commerce use deep learning models to enhance security, detect anomalies, and improve predictive analytics.

*Figure 1. Key AI Technologies*

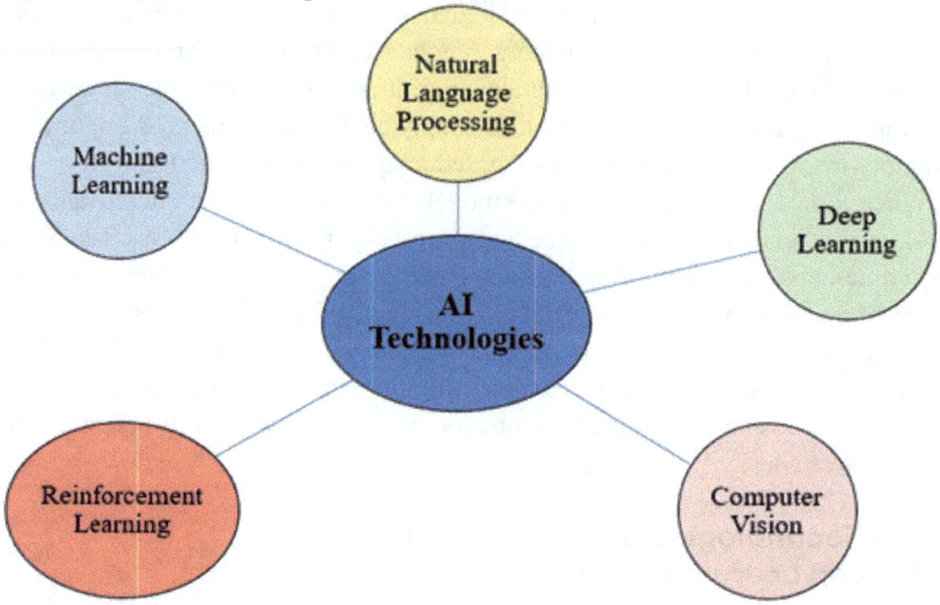


In addition to ML, NLP, and DL, businesses are adopting computer vision and reinforcement learning to enhance automation and decision-making. Computer vision allows machines to interpret and process visual information, leading to applications in surveillance, quality control, and autonomous vehicles. Reinforcement learning, on the other hand, helps AI systems learn optimal strategies through trial and error, making it valuable in robotics and supply chain optimization. These AI technologies are shaping the future of business systems by enabling smarter automation, data-driven decision-making, and enhanced customer engagement.

## Evolution of AI in Business Applications

The use of AI in business has evolved significantly over the decades. Initially, AI applications were limited to rule-based expert systems, where predefined rules guided decision-making. These early AI models lacked adaptability and required constant updates to remain effective. During the 1990s, businesses started integrating data-driven AI models, leveraging statistical techniques to analyse trends and improve forecasting (Russell & Norvig, 2021). However, these systems were still constrained by computational limitations and limited access to large datasets.

The early 2000s marked a significant shift in AI adoption, as advancements in cloud computing and big data enabled businesses to process vast amounts of information in real time. Companies began using machine learning algorithms for personalized recommendations, automated customer support, and targeted marketing campaigns (Buxmann & Schmidt, 2021). AI-powered CRM systems allowed businesses to predict customer needs, optimize sales strategies, and improve overall customer retention.

In recent years, the rise of Deep Learning and neural networks has further revolutionized AI applications in business. AI models can now analyse unstructured data, such as images, videos, and social media content, providing businesses with deeper insights into consumer behaviour (Gentsch, 2019). AI-driven automation is now widely used in manufacturing, logistics, finance, and healthcare, leading to improved efficiency, reduced costs, and enhanced decision-making capabilities. The evolution of AI has transformed traditional business operations into intelligent, adaptive systems capable of continuous learning and improvement.

## AI vs. Traditional Business Systems

The comparison between AI-driven business systems and traditional business models highlights the advantages AI brings to modern enterprises. Traditional business systems rely heavily on manual processes, human expertise, and historical data for decision-making. These systems are often slow, prone to errors, and limited in scalability. AI-powered business systems, on the other hand, automate repetitive tasks, process real-time data, and generate predictive insights, allowing businesses to respond quickly to market changes (Makridakis, 2017).

One major difference between AI and traditional business systems is data processing capabilities. Traditional systems are designed to handle structured data, such as spreadsheets and databases, whereas AI-driven systems can analyse both structured and unstructured data, including emails, social media content, and sensor data (Kaplan & Haenlein, 2019). This ability allows businesses to make more accurate predictions, improve customer engagement, and enhance operational efficiency.

In customer service, traditional business models require human agents to handle queries, often leading to long wait times and inconsistent service quality. AI-driven chatbots and virtual assistants provide instant responses, personalized recommendations, and 24/7 support, significantly improving customer experience (Huang & Rust, 2021). Similarly, AI-powered fraud detection systems in banking analyse transaction patterns in real time, preventing fraudulent activities faster than traditional methods.

AI also enhances supply chain management by optimizing inventory levels, predicting demand fluctuations, and reducing operational costs. Traditional supply chain models rely on fixed forecasting techniques, whereas AI-driven models continuously learn from new data, ensuring better accuracy and efficiency (Goyal et al., 2022). AI-driven business systems also minimize human biases, making decision-making 3more objective and data-centric. Traditional business decisions are often influenced by personal judgment and experience, whereas AI evaluates multiple factors simultaneously, ensuring better outcomes.

Despite its advantages, AI adoption comes with challenges. Businesses must address ethical concerns, data privacy issues, and the need for skilled AI professionals (Rahwan et al., 2019). Unlike traditional business models that operate within well-defined rules, AI requires continuous monitoring to ensure transparency and fairness. Companies must invest in AI governance frameworks to prevent biases, ensure compliance with regulations, and build trust among stakeholders.

Looking forward, AI-driven business systems will continue to evolve, integrating with other emerging technologies such as blockchain and the Internet of Things (IoT). These integrations will create more intelligent and interconnected business environments, improving efficiency, security, and decision-making (Dwivedi et al., 2021). Organizations that embrace AI will gain a competitive advantage, enabling them to adapt to market changes and enhance customer satisfaction in an increasingly digital world.

## ARTIFICIAL INTELLIGENCE-DRIVEN INNOVATIONS IN BUSINESS PROCESSES

Artificial Intelligence is revolutionizing business operations by introducing automation, predictive analytics, and data-driven decision-making. AI-powered systems allow organizations to operate more efficiently, minimize costs, and enhance customer experiences. By automating repetitive tasks, analysing vast amounts of data, and providing real-time insights, AI is reshaping how businesses function. From intelligent automation to optimizing supply chain management, AI plays a crucial role in improving overall business performance.

One of the most significant advantages of AI is its impact on decision-making. Traditional decision-making relied on historical data and human intuition, which could be slow and prone to errors. AI, however, can process large datasets instantly, identify patterns, and provide data-driven recommendations that enhance accuracy and speed. This is particularly beneficial in finance, healthcare, and marketing, where AI assists in fraud detection, patient diagnostics, and personalized advertising campaigns.

*Figure 2. AI-Driven Innovations in Business Processes*

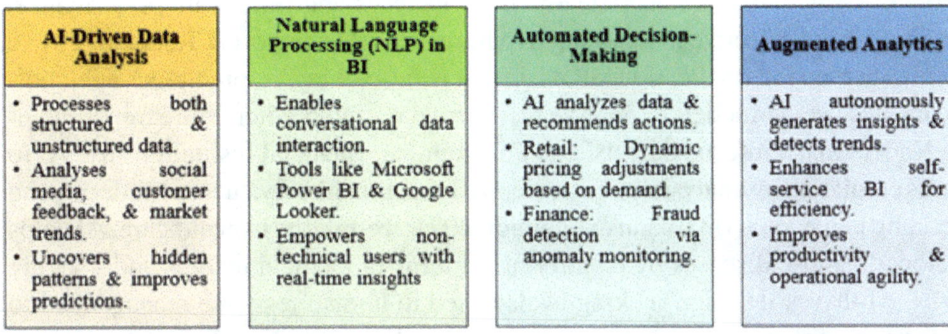


In customer relationship management (CRM), AI is improving interactions by enabling businesses to offer personalized services. AI-powered chatbots and virtual assistants provide instant responses, reducing wait times and enhancing customer satisfaction. Advanced AI-driven CRM systems analyse customer behaviour, predict preferences, and recommend tailored products or services. This helps businesses build stronger relationships with customers and improve retention rates.

AI is also transforming supply chain management by enhancing efficiency and predictive capabilities. AI algorithms optimize inventory management by forecasting demand based on historical trends and market conditions. Companies use AI-powered logistics solutions to determine the most efficient delivery routes, reduce transportation costs, and improve order fulfilment. Businesses leveraging AI in supply chains experience fewer disruptions and increased operational efficiency.

By integrating AI into core business processes, organizations can enhance productivity, reduce costs, and remain competitive in the evolving digital landscape. As AI technology continues to advance, its applications in business will expand, enabling companies to adapt to market changes, improve decision-making, and deliver better services. Businesses that embrace AI-driven innovations will position themselves for long-term success in an increasingly technology-driven world.

## Intelligent Automation and Decision-Making

AI-driven intelligent automation is one of the most significant advancements in business operations. Traditional automation systems relied on predefined rules and workflows, limiting their ability to handle complex scenarios. AI-powered automation, however, uses machine learning and natural language processing (NLP) to adapt and improve decision-making processes over time (Kaplan & Haenlein, 2019). AI enables Robotic Process Automation (RPA), which automates repetitive tasks such as data entry, invoice processing, and customer support. Unlike conventional automation, AI-enhanced RPA learns from patterns and refines its performance, making it more effective in handling dynamic tasks (Davenport & Ronanki, 2018).

Another major application of AI in decision-making is predictive analytics. Businesses use AI models to analyse historical data and predict future trends, helping leaders make informed decisions. For example, financial institutions use AI to assess credit risk by analysing a customer's transaction history, income patterns, and spending behaviour (Buxmann & Schmidt, 2021). Similarly, in healthcare, AI helps doctors diagnose diseases by identifying patterns in medical records and imaging scans. AI-driven decision-making is also used in human resource management to screen job applicants and predict employee performance based on data analysis (Huang & Rust, 2021).

AI-powered chatbots and virtual assistants further enhance decision-making by providing real-time insights and recommendations. These AI tools can analyse customer interactions, detect sentiment, and provide personalized responses, improving engagement and service quality. Businesses use AI-driven analytics platforms to optimize marketing campaigns by identifying the most effective advertising channels and predicting customer behaviour (Dwivedi et al., 2021). The ability of AI to process vast amounts of data and provide actionable insights gives businesses a strategic advantage in making faster and more accurate decisions.

## AI in Customer Relationship Management

Customer relationship management has evolved significantly with the integration of AI. Traditional CRM systems required manual data entry and human analysis, making them time-consuming and error-prone. AI-powered CRM solutions, however, automate data collection, improve customer segmentation, and enhance engagement strategies (Gentsch, 2019). Businesses use AI-driven CRM tools to personalize interactions, predict customer needs, and improve customer satisfaction.

One of the key applications of AI in CRM is customer sentiment analysis. AI algorithms analyse social media comments, emails, and chat messages to determine customer emotions and preferences. This helps businesses tailor their marketing strategies and improve customer service (Huang & Rust, 2021). AI-driven recommendation systems, such as those used by Amazon and Netflix, analyse customer behaviour to suggest products and content based on individual preferences. These systems enhance customer experience by providing relevant and timely recommendations.

Another important aspect of AI in CRM is chatbots and virtual assistants. AI-powered chatbots provide 24/7 customer support, answering queries, resolving issues, and even processing transactions without human intervention. Businesses use AI chatbots on websites, mobile apps, and messaging platforms to enhance customer engagement and reduce response times (Buxmann & Schmidt, 2021). AI also helps businesses manage customer interactions by analysing call centre conversations and identifying areas for improvement.

AI-powered CRM tools assist sales teams by prioritizing leads based on customer behaviour and historical data. AI-driven lead scoring helps businesses identify high-potential customers and focus their sales efforts accordingly. AI also automates follow-up emails and reminders, ensuring better customer engagement. By integrating AI into CRM, businesses can improve efficiency, enhance personalization, and build stronger relationships with their customers.

## AI-Driven Supply Chain Optimization

AI is playing a crucial role in supply chain management, helping businesses optimize inventory, reduce costs, and improve logistics efficiency. Traditional supply chain models relied on historical data and manual planning, leading to inefficiencies and delays. AI-powered supply chain solutions, on the other hand, use real-time data and predictive analytics to enhance decision-making (Goyal et al., 2022).

One of the key applications of AI in supply chain optimization is demand forecasting. AI models analyse historical sales data, market trends, and external factors such as weather conditions to predict future demand. This helps businesses adjust inventory levels, reduce stock shortages, and minimize excess inventory costs. Retailers use AI-driven demand forecasting to optimize product availability and improve customer satisfaction (Baryannis et al., 2019).

AI also enhances route optimization in logistics and transportation. AI-powered logistics platforms analyse traffic patterns, delivery schedules, and fuel consumption to determine the most efficient routes for delivery trucks. Companies like Amazon and FedEx use AI to optimize last-mile delivery, reducing transit times and operational costs (Dwivedi et al., 2021). AI-driven route planning ensures that goods reach customers faster, improving overall supply chain efficiency.

Another significant impact of AI in supply chain management is predictive maintenance. AI-powered systems monitor equipment and machinery in real time, detecting potential failures before they occur. This proactive approach reduces downtime, extends the lifespan of machinery, and lowers maintenance costs (Goyal et al., 2022). AI-driven warehouse automation further improves efficiency by using robotics and machine learning algorithms to manage inventory, pack orders, and streamline operations.

AI is also transforming supplier management by analysing supplier performance, identifying risks, and recommending the best procurement strategies. Businesses use AI-powered procurement tools to negotiate better contracts, reduce costs, and ensure a steady supply of raw materials. AI-driven blockchain integration in supply chain management enhances transparency and traceability, reducing fraud and ensuring ethical sourcing practices (Kaplan & Haenlein, 2019).

AI-driven innovations are reshaping business processes across industries, from intelligent automation to customer relationship management and supply chain optimization. AI enhances decision-making, improves efficiency, and personalizes customer interactions, giving businesses a competitive edge in the digital economy. As AI technology continues to evolve, businesses must invest in AI-powered solutions to streamline operations, enhance customer engagement, and optimize supply chains. By embracing AI-driven innovations, organizations can improve productivity, reduce costs, and create better experiences for customers. The future of business operations lies in AI-driven automation and data-driven decision-making, making AI an essential component of modern business strategies.

## CHALLENGES AND ETHICAL CONSIDERATIONS IN AI-DRIVEN BUSINESS SYSTEMS

The adoption of Artificial Intelligence (AI) in business has greatly enhanced efficiency, decision-making, and customer engagement. AI-driven systems automate processes, analyse vast amounts of data, and provide valuable insights that help businesses operate more effectively. However, the growing reliance on AI also brings several challenges, particularly concerning data privacy, ethical considerations, and regulatory compliance. Addressing these challenges is essential for businesses to ensure responsible AI implementation and maintain public trust.

*Figure 3. Challenges and Ethical Considerations in AI-Driven Business Systems*

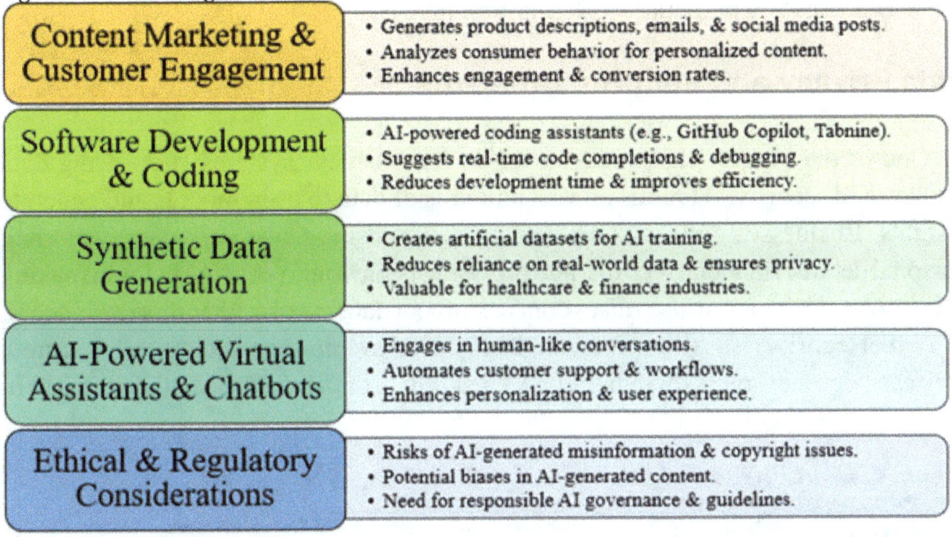


One of the primary concerns in AI adoption is data privacy and security. AI systems rely on large datasets to train models and improve decision-making. However, handling sensitive customer information increases the risk of data breaches, unauthorized access, and misuse of personal data. Companies must implement robust cybersecurity measures and encryption techniques to safeguard customer data. Additionally, compliance with data protection laws such as the General Data Protection Regulation (GDPR) and the California Consumer Privacy Act (CCPA) is crucial to ensure ethical data handling.

Another major issue is bias and fairness in AI models. AI algorithms learn from historical data, which may contain inherent biases. If not carefully managed, these biases can lead to unfair decision-making in hiring, lending, and law enforcement. For example, AI-powered hiring tools have been criticized for favouring certain demographics over others. To ensure fairness, businesses must regularly audit AI models, use diverse training datasets, and implement bias detection mechanisms.

Regulatory compliance is also a significant challenge. AI technologies are advancing faster than the regulatory frameworks governing them. Many governments are now introducing AI-specific laws and guidelines to ensure responsible AI use. Businesses must stay informed about emerging regulations and develop internal AI governance policies to ensure transparency and accountability.

As AI continues to transform industries, businesses must adopt ethical AI practices, prioritize security, and comply with legal requirements. Responsible AI implementation will not only enhance efficiency and trust but also enable sustainable AI adoption in the long run. By proactively addressing these challenges, organizations can maximize AI's potential while minimizing risks.

## Data Privacy and Security Concerns

One of the biggest challenges in AI-driven business systems is ensuring data privacy and security. AI relies on vast amounts of data to train models and generate insights. Businesses collect, store, and process sensitive customer data, including personal details, financial records, and browsing behaviour. While AI helps in making data-driven decisions, it also raises concerns about data misuse, unauthorized access, and cybersecurity risks (Sharma et al., 2022). If AI systems are not properly secured, they can become targets for cyberattacks, leading to data breaches and identity theft.

*Figure 4. Data Privacy and Security Concerns*

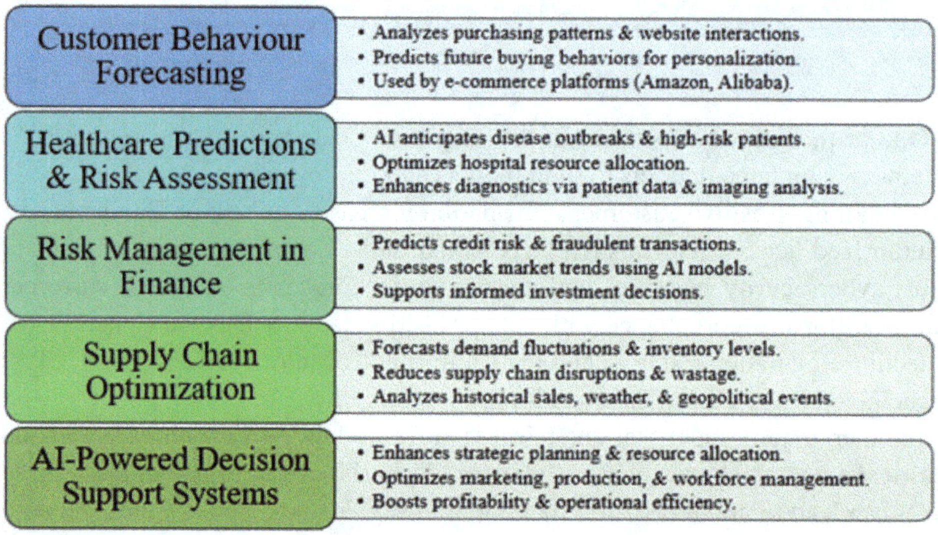


Another concern is informed consent and data ownership. Many businesses collect user data without clear consent, raising ethical questions about privacy. Consumers often remain unaware of how their data is used, shared, or stored. Regulations like the General Data Protection Regulation (GDPR) and the California Consumer Privacy Act (CCPA) require businesses to disclose data collection practices and give users control over their information (Zhang & Dafoe, 2020). However, many companies struggle to comply with these regulations while balancing AI innovation.

AI-driven automated decision-making also raises security concerns. Many financial institutions use AI to approve loans or screen job applicants. If these AI models are hacked or manipulated, they can lead to biased or fraudulent outcomes. Businesses must invest in strong cybersecurity frameworks, encryption techniques, and ethical AI governance to ensure AI-driven systems remain secure and trustworthy (Mukherjee et al., 2021).

## Ethical AI and Bias Mitigation

AI systems are designed to learn from historical data, but if the data itself contains biases, AI models can produce discriminatory or unfair outcomes. Bias in AI occurs when algorithms favour one group over another due to imbalanced training data, flawed model design, or human prejudices (Mehrabi et al., 2021). A common example of AI bias is in hiring systems, where AI models trained on past hiring data might favour male candidates over female candidates due to historical gender biases in the industry.

AI bias is also seen in facial recognition technology, where algorithms perform better for certain demographics while showing higher error rates for others. This has serious ethical implications, especially in law enforcement and security applications. Fairness in AI decision-making is crucial to prevent discriminatory practices and ensure equal treatment of individuals. To address these concerns, businesses must adopt bias detection techniques, diverse training datasets, and transparency in AI decision-making (Whittaker et al., 2022).

Another ethical challenge is the explainability of AI models. Many AI-driven business systems operate as "black boxes," meaning their decision-making processes are complex and difficult to interpret. This lack of transparency raises concerns about accountability, particularly in high-stakes applications such as healthcare, finance, and criminal justice. If an AI system denies a loan application or makes a medical diagnosis, users should have the right to understand how that decision was made (Floridi & Cowls, 2019).

To mitigate bias and enhance transparency, businesses are adopting Explainable AI (XAI) techniques, which allow stakeholders to understand AI decisions. Ethical AI frameworks also emphasize regular auditing of AI models, diversity in AI development teams, and continuous monitoring for fairness. Businesses that fail to address AI bias risk legal consequences, reputational damage, and loss of customer trust (Jobin et al., 2019).

## Regulatory and Compliance Challenges

The rapid adoption of AI in business systems has created regulatory gaps, as existing laws struggle to keep up with technological advancements. AI operates across different industries and jurisdictions, making it difficult to establish global regulatory standards. Governments and policymakers are working to create AI-specific laws that ensure ethical usage while promoting innovation (Wirtz et al., 2022).

*Figure 5. Regulatory and Compliance Challenges in AI*

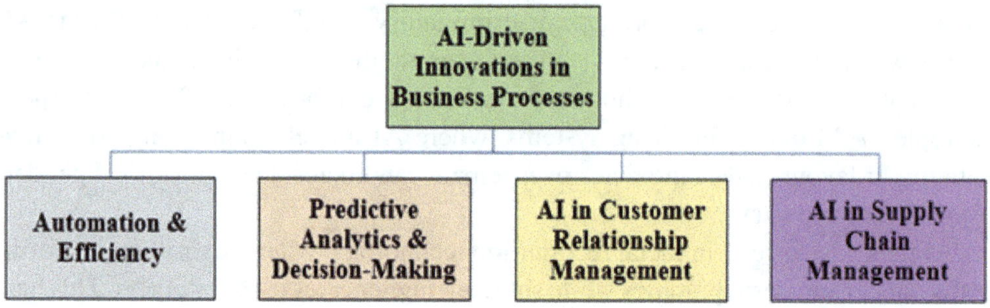


One of the major regulatory challenges is data protection and compliance with privacy laws. Laws like GDPR and CCPA require businesses to obtain explicit user consent before collecting data. However, AI systems often analyse unstructured data from multiple sources, making it difficult to track data flows and ensure compliance. Businesses using AI for personalized advertising must ensure they do not violate privacy laws while targeting consumers based on behavioural data (Leslie, 2020).

Another challenge is accountability in AI decision-making. If an AI system makes an incorrect or harmful decision, determining responsibility can be complex. Should the developer, business, or AI system itself be held accountable? AI regulations must establish clear liability frameworks to address such concerns. Companies using AI in autonomous vehicles, healthcare diagnostics, and financial services must comply with industry-specific AI regulations to ensure safety and fairness (Vinuesa et al., 2020).

Additionally, there is growing concern over AI governance in workplaces. As businesses use AI for employee monitoring and performance evaluation, questions arise about employee privacy and workplace ethics. Governments are introducing labor laws that regulate AI surveillance, automated hiring processes, and AI-driven productivity tracking (Coeckelbergh, 2020).

To navigate these regulatory challenges, businesses should adopt proactive compliance strategies. This includes conducting AI impact assessments, establishing AI ethics committees, and ensuring AI systems align with ethical guidelines. Organizations that prioritize ethical AI governance and legal compliance will be better positioned to gain public trust and regulatory approval.

While AI brings numerous benefits to business systems, addressing its ethical, security, and regulatory challenges is crucial for sustainable AI adoption. Companies must invest in data security measures, fairness-driven AI development, and compliance with evolving AI regulations. AI-driven businesses should focus on transparency, accountability, and ethical responsibility to ensure AI remains a trustworthy and beneficial tool in modern business operations. As governments and industry leaders continue to refine AI policies, businesses must stay informed and proactive in implementing responsible AI solutions.

## CASE STUDIES AND REAL-WORLD APPLICATIONS

Artificial Intelligence (AI) is revolutionizing industries across the globe by helping businesses streamline operations, enhance customer experiences, and improve decision-making. With its ability to process vast amounts of data, detect patterns, and automate tasks, AI is reshaping the way businesses function. Industries such as finance and banking, retail and e-commerce, and human resource (HR) management have particularly benefited from AI-driven advancements. By integrating AI-powered solutions, businesses can increase efficiency, reduce operational costs, and make more informed decisions. AI plays a crucial role in fraud detection, personalized customer interactions, and workforce management, making businesses more agile and competitive.

In the finance and banking sector, AI has become essential for fraud detection, risk assessment, and customer service automation. Traditional fraud detection relied on static rule-based systems, which struggled to adapt to evolving financial crimes. AI-driven fraud detection models, on the other hand, use machine learning algorithms to analyse transaction patterns, detect anomalies, and flag suspicious activities in real time. Banks like JPMorgan Chase and PayPal use AI-based fraud prevention systems to protect customer accounts from cyber threats. Additionally, AI enhances credit risk assessment by considering alternative data sources such as spending habits, transaction histories, and even social media activity, allowing financial institutions to make more accurate lending decisions. AI-powered chatbots and virtual assistants further improve customer service by handling routine banking inquiries, reducing wait times, and enhancing overall user satisfaction.

The retail and e-commerce industry has also embraced AI to personalize shopping experiences, optimize inventory management, and enhance marketing strategies. AI-powered recommendation engines analyse customer browsing habits, past purchases, and preferences to suggest relevant products, significantly improving sales and customer engagement. Companies like Amazon and Netflix leverage AI to offer personalized content and product recommendations, increasing user retention. AI is also transforming supply chain management by predicting demand fluctuations and optimizing stock levels, ensuring retailers maintain adequate inventory while minimizing waste. Additionally, AI-driven virtual shopping assistants and chatbots enhance customer support by providing instant responses, resolving issues, and guiding users through their shopping journey.

In human resource management, AI is automating recruitment, employee engagement, and workforce planning. AI-driven applicant tracking systems (ATS) efficiently scan resumes, match candidates to job roles, and predict their suitability based on previous hiring data. Major companies such as Unilever and Hilton use AI-powered recruitment tools to speed up hiring processes and reduce bias. AI is also being used for employee sentiment analysis, analysing feedback and workplace interactions to help businesses improve employee satisfaction and productivity. Furthermore, AI-powered workforce planning tools assist HR teams in forecasting staffing needs, ensuring efficient resource allocation.

Across finance, retail, and HR, AI is proving to be a transformative force, allowing businesses to automate processes, enhance decision-making, and create more personalized experiences. As AI continues to evolve, its applications will expand, helping industries remain competitive and innovative in the ever-changing digital landscape.

## AI in Finance and Banking

The finance and banking industry has been a frontrunner in adopting AI technologies to improve security, enhance customer service, and streamline operations. AI-powered fraud detection has become essential in preventing financial crimes. Traditional fraud detection systems relied on rule-based approaches, which were often ineffective against sophisticated cyber threats. In contrast, AI algorithms analyse vast amounts of transaction data in real-time to detect anomalies and flag fraudulent activities (Nasr et al., 2022). For example, financial institutions like JPMorgan Chase and PayPal use AI-driven fraud detection models to identify suspicious transactions based on behavioural patterns and spending histories.

*Figure 6. AI in Finance and Banking*

Another key AI application in banking is automated risk assessment. AI-driven credit scoring models assess a customer's financial history, spending behaviour, and other factors to determine creditworthiness. Unlike traditional credit evaluation methods, AI can analyse alternative data sources, such as social media activity and online purchases, to make more accurate predictions (Baesens et al., 2021). This approach allows banks to offer loans to underserved populations who may not have traditional credit histories.

AI-powered chatbots and virtual assistants have also improved customer service in the banking sector. Bank of America's AI chatbot, Erica, provides customers with real-time financial insights, transaction alerts, and budgeting assistance. By automating routine banking inquiries, AI chatbots reduce wait times and improve customer satisfaction (Goyal et al., 2022). Additionally, AI-driven algorithmic trading is widely used in investment firms to execute trades at high speeds based on market trends, economic indicators, and news sentiment analysis (Feng et al., 2018).

## AI in Retail and E-Commerce

The retail and e-commerce industry has embraced AI to enhance customer experience, optimize inventory management, and drive personalized marketing strategies. AI-powered recommendation engines analyse customer behaviour, purchase history, and browsing patterns to suggest products tailored to individual preferences. Companies like Amazon and Netflix leverage AI algorithms to personalize content recommendations, increasing customer engagement and boosting sales (Jia et al., 2020).

*Figure 7. AI in Retail and E-Commerce*

AI also plays a crucial role in customer service automation. Many e-commerce platforms deploy AI-driven chatbots and virtual assistants to handle customer inquiries, process refunds, and provide personalized shopping assistance. AI-powered visual search allows customers to upload images and find similar products, enhancing the shopping experience (Dzyabura & Hauser, 2021).

Another significant AI application in retail is dynamic pricing optimization. AI models analyse competitor pricing, demand fluctuations, and customer purchasing behaviour to adjust product prices in real-time. This pricing strategy helps retailers maximize profits while remaining competitive in the market. For instance, Walmart and Target use AI-driven pricing algorithms to optimize discounts and promotional offers based on consumer demand (Kaplan & Haenlein, 2019).

AI has also transformed supply chain and inventory management in retail. Retailers use AI-driven demand forecasting to predict future sales trends, ensuring optimal inventory levels and reducing overstocking or shortages (Goyal et al., 2022). AI-powered robotic automation in warehouses, such as Amazon's fulfilment centres, enables faster order processing and delivery through machine learning-based logistics optimization (Dwivedi et al., 2021).

## AI-Driven HR and Workforce Management

AI is revolutionizing human resource (HR) management by automating recruitment, improving employee engagement, and optimizing workforce planning. One of the most prominent applications of AI in HR is AI-driven recruitment. Traditional hiring processes involve manual screening of resumes, which is time-consuming and prone to human bias. AI-powered applicant tracking systems (ATS) streamline recruitment by scanning resumes, identifying the best candidates, and predicting job fit based on skills and experience (Suen et al., 2019). Companies like Unilever and Hilton use AI-driven hiring platforms to screen applicants and conduct video interviews with automated assessments.

*Figure 8. AI-Driven HR and Workforce Management*

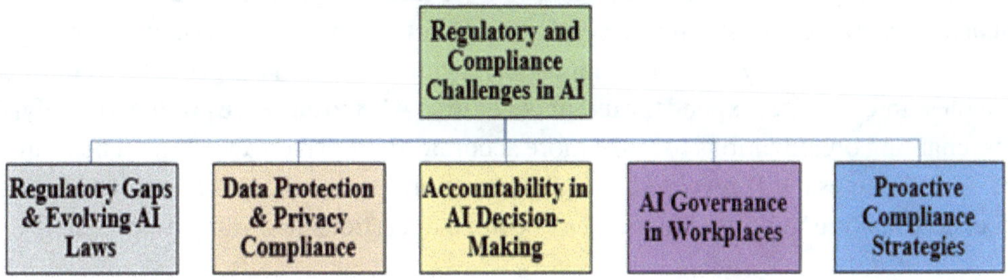


AI also enhances employee engagement and performance evaluation. AI-powered HR analytics platforms monitor employee productivity, track work patterns, and provide insights into employee well-being. AI-driven sentiment analysis tools assess employee feedback from surveys, emails, and workplace communications to identify areas for improvement and enhance workplace culture (Prikshat et al., 2021).

Another significant AI application in HR is workforce planning and predictive analytics. AI models analyse historical workforce data to predict future staffing needs, helping companies allocate resources efficiently. AI-driven chatbots for HR assist employees with administrative tasks such as payroll inquiries, benefits enrolment, and leave requests, reducing HR workload and improving response times (Cappelli et al., 2020).

AI is also used in training and development through personalized learning platforms. AI-powered adaptive learning systems recommend training programs based on employee skills, career goals, and performance evaluations, ensuring continuous skill development (Sharma & Sharma, 2022). Companies use virtual reality (VR) and AI-powered simulations to train employees in real-world scenarios, improving retention and engagement.

AI has transformed business operations across various industries, including finance, retail, and human resource management. AI-driven technologies improve fraud detection, customer service, inventory management, recruitment, and workforce planning. As AI continues to evolve, businesses must embrace these innovations to enhance efficiency, improve decision-making, and create personalized experiences for customers and employees. By leveraging AI-driven solutions, businesses can remain competitive and adapt to changing market demands in the digital era.

## FUTURE TRENDS AND EMERGING TECHNOLOGIES

Artificial Intelligence (AI) is progressing rapidly, transforming how businesses operate, strategize, and make decisions. As AI technologies become more sophisticated, companies must embrace emerging trends to maintain a competitive edge in the digital economy. The continuous advancement of AI is expected to redefine business intelligence, expand the use of generative AI, and enhance predictive analytics, enabling organizations to make more accurate, data-driven decisions. The future of AI in business will revolve around automation, personalization, and intelligent decision-making, helping businesses optimize operations and improve efficiency.

*Figure 9. Key AI Trends in Business*

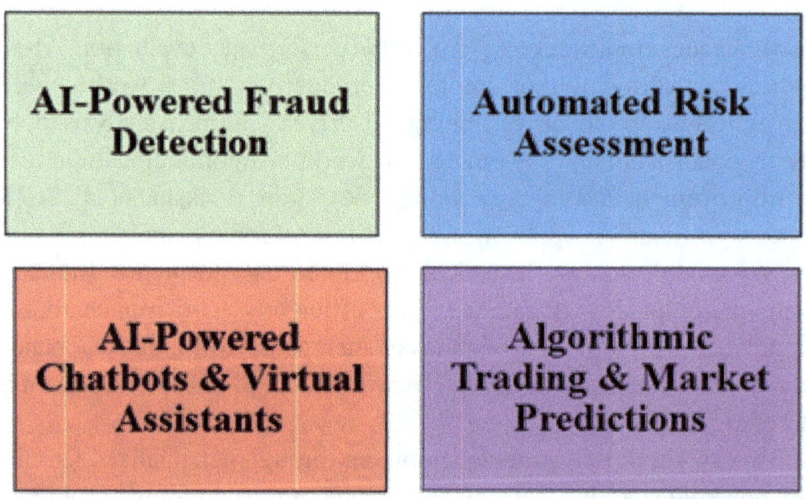


One of the most significant areas where AI will continue to evolve is business intelligence (BI). Traditional BI systems relied on historical data and manual analysis, often leading to delays in decision-making. AI-powered BI, on the other hand, enables real-time data processing, automated insights, and predictive forecasting. Businesses will increasingly use AI-driven BI tools to analyse structured and unstructured data, identify trends, and suggest strategic actions. Moreover, the integration of natural language processing (NLP) in BI platforms will allow business users to interact with data more naturally, making insights accessible to non-technical professionals. AI-driven self-service analytics will further democratize data, allowing organizations to make informed decisions without relying heavily on data specialists.

Another transformative AI development is generative AI, which is revolutionizing content creation, automation, and problem-solving. Generative AI models can produce text, images, code, and even synthetic data, helping businesses in areas such as marketing, customer engagement, and software development. AI-driven tools like ChatGPT, DALL-E, and Codex are already being used to generate personalized content, automate creative processes, and assist developers in writing code. As generative AI continues to improve, businesses will leverage it to enhance customer interactions, develop new products, and streamline content production.

Predictive analytics is another AI-driven innovation shaping the future of business decision-making. By analysing vast datasets, AI-powered predictive models can anticipate market trends, customer behaviour, and operational risks. Businesses in industries such as finance, healthcare, and retail will rely on AI-driven forecasting tools to reduce uncertainties, optimize resources, and improve strategic planning. AI-powered decision-making systems will provide leaders with actionable insights, helping them navigate complex business environments more effectively.

As AI continues to evolve, its role in business intelligence, generative AI applications, and predictive analytics will expand, allowing companies to make smarter, data-driven decisions. Organizations that embrace these advancements will gain a competitive advantage, enabling them to innovate, optimize, and thrive in an AI-powered future.

## AI and the Future of Business Intelligence

Business intelligence (BI) refers to the use of data analysis tools and methodologies to improve decision-making within organizations. Traditionally, BI relied on structured data and rule-based models to generate insights. However, AI-driven BI systems are transforming the field by enabling real-time data processing, predictive analytics, and automation (Chen et al., 2022). With AI, businesses can analyse both structured and unstructured data, including social media interactions, customer feedback, and market trends, to uncover hidden patterns and make more accurate predictions.

*Figure 10. AI and the Future of Business Intelligence*

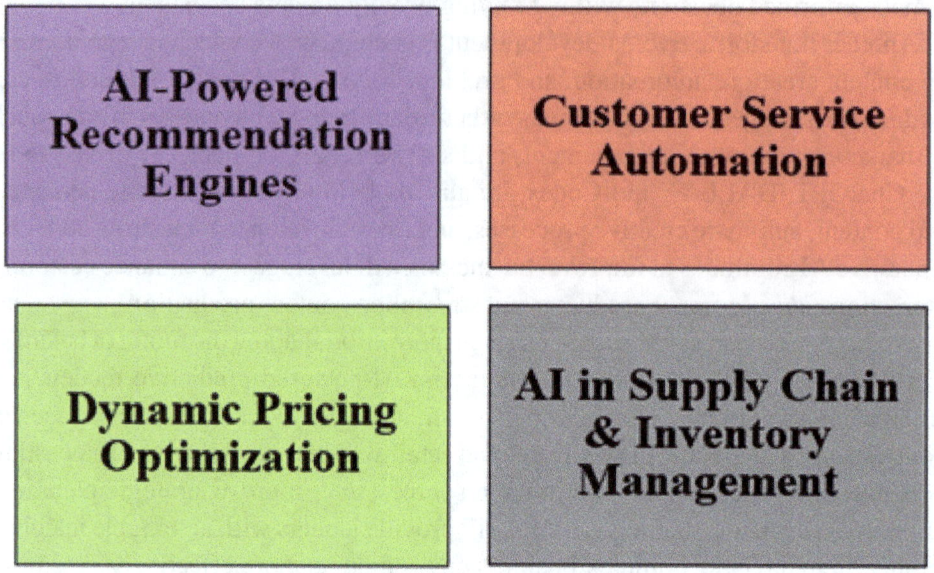


One of the most significant advancements in AI-powered BI is natural language processing (NLP), which allows business users to interact with data using conversational language. AI-powered BI tools, such as Microsoft Power BI and Google Looker, enable employees to ask questions and receive insights in real time without requiring advanced data analysis skills (Gandomi & Haider, 2022). This democratization of data analytics allows organizations to make faster, more informed decisions at all levels.

Another key trend is automated decision-making in BI. AI algorithms can analyse vast datasets and recommend actions based on real-time insights. For example, AI-powered BI platforms in retail can adjust pricing dynamically based on demand fluctuations, competitor pricing, and consumer behaviour. Similarly, financial institutions use AI to monitor transactions and detect anomalies, reducing fraud risks (Choudhury & Jones, 2021).

AI-driven BI is also advancing with the integration of augmented analytics, where AI automatically generates insights, detects anomalies, and predicts trends without human intervention. This shift towards self-service BI empowers businesses to make data-driven decisions efficiently, improving productivity and operational agility (Sun et al., 2021).

## The Role of Generative AI in Business

Generative AI, a subset of AI that creates content, is revolutionizing industries by enabling businesses to generate text, images, code, and even synthetic data. Tools like OpenAI's GPT-4, Google Bard, and DALL-E have demonstrated the potential of generative AI in content creation, software development, and business automation (Bommasani et al., 2021).

One of the most promising applications of generative AI is content marketing and customer engagement. Businesses are using AI-generated content to create product descriptions, personalized email campaigns, and social media posts at scale. AI can analyse consumer behaviour and generate content that resonates with target audiences, improving engagement and conversion rates (Dwivedi et al., 2022).

*Figure 11. Role of Generative AI in Business*

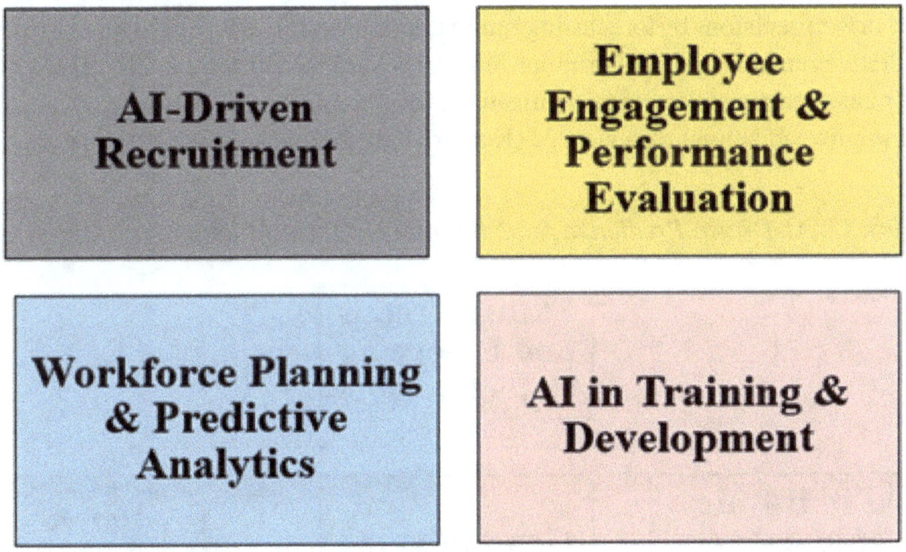


Generative AI is also transforming software development and coding. AI-powered coding assistants, such as GitHub Copilot and Tabnine, help developers write code faster by suggesting real-time code completions and debugging solutions. This significantly reduces development time and allows businesses to build applications more efficiently (Zhang et al., 2022).

Another critical area where generative AI is making an impact is synthetic data generation. AI models can create synthetic datasets to train machine learning algorithms, reducing reliance on real-world data while ensuring privacy compliance. This is particularly valuable in healthcare and finance, where access to large, high-quality datasets is often restricted due to privacy concerns (Ali et al., 2022).

AI-generated virtual assistants and chatbots are also becoming more sophisticated. Unlike traditional rule-based chatbots, generative AI models can engage in human-like conversations, improving customer support and personalization. Businesses use AI-powered virtual agents to handle customer inquiries, automate workflows, and provide personalized recommendations, enhancing user experience (Lin et al., 2022).

As generative AI continues to evolve, businesses will need to navigate ethical and regulatory challenges, including AI-generated misinformation, copyright concerns, and biases in AI-generated content. Companies must establish guidelines to ensure responsible AI usage while leveraging its potential for innovation (Goel et al., 2022).

## AI-Driven Predictive Analytics and Decision-Making

Predictive analytics, powered by AI, is enabling businesses to make proactive, data-driven decisions by forecasting future trends based on historical data. AI-driven predictive analytics is transforming industries such as finance, healthcare, retail, and manufacturing, allowing organizations to anticipate risks, optimize operations, and improve customer experiences (Kumar et al., 2021).

*Figure 12. AI-Driven Predictive Analytics and Decision-Making*

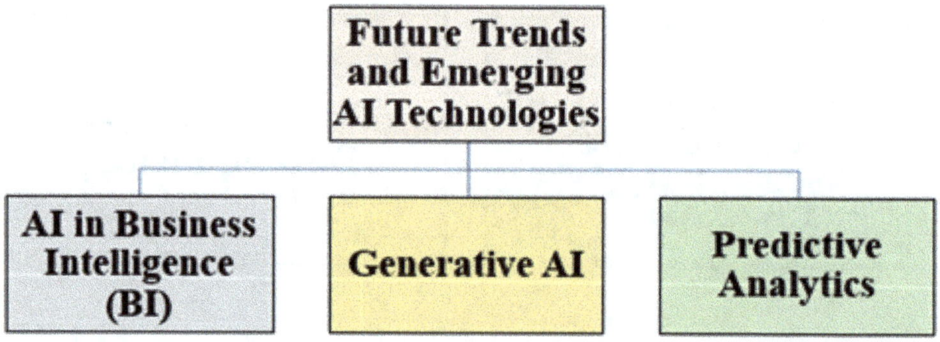


One of the primary applications of AI-driven predictive analytics is customer behaviour forecasting. Businesses use AI models to analyse past purchasing patterns, website interactions, and demographic data to predict future buying behaviours. E-commerce platforms like Amazon and Alibaba use predictive analytics to optimize inventory, recommend products, and personalize customer interactions, increasing sales and customer satisfaction (Gopalakrishnan et al., 2022).

In healthcare, predictive analytics is being used to anticipate disease outbreaks, identify high-risk patients, and optimize hospital resource allocation. AI-powered diagnostic tools analyse patient records, genetic data, and imaging scans to predict potential health risks, allowing doctors to take preventive measures and improve patient outcomes (Chakraborty & Saha, 2021).

AI-driven predictive analytics is also reshaping risk management in finance. Banks and insurance companies use AI models to assess credit risk, detect fraudulent transactions, and predict stock market trends. These predictive models analyse market fluctuations, macroeconomic indicators, and geopolitical events, helping investors make informed decisions and minimize financial risks (Sharma et al., 2022).

Another significant impact of AI-driven predictive analytics is in supply chain management. AI models analyse historical sales data, weather patterns, and geopolitical events to predict demand fluctuations and optimize inventory levels. Companies use predictive analytics to anticipate supply chain disruptions, reduce wastage, and enhance operational efficiency (Jiang et al., 2021).

AI-powered decision support systems (DSS) are becoming more prevalent in business environments. These systems use AI-driven insights to assist managers in strategic planning, resource allocation, and operational efficiency. AI-driven DSS is helping businesses optimize marketing strategies, streamline production processes, and enhance workforce management, leading to improved profitability and productivity (Shah et al., 2022).

The future of AI in business is centred around intelligent decision-making, generative AI, and predictive analytics. AI-powered business intelligence is revolutionizing data analysis by automating insights and enabling real-time decision-making. Generative AI is reshaping content creation, software development, and virtual interactions, while predictive analytics is allowing businesses to anticipate risks and optimize operations. As AI continues to advance, businesses must embrace ethical AI governance, data privacy compliance, and continuous innovation to stay competitive in a rapidly evolving digital landscape.

## FUTURE RESEARCH DIRECTIONS

### The Future of AI-Driven Business Systems

The future of AI in business will be shaped by continuous advancements in AI technologies, deeper human-AI collaboration, and emerging AI trends. Some key developments that will shape the next phase of AI adoption include:

## AI-Powered Hyper Automation

Hyper automation is the next evolution of automation, where AI, robotic process automation (RPA), and machine learning (ML) work together to automate complex business processes. Organizations will increasingly adopt AI-driven automation tools to handle repetitive tasks, optimize workflows, and reduce operational costs. AI-powered document processing, customer service automation, and intelligent workflow management will improve business efficiency.

## AI and the Internet of Things

The integration of AI with IoT devices will lead to smarter business operations and predictive maintenance. AI-powered IoT systems will analyse sensor data in real-time, allowing businesses to predict machine failures, optimize energy consumption, and enhance supply chain efficiency. Smart factories, AI-driven logistics networks, and connected healthcare systems will benefit from this integration.

## The Rise of Explainable and Trustworthy AI

As AI adoption grows, businesses and regulators will demand greater transparency in AI decision-making. Explainable AI (XAI) will become a standard practice, ensuring that AI models provide clear, understandable, and justifiable explanations for their predictions. This will be particularly important in finance, healthcare, and legal applications, where AI decisions can have significant consequences.

## The Expansion of AI in Small and Medium Enterprises

AI was once limited to large enterprises due to high costs and technical complexities. However, with the rise of cloud-based AI services and AI-as-a-Service (AIaaS) platforms, small and medium businesses (SMEs) can now leverage AI for customer insights, marketing automation, and business analytics. AI adoption among SMEs will increase, leading to more competitive and innovative business landscapes.

## AI-Driven Sustainability and Green AI

AI will play a crucial role in achieving sustainability goals. AI models will help businesses optimize energy usage, reduce waste, and develop eco-friendly supply chain practices. AI-driven climate models will assist governments and organizations in monitoring environmental impact and predicting climate change patterns. Green

AI initiatives, focusing on energy-efficient AI models, will become a priority to reduce the carbon footprint of AI systems.

## Summary of Key Findings

AI has proven to be a game-changer in several business domains. In finance and banking, AI enhances fraud detection, credit risk assessment, and algorithmic trading. AI-powered chatbots provide instant customer support, reducing human workload. In retail and e-commerce, AI personalizes customer experiences, optimizes inventory management, and drives dynamic pricing strategies. AI-driven supply chain management ensures demand forecasting, reduces logistics costs, and improves efficiency. In HR and workforce management, AI automates recruitment, predicts employee attrition, and enhances workforce planning.

The impact of AI on decision-making and business intelligence is also significant. AI-driven predictive analytics helps businesses forecast trends, anticipate risks, and make data-driven decisions. The rise of generative AI is opening new possibilities in content creation, marketing, and software development. AI-driven business intelligence (BI) tools enable real-time insights and strategic decision-making, allowing organizations to remain competitive.

However, the adoption of AI also brings challenges. Data security and privacy concerns remain critical, as AI systems process vast amounts of sensitive information. Regulatory compliance is another major issue, as governments introduce new AI-related laws to ensure responsible AI use. AI bias and fairness must also be addressed to prevent discriminatory outcomes in hiring, finance, and law enforcement.

## The Role of Ethical AI in Future Business Applications

As businesses continue to integrate AI into their operations, ensuring ethical AI practices will be essential. Fairness, transparency, and accountability must be at the core of AI implementation. Organizations should focus on explainable AI (XAI), which ensures that AI-driven decisions are understandable and justifiable. Transparency in AI models can build trust among customers, employees, and stakeholders.

To mitigate bias in AI algorithms, businesses must train AI models on diverse datasets and regularly audit them for fairness. AI systems should be designed to minimize discrimination in recruitment, financial lending, and customer segmentation. The development of AI ethics committees in organizations can help ensure compliance with ethical standards and promote responsible AI governance.

Another critical aspect of ethical AI is data privacy and security. Businesses must implement strong cybersecurity measures to protect customer data from breaches and unauthorized access. AI models should comply with global data protection regulations such as GDPR (General Data Protection Regulation) and CCPA (California Consumer Privacy Act) to maintain customer trust.

### Preparing Businesses for the AI-Driven Future

To thrive in an AI-powered future, businesses must take proactive steps to integrate AI into their operations. The following strategies will help organizations maximize AI's potential:

- ***Invest in AI Talent and Training***: Businesses must upskill employees to work with AI technologies. AI literacy programs and AI training workshops should be implemented to equip the workforce with AI-related skills.
- ***Adopt AI with a Clear Strategy***: Organizations should align AI implementation with business goals, ensuring that AI solutions provide real value. AI-driven projects should be scalable and adaptable to changing business needs.
- ***Develop AI Governance Frameworks***: Businesses should establish AI governance policies to ensure ethical AI use, compliance with regulations, and data privacy protection. AI frameworks must address bias detection, transparency, and risk management.
- ***Collaborate with AI Research Institutions***: Partnering with universities and AI research centres will help businesses stay updated with the latest AI advancements and drive innovation in AI applications.
- ***Monitor AI Trends and Emerging Technologies***: Organizations must continuously explore emerging AI trends, such as federated learning, quantum AI, and neuromorphic computing, to stay ahead in the competitive market.

## CONCLUSION

Artificial Intelligence has become an essential part of modern business, transforming the way organizations operate, make decisions, and engage with customers. Throughout this book chapter, this paper have explored how AI-driven business systems are revolutionizing industries, improving efficiency, and enabling data-driven strategies. From intelligent automation and AI-powered customer relationship management to predictive analytics and generative AI, AI continues to reshape business operations.

However, despite its many advantages, AI adoption also presents challenges related to data privacy, ethical concerns, and regulatory compliance. Businesses must ensure responsible AI usage by addressing issues like algorithmic bias, security threats, and transparency. As AI continues to evolve, organizations need to develop governance frameworks, invest in skilled personnel, and stay updated on emerging AI trends. The future of AI in business lies in continuous innovation, ethical AI development, and strategic adoption of new AI technologies.

## REFERENCES

Ali, M., Khan, N., & Akhtar, Z. (2022). Synthetic data generation using AI: Applications and ethical concerns. *Journal of Data Science and Technology*, *5*(3), 112–130.

Ashta, A., & Herrmann, H. (2021). Artificial intelligence and financial fraud detection: A review of the literature. *Financial Innovation*, *7*(1), 1–25.

Baesens, B., Van Vlasselaer, V., & Verbeke, W. (2021). *Fraud analytics using descriptive, predictive, and social network techniques: A guide to data science for fraud detection*. John Wiley & Sons.

Baryannis, G., Validi, S., Dani, S., & Antoniou, G. (2019). Supply chain risk management and artificial intelligence: State of the art and future research directions. *International Journal of Production Research*, *57*(7), 2179–2202. DOI: 10.1080/00207543.2018.1530476

Binns, R. (2018). Fairness in machine learning: Lessons from political philosophy. *Proceedings of the 2018 Conference on Fairness, Accountability, and Transparency*, 149-159. ACM.

Bommasani, R., Hudson, D., & Tang, E. (2021). On the opportunities and risks of foundation models. *Journal of Artificial Intelligence Research*, *71*(2), 1–35.

Brock, J. K.-U., & Von Wangenheim, F. (2019). Demystifying AI: What digital transformation leaders can teach you about real AI use in business. *Business Horizons*, *62*(2), 179–188.

Brynjolfsson, E., & McAfee, A. (2017). *Machine, platform, crowd: Harnessing our digital future*. W.W. Norton & Company.

Buxmann, P., & Schmidt, H. (2021). *Artificial Intelligence in Business: Balancing Risk and Innovation*. Springer.

Cambria, E., White, B., & Huang, G. (2017). Sentic computing for business analytics: A review. *Big Data Research*, *10*, 1–19.

Cappelli, P., Tambe, P., & Yakubovich, V. (2020). Artificial intelligence in human resources management: Challenges and a path forward. *Journal of Business Ethics*, *167*(4), 647–662.

Chakraborty, S., & Saha, P. (2021). AI in healthcare: Predictive analytics for early disease detection. *Healthcare Technology Review*, *34*(6), 89–102.

Chen, T., Wang, S., & Li, Y. (2022). AI-driven business intelligence: A new era of decision-making. *International Journal of Business Analytics*, *10*(4), 45–62.

Choudhury, A., & Jones, L. (2021). The rise of AI-powered BI: Transforming data into insights. *Journal of Business Intelligence*, *19*(1), 67–85.

Chui, M., Manyika, J., & Miremadi, M. (2018). What AI can and can't do (yet) for your business. *The McKinsey Quarterly*, •••, 1–8.

Coeckelbergh, M. (2020). *AI ethics*. MIT Press. DOI: 10.7551/mitpress/12549.001.0001

Davenport, T. H., & Ronanki, R. (2018). Artificial intelligence for the real world. *Harvard Business Review*, *96*(1), 108–116.

Davenport, T. H., & Ronanki, R. (2018). Artificial intelligence for the real world. *Harvard Business Review*, *96*(1), 108–116.

Dwivedi, Y. K., Hughes, L., & Ismagilova, E. (2021). Artificial intelligence (AI): Multidisciplinary perspectives on emerging challenges, opportunities, and research agenda. *International Journal of Information Management*, *57*, 102141. DOI: 10.1016/j.ijinfomgt.2019.08.002

Dwivedi, Y. K., Hughes, L., & Ismagilova, E. (2022). Generative AI in business: Challenges, opportunities, and future directions. *International Journal of Information Management*, *60*, 102379.

Dzyabura, D., & Hauser, J. R. (2021). AI-powered product recommendation and consumer behaviour. *Marketing Science*, *40*(1), 24–42.

Feng, Y., Jiang, L., & Zhu, W. (2018). Deep learning for financial trading: A survey. *Computational Economics*, *52*(4), 1401–1423.

Floridi, L., & Cowls, J. (2019). A unified framework of five principles for AI in society. *Harvard Data Science Review*, *1*(1).

Gandomi, A., & Haider, M. (2022). Augmented analytics and the future of business intelligence. *Journal of Big Data*, *9*(1), 45–58. PMID: 35495077

Gentsch, P. (2019). *AI in marketing, sales and service: How marketers without a data science degree can use AI, big data and bots*. Springer. DOI: 10.1007/978-3-319-89957-2

Goel, V., Agarwal, R., & Sinha, P. (2022). Ethical concerns in generative AI: Mitigating biases and misinformation. *AI & Society*, *37*(2), 281–299.

Gopalakrishnan, V., Patel, D., & Singh, M. (2022). Predictive analytics in e-commerce: A case study of personalized recommendations. *Journal of Retailing and Consumer Services*, *65*, 102884.

Goyal, K., Aggarwal, P., & Garg, R. (2022). AI applications in supply chain management: A systematic literature review. *Operations Research Perspectives*, *9*, 100244.

Huang, M. H., & Rust, R. T. (2021). A strategic framework for artificial intelligence in marketing. *Journal of the Academy of Marketing Science*, *49*(1), 30–50. DOI: 10.1007/s11747-020-00749-9

Jia, Y., Zhao, J., & Wang, Y. (2020). AI-powered customer experience in e-commerce: A case study of recommendation systems. *Electronic Commerce Research and Applications*, *39*, 100919.

Jiang, H., Zhao, L., & Wang, R. (2021). AI-driven predictive analytics for supply chain optimization. *Operations Research Perspectives*, *10*, 100217.

Jobin, A., Ienca, M., & Vayena, E. (2019). The global landscape of AI ethics guidelines. *Nature Machine Intelligence*, *1*(9), 389–399. DOI: 10.1038/s42256-019-0088-2

Jordan, M. I., & Mitchell, T. M. (2015). Machine learning: Trends, perspectives, and prospects. *Science*, *349*(6245), 255–260. DOI: 10.1126/science.aaa8415 PMID: 26185243

Kaplan, A., & Haenlein, M. (2019). Siri, Alexa, and other digital assistants: The future of customer service? *Journal of Business Research*, *116*, 1–16.

Kelleher, J. D. (2019). *Deep learning*. MIT Press. DOI: 10.7551/mitpress/11171.001.0001

Kumar, A., Gupta, S., & Sharma, K. (2021). AI-based decision support systems: Transforming business strategy. *Decision Support Systems*, *145*, 113524.

Leslie, D. (2020). *Understanding artificial intelligence ethics and safety*. The Alan Turing Institute.

Lin, B., Chen, F., & Yu, X. (2022). The evolution of AI chatbots: Enhancing customer service with NLP. *Computers in Human Behavior*, *132*, 107290.

Manyika, J., Chui, M., Brown, B., Bughin, J., Dobbs, R., Roxburgh, C., & Byers, A. H. (2017). *Big data: The next frontier for innovation, competition, and productivity*. McKinsey Global Institute.

McKinsey Global Institute. (2020). The state of AI in 2020. McKinsey & Company. https://www.mckinsey.com/

Mehrabi, N., Morstatter, F., Saxena, N., Lerman, K., & Galstyan, A. (2021). A survey on bias and fairness in machine learning. *ACM Computing Surveys*, *54*(6), 1–35. DOI: 10.1145/3457607

Mukherjee, S., Sharma, V., & Singh, S. (2021). Cybersecurity challenges in AI-driven business applications. *Journal of Business Ethics*, *171*(3), 647–662.

Nasr, A., Kamalov, F., & Balogun, A. O. (2022). Fraud detection in finance using machine learning. *Journal of Risk and Financial Management*, *15*(2), 1–22.

Russell, S., & Norvig, P. (2021). *Artificial intelligence: A modern approach* (4th ed.). Pearson.

Schmidhuber, J. (2015). Deep learning in neural networks: An overview. *Neural Networks*, *61*, 85–117. DOI: 10.1016/j.neunet.2014.09.003 PMID: 25462637

Shah, R., Patel, A., & Mehta, P. (2022). AI in risk management: Predictive analytics in financial decision-making. *Journal of Risk and Financial Management*, *15*(4), 108–124.

Sharma, R., Gupta, N., & Rathore, H. (2022). Data security risks in artificial intelligence applications. *Information Systems Frontiers*, *24*(4), 887–901.

Sharma, R., Gupta, N., & Verma, S. (2022). AI-driven forecasting models for business decision-making. *Expert Systems with Applications*, *189*, 116048.

Suen, H. Y., Hung, K. E., & Lin, Z. P. (2019). AI-powered recruitment and hiring: Challenges and future directions. *Computers in Human Behavior*, *99*, 224–234.

Sun, J., Li, H., & Wang, Q. (2021). AI-powered self-service business intelligence: A review and future directions. *Journal of Information Technology*, *36*(2), 184–201.

Taddy, M. (2019). The technological singularity: A business leader's guide to artificial intelligence. McGraw-Hill Education. Goyal, K., Aggarwal, P., & Garg, R. (2022). AI applications in supply chain management: A systematic literature review. *Operations Research Perspectives*, *9*, 100244.

Vinuesa, R., Azizpour, H., Leite, I., Balaam, M., Dignum, V., Domisch, S., & Nerini, F. F. (2020). The role of artificial intelligence in achieving the Sustainable Development Goals. *Nature Communications*, *11*(1), 1–10. DOI: 10.1038/s41467-019-14108-y PMID: 31932590

Whittaker, M., Alper, M., Brown, B., & Crawford, K. (2022). Addressing AI bias in practice. *AI Now Institute Report.*

Wirtz, B. W., Weyerer, J. C., & Geyer, C. (2022). Artificial intelligence and regulation. *Government Information Quarterly*, *39*(2), 101679.

# Chapter 13
# Emerging Trends and Innovation in AI for Business and Management Education: A Future-Ready Approach

**Kumar R. Rakshith**
https://orcid.org/0009-0000-9442-221X
*Dayananda Sagar College of Engineering, India*

**Roopa U**
https://orcid.org/0000-0002-1813-7203
*Dayananda Sagar College of Engineering, India*

## ABSTRACT

*AI is revolutionizing the provision of business and management programs. For example, it is enabling personalized learning approaches that capitalize on intelligent tutoring and adaptable e-learning platforms, virtual simulations, AI-based assessments, and reshaping learning experiences in business, finance, operations, marketing, and entrepreneurship education. Ethical dilemmas present themselves in terms of AI slant, data privacy, and dependence of operations in synchronously and asynchronously designed applications. Global case studies from institutions such as INSEAD, Wharton, MIT Sloan, National University of Singapore, and ISB illustrate how AI is reshaping classrooms and career services. Corporate training is also being transformed, with customized upskilling strategies. Yet more importantly, this has broadened horizons to embrace strategic, ethical, and policy considerations to provide equitable future-proof business education.*

DOI: 10.4018/979-8-3373-2150-9.ch013

## INTRODUCTION

Artificial Intelligence (AI) is no longer an emerging concept; it is a driving force behind transformation across business sectors and is rapidly becoming central to management education. As industries pivot towards AI-powered decision-making, automation, and data-driven strategies, business schools are under growing pressure to modernize their curricula. The role of AI in education extends far beyond technological tools; it fundamentally shifts how students learn, how faculty teach, and how universities operate. The opportunity for AI to positively impact learning outcomes while creating academic experiences reflective of evolving and realistic industry practices is limitless.

In response to this evolution, leading institutions worldwide are adopting intelligent tutoring systems, virtual simulations, AI-informed assessments, and adaptive learning technologies that leverage AI to create personalized learning. These technologies will equip graduates with capabilities beyond those of prepared graduates to create the next generation of leaders who are fluent in AI, ethical decision makers, and taught to appeal to rational and critical conditions described as strategic agility. The aim of business schools is to prepare students for the future of leadership that exemplifies both human-centered thinking, work, and conversations enlivened by technology.

This chapter examines the different ways AI is currently transforming the organization of business and management education, as well as the content and delivery of that education. The chapter takes a global viewpoint using examples from Wharton, MIT Sloan, NUS, and IIM Ahmedabad as it critically considers AI across the core specializations in MBA programs, virtual learning spaces, start-up level innovation, and corporate training. It will also encapsulate some of the ethical, institutional, and pedagogic tensions that arise from the integration of AI and propose recommendations for developing more balanced, future-oriented, and responsible AI-led educational systems.

### Background: A Growing Role of AI in Management Education

Having outlined the growing relevance of AI in the broader education landscape, it becomes essential to examine its specific significance within business and management education. The increased reliance on AI across the majority of industries in the economy implies that business students must become AI-fluent and analytically proficient. Traditional management education has long been case-based, financial modeling-focused, and human decision-making oriented, but current business worlds expect and require some degree of a combination between enhanced decision making with the aid of AI, data-driven decisions, and AI-enabled fluency (Besiri,

2024). AI, thus, is fundamentally transforming a number of areas in management education in the following ways:

- Customization of Learning Experiences: AI systems adapt course material focused on the strengths and weaknesses of students, establishing precise learning paths (Mollick & Mollick, 2023).
- Case Studies Simulations: AI-developed case studies enable students to analyze data in real-time, determine market trends, and assess risk factors to make informed business decisions (Banerjee & Namboodiri, 2023).
- Business Analytics and Forecasting: Predictive analytics and machine learning algorithms train students to anticipate trends in the market, assess financial risk, and model consumer behaviors (Rust & Huang, 2022).
- Administrative and Assessment Automation: AI grades, provides feedback, and even personalized mentoring, allowing teachers to concentrate on higher-order thinking and student interaction (Selwyn, 2023).
- AI for Decision Support Systems: Artificial intelligence-based technologies allow students to use computer-based decision-making models that build student competencies for financial risk analysis, operational effectiveness, and strategic planning (Wilson & Daugherty, 2018).
- AI Facilitated Collaboration and Networking: AI technologies augment networking possibilities by linking students to colleagues, mentors, and professional leaders with shared professional interests and expertise (Nguyen & Henderson, 2022).

## AI and the Future of the MBA Programme

With AI becoming increasingly ubiquitous, MBA programs will need to redevelop their curriculum to ensure that students exiting the program will have AI competencies. Business schools around the world are looking into creating courses on AI marketing, automation in finance, HR analytics, and AI-based supply chain management. AI literacy is now considered a baseline skill for graduates of MBA programs and is a key area for students to feel confident that they are able to articulate their understanding and use of AI in business decision making by their graduation (Wilson & Daugherty, 2018).

AI also encourages a data-centered focus on leadership. Business leaders in the past relied more heavily on intuition and experience; nowadays, there are AI-enabled decision support systems that allow the business leader to provide ongoing data-driven insight to inform corporate strategy in real-time. Business schools have sought to develop AI as part of their leadership development programs that offer student engagement in AI-enabled, scenario-based decision-making models (Pendy, 2023).

This is an important addition and would ensure business students are leaders who have both strategic thinking skills and AI abilities. AI-enabled translation technology, virtual learning environments, and an international networking perspective are other ways AI is transforming the globalization of MBA programs (Tiwari, 2023).

Despite the considerable advantages AI has to offer, there remain barriers to its fusion within business education. Ethical implications, faculty preparedness, and budgets are considerations to ensure AI is integrated successfully. These barriers will be considered in greater depth later in this study.

## Research Scope and Objective

This research examines the potential impact and future of AI in business education, with particular emphasis on:

- AI has implications for MBA curricula, faculty roles, educational technology, and student engagement.
- AI in terms of opportunities for integration into finance, marketing, human resources, and strategic management courses.
- The future of AI-integrated business education in corporate training and leadership.
- Challenges and considerations of dismantling AI and the adoption of AI business education within business schools.
- Directions and implications for business schools to move forward with the AI movement responsibly and successfully into degree education.

## AI-Powered Innovation in Business Education

To contextualize AI's relevance in business education, it is first essential to understand the specific ways it transforms core learning principles and prepares students for evolving managerial landscapes

***Adaptive Learning Models:*** AI has a huge influence on business education as adaptive learning systems are integrated with the teaching process. Institutions that implement AI-driven adaptive learning systems typically represent leading or innovative business schools that prioritize personalized, data-driven education models. And by ongoing measuring of students' performance, their curriculum is altered immediately for each student (Luckin, 2022). Machine learning algorithms in these systems can effectively track student engagement and learning obstacles to improve recommendations for personalised adaptive learning (Siemens & Baker, 2023).

Adaptive learning helps students to better comprehend ideas, retain information for longer periods of time, and become critical thinkers. The process of adaptive learning is a perfect fit for MBA education as students enrolled in MBA programmes come from different academic and professional backgrounds. IBM Watson Education and Coursera AI tutor work together as an AI-based platform to create learning plans based on students' weaknesses in a particular subject. Adaptive learning methods allow learners to learn at their own pace while keeping the cognitive complexity of the theory and business principles complex yet at proper levels that will not go beyond their cognitive capacity. LinkedIn Learning can be considered an example of the use of AI to assess students' pace and match their knowledge level (Zawacki-Richter et al., 2022).

***AI-Powered Business Simulations:*** Artificial intelligence has changed the practices of business simulations, as students engage in decision-making, which stimulates real business activities, and poses a high risk. While studying these cases, students do a manual analysis of the business cases using outdated static data. AI-based business simulations from Harvard Business Publishing, along with MIT Sloan, deliver dynamic business scenarios composed of real-time data interactions.

In AI-based systems, MBA students perform virtual leadership training and explore financial strategy planning as well as market strategy testing. AI gives students the ability to develop predictive models through which students can predict specific business risks before making decisions (Rust & Huang, 2022). Educational organizations achieve a bridge between educational theory and actual business procedures by implementing AI-based business simulation approaches into their curriculum.

***AI in Virtual Classrooms and Hybrid Learning:*** Educational delivery in business experiences has undergone transformation since AI implementation allows for digital classroom development, together with traditional classroom integration of online learning principles. Students benefit from automatic feedback via AI-based educational platforms, while the platforms also provide participation tools to boost the quality of remote learning (Nguyen & Henderson, 2022). Virtual learning platforms start by assessing student engagement through artificial intelligence machines, after which personalized recommendations modify the educational content.

Machine-aided transcription procedures combined with real-time translation capabilities are the cutting edge of what AI can offer or be incorporated in today's virtual classroom. AI-supported translation methods with speech recognition procedures provide opportunities for students belonging to all socio-demographics and often disparate language-speaking societies, thus improving enrollment possibilities from populations with a wider diversity. Continuous AI-supported intermediary support systems, such as chatbots and virtual assistants, offer themselves to students during their virtual MBA education around the globe, twenty-four hours a day (Davenport & Ronanki, 2018).

The learning experience is enhanced as students can have a combination of an AI-based chatbot providing them answers and an AI-supported virtual assistant supplying course information during their educational process because of instructor-proportional assistant cognitive processes plus AI-assisted administrative decision processes, which can assist in improving enrollment management. AI-assisted online analytic systems build predictive capacity to assist in monitoring students' academic performance, which allows for interventions to occur before a student falls to academic merit status at a virtual learning institution. The prediction ability serves to provide rapid educational assistance referrals with the implementation of AI technology (Baker & Smith, 2021).

***AI-Driven Personalization and Collaboration in MBA Learning:*** The integration of artificial intelligence drives fundamental transformations in Master of Business Administration education through individualized educational methods accompanied by a team-based learning environment redesign. Squirrel AI and Carnegie Learning's AI Tutor are both intelligent tutoring systems that adjust their instruction in financial modeling and strategic analysis based on individual learner behaviors, or even student errors, but also allow reconstruction of the pace of the student's learning. Grammarly and Turnitin provide feedback on the quality of writing and will track mistakes to help develop better writing skills for academic purposes (Selwyn, 2023). VMock is an AI-type platform that assists individuals in positioning themselves in the job market by analyzing their resume according to how it relates to contemporary information about the job market (Banerjee & Namboodiri, 2023).

The important dimensions of teamwork in MBA schooling are all being transformed with advancements in AI technology. The integration of advanced technology and artificial intelligence gives students the opportunity to collaborate with group members known for diverse skills to create teams that will perform at remarkable levels. The collection of Microsoft Teams AI, Zoom AI Companion, and Google Workspace AI allows students to pull from and develop tools to coordinate academic projects and deliver project work through collaboration, even if team members are in different geographical areas and time zones (Tiwari, 2023). The AI-enhanced conflict management tool observes how team members interact and reports to help predict adjustments in behavior that will most likely improve the work performance of the group (Davenport & Ronanki, 2018). Advanced technology will enable business education to provide team-based work at both a better workplace collaborative level of development, and at a fundamental redesign of the learning structure.

While innovations like adaptive learning and simulations have transformed the tools used in classrooms, their true impact is most evident in how they reshape the pedagogical experience for students and educators alike.

## AI's Impact on Pedagogical Approaches in Business Schools

***Revolutionizing Teaching Methods with AI:*** Artificial Intelligence (AI) is fundamentally transforming business education as it moves away from the traditional lecture-based format towards interactive, AI-generated learning environments. Case-based pedagogy, a new way to educate students in business, has been used in business schools for years alongside faculty-based assessment strategies. AI provinces pedagogical systems that create opportunities to adapt with data, personalizing the experience of learning to the learning needs of a specific learner (Luckin's, 2022).

Adaptive learning by AI is the most significant disruption to how education is delivered within higher education. These digital learning systems provide say adaptability based on assessments in the platforms used - Coursera AI, edX Learning Assistant, and IBM Watson Education (Siemens & Baker, 2023). For example, MBA students benefit from these systems by selecting study/learning topics that focus on improvement instead of building experience, selecting familiar content that they studied, video, white papers, and articles for the type of material that matches their knowledge base. Furthermore, adaptive systems support learning and retention of knowledge for both students and business schools, who develop richer understandings of the types of students.

In addition, AI-enabled faculty support systems provide an alternative to augment faculty work in managing a higher education course. ChatGPT for Educators and Squirrel AI provides assistance to faculty teaching when managing course materials, summarizing syllabi, and generating discussion prompts from recent academic readings (Nguyen & Henderson, 2022). Faculty are not being replaced - they are being supported through educational AI that expands their ability to personalize the support they are able to provide to their learners while shifting faculty attention toward strategic mentoring, instead of back-to-compliance-driven administrative tasks.

***AI in Automated Grading, Assessments, and Student Feedback:*** There are several avenues available to implement AI for business education, either through scoring modalities or evaluation procedures. Assignment evaluations via Artificial Intelligence can be as simple as Turnitin AI and as complex as Gradescope or EvalAI, which rely on NLP and machine learning to assess the variety of academic and business projects (Tiwari, 2023). The computer programs give instant evaluative feedback on the quality of the content and the structure of the argument, as well as the coherence of the terms discussed, which gives professors a good grading effort while advocating for greater consistency in grading.

The implementation of automated grading systems, or algorithmic scoring, in examinations is an additional efficient grading system that reduces human bias when scoring multiple-choice items. AI assessment toolkits are producing case studies and simulations via automation at a faster rate by generating quiz-based scenarios in finance/programs, as well as data analytics. Business education assessments are in the process of changing from providing theoretical knowledge to applying that theoretical knowledge to real-world business problems; for business domains, this creates a more applicable experience for students.

When trials are evaluated through surveillance learning means, AI-powered feedback systems will lift the student's performance in assessment. The business school journey is characterized by considering the outputs of delayed feedback for various reasons, ranging from teaching workloads to immediate individualized improvement recommendations. AI tutors in the academic space create educational assessment means through students' synthesized decision-making and provide recommendations for improvement to: simulation-based assessments, a business strategy feedback component, leader circle evaluations, and financial plans.

***The Role of AI in Faculty Development and Curriculum Enhancement:*** The educational experience of students changes through AI, while faculty members use AI tools to improve their instructional techniques. AI-powered developmental instruments monitor faculty teaching practices, including assessment of instructional methods, student interaction, and course plan effectiveness (Baker & Smith, 2019). AI systems also track classroom engagement and help faculty adapt accordingly.

AI insights also provide teachers the opportunity to align the content to industry relevance and up-to-date practices, while curriculum redesigns from predictive analytics can serve topics such as AI-infused finance, digital marketing, and operations.

As AI technologies become increasingly embedded in business education, faculty roles are also changing in relation to the content. educators must now engage with AI-enabled tools, decipher learning analytics, and support students to address ethical and strategic issues in how they engage with technology. Yet amid these changes, fundamental challenges persist: anxieties about becoming irrelevant, worries about losing control of the classroom, and a lack of technical training to use AI effectively.

To bridge the gap, institutions should create structured pathways to faculty development. Programs like INSEAD's AI for Educators provide hands-on exposure to AI tools in the classroom and allow faculty to co-design curriculum using adaptive systems. Bootcamps, co-teaching pilots, and academic design labs can allow educators to refactor their pedagogies while allowing for academic freedom of thought and human-centered mentoring. By creating opportunities for faculty to develop AI literacy, institutions will advance the implementation of AI technologies, as well as confidence, creativity, and innovation, when designing instructional experiences.

## Challenges in AI-Driven Pedagogy: The Need for Human Oversight

While AI can be beneficial in education, there are also negative aspects to consider. The primary negative aspect is that using AI-driven teaching tools can suppress social interaction and higher-order thinking. Business education fundamentally relies on interpersonal engagement and soft skills development, such as leadership, negotiation, and ethical reasoning.

Second, there are potential biases in grading and learning recommendations that come with AI-based assessments. If learning models are trained or tested using data containing shared historical biases or privileges to a specific learning style, context, or location, it could even create a greater inequality and show a greater impact on access to educational programming (Mehrabi et al., 2022). Business schools need to have continuing reviews of AI automated processes and algorithms in order to be purposeful in avoiding algorithmic discrimination.

A third issue is with the instructors, or the area of study, with practices and cultural training, supporting the adoption of AI. Many of the professors in business schools do not understand AI and are used to the notion of teaching methodologies. When adopting an AI/tool, educators have to recognize the devastating thought process in cultural mindset, and who will support in any Trainer/Professional Development training will never happen (Selwyn, 2023). Universities need to have and develop AI literacy programs for educators, so they can adopt AI tools as an augmentation to the learning environment, and not succumb to the thought of fear of being replaced as educators.

## Finding the Right Balance: AI and Human-Centered Learning

Business schools must incorporate AI into a hybrid approach to learning that ensures human-led business education and captures the benefits of AI. This hybrid approach must rethink how teaching, mentorship, and learning communities integrate to enhance student possibilities (Dede, Richards & Saxberg, 2020).

Strategies to promote a positive and human-centered adoption of AI in schools of business include:

- Blended learning - Combination of an AI-automation assisted human-led case discussion with faculty, human-mentored project-based experiential learning.
- AI-enhanced coaching and mentoring capabilities - AI should assist in analyzing student performance, but the intervention around career counseling

and leadership training should be retained through human mentoring roles (Terblanche, 2024).

- Regularly auditing AI in use - Business schools that adopt an ethics-based policy around AI must be audited regularly to ensure that their AI learning remains inclusive, transparent, and equitable (Rust & Huang, 2022).

Once business schools discover the right balance, business education can grow in capacity to take advantage of the possibilities offered by AI relative to efficiency and personalization, and maintain a human experience around leadership, innovation, and ethical business, leading decisions.

While AI is reshaping pedagogy and faculty development, its impact is perhaps most visible in how it transforms each core specialization within MBA programs, redefining finance, marketing, HR, and operations through data-driven decision-making and intelligent systems.

## AI in MBA Core Specialization

***AI in Finance:*** Artificial Intelligence has revolutionized how we make financial decisions by rendering things faster, data-driven, and more precise. At business schools, professors are utilizing AI to teach students investment strategy, financial modeling, and how to manage risk to prepare MBA degrees for a technology-based financial services industry (Tambe, Cappelli & Yakubovich, 2019).

Perhaps one of the largest transformational uses of AI in finance is in algorithmic trading. In algorithmic trading, machine-learning models analyze market data, identify trends in the market data, and make trades in fractions of a second. Platforms like Kavout and MetaTrader AI allow users to create simulated worlds to trade and utilize actual market interactions with trends. They leverage machine learning algorithms to provide a great deal of analysis with a lot of data to allow for good trading strategies (Jansen, 2020).

Artificial intelligence and machine learning are refining risk assessment in finance through their predictions of the likelihood of loan default and investment risk, while also detecting fraudulent transactions. For instance, financial institutions and banking models have embraced AI-based credit ratings that take non-traditional data points, such as an individual's social media behavior and their spending behavior, to ascertain how creditworthy an individual is. These new methodologies will provide a more complete assessment of an individual's entire financial behavior (Goetghebuer, 2021). AI-embedded transactions also track or predict fraud by using algorithms for detecting an anomaly or recognizing a pattern to detect abnormal transactions that lead to greater overall financial risk (Langenbucher & Corcoran, 2021).

In addition, robo-advisors that utilize AI technologies, such as Wealthfront or Betterment, offer automated investment recommendations based on a person's risk tolerance, financial goals, and market conditions as a way to automate investment management. Finally, finance students in education can now interactively engage with robotics against criteria outlining Aiken's levels of Learning through a theory and practice of text in assessing portfolio diversification, asset allocation, and/or predictive strategies.

Recent research has shown that generative AI also enhances real-time financial forecasting and portfolio simulation in MBA classrooms, creating dynamic learning labs for students (Besiri, 2024).

***AI in Marketing:*** The advancement of Artificial Intelligence (AI) has significantly transformed marketing, including personalized customer experiences, data-driven decisions, and automated marketing efforts. In the "good old days" marketers had to base decisions on consumer purchase intention surveys, focus groups, and historical sales data to formulate and execute a marketing plan, however, that's all changed and now marketers can analyze real-time consumer behavior, sentiment, and preferences, allowing for highly personalized marketing strategies through AI (Anitsal, 2024).

An area of application where predictive analytics is a popular area for tuning AI into marketing is where marketers are leveraging AI to determine customer needs and to optimize marketing strategies. AI-based platforms such as Salesforce Einstein analyze customer interactions, social media interactions, thinking, and purchase behaviors to assist marketers in designing effective and targeted choices in utilizing their marketing strategies with consumers and customers (Salesforce, 2024).

AI is also sparking a renaissance in digital advertising in programmatic advertising, which is where machine learning algorithms optimally decide which ad placement bid, using analysis of targeted audience members with the machine learning algorithms in real-time bidding on the ad placement (Viant Technology, 2024). Another expanding area is AI-generated content.

AI processes can create personalized email campaigns, ad copy, and blog post types of content using tools like Jasper AI to engage audiences and improve conversion rates (Slavin, 2023). AI is also providing solutions through search engine optimization (SEO) tools to assist marketers in creating and optimizing content strategies to improve visibility and search rankings.

***AI in Human Resources:*** AI is changing HR through automation in hiring processes, better workforce planning, and enhanced employee engagement strategies. HR has traditionally demanded a high level of manual resume review and possibly prejudiced assessments in the interview process. Today, systems that use AI allow SME HR to benefit from the use of data to assess candidates for recruitment and performance review tasks (Daramola, 2023).

Also, hiring platforms with AI capabilities, such as HireVue and Pymetrics, offer assessments of behavior and skill sets to assess candidates for the best fit. They analyze video interviews, speech patterns, and facial expressions to determine soft skills metrics and cultural fit and increase the accuracy and efficiency of the hiring process (Hemalatha & Prabhu, 2023).

Additionally, AI has transformed employee retention strategies, as HR now analyses workplace sentiment and engagement and performance data through the use of HR analytics tools like Workday AI and Visier that highlight attrition risk and recommend employee-specific career development plans (Kumar & Singh, 2023).

In the area of learning and development, AI-equipped corporate training platforms such as LinkedIn Learning AI and Coursera for Business provide tailored training modules based on employee skill gaps to support employee growth (Arakawa & Yakura, 2024). Additionally, AI-powered coaching chatbots provide immediate feedback on well-developed leadership and soft skills to MBA students and corporate professionals (Van Nuland, 2023).

Moreover, an AI-based performance management system gives immediate feedback on various employees' performance outcomes, changing assessment from annual reviews to continuously assessing employee performance. Performance management systems leverage natural language processing (NLP) and predictive analytics to assess work patterns, levels of productivity, and leadership potential (ClearCompany, 2023).

***AI in Operations and Supply Chain Management:*** The supply chain management (SCM) and operations landscape has changed with artificial intelligence (AI) being leveraged to improve logistics efficiencies, lower costs, and improve demand forecasting. With this new AI-based technology emerging, MBA programs are incorporating AI-enabled SCM platforms into their curricula, and in some cases, offering students access to AI global SCM networks designed to analyze real-time global data (Jackson et al., 2024).

AI-enabled demand forecasting tools, such as SAP Integrated Business Planning and Oracle SCM AI, leverage historical sales data and data trends around climate change and geopolitical tensions to predict the likelihood of global supply chain disruptions. This information enables businesses to maximize working capital through improved inventory management to minimize lost sales from an out-of-stock inventory and overproduction (Patil, 2025).

AI-enhanced warehouse and distribution automation systems use robotic process automation (RPA), along with smart inventory management, to improve efficiency by reducing human error, better using existing storage, and automating order fulfillment. Companies like Amazon and Walmart use AI-powered robotics to perform independently in the management of logistics and are able examples used as case studies to teach students in MBA operations management courses (Winkelhaus & Grosse, 2020).

In enhancing the last-mile segment of deliveries, companies are employing artificial intelligence (AI)-enabled optimization of original algorithms with autonomous delivery drones. AI-capable logistics platforms, Route4Me, for example, or FedEx's SenseAware utilize data-driven algorithms to facilitate time-efficiency capabilities by both analyzing possible downtimes for deliveries and providing alternate routes in real time (Boysen et al., 2021).

AI is also evolving into automating contract negotiations, evaluating risk factors, and aiding procurement strategies for organizations to plan for effective supplier relationship management (SRM). AI-enabled SRM technologies like GEP Smart and JAGGAER AI Procurement use supplier performance data combined with cost and risk awareness to support procurement decisions (Handfield et al., 2020).

## AI's Future in MBA Specializations

As AI develops, business schools are restructuring their MBA programs with AI-specific concentrations. Business leaders of the future will have to understand how to use AI for decision-making, predictive analytics, and automation-based strategies in finance, marketing, HR, and operations (Bagai & Mane, 2024).

AI-based business education will also continue to include emphasis on data-oriented leaders, ethics of AI, and AI and human collaboration so that MBA graduates are prepared to situate their technical AI skills within the framework of strategic leadership and also offer guidance to those interfacing with AI in operational capacities.

## Artificial Intelligence in Startup Lifecycle

Outside formal education systems, AI is also transforming entrepreneurship, especially in fast-moving startup ecosystems. This section investigates AI's influence across the startup lifecycle, from ideation to scaling.

Artificial Intelligence is no longer an abstraction of the future; it is the infrastructure upon which contemporary entrepreneurs design, build, and operate their businesses. In a particularly agile startup context like India, and across the globe, AI-driven models are paving the way for previous traditional modes and markers of ideation, investment/funding, product development, scaling to market, and long-term innovation. The following section details and unpacks the integration of AI and guides in the unique journey of an entrepreneur at different levels and processes of AI infusion through each, and an overview of the different levelling effects to each approach.

## AI in Startup Ideation and Business Model Innovation

AI will play a role in the ideation phase as it will allow entrepreneurs to create ideas rapidly, transform them into prototypes, and validate their approaches based on predictive models, trend analysis, and simulations of customer behavior. Many entrepreneurs are creating AI-driven startups that help not only to create ideas but also support entire business ideas based on data-informed feasibility analysis.

For example, you can use NLP and machine learning algorithms to effectively scan the "digital universe" research databases, social media blogs, and patent databases, to identify problems that haven't previously been solved or discover new demand from customers (Wang & Demszky, 2023). Novel value propositions can emerge from using AI that may be worth a significant amount to the market in some cases.

Secondly, AI can enable a new phase of entrepreneur engagement when it comes to developing frameworks for business models. Instead of relying on their instincts or stale reporting from conventional sources on the market and potential changes in it, founders can now develop frameworks of business models in which real-time, responsive, and mediated market conditions are incorporated into the framework using scenario planning, AI-driven SWOT analysis, or customer-segmentation algorithms (Haefner et al., 2021). Eventually, what those frameworks will embed into business models will be the ability to respond to market disruption in real-time, and be beneficial in a reactive fashion in situations that are less predictable (or unstable), i.e., Tier 2 and Tier 3 startup hubs in India.

AI-driven ideation platforms are enabling startups to rapidly validate business models, simulate customer journeys, and test minimum viable products with minimal technical input.

AI-driven platforms such as Lean Canvas AI, or generative ChatGPT-based business turbo-chargers, help entrepreneurs in the embryonic stages of start-up thinking and rethinking about their ideas to define narrowed-down unique selling points, return to market possibilities, and iteration, alongside reduced time and better product-to-market fit. These AI-driven platforms and tools create a testing environment for business ideas and hypotheses against historical data sets, and sentiment analysis to mitigate failure at the earliest stage of new ventures.

## AI in Product Development and Personalization

AI brings significant competitive advantages in the product development space. Startups that utilize technologies like computer vision, natural language processing, and recommendation engines are able to build significantly more personalized products and product experiences, while AI systems allow for continuous product iteration through feedback loops, leveraging data on how customers are using their products to inform iterations in product features or user experience.

Health Tech startups enabled through AI tools - like CureSkin or PharmEasy in India - use machine learning-informed technology to reach diagnostics and develop personalized treatment recommendations. Such platforms offer intended journeys for users based on data from wearables, historical health data, or generated from application activity, intended to promote goals and outcomes while lowering costs.

From a development perspective, AI enables the rapid and low-risk creation of product prototypes, accelerating the iteration process. Generative design tools or no-code/low-code AI tools can also allow non-technical founders to create working prototypes of products without any coding knowledge (Ghosh et al., 2021). This democratizing of technology development also inspires new opportunities for entrepreneurship for a wider segment of the population that may have been outside historically identified categories and experiences.

Along with the above, developments in AI also improve customer experience, e.g., AI-based A/B testing to provide consistent UX iterations that respond to user interface behavior, data, and dynamically change without human interaction.

Recent studies highlight that generative AI tools such as ChatGPT and DALL·E are being used in early-stage product design, allowing for rapid prototyping and user testing in lean startup environments (Banerjee & Namboodiri, 2023).

## The Growing Importance of AI in Startup Funding, Growth, and Ethical Risk Management

With increased investment into startup ecosystems that are focused on funding and scaling startup companies, artificial intelligence is slowly emerging as a larger and larger enabler. In other words, while entrepreneurs are determining use for an initial pitch deck, financial modeling, and predicting investor behavior based on observed trends in funding rounds could include AI tools (e.g., Equidam, funded.ai, and ChatGPT). Similarly, investors (e.g., venture capitalists, angel syndicates, and possibly their respective firms) often will use AI. In either event, the startup should be prepared to deliver information, solely or in part, as machine-readable information or formatted for machine-readable purposes to remain competitive (Ozince & Ihlamur, 2024). As companies grow and scale their operations, machine intelligence increases operational efficiencies of existing businesses with tools developed for utilization in intelligent inventory management systems, robotic process automation (RPA), and dynamic pricing. Meesho and Zepto are examples of very large startups in India that use the skills of machine intelligence for just-in-time inventory management and delivery routes in real time. In addition, AI-driven growth hacking tools - both Meta's Advantage and Google's Performance Max - help startups micro-target audiences, optimize ad spend, and ultimately compete with larger incumbents, democratizing digital marketing practices.

While AI has its benefits for entrepreneurial activity, it is not without ethical and operational challenges. For example, there are significant issues around the use of user data, even with policies such as the EU's General Data Protection Regulation and India's Digital Personal Data Protection Act, 2023. There are also concerns about bias in AI models that can lend itself to discrimination and exclusion in places where such bias can lead to bad decisions, such as in recruitment (West et al., 2019) or hiring. Founders ought to consider principles of explainable AI (XAI) and work toward reducing bias in its application. On the operational side, over-reliance on AI may diminish human evaluative judgment when validity and empathy are required or cultural competency is needed. Complimenting this, due to the complexity of these issues, start-ups are creating ethical review boards and internal compliance frameworks as a form of anticipatory governance. The development of such practices suggests the responsible integration of AI systems is not just a technical issue, but an emergent responsibility of leadership for the emerging generation of entrepreneurs.

## Transforming Traditional Startup Models through AI

Artificial intelligence represents a departure from the previous constructs; it is changing them. The previous construct for a startup was a linear growth model, linear business growth, linear scaling, and human-based decision making to run the model.

Now, because of AI, startups are building new adaptive constructs based on data, they are scaling models through non-linear scaling, dynamically learning and adapting to decentralized decision-making models (Bughin, Catlin & LaBerge, 2019). An example of an AI-native startup is one that has infused this idea into the first sequence of its startup and business process. We see this in fintech with startups such as Cred or ZestMoney, as both have built their AI, by definition, into their settlement as they are providing products to finance that are responsive to their customer, to name a few.

AI has also built adaptive systems into the platform economy, where two sided marketplaces are being built through dynamic algorithms using AI in edtech (sections like Leverage Edu), in agritech (for example, DeHaat), even in jobtech (for example, Apna), where friction is low, scalable, and at little or no incremental cost. AI is reshaping the way experiences in startups have evolved from the integration of AI technologies into products. It is signaling a new paradigm shift of entrepreneurial thinking where information used in embedded systems and algorithmic thinking is becoming center stage.

As the integration of AI deepens across business education, institutions must confront not only their operational challenges but also their long-term ethical, strategic, and global implications.

## Future Implications and Challenges in AI-Driven Business Education

As Artificial Intelligence continues to revolutionize business education, it opens up a number of opportunities for growth and innovation, but it also comes with a number of important implications and challenges that institutions must tackle in a thoughtful and strategic manner.

1. ***Ethical and Algorithmic Risks:*** AI-based systems can create unintended bias, particularly in student admissions, grades, and hiring. If left to run unchecked, these algorithm-based models may even reinforce existing inequalities based on race, gender, or geographical region. Institutions will need to implement a series of measures, such as explainable AI (XAI), bias audits, and diverse data representation, in order to combat these ethical and algorithmic risks. (Mehrabi et al., 2022)
2. ***Data Privacy and Consent:*** AI-driven learning platforms also rely on data about students, and the sensitive, personal data they collect not only personalizes student learning but also creates privacy concerns, particularly with regions having various regulatory controls like the GDPR or India's Digital Personal Data Protection Act (Government of India, 2023). Institutions will need to craft strong policies around data stewardship/due diligence and allow students to have control over the sensitive data that makes up their own consent dashboards and online profiles (UNESCO, 2023)
3. ***Faculty Preparedness and Resistance:*** They may lack the training, confidence, competence, or simply be resistant to attempting to integrate the potentially disruptive AI tools into their teaching. Their resistance to these often disruptive technology tools may be based on being replaced by AI as faculty, along with a lack of institutional support in implementing and using AI in teaching, and other institutional factors. Schools need to provide opportunities for AI literacy techniques and training boot camps, as well as models (i.e., co-teaching) which include in-person and digital training (i.e., AI tools) and programs like INSEAD's "AI for Educators" (Baidoo-Anu & Owusu-Ansah, 2023)
4. ***Human Judgment and Soft Skills:*** As AI technologies become more ubiquitous, one danger is that managers might lose important management skills, including empathy, negotiation, and critical thinking. Managers must still rely upon the soft knowledge we gain through human mentorship and in-person,

“in-class” interaction, while still being able to contemplate the inclusion of AI into their practices (as a supplemental mechanism to human judgment, not a direct replacement). (Dede, Richards & Saxberg, 2020)

5. ***Access and Equity in the Global South:*** Most efforts for AI integration remain relegated to elite institutions. Most business schools in developing regions lack the foundation and qualified faculty to implement and deploy AI with adequate consideration. There is an increasing need to level this digital playing field through scalable, low-cost AI tools and cross-regional collaborations (UNESCO, 2023)
6. ***Scenarios and Readiness Models:*** Schools must be prepared to not only address technological changes-being open to changing the culture and organization of the institution. These scenarios span the range of optimistic scenarios for personalized, equitable learning experiences to cautionary accounts about over-automated learning, data sharing, and exploitation. schools might even consider AI readiness maturity models to consider and better understand their capabilities across factors like governance, pedagogy, and engagement and involvement with their students as stakeholders.

In light of these challenges, business schools must be considerate of how they are pursuing accountability in a way that balances innovative thinking, creativity, and experimentation with AI technologies. A future-ready approach to AI demands a thoughtful integration process-using human-centered design, ethical considerations, and inclusivity, that must precede implementation.

As business education continues to evolve alongside AI, understanding the trends that will define the next generation of teaching and learning becomes critical. The next section outlines key trajectories likely to influence the design and delivery of MBA programs in the coming years.

## Future Trends in AI For Business Schools

**Adaptive Curriculum Development and Market Synchronization:** In the future, MBA programs will feature an agile, AI-supported curriculum that dynamically adapts to critical industry signals and student data. Advanced machine learning algorithms can analyze job boards, forecast employer expectations, and take stock of company strategy documents to build predictive models of skill needs to plan for (Yoon & Rao, 2023). For instance, if demand for hiring for ESG peaks, the institution could add more sustainability analytics modules to their program, in weeks instead of years, as skills change.

This responsiveness sharpens graduation preparedness, all while ensuring graduates are able to evolve with business needs. If we view emotional intelligence analytics as part of the MBA experience, the approach could help inform "leadership development pathways for individuals." So, a learner demonstrates aptitude in conflict resolution but lacks assertiveness. Once they are flagged, dynamic AI could recommend you as a micro-module designer or as a mentor.

**AI-Augmented Experiential Learning:** Experiential learning is changing. Technologies augmented with AI now allow students to interact with digital replicas of real companies' digital twins in order to evaluate strategy in a live-market context. Imagine a student managing a digital twin of Tesla's supply chain while dealing with simulated events such as disruptions in the availability of raw materials or changes in governmental policy.

These platforms can also include cross-border collaborations. One to think of would be a worldwide AI consulting challenge, where MBA teams on different continents studied and worked together to solve real-world business problems (going from London to Jinjiang spontaneously), consistent with what a multinational consulting engagement would be like. This kind of experiential learning would help build problem-solving agility and readiness for the international/global world we live in today.

Institutions like Harvard and INSEAD are piloting AI-powered simulations where MBA students engage with dynamic scenarios using real-time data and NLP-based coaching systems.

**AI-Enhanced Faculty Intelligence and Teaching Optimization:** While AI facilitates hyper-personalization for learners, it also enhances instructor behaviors. Intelligent analytics platforms can recognize micro-patterns in student engagement, such as pauses within lectures, the speed of note-taking, or the level of interactivity within peer forums. Educators can use these learning insights to modify content, delivery, and pacing in real-time.

Professors may develop globally connected faculty networks where AI platforms curate and share pedagogical innovations based on disciplinary needs, geographical locations, and teaching styles. For instance, a finance professor in Singapore can utilize teaching resources created in real time from Canada, based on AI-filtered metrics based on student feedback from the lecture environment.

**Continuous Upskilling Through AI-Led Executive Education:** The half-life of most skills is diminishing, making continuous learning an important necessity. Today, AI-enabled platforms help executives with just-in-time executive education. If a CFO anticipates their organization needs to implement anticipated regulatory changes in sustainability reporting, an AI-enabled learning path can be developed, from understanding global regulations to simulation-based compliance workshops, entirely created by AI platforms.

Within the next five to ten years, we may see AI-supported career mentors become the norm to create learning and development plans for professionals. These agents, trained on thousands of professional journeys, would allow for behavioral nudges, opportunity forecasts, and personalized development maps for the individual. More importantly, these AI-enabled mentors will create a combined experience of hard data with emotional analytics to provide a holistic mentoring experience instead of the career tools used today.

**Integrating Ethics and Personalization in Business Education Driven by AI:** AI is transforming career personalization in business education by enabling deeper matching between students and employers based on analysis of student communication styles, leadership characteristics, and workplace cultural fit, going beyond simple resume screening. Technological advances like AI reputation scores, even probationary ones based on academic and behavioral metrics, provide a more nuanced portrait of candidates, while simultaneously raising ethical issues. To encourage responsible use, business schools are adopting ethical structures, such as co-design processes, ethical sandboxes, and "Responsible AI Studios" in which students think collaboratively about questions of developing AI governance models. Ethics training is shifting towards a focus on foresight and real-world application, preparing future managers to be prepared to be ethical, not simply users of AI, but architects of AI use in business and society.

As AI maturity continues to rise across educational institutions, schools can adopt readiness models such as the OECD's "AI in Education Maturity Matrix"(OECD, 2023) to assess preparedness across domains like governance, pedagogy, equity, and infrastructure.

## Case Studies and Global Best Practices in AI-Driven Business Education

Several leading business schools have already begun implementing AI-driven strategies. The following case studies illustrate how these practices are being applied in diverse institutional contexts.

A key instance of the adoption of Artificial Intelligence (AI) into the education of business leaders is through leading global business schools committed to accelerating their practice. These examples illustrate how the world's best business schools are now adopting AI into the engagement of business education, learning constructs, and the design of curricula. The instantiation of AI education in management programs involves the individuation of courses and programs of varying quality, like the following case studies from Wharton, MIT Sloan, NUS, and IIM Ahmedabad.

## The Wharton School, University of Pennsylvania (USA)

The Wharton School is leading the way in research and pedagogy on AI for business education in its AI for Business initiative, which is housed under the Analytics at Wharton Research Center. The AI for Business Initiative is developed as both a research center and a hub for curriculum development and pedagogy. Wharton engages MBA and Executive MBA cohorts in the following AI-enabled courses: AI for Business, Analytics for Decision-Making, and People Analytics (Wharton School, 2023). Wharton is also integrating AI into career services through predictive modeling to match student profiles to job opportunities more accurately. In collaboration with partners in industry, students engage with real datasets developed by industry partners, while critically thinking about algorithmic bias, explainability, and decision-making (Wharton School, 2023).

## MIT Sloan School of Management (USA)

MIT Sloan's main program for executives, Artificial Intelligence: Implications for Business Strategy, is widely viewed as a leader in AI-related business programs and education. Co-developed with the MIT Computer Science and Artificial Intelligence Laboratory (CSAIL), this program is designed to enable MBA students and mid-career professionals to incorporate AI into business decision-making.

This program promotes cross-functional thinking and links among the areas of the program, including Innovations in AI, marketing, operations, finance, and managerial leadership. Students were presented with opportunities to engage with multiple applications of machine learning, case simulations, and ethical decision-making tasks. Additional educational opportunities are available in the MIT Sloan virtual AI sandboxes, where students can test AI algorithms in simulated business settings.

This program represents an intersection of technical knowledge in the context of business strategy; it is a direct response to the interdisciplinary and multi-functional expectations made of leaders for an AI world.

## National University of Singapore (NUS)

Business School The NUS Business School has employed a deliberate strategy for embedding analytics and AI as part of the programming in modules in its MBA and Executive MBA programs. Specifically, courses such as Analytics for Managers, AI in Marketing, and Leadership in an Age of AI all embed AI as part of the learning experience (National University of Singapore Business School, 2022). A unique example is the use of learning platforms that use AI and adaptive learning to present content as well as personalize content and assessments based on students' performance, engagement, and usage patterns.

Additionally, NUS utilizes chatbots and virtual assistants in its career guidance services, making resume screening, interview practice, and networking recommendations more efficient through data-based algorithms. Such AI-based functionalities have not only enhanced operational efficiency but also student satisfaction and placement rates (Tan & Heng, 2021).

This online-first stance enforces the ambition of the school to become a center of future-ready leadership in Asia.

## Indian Institute of Management Ahmedabad (India)

IIM Ahmedabad is at the forefront of the effort made by Indian institutions to include AI in its Post Graduate Programme in Management, but also in executive education. For example, it has introduced elective classes such as AI for Managers, Machine Learning in Business that offer participants both theoretical and experiential elements (IIM Ahmedabad, 2023).

IIM-A has collaborated with the Centre for Digital Transformation to involve students in applied research projects that will generate AI case studies from the banking, health, and retail sectors, which are then used to connect theory-based student learning with simulated theoretical principles using pedagogic assessments in the classroom.

Similarly, IIM-A has started to investigate AI tools for peer assessment, plagiarism detection, and moderation, as well as a mechanism for personal feedback to enhance all assessments.

The evidence for the emergence of AI-led pedagogical advancement in the global context of developed and developing economies is demonstrated through this case study, and particularly in the Indian management education context.

## Strategic Outlook: AI Beyond the Classroom and the Future of Business Education

While artificial intelligence is reshaping business education in higher education institutes, it is also beginning to proliferate outside of formal education in corporate training, executive learning, and institutional strategy. The push for a continuous, adaptive, and lifelong learning approach makes education enhanced by artificial intelligence an essential ingredient for learning for both individual and organizational learning.

**AI in Corporate Training and Executive Education:** Leading global corporations and business schools are utilizing AI to create personalized learning journeys, reduce skills gaps, and simplify leadership development. AI can recommend content using employee performance data and organizational goals and is being employed by corporate universities and training departments of companies like LinkedIn Learning, Coursera for Business, and Degreed. Executive programs have been launched by institutions like INSEAD and MIT Sloan that integrate AI-powered coaching, adaptive dashboards, and natural language processing-based simulations to enhance communication and decision making (Mollick & Mollick, 2023). IBM's Watson is also being used in combination with instantaneous microlearning to reinforce knowledge retention under high-pressure working conditions. These initiatives highlight evidence of a new logic for education; it is no longer a one-off event, it is a lifelong partnership formed and informed by real-time AI analytical insights and learner requirements.

However, increased reliance on AI tools comes with important concerns. Ethical risks such as bias in algorithms, invasive data use, and excessive automation continue to pose challenges to learner autonomy and institutional trust. As AI becomes woven into strategic HR and learning activities, business schools and corporate educators alike must be involved in strong frameworks for human oversight, transparency, and inclusive access (West et al., 2019).

**Strategic Shifts for the AI-Enabled Business School:** To take advantage of the opportunities and mitigate the risks associated with the integration of AI, business schools need to act proactively with an eye toward securing a future-ready approach. This can be achieved through a few strategic directions to consider:

1. ***Develop Institutional AI Strategies:*** Schools should have AI governance policies, make investments in reskilling faculty, and build a strong digital infrastructure to ensure sustainable integration (Davenport & Ronanki, 2018).
2. ***Co-Create Human-Centered Curricula:*** AI should not replace human judgment but work alongside it. Courses must embed ethics, critical thinking, and interdisciplinary perspectives to foster responsible AI leadership (Selwyn, 2023).
3. ***Facilitate Industry-Academic Collaboration:*** Business schools should partner with startups, corporations, and policymakers to co-develop labs, capstones, and experiential modules grounded in real-world problems (Gans, Goldfarb, & Agrawal, 2018).

4. ***Democratize Access and Inclusion:*** For example, AI tools that transcribe or translate in real-time, or develop personalized learning paths, can shift elite education to poor or underrepresented learners in a global atmosphere of inclusivity (Luckin, 2022).
5. ***Reframe Leadership as Adaptive and Ethical:*** Business education must pivot from building technical managers to developing adaptive, ethical leaders who care about the societal impacts of AI (Baidoo-Anu & Owusu-Ansah, 2023).

## Targeted Responses to Institutional Challenges

To operationalize these strategic shifts, the following interventions address key barriers that institutions commonly face when integrating AI into business education:

- Faculty resistance to AI can be reduced by providing AI literacy programs, bootcamps, and co-teaching approaches to develop familiarity and competence with new technologies.
- Bias in algorithms must be addressed with explainable AI (XAI), fairness audits, and proactive efforts to diversify training data and outcomes.
- Data privacy issues will require advanced consent management dashboards, clear data governance policies, and effective student management of their profiles.
- Equity and access challenges, particularly with lower-resource contexts, can be addressed through the plethora of scalable, low-bandwidth AI applications and global institutional partnerships.
- The erosion of human-centric learning should be countered by pairing AI simulations with live mentorship and socio-emotional skill development to preserve the human dimension of education.

AI will not supplant business educators or leaders but augment their ability to perpetuate new innovations. The business school of the future will be a human and machine fusion that promotes innovation, inclusion, and ethical leadership. Business schools that intelligently combine AI into their instructional delivery while protecting their core educational mission will lead a new era of business education globally.

# CONCLUSION

The inclusion of Artificial Intelligence in business education is transforming the engagement of students, teachers, and business practitioners with learning, creativity, and organizational effectiveness. AI-enabled tools that have emerged in business education, including adaptive learning systems, predictive analytics, and machine learning-based smart simulations, are improving MBA programs to be more personalized, efficient, and well-suited to the new learning expectations for the business workforce of a growing AI-first world. These innovations not only augment academic delivery for students and faculty, but they also allow graduates to develop the data-driven decision-making and problem-solving capabilities necessary for future-proof leadership.

One of the most striking aspects of AI in business education is the capacity to customize real-time feedback about learning outcomes, automate assessment, and individualize instructional design. Business schools are emerging from static curriculum models and beyond static content, moving forward to build opportunities to develop dynamic, AI-powered content wherever there are opportunities to speed up the educational transition to better support change in the workplace. Meanwhile, in corporate and executive education, AI is elevating experiences based on immersive simulations, AI-connected leadership diagnostics, and employee upskilling platforms that deepen strategic learning. As companies leverage AI to optimize workforce performance, executive learners are being trained to engage in high-stakes decision-making founded on data.

Despite these benefits, it will also offer considerable new challenges. Algorithmic bias, data privacy issues, and the dangers of over-automation all require governance systems and structures to exist in business schools. In other words, AI will not replace human-led learning, but it will serve as a complementary way to add a layer to mentoring, ethical reasoning, and the human side of leadership and creativity. MBA programs of the future need to put AI literacy and ethical uplift at the center of learning and prepare students to lead responsibly in an increasingly automated context.

Moving ahead requires balancing technology disruption with human-centered values. Responsible implementation, ongoing faculty training, and ethical co-design of AI tools will be key to success, and institutions need to embrace this balance, leveraging the strengths of machine intelligence and human reason if they would like to stay relevant, but shape the learning experience of the next generation of business leaders to thrive in an AI-powered environment.

## REFERENCES

Ahmedabad, I. I. M. (2024, August 23). *IIMA report reveals that employees are ready to embrace AI-driven transformations - the gap in AI education and upskilling needs to be filled*.https://www.iima.ac.in/inmediaiima-report-reveals-employees-are-ready-embrace-ai-driven-transformations-gap-ai-education

Anitsal, I. (2024, October 3). *How AI is transforming marketing*. Missouri State University News.

Arakawa, R., & Yakura, H. (2024). Coaching copilot: Blended form of an LLM-powered chatbot and a human coach to effectively support self-reflection for leadership growth. *arXiv*. https://doi.org//arXiv.2405.15250DOI: 10.1145/3640794.3665549

Bagai, R., & Mane, V. (2024). Designing an AI-powered mentorship platform for professional development: Opportunities and challenges. *arXiv*. https://doi.org//arXiv.2407.20233DOI: 10.48550

Baidoo-Anu, D., & Owusu Ansah, L. K. (2023). Education in the era of generative AI: Threat or opportunity? *Education and Information Technologies*.

Baker, T., & Smith, L. (2019). *Educ AI tion rebooted? Exploring the future of artificial intelligence in schools and colleges*. Nesta Foundation.

Banerjee, A., & Namboodiri, V. (2023). The impact of generative AI on personalized business learning. *Technovation*.

Besiri, D. (2024). *AI-driven predictive analytics: Transforming decision-making in business. Human Computer Interaction, 12*(2), Article 8ny1ww06.

Boysen, N., Briskorn, D., & Schwerdfeger, S. (2021). Delivery by drone: An evaluation of unmanned aerial vehicle technology in logistics. *Transportation Research Part C, Emerging Technologies, 124*, 102977.

Bughin, J., Catlin, T., & LaBerge, L. (2019). The four fundamentals of workplace automation. *McKinsey Quarterly*.https://www.mckinsey.com/business-functions/mckinsey-digital/our-insights/the-four-fundamentals-of-workplace-automation

ClearCompany. (2023). *AI-powered talent management: Transforming recruitment and development*.https://www.clearcompany.com/resources/ai-talent-management

Daramola, O. (2023). The impact of artificial intelligence on recruitment processes: A comprehensive review. *Open journal of business and management*, 11(5), 2075–2092.

Davenport, T. H., & Ronanki, R. (2018). Artificial intelligence for the real world. *Harvard Business Review*, *96*(1), 108–116.

Dede, C., & Richards, J. (2020). *Learning in the age of AI: Hybrid approaches to teacher-supported AI classrooms*. Harvard Education Press.

Gans, J. S., & Goldfarb, A. (2018). *Prediction, judgment, and complexity: A theory of decision-making and artificial intelligence*. National Bureau of Economic Research.

Ghosh, S., & Ghosh, S. (2021). Classifying speech acts using a multi-channel deep attention network for task-oriented conversational search agents. *Proceedings of the 2021 conference on human information interaction and retrieval*, 267–272. DOI: 10.1145/3406522.3446057

Goetghebuer, J. (2021). AI and Creditworthiness Assessments: The Tale of Credit Scoring and Consumer Protection. In De Bruyne, J., & Vanleenhove, C. (Eds.), *Artificial Intelligence and the Law* (pp. 429–460). Intersentia. DOI: 10.1017/9781839701047.017

Government of India. (2023). *The Digital Personal Data Protection Act, 2023* (No. 12 of 2023). Ministry of Electronics & Information Technology. https://www.meity.gov.in/writereaddata/files/Digital_personal_data_protection_bill.pdf

Haefner, N., Wincent, J., Parida, V., & Gassmann, O. (2021). Artificial intelligence and innovation management: A review, framework, and research agenda. *Technological Forecasting and Social Change*, *162*, 120392. DOI: 10.1016/j.techfore.2020.120392

Handfield, R. B., Jeong, S., & Choi, T. (2020). Emerging procurement technology: Data analytics and cognitive analytics. *Journal of Purchasing and Supply Management*, *26*(2), 100621.

Hemalatha, S., & Prabhu, J. (2023). A review of machine learning applications in the talent acquisition process. *Computational Intelligence and Neuroscience Advances*, 2023, Article 1261.

Jansen, S. (2020). *Machine learning for algorithmic trading* (2nd ed.). Packt Publishing.

Kumar, R., & Singh, M. (2023). Predictive analytics in employee retention and engagement strategies. *International Journal of Human Resource Studies*, *13*(2), 45–60.

Langenbucher, K., & Corcoran, P. (2021). Responsible AI credit scoring - A lesson from Upstart.com. In *Digital finance in Europe: Law, regulation, and governance* (Book 5 in the *European Company and Financial Law Review - Special Volume* series). University Press Library Open.

Luckin, R., George, K., & Cukurova, M. (2022). *AI for School Teachers*. Routledge. DOI: 10.1201/9781003193173

Mehrabi, N., Morstatter, F., Saxena, N., Lerman, K., & Galstyan, A. (2022). A survey on bias and fairness in machine learning. *ACM Computing Surveys*, *55*(3), 1–35. DOI: 10.1145/3457607

Mollick, E., & Mollick, L. (2023). Assigning AI: Seven Approaches for Students with Prompts. *SSRN*. DOI: 10.2139/ssrn.4475995

National University of Singapore Business School. (2022). *The NUS MBA: Programme structure and curriculum overview* [Web page].https://mba.nus.edu.sg/the-programme/

Nguyen, A., & Henderson, M. (2022). AI-powered peer learning: The role of intelligent systems in shaping professional development. *International Journal of Educational Technology in Higher Education*, *19*(1), 23. PMID: 35434266

OECD. (2023). *Digital Education Outlook 2023: Towards an effective digital education ecosystem*. OECD Publishing.

Ozince, E., & Ihlamur, Y. (2024, July 5). *Automating venture capital: Founder assessment using LLM-powered segmentation, feature engineering, and automated labeling techniques*. Preprint. arXiv.https://doi.org//arXiv.2407.04885DOI: 10.48550

Patil, D. (2024). *Artificial intelligence-driven supply chain optimization: Enhancing demand forecasting and cost reduction. SSRN* https://doi.org/DOI: 10.2139/ssrn.5057408

Pendy, B. (2023). Role of AI in business management. *Brilliance: Research of Artificial Intelligence*, *3*(1), 48–55. DOI: 10.47709/brilliance.v3i1.2191

Rust, R. T., & Huang, M. H. (2022). The AI marketing canvas: A five-stage roadmap to implementing artificial intelligence in marketing. *Journal of Business Research*, *140*, 781–789.

Salesforce. (2024). *Discover how AI is transforming education*. https://www.salesforce.com/campaign/experience/edu-ai-data/

Selwyn, N. (2023). *Should robots replace teachers? AI and the future of education*. Polity Press.

Siemens, G., & Baker, R. S. (2023). The state of learning analytics in 2023. *Computers & Education*, *203*, 104624.

Slavin, A. (2023, March 19). *How AI can support educators to make their lives easier* [Blog post]. Jasper.https://www.jasper.ai/blog/amanda-slavin-how-ai-can-support-educators-to-make-their-lives-easier

Tambe, P., Cappelli, P., & Yakubovich, V. (2019). Artificial intelligence in human resources management: Challenges and a path forward. *California Management Review*, *61*(4), 15–42. DOI: 10.1177/0008125619867910

Tan, C. Y., & Heng, S. H. (2021). Integrating AI in business education: A Singapore perspective. *Asian Journal of Management Education*, *18*(2), 77–89.

Terblanche, N. H. D. (2024). Artificial intelligence coaching: Redefining people development and organizational performance. *The Journal of Applied Behavioral Science*, *23*(1), 384–393. DOI: 10.1177/00218863241283919

Tiwari, R. (2023, February). *The integration of AI and machine learning in education and its potential to personalize and improve student learning experiences. International journal of scientific research in engineering and management, 7*(2)

UNESCO. (2023). *Technology in education: A tool on whose terms? Global Education Monitoring Report*.https://unesdoc.unesco.org/ark:/48223/pf0000385723

Van Nuland, H. J. (2023). The role of AI in transforming leadership and organizational management. *Journal of Organizational Change Management*, *36*(2), 123–139.

Viant Technology. (2024, January 15). *Understanding AI in programmatic advertising*. [Blog post]. Viant Technology Blog.https://www.viantinc.com/blog/understanding-ai-in-programmatic-advertising/

Wang, R. E., & Demszky, D. (2023). Is ChatGPT a good teacher coach? Measuring zero-shot performance for scoring and providing actionable insights on classroom instruction. *arXiv*.https://doi.org//arXiv.2306.03090DOI: 10.18653/v1/2023.bea-1.53

West, S. M., Whittaker, M., & Crawford, K. (2019). *Discriminating systems: Gender, race, and power in AI*[PDF]. AI Now Institute.https://ainowinstitute.org/wp-content/uploads/2023/04/discriminatingsystems.pdf

Wharton School. (2023). *AI for business*.https://ai.wharton.upenn.edu/

Wilson, H. J., & Daugherty, P. R. (2018). Collaborative intelligence: Humans and AI are joining forces. *Harvard Business Review*, *96*(4), 114–123.

Winkelhaus, S., & Grosse, E. H. (2020). Logistics 4.0: A systematic review towards a new logistics system. *International Journal of Production Research*, *58*(1), 18–43. DOI: 10.1080/00207543.2019.1612964

Yoon, S., & Rao, K. (2023). Personalized learning analytics and AI-driven MBA programs. *Journal of Management Education*, *47*(2), 188–207.

Zawacki-Richter, O., Marín, V. I., & Bond, M. (2022). Systematic review of research on AI in higher education. *Educational Technology Research and Development*, *70*, 1345–1370.

## ADDITIONAL READING

Al Daraai, S. B., Al Maqrashi, M., Al Zakwani, M., & Al Shaikh, Z. (2024). Integrating AI in higher education. In Al-Ani, S. (Ed.), *Handbook of research on teaching methods in language translation and interpretation* (pp. 212–228).

Hall, A. A., Bailey, J., & Garcia-Lopez, A. (2024). Artificial intelligence in education. In Cruz-Cunha, M. L. (Ed.), (pp. 95–113). Advances in business information systems and analytics.

## KEY TERMS AND DEFINITIONS

**Adaptive Learning:** A method of teaching where the learning content adjusts to the student's performance and pace, making sure everyone gets a more personalized experience.

**AI-Driven Pedagogy:** This refers to the way teaching is changing because of AI, bringing in tools and techniques that make learning more interactive, personalized, and efficient.

**Algorithmic Bias:** Unintended discrimination or inequality that arises when AI systems produce outcomes based on biased training data or flawed algorithms.

**Artificial Intelligence (AI):** A smart technology that helps machines perform tasks we usually expect from humans, like solving problems, making decisions, or learning from data. In this chapter, AI is at the core of transforming business education.

**Business Simulation:** Real-world business scenarios are used in classrooms where students can try out strategies and decisions in a risk-free, virtual setting, often guided by AI tools.

**Ethical AI in Education:** The responsible use of AI in educational settings, ensuring fairness, transparency, data privacy, and accountability.

**Virtual Classrooms:** Online learning spaces that bring students and teachers together digitally, often with AI features like instant feedback, language translation, or smart tutoring.

# Compilation of References


AACSB. (2025, February). *GenAI adoption in business schools: Deans and faculty respond* [Report]. https://www.aacsb.edu/insights/reports/2025/genai-adoption-in-business-schools-deans-and-faculty-respond

Abad-Segura, E., González-Zamar, M.-D., Infante-Moro, J. C., & Ruipérez García, G. (2020). Sustainable Management of Digital Transformation in Higher Education: Global Research Trends. *Sustainability (Basel)*, *12*(5), 2107. DOI: 10.3390/su12052107

Abdulmuhsin, A. A., Alkhwaldi, A. F., Dbesan, A. H., & Tarhini, A. (2025). *Empirical insights on organisational sustainability: Exploring the influence of communities of practice and associated technologies*. Sustainability Accounting, Management and Policy Journal., DOI: 10.1108/SAMPJ-02-2024-0155

Abe, M., & Nakagawa, K. (2020, May). Cross-sectional stock price prediction using deep learning for actual investment management. In *Proceedings of the 2020 Asia Service Sciences and Software Engineering Conference* (pp. 9–15). DOI: 10.1145/3399871.3399889

Abey, J., Velmurugan, R., & Shaikh, Z. H. (2025). Analyzing the Performance of a Deep Learning-Based Model for Stock Market Trend Prediction. In Hamdan, R. K. (Ed.), *Sustainable Data Management. Studies in Big Data* (Vol. 170). Springer., DOI: 10.1007/978-3-031-83915-3_59

Acharya, M. S., Armaan, A., & Antony, A. S. (2019, February). A comparison of regression models for prediction of graduate admissions. In *2019 international conference on computational intelligence in data science (ICCIDS)* (pp. 1-5). IEEE. DOI: 10.1109/ICCIDS.2019.8862140

Achiam, J., Adler, S., Agarwal, S., Ahmad, L., Akkaya, I., Aleman, F. L., . . . McGrew, B. (2023). Gpt-4 technical report. *arXiv preprint arXiv:2303.08774.*

Açıkgöz, A., & Latham, G. P. (2022). Self-Set learning goals and service performance in a gig economy: A Moderated-Mediation role of improvisation and mindful metacognition. *Journal of Business Research, 139*, 1553–1563. DOI: 10.1016/j.jbusres.2021.10.074

Act, E. U.-A. I. https://digital-strategy.ec.europa.eu/en/policies/regulatory-framework-ai, Retrieved 11:00, February 22, 2025.

Adamopoulou, E., & Moussiades, L. (2020). An overview of chatbot technology. In *Artificial Intelligence Applications and Innovations: 16th IFIP WG 12.5 International Conference, AIAI 2020, Neos Marmaras, Greece, June 5–7, 2020* [Springer International Publishing.]. *Proceedings, 16*(Part II), 373–383.

Adarkwah, M. A. (2024). GenAI-Infused Adult Learning in the Digital Era: A Conceptual Framework for Higher Education. *Adult Learning*. Advance online publication. DOI: 10.1177/10451595241271161

Adcroft, A., Dhaliwal, S., & Willis, R. (2005). Insatiable demand or academic supply: The intellectual context of entrepreneurship education. *European Business Review, 17*(6), 518–531. DOI: 10.1108/09555340510630554

Adedoyin, F. F., & Christiansen, B. (Eds.). (2024). *Generative AI and Multifactor Productivity in Business*. IGI Global. DOI: 10.4018/979-8-3693-1198-1

Adeleye, O. O., Eden, C. A., & Adeniyi, I. S. (2024). Innovative teaching methodologies in the era of artificial intelligence: A review of inclusive educational practices. *World Journal of Advanced Engineering Technology and Sciences, 11*(2), 069-079.

Agrawal, A. (2021, November 14th). Has the Pandemic made business education less relevant? *Business Today (Norwich)*, •••, 102.

Agudo-Peregrina, Á. F., Hernández-García, Á., & Pascual-Miguel, F. J. (2014). Behavioral intention, use behavior and the acceptance of electronic learning systems: Differences between higher education and lifelong learning. *Computers in Human Behavior, 34*, 301–314. DOI: 10.1016/j.chb.2013.10.035

Ahammad, I., Sarkar, W. A., Meem, F. A., Ferdus, J., Ahmed, M. K., Rahman, M. R., ... & Islam, M. S. (2024). Advancing stock market predictions with time series analysis including LSTM and ARIMA. *Cloud Computing and Data Science*, 226–241.

Ahmad, S. F., Alam, M. M., Rahmat, M. K., Mubarik, M. S., & Hyder, S. I. (2022). Academic and administrative role of artificial intelligence in education. *Sustainability (Basel), 14*(3), 1101. DOI: 10.3390/su14031101

Ahmedabad, I. I. M. (2024, August 23). *IIMA report reveals that employees are ready to embrace AI-driven transformations - the gap in AI education and upskilling needs to be filled*.https://www.iima.ac.in/inmediaiima-report-reveals-employees-are-ready-embrace-ai-driven-transformations-gap-ai-education

Ahmed, Y., Ahmed, T., Raza, A., & Jan, I. (2024). *Harnessing AI for Personalized Learning*. Equity, and Administrative Efficiency in Transnational Higher Education., DOI: 10.4018/979-8-3693-7016-2.ch009

*AI Tools and Platforms for Personalized Learning*. (2025). (pp. 25–60)., DOI: 10.4018/979-8-3693-3474-4.ch003

Akbar, K., Nyika, F. D., & Mbonye, V. (2024). Revolutionizing Creative Education: The Role of Generative AI in Enhancing Innovation and Learning in Higher Education. In *Impacts of Generative AI on Creativity in Higher Education* (pp. 307-330). IGI Global.

Akinradewo, O., Hafez, M., Aliu, J., Oke, A., Aigbavboa, C., & Adekunle, S. (2025). Barriers to the Adoption of Augmented Reality Technologies for Education and Training in the Built Environment: A Developing Country Context. *Technologies*, *13*(2), 62. DOI: 10.3390/technologies13020062

Akpan, I. J., Razavi, R., & Akpan, A. A. (2025). Evolutionary Trends in Decision Sciences Education Research from Simulation and Games to Big Data Analytics and Generative Artificial Intelligence. *Big Data*, big.2024.0128. DOI: 10.1089/big.2024.0128 PMID: 40019821

AlAli, R., & Wardat, Y. (2024). Opportunities and challenges of integrating generative artificial intelligence in education. *International Journal of Religion*, *5*(7), 784–793. DOI: 10.61707/8y29gv34

Al-Amri, S., & Ali, Z. (2016). Systematic review of computer based assessments in medical education. *Saudi Journal of Medicine & Medical Sciences*, *4*(2), 79–88. DOI: 10.4103/1658-631X.178288 PMID: 30787703

Albert, S., & Grzeda, M. (2015). Reflection in Strategic Management Education. *Journal of Management Education*, *39*(5), 650–669. DOI: 10.1177/1052562914564872

Alenezi, H. S., & Faisal, M. H. (2020). Utilizing crowdsourcing and machine learning in education: Literature review. *Education and Information Technologies*, *25*(4), 2971–2986. DOI: 10.1007/s10639-020-10102-w

Alhusban, M. I., Alshurafat, H., & Khatatbeh, I. N. (2025). Exploring professional perspectives on integrating generative artificial intelligence into corporate learning and development: An organizational change perspective. *Development and Learning in Organizations*, *39*(2), 21–24. DOI: 10.1108/DLO-05-2024-0131

Ali, M., Khan, N., & Akhtar, Z. (2022). Synthetic data generation using AI: Applications and ethical concerns. *Journal of Data Science and Technology*, *5*(3), 112–130.

ALPAC, L. (1966). Machines: Computers in Translation and Linguistics, Report by the Automatic Language Processing Advisory Committee, Division of Behavioral Sciences. *National Academy of Sciences, National Research Council, Publication, 1416*.

Alpaydin, E. (2020). *Introduction to machine learning*. MIT press.

Alrefaee, S., Khan, M., & Alrefaee, Y. M. H. A. (2025). *A Bibliometric Analysis of Online Education Research in India (2014-2024): Trends, Patterns, and Future Directions*. In Review. DOI: 10.21203/rs.3.rs-5830161/v2

Alsbou, M. K. K., & Alsaraireh, R. A. I. (2024). Data-Driven Decision-Making in Education: Leveraging AI for School Improvement. *2024 International Conference on Knowledge Engineering and Communication Systems (ICKECS)*, 1–6. DOI: 10.1109/ICKECS61492.2024.10616616

Al-Smadi, M. (2023). ChatGPT and beyond: The generative AI revolution in education. *arXiv preprint arXiv:2311.15198*.

Alvero, A. J., Arthurs, N., Antonio, A. L., Domingue, B. W., Gebre-Medhin, B., Giebel, S., & Stevens, M. L. (2020, February). AI and holistic review: informing human reading in college admissions. In *Proceedings of the AAAI/ACM Conference on AI, Ethics, and Society* (pp. 200-206). DOI: 10.1145/3375627.3375871

Al-Zubidy, A., & Carver, J. C. (2019). Identification and prioritization of SLR search tool requirements: An SLR and a survey. *Empirical Software Engineering*, *24*(1), 139–169. DOI: 10.1007/s10664-018-9626-5

Amankwah-Amoah, J., Abdalla, S., Mogaji, E., Elbanna, A., & Dwivedi, Y. K. (2024). The impending disruption of creative industries by generative AI: Opportunities, challenges, and research agenda. *International Journal of Information Management*, *79*, 102759. DOI: 10.1016/j.ijinfomgt.2024.102759

Ambhika, C., Gayathri, S., Anish, T. P., & Sheena, B. G. (2024, August). Enhancing Predictive Modeling in High Dimensional Data Using Hybrid Feature Selection. In *2024 5th International Conference on Electronics and Sustainable Communication Systems (ICESC)* (pp. 873-879). IEEE. DOI: 10.1109/ICESC60852.2024.10690153

Amdan, M. A. B., Janius, N., & Kasdiah, M. A. H. B. (2024). Concept paper: Efficiency of Artificial Intelligence (AI) tools for STEM education in Malaysia. *International Journal of Science and Research Archive, 12*(2), 553–559. DOI: 10.30574/ijsra.2024.12.2.1273

Amitabh, B. (2020, September 10). *NEP: Ambitious targets set for education sector*. The Deccan Chronicle, p. 10.

Anderson, J. R., Boyle, C. F., & Reiser, B. J. (1985). Intelligent tutoring systems. *Science, 228*(4698), 456–462. DOI: 10.1126/science.228.4698.456 PMID: 17746875

Anderson, L., Ellwood, P., & Coleman, C. (2017). The impactful academic: Relational management education as an intervention for impact. *British Journal of Management, 28*(1), 14–28. DOI: 10.1111/1467-8551.12202

Angeioplastis, A., Aliprantis, J., Konstantakis, M., & Tsimpiris, A. (2025). Predicting Student Performance and Enhancing Learning Outcomes: A Data-Driven Approach Using Educational Data Mining Techniques. *Computers, 14*(3), 83. DOI: 10.3390/computers14030083

Anitsal, I. (2024, October 3). *How AI is transforming marketing*. Missouri State University News.

Anozie, N., & Junker, B. W. (2006, July). Predicting end-of-year accountability assessment scores from monthly student records in an online tutoring system. Educational Data Mining: Papers from the AAAI Workshop. Menlo Park, CA: AAAI Press.

Ansari, G., Gupta, S., & Singhal, N. (2021). Natural Language Processing in Online Reviews. In *Natural Language Processing for Global and Local Business* (pp. 40–64). IGI Global Scientific Publishing. DOI: 10.4018/978-1-7998-4240-8.ch003

Arakawa, R., & Yakura, H. (2024). Coaching copilot: Blended form of an LLM-powered chatbot and a human coach to effectively support self-reflection for leadership growth. *arXiv*. https://doi.org//arXiv.2405.15250DOI: 10.1145/3640794.3665549

Argal, A., Gupta, S., Modi, A., Pandey, P., Shim, S., & Choo, C. (2018, January). Intelligent travel chatbot for predictive recommendation in echo platform. In *2018 IEEE 8th annual computing and communication workshop and conference (CCWC)* (pp. 176-183). IEEE. DOI: 10.1109/CCWC.2018.8301732

Arulkumaran, K., Cully, A., & Togelius, J. (2019, July). Alphastar: An evolutionary computation perspective. In *Proceedings of the genetic and evolutionary computation conference companion* (pp. 314-315). DOI: 10.1145/3319619.3321894

Arya, V., Saraf, A., Chichkanov, N., Papa, A., & Romano, M. (2025). AI-enhanced competency transfer hubs: A conceptual framework for university-industry engagement and knowledge sharing. *The Journal of Technology Transfer*. Advance online publication. DOI: 10.1007/s10961-025-10233-7

Asad, M. M., & Ajaz, A. (2024). Impact of ChatGPT and generative AI on lifelong learning and upskilling learners in higher education: Unveiling the challenges and opportunities globally. *The International Journal of Information and Learning Technology*, *41*(5), 507–523. DOI: 10.1108/IJILT-06-2024-0103

Asakura, K., Occhiuto, K., Todd, S., Leithead, C., & Clapperton, R. (2020). A call to action on artificial intelligence and social work education: Lessons learned from a simulation project using natural language processing. *Journal of Teaching in Social Work*, *40*(5), 501–518. DOI: 10.1080/08841233.2020.1813234

Ashford, S. J., Caza, B. B., & Reid, E. M. (2018). From surviving to thriving in the gig economy: A research agenda for individuals in the new world of work. *Research in Organizational Behavior*, *38*, 23–41. DOI: 10.1016/j.riob.2018.11.001

Ashish, V. (2017). Attention is all you need. *Advances in Neural Information Processing Systems*, *30*, I.

Ashta, A., & Herrmann, H. (2021). Artificial intelligence and financial fraud detection: A review of the literature. *Financial Innovation*, *7*(1), 1–25.

Aswini, J., Sudha, K., Ganesh, G., Subramanian, S., & Ghinea, G. (2024). AI-powered parallel computing architecture and its applications. In *The convergence of self-sustaining systems with AI and IoT* (pp. 23–39). IGI Global. DOI: 10.4018/979-8-3693-1702-0.ch002

Ateş, H. (2025). Integrating augmented reality into intelligent tutoring systems to enhance science education outcomes. *Education and Information Technologies*, *30*(4), 4435–4470. DOI: 10.1007/s10639-024-12970-y

Aure, P. A., & Cuenca, O. (2024). Fostering social-emotional learning through human-centered use of generative AI in business research education: An insider case study. *Journal of Research in Innovative Teaching and Learning*, *17*(2), 168–181. DOI: 10.1108/JRIT-03-2024-0076

Aydın, Ö. (2023). Google Bard generated literature review: Metaverse. *Journal of AI*, *7*(1), 1–14. DOI: 10.61969/jai.1311271

Aydın, Ö., & Karaarslan, E. (2023). Is ChatGPT leading generative AI? What is beyond expectations? *Academic Platform Journal of Engineering and Smart Systems*, *11*(3), 118–134. DOI: 10.21541/apjess.1293702

Baesens, B., Van Vlasselaer, V., & Verbeke, W. (2021). *Fraud analytics using descriptive, predictive, and social network techniques: A guide to data science for fraud detection*. John Wiley & Sons.

Bagai, R., & Mane, V. (2024). Designing an AI-powered mentorship platform for professional development: Opportunities and challenges. *arXiv*. https://doi.org// arXiv.2407.20233DOI: 10.48550

Bahroun, Z., Anane, C., Ahmed, V., & Zacca, A. (2023). Transforming education: A comprehensive review of generative artificial intelligence in educational settings through bibliometric and content analysis. *Sustainability (Basel)*, *15*(17), 12983. DOI: 10.3390/su151712983

Baidoo-Anu, D., & Owusu Ansah, L. K. (2023). Education in the era of generative AI: Threat or opportunity? *Education and Information Technologies*.

Baig, M. I., & Yadegaridehkordi, E. (2025). Factors influencing academic staff satisfaction and continuous usage of generative artificial intelligence (GenAI) in higher education. *International Journal of Educational Technology in Higher Education*, *22*(1), 5. DOI: 10.1186/s41239-025-00506-4

Baker, T., & Smith, L. (2019). *Educ AI tion rebooted? Exploring the future of artificial intelligence in schools and colleges*. Nesta Foundation.

Banerjee, A., & Namboodiri, V. (2023). The impact of generative AI on personalized business learning. *Technovation*.

Barnes, L. B., Christensen, C. R., & Hansen, A. J. (1994). *Teaching and the case method: Text, cases, and readings*. Harvard Business Press.

Bartle, E. (2015). Personalised learning: An overview. *The Institute for Teaching and Learning Innovation, Queensland University. Retrieved from* https://itali. uq. *edu. au/filething/get/1865/Personalised_learning_overview_Final_16_Mar_15.pdf.*

Baryannis, G., Validi, S., Dani, S., & Antoniou, G. (2019). Supply chain risk management and artificial intelligence: State of the art and future research directions. *International Journal of Production Research*, *57*(7), 2179–2202. DOI: 10.1080/00207543.2018.1530476

Bates, S. (2014). Personalised learning: Implications for curricula, staff and students. *Universitas (Accra)*, •••, 21.

Bathla, G. (2020, November). Stock price prediction using LSTM and SVR. In *2020 Sixth International Conference on Parallel, Distributed and Grid Computing (PDGC)* (pp. 211–214). IEEE. DOI: 10.1109/PDGC50313.2020.9315800

Batista, J., Mesquita, A., & Carnaz, G. (2024). Generative AI and Higher Education: Trends, Challenges, and Future Directions from a Systematic Literature Review. In *Information (Switzerland)* (Vol. 15, Issue 11). Multidisciplinary Digital Publishing Institute (MDPI). DOI: 10.3390/info15110676

Batley, T. (1990). Management Education for Professional Engineers. *Journal of European Industrial Training*, *14*(7). Advance online publication. DOI: 10.1108/03090599010135168

Baton, A. (2023) Management Education in a VUCA world, Business World, 16th December 2023, P.6.

Bell, R., & Bell, H. (2023). Entrepreneurship education in the era of generative artificial intelligence. *Entrepreneurship Education*, *6*(3), 229–244. DOI: 10.1007/s41959-023-00099-x

Benmamoun, M. (2024). Reinventing international business education: Integrating the power of generative AI. *AIB Insights*, *24*(1), 1–7.

Bennett, R. E. (2011). Formative assessment: A critical review. *Assessment in Education: Principles, Policy & Practice*, *18*(1), 5–25. DOI: 10.1080/0969594X.2010.513678

Besiri, D. (2024). *AI-driven predictive analytics: Transforming decision-making in business. Human Computer Interaction, 12*(2), Article 8ny1ww06.

Bhandari, H. N., Rimal, B., Pokhrel, N. R., Rimal, R., Dahal, K. R., & Khatri, R. K. (2022). Predicting stock market index using LSTM. *Machine Learning with Applications*, *9*, 100320. DOI: 10.1016/j.mlwa.2022.100320

Bhaskar, P., & Gupta, P. K. K. (2024). Delving into educators' perspectives on ChatGPT in management education: A qualitative exploration. *Interactive Technology and Smart Education*, *21*(4), 645–671. DOI: 10.1108/ITSE-08-2023-0169

Bhattacharya, R., & Bhattacharya, S. (2020, September 20). *A room not for her own*. The Economic Times, p. 12.

Bhattacharyya, R. (2020, November 14). *FMCG adds new campuses to hiring list*. The Economic Times, p. 1.

Biloslavo, R., Edgar, D., Aydin, E., & Bulut, C. (2024). Artificial intelligence (AI) and strategic planning process within VUCA environments: A research agenda and guidelines. *Management Decision*. Advance online publication. DOI: 10.1108/MD-10-2023-1944

Binns, R. (2018). Fairness in machine learning: Lessons from political philosophy. *Proceedings of the 2018 Conference on Fairness, Accountability, and Transparency*, 149-159. ACM.

Böhm, S., Carrington, M., Cornelius, N., De Bruin, B., Greenwood, M., Hassan, L., Jain, T., Karam, C., Kourula, A., Romani, L., Riaz, S., & Shaw, D. (2022). Ethics at the Centre of Global and Local Challenges: Thoughts on the Future of Business Ethics. *Journal of Business Ethics, 180*(3), 835–861. DOI: 10.1007/s10551-022-05239-2 PMID: 36212626

Bommasani, R., Hudson, D., & Tang, E. (2021). On the opportunities and risks of foundation models. *Journal of Artificial Intelligence Research, 71*(2), 1–35.

Boysen, N., Briskorn, D., & Schwerdfeger, S. (2021). Delivery by drone: An evaluation of unmanned aerial vehicle technology in logistics. *Transportation Research Part C, Emerging Technologies, 124*, 102977.

Braddick, W. A. G. (1991). European Management Education: Internationalization and Harmonization. *Industry and Higher Education, 5*(3), 138–142. DOI: 10.1177/095042229100500303

Brew, C., & Leacock, C. (2013). Automated short answer scoring: Principles and prospects. In *Handbook of Automated Essay Evaluation* (pp. 136–152). Routledge.

Brock, J. K.-U., & Von Wangenheim, F. (2019). Demystifying AI: What digital transformation leaders can teach you about real AI use in business. *Business Horizons, 62*(2), 179–188.

Brown, M., & Klein, C. (2020). Whose Data? Which Rights? Whose Power? A Policy Discourse Analysis of Student Privacy Policy Documents. *The Journal of Higher Education, 91*(7), 1149–1178. DOI: 10.1080/00221546.2020.1770045

Brown, N., & Sandholm, T. (2018). Superhuman AI for heads-up no-limit poker: Libratus beats top professionals. *Science, 359*(6374), 418–424. DOI: 10.1126/science.aao1733 PMID: 29249696

Brynjolfsson, E., & McAfee, A. (2017). *Machine, platform, crowd: Harnessing our digital future*. W.W. Norton & Company.

Budhwar, P., Chowdhury, S., Wood, G., Aguinis, H., Bamber, G. J., Beltran, J. R., Boselie, P., Lee Cooke, F., Decker, S., DeNisi, A., Dey, P. K., Guest, D., Knoblich, A. J., Malik, A., Paauwe, J., Papagiannidis, S., Patel, C., Pereira, V., Ren, S., & Varma, A. (2023). Human resource management in the age of generative artificial intelligence: Perspectives and research directions on ChatGPT. *Human Resource Management Journal, 33*(3), 606–659. DOI: 10.1111/1748-8583.12524

Bughin, J., Catlin, T., & LaBerge, L. (2019). The four fundamentals of workplace automation. *McKinsey Quarterly*.https://www.mckinsey.com/business-functions/mckinsey-digital/our-insights/the-four-fundamentals-of-workplace-automation

Bunjak, A., Černe, M., & Popovič, A. (2021). Absorbed in technology but digitally overloaded: Interplay effects on gig workers' burnout and creativity. *Information & Management*, *58*(8), 103533. DOI: 10.1016/j.im.2021.103533

Buxmann, P., & Schmidt, H. (2021). *Artificial Intelligence in Business: Balancing Risk and Innovation*. Springer.

Calleja, J., & Camilleri, P. (2025). Primary school teachers' perceptions towards the use of generative AI in teaching using lesson study. *International Journal for Lesson and Learning Studies*. DOI: 10.1108/IJLLS-11-2024-0268

Cambria, E., White, B., & Huang, G. (2017). Sentic computing for business analytics: A review. *Big Data Research*, *10*, 1–19.

Campus Technology. (August 27, 2024). Share of higher education students using artificial intelligence (AI) tools for schoolwork worldwide as of July 2024 [Graph]. In *Statista*. Retrieved January 16, 2025, from https://www.statista.com/statistics/1498309/usage-of-ai-by-students-worldwide/

Cappelli, P., Tambe, P., & Yakubovich, V. (2020). Artificial intelligence in human resources management: Challenges and a path forward. *Journal of Business Ethics*, *167*(4), 647–662.

Chacko, A. S. (2024). *Exploring Design Education in the Age of Generative Artificial Intelligence: Opportunities and Challenges* (Master's thesis, Georgetown University).

Chakraborty, S., & Saha, P. (2021). AI in healthcare: Predictive analytics for early disease detection. *Healthcare Technology Review*, *34*(6), 89–102.

Chakraborty, U., Roy, S., & Kumar, S. (2023). *Rise of Generative AI and ChatGPT: Understand how Generative AI and ChatGPT are transforming and reshaping the business world (English Edition)*. BPB Publications.

Chan, C. K. Y. (2023). A comprehensive AI policy education framework for university teaching and learning. *International Journal of Educational Technology in Higher Education*, *20*(1), 38. DOI: 10.1186/s41239-023-00408-3

Chan, C. K. Y., & Hu, W. (2023). Students' voices on generative AI: Perceptions, benefits, and challenges in higher education. *International Journal of Educational Technology in Higher Education*, *20*(1), 43. DOI: 10.1186/s41239-023-00411-8

Chen, J. J., & Perez, C. (2023). Enhancing Assessment and Personalized Learning Through Artificial Intelligence. *Childhood Education*, *99*(6), 72–79. DOI: 10.1080/00094056.2023.2282903

Chen, L., Ifenthaler, D., Yau, J. Y.-K., & Sun, W. (2024). Artificial intelligence in entrepreneurship education: A scoping review. *Education + Training*, *66*(6), 589–608. DOI: 10.1108/ET-05-2023-0169

Chen, T., Wang, S., & Li, Y. (2022). AI-driven business intelligence: A new era of decision-making. *International Journal of Business Analytics*, *10*(4), 45–62.

Chiang, R. H., Goes, P., & Stohr, E. A. (2012). Business intelligence and analytics education, and program development: A unique opportunity for the information systems discipline. [TMIS]. *ACM Transactions on Management Information Systems*, *3*(3), 1–13. DOI: 10.1145/2361256.2361257

Chiu, T. K. F. (2023). The impact of Generative AI (GenAI) on practices, policies and research direction in education: A case of ChatGPT and Midjourney. *Interactive Learning Environments*. Advance online publication. DOI: 10.1080/10494820.2023.2253861

Chiu, T. K. F. (2024). Future research recommendations for transforming higher education with generative AI. *Computers and Education: Artificial Intelligence*, *6*, 100197. Advance online publication. DOI: 10.1016/j.caeai.2023.100197

Choudhury, A., & Jones, L. (2021). The rise of AI-powered BI: Transforming data into insights. *Journal of Business Intelligence*, *19*(1), 67–85.

Chowdhary, K. R. (2020). Natural Language Processing. In *Fundamentals of Artificial Intelligence* (pp. 603–649). Springer India., DOI: 10.1007/978-81-322-3972-7_19

Chowdhury, R. H.Rakibul Hasan Chowdhury. (2024). The evolution of business operations: Unleashing the potential of Artificial Intelligence, Machine Learning, and Blockchain. *World Journal of Advanced Research and Reviews*, *22*(3), 2135–2147. DOI: 10.30574/wjarr.2024.22.3.1992

Chowdhury, S., Dey, P., Joel-Edgar, S., Bhattacharya, S., Rodriguez-Espindola, O., Abadie, A., & Truong, L. (2023). Unlocking the value of artificial intelligence in human resource management through AI capability framework. *Human Resource Management Review*, *33*(1), 100899. DOI: 10.1016/j.hrmr.2022.100899

Chugh, R., Turnbull, D., Morshed, A., Sabrina, F., Azad, S., Md Mamunur, R., Kaisar, S., & Subramani, S. (2025). The promise and pitfalls: A literature review of generative artificial intelligence as a learning assistant in ICT education. *Computer Applications in Engineering Education*, *33*(2), e70002. DOI: 10.1002/cae.70002

Chui, M., Manyika, J., & Miremadi, M. (2018). What AI can and can't do (yet) for your business. *The McKinsey Quarterly*, •••, 1–8.

Chusniyah, A., Makruf, I., & Supriyanto, . (2025). Two decades of sustainable development studies in higher education management: A bibliometric analysis. *International Journal of Sustainability in Higher Education*, *26*(3), 614–632. DOI: 10.1108/IJSHE-11-2023-0546

Clayton, P. R., & Clopton, J. (2019). Business curriculum redesign: Integrating data analytics. *Journal of Education for Business*, *94*(1), 57–63. DOI: 10.1080/08832323.2018.1502142

ClearCompany. (2023). *AI-powered talent management: Transforming recruitment and development*.https://www.clearcompany.com/resources/ai-talent-management

Clegg, S., & Sarker, S. (2024). Artificial intelligence and management education: A conceptualization of human-machine interaction. *International Journal of Management Education*, *22*(3), 101007. DOI: 10.1016/j.ijme.2024.101007

Cloudforce. (2025, June 12). *London Business School becomes first UK business school to provide AI for all* [Press release]. PR Newswire. https://www.prnewswire.com/news-releases/london-business-school-becomes-first-uk-business-school-to-provide-ai-for-all-302480049.html

Coeckelbergh, M. (2020). *AI ethics*. MIT Press. DOI: 10.7551/mitpress/12549.001.0001

Conati, C., Porayska-Pomsta, K., & Mavrikis, M. (2018). AI in Education needs interpretable machine learning: Lessons from Open Learner Modelling. *arXiv preprint arXiv:1807.00154*.

Cordeschi, R. (2006). AI's half century. On the thresholds of the Dartmouth conference. *IA Retrospettiva*, *3*, 1–2.

Cortes, C., & Vapnik, V. (1995). Support-vector networks. *Machine Learning*, *20*(3), 273–297. DOI: 10.1023/A:1022627411411

Costan, E., Gonzales, G., Gonzales, R., Enriquez, L., Costan, F., Suladay, D., Atibing, N. M., Aro, J. L., Evangelista, S. S., Maturan, F., Selerio, E.Jr, & Ocampo, L. (2021). Education 4.0 in Developing Economies: A Systematic Literature Review of Implementation Barriers and Future Research Agenda. *Sustainability (Basel)*, *13*(22), 12763. DOI: 10.3390/su132212763

Creely, E. (2024). Exploring the role of generative AI in enhancing language learning: Opportunities and challenges. *International Journal of Changes in Education*, *1*(3), 158–167. DOI: 10.47852/bonviewIJCE42022495

Cronin, I. (2024). *Understanding Generative AI Business Applications*. Springer Nature. DOI: 10.1007/979-8-8688-0282-9

Cui, L., Huang, S., Wei, F., Tan, C., Duan, C., & Zhou, M. (2017, July). Superagent: A customer service chatbot for e-commerce websites. In *Proceedings of ACL 2017, system demonstrations* (pp. 97-102). DOI: 10.18653/v1/P17-4017

D'Souza, R. (2024). Scope of Artificial Intelligence in Education. *International Journal of Emerging Knowledge Studies, 03*(09), 670–678. DOI: 10.70333/ijeks-03-09-035

Dai, Y., Liu, A., & Lim, C. P. (2023). Reconceptualizing ChatGPT and generative AI as a student-driven innovation in higher education. *Procedia CIRP*, *119*, 84–90. DOI: 10.1016/j.procir.2023.05.002

Đambić, G., Krajcar, M., & Bele, D. (2016). Machine learning model for early detection of higher education students that need additional attention in introductory programming courses. *International journal of digital technology & economy, 1*(1), 1-11.

Daniel, K., Msambwa, M. M., & Wen, Z. (2025). Can Generative AI Revolutionise Academic Skills Development in Higher Education? A Systematic Literature Review. *European Journal of Education*, *60*(1), e70036. DOI: 10.1111/ejed.70036

Daramola, O. (2023). The impact of artificial intelligence on recruitment processes: A comprehensive review. *Open journal of business and management*, 11(5), 2075–2092.

Das, H. (2024). Adopting to a new era. *Business Today (Norwich)*, *13*(October), 98–99.

Davenport, T. H., & Ronanki, R. (2018). Artificial intelligence for the real world. *Harvard Business Review*, *96*(1), 108–116.

Dayal, I. (2011). Globalizing Management Education. *Global Business Review*, *12*(3), 473–478. DOI: 10.1177/097215091101200309

Debroy, B. (2020, September 10). *The NEP reboot*. The Indian Express, p. 11.

Dede, C., & Richards, J. (2020). *Learning in the age of AI: Hybrid approaches to teacher-supported AI classrooms*. Harvard Education Press.

Dehler, G. E. (2009). Prospects and possibilities of critical management education: Critical beings and a pedagogy of critical action. *Management Learning*, *40*(1), 31–49. DOI: 10.1177/1350507608099312

Delipetrev, B., Tsinaraki, C., & Kostic, U. (2020). Historical evolution of artificial intelligence.

Demartini, C. G., Sciascia, L., Bosso, A., & Manuri, F. (2024). Artificial intelligence bringing improvements to adaptive learning in education: A case study. *Sustainability (Basel)*, *16*(3), 1347. DOI: 10.3390/su16031347

Deng, J., Dong, W., Socher, R., Li, L. J., Li, K., & Fei-Fei, L. (2009, June). Imagenet: A large-scale hierarchical image database. In *2009 IEEE conference on computer vision and pattern recognition* (pp. 248-255). Ieee. DOI: 10.1109/CVPR.2009.5206848

Detrick, G. (2002). Russell L Ackoff: Interview by Glenn Detrick. *Academy of Management Learning & Education*, *1*(1), 56–63. DOI: 10.5465/amle.2002.7373640

Dias, S. B., Hadjileontiadou, S. J., Hadjileontiadis, L. J., & Diniz, J. A. (2015). Fuzzy cognitive mapping of LMS users' quality of interaction within higher education blended-learning environment. *Expert Systems with Applications*, *42*(21), 7399–7423. DOI: 10.1016/j.eswa.2015.05.048

Díaz-Rodríguez, N., Del Ser, J., Coeckelbergh, M., López De Prado, M., Herrera-Viedma, E., & Herrera, F. (2023). Connecting the dots in trustworthy Artificial Intelligence: From AI principles, ethics, and key requirements to responsible AI systems and regulation. *Information Fusion*, *99*, 101896. DOI: 10.1016/j.inffus.2023.101896

Dimitriadou, E., & Lanitis, A. (2023). A critical evaluation, challenges, and future perspectives of using artificial intelligence and emerging technologies in smart classrooms. *Smart Learning Environments*, *10*(1), 12. DOI: 10.1186/s40561-023-00231-3 PMID: 40478141

Ding, G., & Qin, L. (2020). Study on the prediction of stock price based on the associated network model of LSTM. *International Journal of Machine Learning and Cybernetics*, *11*(6), 1307–1317. DOI: 10.1007/s13042-019-01041-1

Djokic, I., Milicevic, N., Djokic, N., Maleic, B., & Kalas, B. (2024). STUDENTS' PERCEPTIONS OF THE USE OF ARTIFICIAL INTELLIGENCE IN EDUCATIONAL SERVICES. *Amfiteatru Economic*, *26*(65), 294–310. DOI: 10.24818/EA/2024/65/294

Dubey, P. K. (2024). *Personalized Learning and Pedagogy*., DOI: 10.4018/979-8-3693-6130-6.ch004

Dwivedi, P. P., & Sharma, D. K. (2025). Performance measures of sustainable development goals using SWI MCDM methods: A case of the Indian states. *International Transactions in Operational Research*, itor.13609. DOI: 10.1111/itor.13609

Dwivedi, Y. K., Hughes, L., & Ismagilova, E. (2021). Artificial intelligence (AI): Multidisciplinary perspectives on emerging challenges, opportunities, and research agenda. *International Journal of Information Management*, *57*, 102141. DOI: 10.1016/j.ijinfomgt.2019.08.002

Dwivedi, Y. K., Hughes, L., & Ismagilova, E. (2022). Generative AI in business: Challenges, opportunities, and future directions. *International Journal of Information Management*, *60*, 102379.

Dwivedi, Y. K., Ismagilova, E., Hughes, D. L., Carlson, J., Filieri, R., Jacobson, J., Jain, V., Karjaluoto, H., Kefi, H., Krishen, A. S., Kumar, V., Rahman, M. M., Raman, R., Rauschnabel, P. A., Rowley, J., Salo, J., Tran, G. A., & Wang, Y. (2021). Setting the future of digital and social media marketing research: Perspectives and research propositions. *International Journal of Information Management*, *59*, 102168. DOI: 10.1016/j.ijinfomgt.2020.102168

Dyer, S. L., & Hurd, F. (2016). "What's going on?" Developing reflexivity in the management classroom: From surface to deep learning and everything in between. *Academy of Management Learning & Education*, *15*(2), 287–303. DOI: 10.5465/amle.2014.0104

Dzyabura, D., & Hauser, J. R. (2021). AI-powered product recommendation and consumer behaviour. *Marketing Science*, *40*(1), 24–42.

Eapen, J., Bein, D., & Verma, A. (2019, January). Novel deep learning model with CNN and bi-directional LSTM for improved stock market index prediction. In *2019 IEEE 9th Annual Computing and Communication Workshop and Conference (CCWC)* (pp. 264–270). IEEE. DOI: 10.1109/CCWC.2019.8666592

Ed-Dafali, S., Adardour, Z., Derj, A., Bami, A., & Hussainey, K. (2025). A PRISMA-Based Systematic Review on Economic, Social, and Governance Practices: Insights and Research Agenda. *Business Strategy and the Environment*, *34*(2), 1896–1916. DOI: 10.1002/bse.4069

El-Alfy, E. S. M., & Abdel-Aal, R. E. (2008). Construction and analysis of educational tests using abductive machine learning. *Computers & Education*, *51*(1), 1–16. DOI: 10.1016/j.compedu.2007.03.003

Elbourn, S. (2024). The Impact of Generative AI on Student Churn and the Future of Formal Education. *arXiv preprint arXiv:2412.00605*.

Ellikkal, A., & Rajamohan, S. (2024). AI-enabled personalized learning: Empowering management students for improving engagement and academic performance. *Vilakshan - XIMB. Journal of Management*. Advance online publication. DOI: 10.1108/XJM-02-2024-0023

Ellikkal, A., & Rajamohan, S. (2024). *AI-enabled personalized learning: empowering management students for improving engagement and academic performance*. Vilakshan-XIMB Journal of Management.

El-Seoud, M. S., Taj-Eddin, I. A., Seddiek, N., El-Khouly, M. M., & Nosseir, A. (2014). E-learning and students' motivation: A research study on the effect of e-learning on higher education. *International Journal of Emerging Technologies in Learning*, *9*(4), 20. DOI: 10.3991/ijet.v9i4.3465

Elshazly, E. (2024). *Promoting Accessibility and Personalizing Learning Experiences Through AI.*, DOI: 10.4018/979-8-3693-5538-1.ch005

Essien, A., Bukoye, O. T., O'Dea, X., & Kremantzis, M. (2024). The influence of AI text generators on critical thinking skills in UK business schools. *Studies in Higher Education*, *49*(5), 865–882. DOI: 10.1080/03075079.2024.2316881

Ezzaim, A., Dahbi, A., Aqqal, A., & Haidine, A. (2024). AI-based learning style detection in adaptive learning systems: A systematic literature review. *Journal of Computers in Education*. Advance online publication. DOI: 10.1007/s40692-024-00328-9

Fellenz, M. R., Hoidn, S., & Brady, M. (2022). *The Future of Management Education*. Routledge., DOI: 10.4324/9781003095903

Feng, Y., Jiang, L., & Zhu, W. (2018). Deep learning for financial trading: A survey. *Computational Economics*, *52*(4), 1401–1423.

Ferrucci, D. A. (2012). Introduction to "this is watson". *IBM Journal of Research and Development, 56*(3.4), 1-1.

Figueroa, E., Batista, E., Palau, R., Unciti, O., Ferre, M., & Ballesté, A. M. (2024). The Use of Artificial Intelligence Techniques in Smart Classrooms is in its Infancy. *IEEE Access : Practical Innovations, Open Solutions*, *12*, 125179–125193. DOI: 10.1109/ACCESS.2024.3454372

Floridi, L., & Chiriatti, M. (2020). GPT-3: Its nature, scope, limits, and consequences. *Minds and Machines*, *30*(4), 681–694. DOI: 10.1007/s11023-020-09548-1

Floridi, L., & Cowls, J. (2019). A unified framework of five principles for AI in society. *Harvard Data Science Review*, *1*(1).

Forbes – Future of Gen AI. https://www.forbes.com/sites/bernardmarr/2024/03/05/the-future-of-generative-ai-6-predictions-everyone-should-know-about/, retrieved 7:00, February 22, 2025.

Fradkov, A. L. (2020). Early history of machine learning. *IFAC-PapersOnLine*, *53*(2), 1385–1390. DOI: 10.1016/j.ifacol.2020.12.1888

Fu, Y., & Weng, Z. (2024). Navigating the ethical terrain of AI in education: A systematic review on framing responsible human-centered AI practices. *Computers and Education: Artificial Intelligence*, *7*, 100306. DOI: 10.1016/j.caeai.2024.100306

Gama, F., & Magistretti, S. (2025). Artificial intelligence in innovation management: A review of innovation capabilities and a taxonomy of AI applications. *Journal of Product Innovation Management*, *42*(1), 76–111. DOI: 10.1111/jpim.12698

Gandomi, A., & Haider, M. (2022). Augmented analytics and the future of business intelligence. *Journal of Big Data*, *9*(1), 45–58. PMID: 35495077

Gans, J. S., & Goldfarb, A. (2018). *Prediction, judgment, and complexity: A theory of decision-making and artificial intelligence*. National Bureau of Economic Research.

Gao, T., & Chai, Y. (2018). Improving stock closing price prediction using recurrent neural network and technical indicators. *Neural Computation*, *30*(10), 2833–2854. DOI: 10.1162/neco_a_01124 PMID: 30148707

Garcia-Brustenga, G., Fuertes-Alpiste, M., & Molas Castells, N. (2018). Briefing paper: chatbots in education. DOI: 10.7238/elc.chatbots.2018

Gartner – Impact of AI in future, https://www.gartner.com/en/topics/generative-ai#:~:text=of%20Gen%20AI-,Which%20industries%20are%20most%20impacted%20by%20generative%20AI%3F,-Generative%20AI%20will, retrieved 6:06, February 22, 2025.

Gentsch, P. (2019). *AI in marketing, sales and service: How marketers without a data science degree can use AI, big data and bots*. Springer. DOI: 10.1007/978-3-319-89957-2

George, A. S. (2023). The potential of generative AI to reform graduate education. *Partners Universal International Research Journal*, *2*(4), 36–50.

Geraldi, J., Locatelli, G., Dei, G., Söderlund, J., & Clegg, S. (2024). AI for Management and Organization Research: Examples and Reflections from Project Studies. *Project Management Journal*, *55*(4), 339–351. DOI: 10.1177/87569728241266938

Ghobakhloo, M., Fathi, M., Iranmanesh, M., Vilkas, M., Grybauskas, A., & Amran, A. (2024). Generative artificial intelligence in manufacturing: Opportunities for actualizing Industry 5.0 sustainability goals. *Journal of Manufacturing Technology Management*, *35*(9), 94–121. DOI: 10.1108/JMTM-12-2023-0530

Ghosh, P., Neufeld, A., & Sahoo, J. K. (2022). Forecasting directional movements of stock prices for intraday trading using LSTM and random forests. *Finance Research Letters*, *46*, 102280. DOI: 10.1016/j.frl.2021.102280

Ghosh, S., & Ghosh, S. (2021). Classifying speech acts using a multi-channel deep attention network for task-oriented conversational search agents. *Proceedings of the 2021 conference on human information interaction and retrieval*, 267–272. DOI: 10.1145/3406522.3446057

Gikas, J., & Grant, M. M. (2013). Mobile computing devices in higher education: Student perspectives on learning with cellphones, smartphones & social media. *The Internet and Higher Education*, *19*, 18–26. DOI: 10.1016/j.iheduc.2013.06.002

Glavič, P. (2020). Identifying Key Issues of Education for Sustainable Development. *Sustainability (Basel)*, *12*(16), 6500. DOI: 10.3390/su12166500

Goel, V., Agarwal, R., & Sinha, P. (2022). Ethical concerns in generative AI: Mitigating biases and misinformation. *AI & Society*, *37*(2), 281–299.

Goetghebuer, J. (2021). AI and Creditworthiness Assessments: The Tale of Credit Scoring and Consumer Protection. In De Bruyne, J., & Vanleenhove, C. (Eds.), *Artificial Intelligence and the Law* (pp. 429–460). Intersentia. DOI: 10.1017/9781839701047.017

Goodfellow, I., Pouget-Abadie, J., Mirza, M., Xu, B., Warde-Farley, D., Ozair, S., & Bengio, Y. (2014). Generative adversarial nets. *Advances in Neural Information Processing Systems*, •••, 27.

Google, A. I. Blog. (2021). Introducing MUM: A new AI milestone for understanding information. https://blog.google/products/search/introducing-mum/, Retrieved 12:33, February 21, 2025.

Gopalakrishnan, V., Patel, D., & Singh, M. (2022). Predictive analytics in e-commerce: A case study of personalized recommendations. *Journal of Retailing and Consumer Services*, *65*, 102884.

Government of India. (2023). *The Digital Personal Data Protection Act, 2023* (No. 12 of 2023). Ministry of Electronics & Information Technology. https://www.meity.gov.in/writereaddata/files/Digital_personal_data_protection_bill.pdf

Goyal, K., Aggarwal, P., & Garg, R. (2022). AI applications in supply chain management: A systematic literature review. *Operations Research Perspectives*, *9*, 100244.

Graesser, A. C., Wiemer-Hastings, K., Wiemer-Hastings, P., & Kreuz, R.Tutoring Research Group. (1999). AutoTutor: A simulation of a human tutor. *Cognitive Systems Research*, *1*(1), 35–51. DOI: 10.1016/S1389-0417(99)00005-4

Grájeda, A., Burgos, J., Córdova, P., & Sanjinés, A. (2024). Assessing student-perceived impact of using artificial intelligence tools: Construction of a synthetic index of application in higher education. *Cogent Education*, *11*(1), 2287917. DOI: 10.1080/2331186X.2023.2287917

Griol, D., Molina, J. M., & Callejas, Z. (2014). An approach to develop intelligent learning environments by means of immersive virtual worlds. *Journal of Ambient Intelligence and Smart Environments*, *6*(2), 237–255. DOI: 10.3233/AIS-140255

Gupta, M., & Singh, A. (2023). Emerging Trends in Artificial Intelligence Education: Advancements, Opportunities, and Impact on Educational Technology. *Quanta Research*, *1*(1), 20–26.

Gupta, P., Mahajan, R., Badhera, U., & Kushwaha, P. S. (2024). Integrating generative AI in management education: A mixed-methods study using social construction of technology theory. *International Journal of Management Education*, *22*(3), 101017. DOI: 10.1016/j.ijme.2024.101017

Gupta, S., Srivastava, R., Shaikh, Z. H., & Irfan, M. (2024). Revolutionizing Rural Finance:Exploring the Impact of FinTech on Financial Inclusion in India. In Irfan, M., Muhammad, K., Naifar, N., & Khan, M. A. (Eds.), *Applications of Block Chain technology and Artificial Intelligence. Financial Mathematics and Fintech.* Springer., DOI: 10.1007/978-3-031-47324-1_3

Hacker, P., Engel, A., & Mauer, M. (2023, June). Regulating ChatGPT and other large generative AI models. In *Proceedings of the 2023 ACM conference on fairness, accountability, and transparency* (pp. 1112-1123). DOI: 10.1145/3593013.3594067

Haefner, N., Wincent, J., Parida, V., & Gassmann, O. (2021). Artificial intelligence and innovation management: A review, framework, and research agenda. *Technological Forecasting and Social Change*, *162*, 120392. DOI: 10.1016/j.techfore.2020.120392

Haleem, A., Javaid, M., & Singh, R. P. (2022). An era of ChatGPT as a significant futuristic support tool: A study on features, abilities, and challenges. *BenchCouncil transactions on benchmarks, standards and evaluations*, *2*(4), 100089.

Haleem, A., Javaid, M., Qadri, M. A., & Suman, R. (2022a). Understanding the role of digital technologies in education: A review. *Sustainable Operations and Computers*, *3*, 275–285. DOI: 10.1016/j.susoc.2022.05.004

Handfield, R. B., Jeong, S., & Choi, T. (2020). Emerging procurement technology: Data analytics and cognitive analytics. *Journal of Purchasing and Supply Management*, *26*(2), 100621.

Harvard Business Review. (2024). Gen AI's impact on the case classroom. Retrieved from https://hbsp.harvard.edu/inspiring-minds/gen-ais-impact-on-the-case-classroom

Hayes-Roth, F., Waterman, D. A., & Lenat, D. B. (1983). *Building expert systems*. Addison-Wesley Longman Publishing Co., Inc.

HEC Paris. (2025, May 7). *Students massively adopt AI tools for schoolwork*. HEC Paris.

Helo, P., & Hao, Y. (2022). Artificial intelligence in operations management and supply chain management: An exploratory case study. *Production Planning and Control*, *33*(16), 1573–1590. DOI: 10.1080/09537287.2021.1882690

Hemalatha, S., & Prabhu, J. (2023). A review of machine learning applications in the talent acquisition process. *Computational Intelligence and Neuroscience Advances*, 2023, Article 1261.

Hibbert, P. (2012). Approaching reflexivity through reflection: Issues for critical management education. *Journal of Management Education*, *37*(6), 803–827. DOI: 10.1177/1052562912467757

Hilbert, S., Coors, S., Kraus, E., Bischl, B., Lindl, A., Frei, M., Wild, J., Krauss, S., Goretzko, D., & Stachl, C. (2021). Machine learning for the educational sciences. *Review of Education*, *9*(3), e3310. DOI: 10.1002/rev3.3310

Hindwan, S. (2020, December 13). *New challenges to education during pandemic*. The Pioneer, p. 3. https://intelitek.com/2018/06/06/intelitek-releases-white-paper-on-changing-education-systems-to-prepare-students-for-the-demands-of-modern-society-and-the-industrial-workspace/

Ho, M. K., Darman, H., & Musa, S. (2021, July). Stock price prediction using ARIMA, neural network and LSTM models. In *Journal of Physics: Conference Series* (Vol. 1988, No. 1, p. 012041). IOP Publishing. DOI: 10.1088/1742-6596/1988/1/012041

Hochreiter, S., & Schmidhuber, J. (1997). Long short-term memory. *Neural Computation*, *9*(8), 1735–1780. DOI: 10.1162/neco.1997.9.8.1735 PMID: 9377276

Holmes, W. (2016). *Intelligence Unleashed: An argument for AI in Education.* https://www.researchgate.net/publication/299561597

Holmström, J., & Carroll, N. (2024). How organizations can innovate with generative AI. *Business Horizons.* Advance online publication. DOI: 10.1016/j.bushor.2024.02.010

Holstein, K., & Doroudi, S. (2021). Equity and artificial intelligence in education: will" aied" amplify or alleviate inequities in education? *arXiv preprint arXiv:2104.12920.*

Hopfield, J. J. (1982). Neural networks and physical systems with emergent collective computational abilities. *Proceedings of the National Academy of Sciences of the United States of America, 79*(8), 2554–2558. DOI: 10.1073/pnas.79.8.2554 PMID: 6953413

Hu, K. (2023). *ChatGPT Sets Record for Fastest-Growing User Base.* Https://Www.Reuters.Com/Technology/Chatgpt-Sets-Record-Fastest-Growinguser-Base-Analyst-Note-2023-02-01/

Huang, L. S., Su, J. Y., & Pao, T. L. (2019). A context aware smart classroom architecture for smart campuses. *Applied Sciences (Basel, Switzerland), 9*(9), 1837. DOI: 10.3390/app9091837

Huang, M. H., & Rust, R. T. (2021). A strategic framework for artificial intelligence in marketing. *Journal of the Academy of Marketing Science, 49*(1), 30–50. DOI: 10.1007/s11747-020-00749-9

Hwang, G. J., Sung, H. Y., Chang, S. C., & Huang, X. C. (2020). A fuzzy expert system-based adaptive learning approach to improving students' learning performances by considering affective and cognitive factors. *Computers and Education: Artificial Intelligence, 1*, 100003. DOI: 10.1016/j.caeai.2020.100003

IBM Deep Blue https://www.ibm.com/history/deep-blue, Retrieved 10:32, February 21, 2025.

IBM GEN AI. https://research.ibm.com/blog/what-is-generative-AI#:~:text=is%20generative%20AI%3F-,Generative%20AI%20refers%20to%20deep%2Dlearning%20models%20that%20can%20generate%20high%2Dquality%20text%2C%20images%2C%20and%20other%20content%20based%20on%20the%20data%20they%20were%20trained%20on.,-Explore%20what%20you, retrieved 6:50, February 21, 2025.

Idroes, G. M., Noviandy, T. R., Maulana, A., Irvanizam, I., & Idroes, R. (2023). Student perspectives on the role of artificial intelligence in education: A survey-based analysis. *Journal of Educational Management and Learning, 1*(1), 8–15. DOI: 10.60084/jeml.v1i1.58

Igbokwe, I. C. (2023). Application of artificial intelligence (AI) in educational management. *International Journal of Scientific and Research Publications, 13*(3), 300–307. DOI: 10.29322/IJSRP.13.03.2023.p13536

Ijaz, K., Bogdanovych, A., & Trescak, T. (2017). Virtual worlds vs books and videos in history education. *Interactive Learning Environments, 25*(7), 904–929. DOI: 10.1080/10494820.2016.1225099

Isaeva, R., Karasartova, N., Dznunusnalieva, K., Mirzoeva, K., & Mokliuk, M. (2025). ENHANCING LEARNING EFFECTIVENESS THROUGH ADAPTIVE LEARNING PLATFORMS AND EMERGING COMPUTER TECHNOLOGIES IN EDUCATION. *Jurnal Ilmiah Ilmu Terapan Universitas Jambi, 9*(1), 144–160. DOI: 10.22437/jiituj.v9i1.37967

Ivanov, S., & Soliman, M. (2023). Game of algorithms: ChatGPT implications for the future of tourism education and research. *Journal of Tourism Futures, 9*(2), 214–221. DOI: 10.1108/JTF-02-2023-0038

Jääskä, E., Aaltonen, K., & Kujala, J. (2021). Game-Based Learning in Project Sustainability Management Education. *Sustainability (Basel), 13*(15), 8204. DOI: 10.3390/su13158204

Jackson, I., Ivanov, D., Dolgui, A., & Namdar, J. (2024). Generative artificial intelligence in supply chain and operations management: A capability-based framework for analysis and implementation. *International Journal of Production Research, 62*(17), 6120–6145. DOI: 10.1080/00207543.2024.2309309

Jafari, D., & Shaterzadeh-Yazdi, Z. (2024). Transforming Education with AI: The Development of a Personalized Learning Algorithm for Individual Learning Styles. *Journal of Algorithms and Computation, 56*(2), 135–150.

Jain, N. (2024, October 13th). Harnessing the Power of AI. *Business Today (Norwich)*, •••, 76–77.

Jalil, N. A., Hwang, H. J., & Dawi, N. M. (2019, July). Machines learning trends, perspectives and prospects in education sector. In *Proceedings of the 3rd International Conference on Education and Multimedia Technology* (pp. 201-205). DOI: 10.1145/3345120.3345147

Jamison, J. (2017, March). Applying machine learning to predict Davidson college's admissions yield. In *Proceedings of the 2017 ACM SIGCSE Technical Symposium on Computer Science Education* (pp. 765-766). DOI: 10.1145/3017680.3022468

Jannai, D., Meron, A., Lenz, B., Levine, Y., & Shoham, Y. (2023). Human or not? A gamified approach to the Turing test. *arXiv preprint arXiv:2305.20010.*

Jansen, S. (2020). *Machine learning for algorithmic trading* (2nd ed.). Packt Publishing.

Jayasinghe, S. (2024). Harnessing generative AI for self-directed learning: Perspectives from top management. *Development and Learning in Organizations*.

Jiang, H., Zhao, L., & Wang, R. (2021). AI-driven predictive analytics for supply chain optimization. *Operations Research Perspectives, 10*, 100217.

Jia, Y., Zhao, J., & Wang, Y. (2020). AI-powered customer experience in e-commerce: A case study of recommendation systems. *Electronic Commerce Research and Applications, 39*, 100919.

Jin, Y., Yan, L., Echeverria, V., Gašević, D., & Martinez-Maldonado, R. (2024). *Generative AI in Higher Education: A Global Perspective of Institutional Adoption Policies and Guidelines*. DOI: 10.1016/j.caeai.2024.100348

Jobin, A., Ienca, M., & Vayena, E. (2019). The global landscape of AI ethics guidelines. *Nature Machine Intelligence, 1*(9), 389–399. DOI: 10.1038/s42256-019-0088-2

Jochem, T., Pomerleau, D., Kumar, B., & Armstrong, J. (1995, September). PANS: A portable navigation platform. In *Proceedings of the Intelligent Vehicles' 95. Symposium* (pp. 107-112). IEEE. DOI: 10.1109/IVS.1995.528266

Jordan, M. I., & Mitchell, T. M. (2015). Machine learning: Trends, perspectives, and prospects. *Science, 349*(6245), 255–260. DOI: 10.1126/science.aaa8415 PMID: 26185243

Kadaruddin, K. (2023). Empowering education through Generative AI: Innovative instructional strategies for tomorrow's learners. *International Journal of Business, Law, and Education, 4*(2), 618–625. DOI: 10.56442/ijble.v4i2.215

Kaggwa, S., Eleogu, T. F., Okonkwo, F., Farayola, O. A., Uwaoma, P. U., & Akinoso, A. (2024). AI in decision making: Transforming business strategies. *International Journal of Innovation and Scientific Research, 10*(12), 423–444. DOI: 10.51244/IJRSI.2023.1012032

Kanbach, D. K., Heiduk, L., Blueher, G., Schreiter, M., & Lahmann, A. (2024). The GenAI is out of the bottle: Generative artificial intelligence from a business model innovation perspective. *Review of Managerial Science, 18*(4), 1189–1220. DOI: 10.1007/s11846-023-00696-z

Kaplan, A., & Haenlein, M. (2019). Siri, Alexa, and other digital assistants: The future of customer service? *Journal of Business Research, 116*, 1–16.

Katsamakas, E., Pavlov, O. V., & Saklad, R. (2024). Artificial Intelligence and the Transformation of Higher Education Institutions: A Systems Approach. *Sustainability (Basel)*, *16*(14), 6118. Advance online publication. DOI: 10.3390/su16146118

Kaushik, M., & Giri, A. K. (2020). Forecasting foreign exchange rate: A multivariate comparative analysis between traditional econometric, contemporary machine learning & deep learning techniques. *arXiv preprint*, arXiv:2002.10247. https://arxiv.org/abs/2002.10247

Kavitha, V., & Lohani, R. (2019). A critical study on the use of artificial intelligence, e-Learning technology and tools to enhance the learners experience. *Cluster Computing*, *22*(S3, Suppl 3), 6985–6989. DOI: 10.1007/s10586-018-2017-2

Kayyali, M. (2024). Future possibilities and challenges of AI in education. In *Transforming education with generative AI: Prompt engineering and synthetic content creation* (pp. 118–137). IGI Global Scientific Publishing. DOI: 10.4018/979-8-3693-1351-0.ch006

Kayyali, M. (2024). Immersive Technologies: Virtual and Augmented Reality in Higher Education. In Braman, J., Brown, A., & Richards, M. J. (Eds.), (pp. 99–114). Advances in Educational Technologies and Instructional Design. IGI Global., DOI: 10.4018/979-8-3693-1310-7.ch007

Kelleher, J. D. (2019). *Deep learning*. MIT Press. DOI: 10.7551/mitpress/11171.001.0001

Kenthapadi, K., Lakkaraju, H., & Rajani, N. (2023, August). Generative ai meets responsible ai: Practical challenges and opportunities. In *Proceedings of the 29th ACM SIGKDD conference on knowledge discovery and data mining* (pp. 5805-5806). DOI: 10.1145/3580305.3599557

Keskar, A. (2024). Driving operational excellence in manufacturing through generative AI: Transformative approaches for efficiency, innovation, and scalability. *International Journal of Research and Analytical Reviews*, *11*, 245–261.

Khan, H., Chetan, V., Hukkeri, S. V., & Neelima, M. (2025). Future of Productivity Management: The Role of Generative AI. In *Generative AI for Business Analytics and Strategic Decision Making in Service Industry* (pp. 89–112). IGI Global Scientific Publishing. DOI: 10.4018/979-8-3693-7026-1.ch004

Khan, N., Khan, Z., Koubaa, A., Khan, M. K., & Salleh, R. B. (2024). Global insights and the impact of generative AI-ChatGPT on multidisciplinary: A systematic review and bibliometric analysis. *Connection Science*, *36*(1), 2353630. DOI: 10.1080/09540091.2024.2353630

Khanna, S., Kaushik, A., & Barnela, M. (2010, March). Expert systems advances in education. In *Proceedings of the National Conference on Computational Instrumentation NCCI-2010. CSIO* (pp. 109-112).

Khan, S., Mazhar, T., Shahzad, T., Khan, M. A., Rehman, A. U., Saeed, M. M., & Hamam, H. (2025). Harnessing AI for sustainable higher education: Ethical considerations, operational efficiency, and future directions. *Discover Sustainability*, *6*(1), 23. DOI: 10.1007/s43621-025-00809-6

Kietzmann, J., Lee, L. W., McCarthy, I. P., & Kietzmann, T. C. (2020). Deepfakes: Trick or treat? *Business Horizons*, *63*(2), 135–146. DOI: 10.1016/j.bushor.2019.11.006

Kinshuk, C., Chen, N.-S., Cheng, I.-L., & Chew, S. W. (2016). Evolution is not enough: Revolutionizing current learning environments to smart learning environments. *International Journal of Artificial Intelligence in Education*, *26*(2), 561–581. DOI: 10.1007/s40593-016-0108-x

Kioupi, V., & Voulvoulis, N. (2019). Education for Sustainable Development: A Systemic Framework for Connecting the SDGs to Educational Outcomes. *Sustainability (Basel)*, *11*(21), 6104. DOI: 10.3390/su11216104

Klašnja-Milićević, A., & Ivanović, M. (2021). E-learning personalization systems and sustainable education. *Sustainability (Basel)*, *13*(12), 6713. DOI: 10.3390/su13126713

Klutka, J., Ackerly, N., & Magda, A. J. (2018). *Artificial intelligence in higher education: Current uses and future applications*. Learning House.

Kohnke, L., Moorhouse, B. L., & Zou, D. (2023). Exploring generative artificial intelligence preparedness among university language instructors: A case study. *Computers and Education: Artificial Intelligence*, *5*, 100156. DOI: 10.1016/j.caeai.2023.100156

Koroteev, M. V. (2021). BERT: a review of applications in natural language processing and understanding. *arXiv preprint arXiv:2103.11943.*

Kose, U., & Arslan, A. (2016). Intelligent e-learning system for improving students' academic achievements in computer programming courses. *International Journal of Engineering Education*, *32*(1), 185–198.

Kozinets, R. V. (2023). Immersive netnography: A novel method for service experience research in virtual reality, augmented reality and metaverse contexts. *Journal of Service Management*, *34*(1), 100–125. DOI: 10.1108/JOSM-12-2021-0481

Krishan, R. G. (2016, February 19). *Boosting industry-academia linkages*. Business Standard, p. 8.

Krizhevsky, A., Sutskever, I., & Hinton, G. E. (2012). Imagenet classification with deep convolutional neural networks. *Advances in Neural Information Processing Systems*, •••, 25.

Kshetri, N., & Hughes, L. (2023). "So what if ChatGPT wrote it?" Multidisciplinary perspectives on opportunities, challenges and implications of generative conversational AI for research, practice and policy. *International Journal of Information Management*, *71*, 102642. DOI: 10.1016/j.ijinfomgt.2023.102642

Kučak, D., Juričić, V., & Đambić, G. (2018). MACHINE LEARNING IN EDUCATION-A SURVEY OF CURRENT RESEARCH TRENDS. *Annals of DAAAM & Proceedings, 29.*

Kulkarni, V. (2020, October 29). *Apprenticeship: Win-win solutions*. The Economic Times (ET Newsmakers), p. 3.

Kumar, C. R. (2015, December 1). *Five steps to revitalise India's higher education system*. The Economic Times.

Kumar, S. (2020, September 10). *Higher education more corporatized and profit-driven*. The Morning India.

Kumar, S., & Sharma, A. (2020, September 21). *Regional universities and challenges before new education policy*. The Daily Guardian, p. 5.

Kumar, A., & Gupta, D. (2021). Sentiment analysis as a restricted NLP problem. In *Natural language processing for global and local business* (pp. 65–96). IGI Global. DOI: 10.4018/978-1-7998-4240-8.ch004

Kumar, A., Gupta, S., & Sharma, K. (2021). AI-based decision support systems: Transforming business strategy. *Decision Support Systems*, *145*, 113524.

Kumar, R., & Singh, M. (2023). Predictive analytics in employee retention and engagement strategies. *International Journal of Human Resource Studies*, *13*(2), 45–60.

Kusuma, K., Sheela, P., Panigrahi, R. R., & Shaikh, Z. H. (2024). Blockchain Technology and Islamic Finance: A Decade of Growth Trends. In Irfan, M., Kadry, S., Sharif, M., & Khan, H. (Eds.), *Fintech Applications in Islamic Finance: AI, Machine Learning, and Blockchain Techniques* (pp. 59–79). IGI Global., DOI: 10.4018/979-8-3693-1038-0.ch004

Labarthe, H., Luengo, V., & Bouchet, F. (2018, June). Analyzing the relationships between learning analytics, educational data mining and AI for education. In *14th International Conference on Intelligent Tutoring Systems (ITS): Workshop Learning Analytics* (pp. 10-19).

Laifa, M., Akhrouf, S., Mohdeb, D., & Belazzoug, M. (2024). Satisfaction of students and teachers with blended learning during COVID-19 pandemic: An Algerian case study. *International Journal of Learning Technology, 19*(3), 273–297. DOI: 10.1504/IJLT.2024.142509

Lakumarapu, S., Nithyanandhan, R., Bhargavi, V. S., Anish, T. P., & Nalini, M. (2024, August). Machine Learning Approaches for Liver Disease Prediction: A Comparative Analysis. In *2024 5th International Conference on Electronics and Sustainable Communication Systems (ICESC)* (pp. 159-164). IEEE. DOI: 10.1109/ICESC60852.2024.10689974

Langenbucher, K., & Corcoran, P. (2021). Responsible AI credit scoring - A lesson from Upstart.com. In *Digital finance in Europe: Law, regulation, and governance* (Book 5 in the *European Company and Financial Law Review - Special Volume* series). University Press Library Open.

Lao, Y., & You, Y. (2024). *Unraveling generative AI in BBC News: application, impact, literacy and governance. Transforming Government: People*. Process and Policy., DOI: 10.1108/TG-01-2024-0022

LeCun, Y., Boser, B., Denker, J. S., Henderson, D., Howard, R. E., Hubbard, W., & Jackel, L. D. (1989). Backpropagation applied to handwritten zip code recognition. *Neural Computation, 1*(4), 541–551. DOI: 10.1162/neco.1989.1.4.541

LeCun, Y., Bottou, L., Bengio, Y., & Haffner, P. (1998). Gradient-based learning applied to document recognition. *Proceedings of the IEEE, 86*(11), 2278–2324. DOI: 10.1109/5.726791

Lee, K., Datta, S., Paek, H., Rastegar-Mojarad, M., Huang, L. C., He, L., . . . Wang, X. (2024). AID-SLR: A Generative Artificial Intelligence-Driven Automated System for Systematic Literature Review. medRxiv, 2024-07. DOI: 10.1101/2024.07.03.24309897

Lee, W. J., Becker, K. and Nobre, H. (2012), Impact of culture on online management education, Cross Cultural Management: An International Journal, Vol. 19 No. 3, pp. 399-420. https://doi.org/DOI: 10.1108/13527601211247116

Lee, D., Arnold, M., Srivastava, A., Plastow, K., Strelan, P., Ploeckl, F., Lekkas, D., & Palmer, E. (2024). The impact of generative AI on higher education learning and teaching: A study of educators' perspectives. *Computers and Education: Artificial Intelligence*, *6*, 100221. Advance online publication. DOI: 10.1016/j.caeai.2024.100221

Leelavathi, R., & Surendhranatha, R. C. (2024). ChatGPT in the classroom: navigating the generative AI wave in management education. *Journal of Research in Innovative Teaching & Learning*, (ahead-of-print).

Leelavathi, R., & Surendhranatha, R. C. (2024). ChatGPT in the classroom: navigating the generative AI wave in management education. *Journal of Research in Innovative Teaching & Learning*. DOI: 10.1108/JRIT-01-2024-0017

Leitch, C. M., & Harrison, R. T. (1999). A process model for entrepreneurship education and development. *International Journal of Entrepreneurial Behaviour & Research*, *5*(3), 83–109. DOI: 10.1108/13552559910284065

Leong, K., & Sung, A. (2025). Introducing airsim: An innovative ai-driven feedback generation tool for supporting student learning. *Technology, Knowledge and Learning*, 1-23.

Leoni, L., Gueli, G., Ardolino, M., Panizzon, M., & Gupta, S. (2024). AI-empowered KM processes for decision-making: Empirical evidence from worldwide organisations. *Journal of Knowledge Management*, *28*(11), 320–347. DOI: 10.1108/JKM-03-2024-0262

Le, Q. V. (2013, May). *Building high-level features using large scale unsupervised learning. In 2013 IEEE international conference on acoustics, speech and signal processing*. IEEE.

Leslie, D. (2020). *Understanding artificial intelligence ethics and safety*. The Alan Turing Institute.

Leung, C. K., Ursino, D., Sajja, R., Erazo Ramirez, C., Li, Z., Demiray, B. Z., Sermet, Y., & Demir, I. (2024). *Integrating Generative AI in Hackathons: Opportunities*. Challenges, and Educational Implications., DOI: 10.3390/bdcc8120188

Liang, J., Stephens, J. M., & Brown, G. T. L. (2025). A systematic review of the early impact of artificial intelligence on higher education curriculum, instruction, and assessment. *Frontiers in Education*, *10*, 1522841. DOI: 10.3389/feduc.2025.1522841

Li, F., Yigitcanlar, T., Nepal, M., Nguyen, K., & Dur, F. (2023). Machine learning and remote sensing integration for leveraging urban sustainability: A review and framework. *Sustainable Cities and Society*, *96*, 104653. DOI: 10.1016/j.scs.2023.104653

Lim, S. C. J., & Lee, M. F. (2024). Rethinking education in the era of artificial intelligence (AI): Towards future workforce competitiveness and business success. In *Emerging Technologies in Business: Innovation Strategies for Competitive Advantage* (pp. 151–166). Springer Nature Singapore. DOI: 10.1007/978-981-97-2211-2_7

Lim, W. M., Gunasekara, A., Pallant, J. L., Pallant, J. I., & Pechenkina, E. (2023). Generative AI and the future of education: Ragnarök or reformation? A paradoxical perspective from management educators. *International Journal of Management Education, 21*(2), 100790. Advance online publication. DOI: 10.1016/j.ijme.2023.100790

Lin, B., Chen, F., & Yu, X. (2022). The evolution of AI chatbots: Enhancing customer service with NLP. *Computers in Human Behavior, 132*, 107290.

Lin, C. C., Huang, A. Y., & Lu, O. H. (2023). Artificial intelligence in intelligent tutoring systems toward sustainable education: A systematic review. *Smart Learning Environments, 10*(1), 41. DOI: 10.1186/s40561-023-00260-y

Linkon, A. A., Shaima, M., Sarker, M. S. U., Badruddowza, B., Nabi, N., Rana, M. N. U., & Chowdhury, F. R. (2024). Advancements and applications of generative artificial intelligence and large language models on business management: A comprehensive review. *Journal of Computer Science and Technology Studies, 6*(1), 225–232. DOI: 10.32996/jcsts.2024.6.1.26

Liu, X., Wang, S., Wang, P., & Wu, D. (2019, May). Automatic grading of programming assignments: an approach based on formal semantics. In *2019 IEEE/ACM 41st International Conference on Software Engineering: Software Engineering Education and Training (ICSE-SEET)* (pp. 126-137). IEEE. DOI: 10.1109/ICSE-SEET.2019.00022

Liu, Y., Zhang, K., Li, Y., Yan, Z., Gao, C., Chen, R., . . . Sun, L. (2024). Sora: A review on background, technology, limitations, and opportunities of large vision models. *arXiv preprint arXiv:2402.17177.*

Liu, Z., & Yushchik, E. (2024). Exploring the prospects of using artificial intelligence in education. *Cogent Education, 11*(1), 2353464. Advance online publication. DOI: 10.1080/2331186X.2024.2353464

López-Meneses, E., Mellado-Moreno, P. C., Gallardo Herrerías, C., & Pelícano-Piris, N. (2025). Educational Data Mining and Predictive Modeling in the Age of Artificial Intelligence: An In-Depth Analysis of Research Dynamics. *Computers, 14*(2), 68. DOI: 10.3390/computers14020068

Lotherington, H., Pegrum, M., Thumlert, K., Tomin, B., Boreland, T., & Pobuda, T. (2024). Exploring opportunities for language immersion in the posthuman spectrum: Lessons learned from digital agents. *Interactive Technology and Smart Education.* Advance online publication. DOI: 10.1108/ITSE-02-2024-0038

Luan, H., Geczy, P., Lai, H., Gobert, J., Yang, S. J. H., Ogata, H., Baltes, J., Guerra, R., Li, P., & Tsai, C.-C. (2020). Challenges and Future Directions of Big Data and Artificial Intelligence in Education. *Frontiers in Psychology*, *11*, 580820. DOI: 10.3389/fpsyg.2020.580820 PMID: 33192896

Luan, H., & Tsai, C. C. (2021). A review of using machine learning approaches for precision education. *Journal of Educational Technology & Society*, *24*(1), 250–266.

Luckin, R., George, K., & Cukurova, M. (2022). *AI for School Teachers*. Routledge. DOI: 10.1201/9781003193173

Luckin, R., & Holmes, W. (2016). *Intelligence Unleashed: An argument for AI in Education*. UCL Knowledge Lab.

Luo, Q. Z., & Hsiao-Chin, L. Y. (2023). The influence of AI-powered adaptive learning platforms on student performance in Chinese classrooms. *Journal of Education*, *6*(3), 1–12. DOI: 10.53819/81018102t4181

Macesar, A. F. (2023, August 3). *How to create marketing images from AI*. The Sustainable Agency. https://thesustainableagency.com/blog/how-to-create-ai-images-for-marketing/

Mah, D. K., Knoth, N., & Egloffstein, M. (2025, March). Perspectives of academic staff on artificial intelligence in higher education: Exploring areas of relevance. []. Frontiers Media SA.]. *Frontiers in Education*, *10*, 1484904. DOI: 10.3389/feduc.2025.1484904

Makinde, A. I., Adeleye, S. A., Oronti, A. O., & Jimoh, I. T. (2024). Revolutionizing education. *Artificial Intelligence for Wireless Communication Systems: Technology and Applications, 103.*

Malhotra, P. (2024). The rise of passive investing: A systematic literature review applying PRISMA framework. *Journal of Capital Markets Studies*, *8*(1), 95–125. DOI: 10.1108/JCMS-12-2023-0046

Mangaiyarkarasi, T., Catherine, S., & Kalaiselvi, K. (2025). Adapting to Generation AI: Navigating the Future of Business and Technology. In *Navigating Data Science in the Age of AI: Exploring Possibilities of Generative Intelligence* (pp. 13-33). Emerald Publishing Limited.

Manyika, J., Chui, M., Brown, B., Bughin, J., Dobbs, R., Roxburgh, C., & Byers, A. H. (2017). *Big data: The next frontier for innovation, competition, and productivity*. McKinsey Global Institute.

Markouh, O., Adadi, A., & Berrada, M. (2024, May). Towards a Blockchain Generative AI Driven Education: An Exploratory Study. In *2024 4th International Conference on Innovative Research in Applied Science, Engineering and Technology (IRASET)* (pp. 1-9). IEEE.

Marr, B. (2024). *Generative AI in practice: 100+ amazing ways generative artificial intelligence is Changing Business and Society*. John Wiley & Sons.

Matos, E. J., Bertoncini, A. L. C., Ames, M. C. F. D. C., & Serafim, M. C. (2024). The (lack of) ethics at generative AI in Business Management education and research. *RAM. Revista de Administração Mackenzie*, *25*(6), eRAMD240061. DOI: 10.1590/1678-6971/eramd240061

Matthew, U. O., Bakare, K. M., Ebong, G. N., Ndukwu, C. C., & Nwanakwaugwu, A. C.Ugochukwu Okwudili MatthewKafayat Motomori BakareGodwin Nse EbongCharles Chukwuebuka NdukwuAndrew Chinonso Nwanakwaugwu. (2023). Generative Artificial Intelligence (AI) Educational Pedagogy Development: Conversational AI with User-Centric ChatGPT4. *Journal of Trends in Computer Science and Smart Technology*, *5*(4), 401–418. DOI: 10.36548/jtcsst.2023.4.003

Mavin, S., Bryans, P., & Waring, T. (2004). Unlearning gender blindness: New directions in management education. *Management Decision*, *42*(3/4), 565–578. DOI: 10.1108/00251740410522287

Mayer, H., Yee, L., Chui, M., & Roberts, R. (2025, January 28). Superagency in the workplace: Empowering people to unlock AI's full potential. McKinsey Digital. https://www.mckinsey.com/capabilities/mckinsey-digital/our-insights/superagency-in-the-workplace-empowering-people-to-unlock-ais-full-potential-at-work

McFarland, T. D., & Parker, R. (1990). Expert systems in education and training. *Educational Technology*.

McGraw-Hill. (October 24, 2023). Share of undergraduate students who have various opinions on the use of artificial intelligence (AI) tools in higher education in the United States in 2023 [Graph]. In *Statista*. Retrieved January 16, 2025, from https://www.statista.com/statistics/1445975/us-undergraduate-students-opinions-on-the-use-of-ai-in-education/

McKinsey & Company. (2024, August 7). *What is digital transformation?* Retrieved from https://www.mckinsey.com/featured-insights/mckinsey-explainers/what-is-digital-transformation

McKinsey Global Institute. (2020). The state of AI in 2020. McKinsey & Company. https://www.mckinsey.com/

McPhail, K., Kafouros, M., McKiernan, P., & Cornelius, N. (2024). Reimagining Business and Management as a Force for Good. *British Journal of Management, 35*(3), 1099–1112. DOI: 10.1111/1467-8551.12846

Meghwal, A. R. (2020, August 31). *On education, looking ahead*. The Indian Express, p. 7.

Mehrabi, N., Morstatter, F., Saxena, N., Lerman, K., & Galstyan, A. (2021). A survey on bias and fairness in machine learning. *ACM Computing Surveys, 54*(6), 1–35. DOI: 10.1145/3457607

Mehtab, S., & Sen, J. (2020, November). Stock price prediction using CNN and LSTM-based deep learning models. In *2020 International Conference on Decision Aid Sciences and Application (DASA)* (pp. 447–453). IEEE. DOI: 10.1109/DASA51403.2020.9317207

Memarian, B., & Doleck, T. (2023). Fairness, Accountability, Transparency, and Ethics (FATE) in Artificial Intelligence (AI) and higher education: A systematic review. *Computers and Education: Artificial Intelligence, 5*, 100152. DOI: 10.1016/j.caeai.2023.100152

Miao, Q., & Nduneseokwu, C. (2024). Advancing Environmental Leadership: Education, Development, and Training. In Q. Miao & C. Nduneseokwu, *Environmental Leadership in a VUCA Era* (pp. 467–538). Springer Nature Singapore. DOI: 10.1007/978-981-96-0324-4_10

Michie, D. (1963). Experiments on the mechanization of game-learning Part I. Characterization of the model and its parameters. *The Computer Journal, 6*(3), 232–236. DOI: 10.1093/comjnl/6.3.232

Microsoft Copilot https://www.microsoft.com/en-us/microsoft-365/blog/2025/01/16/copilot-is-now-included-in-microsoft-365-personal-and-family/, Retrieved 7:25, February 22, 2025.

Millar, J., & Price, M. (2018). Imagining management education: A critique of the contribution of the United Nations PRME to critical reflexivity and rethinking management education. *Management Learning, 49*(3), 346–362. DOI: 10.1177/1350507618759828

Milton, J., & Al-Busaidi, A. (2023). New role of leadership in AI era: Educational sector. In *SHS Web of Conferences* (Vol. 156, p. 09005). EDP Sciences.

Ministry of Human Resource Development. (2020). *India report on digital education – June 2020*. Government of India.

Ministry of Information and Broadcasting. (2020). *India 2020*. Government of India.

Mircea, M., Stoica, M., & Ghilic-Micu, B. (2021). Investigating the impact of the internet of things in higher education environment. *IEEE Access : Practical Innovations, Open Solutions*, *9*, 33396–33409. DOI: 10.1109/ACCESS.2021.3060964

Mishra, P. (2024). Revolutionizing Education With AI and ML. In Reddy, C. (Ed.), *M. Ouaissa, M. Ouaissa, H. Lamaazi, M. El Hamlaoui, & K. K* (pp. 53–94). Advances in Educational Technologies and Instructional Design. IGI Global., DOI: 10.4018/979-8-3693-8151-9.ch003

Mittal, S. Sai, V. Chamola and D. Sangwan. (2024). A Comprehensive Review on Generative AI for Education," in *IEEE Access*. 12, 142733-142759, DOI: 10.1109/ACCESS.2024.3468368

Mittal, U., Sai, S., Chamola, V., & Member, S. (n.d.). (2024). *A Comprehensive Review on Generative AI for Education*. https://doi.org/DOI: 10.1109/ACCESS.2017.DOI

Mnih, V., Kavukcuoglu, K., Silver, D., Rusu, A. A., Veness, J., Bellemare, M. G., ... & Hassabis, D. (2015). Human-level control through deep reinforcement learning. *nature, 518*(7540), 529-533.

Moghar, A., & Hamiche, M. (2020). Stock market prediction using LSTM recurrent neural network. *Procedia Computer Science, 170*, 1168–1173. DOI: 10.1016/j.procs.2020.03.049

Mohamed, A., Faisal, R., & Shaalan, K. (2024, September). Exploring the Impact of AI-Driven Virtual Assistants in AR and VR Environments for Special Needs Education: A Quantitative Analysis. In *International Conference on Extended Reality* (pp. 113-127). Cham: Springer Nature Switzerland. DOI: 10.1007/978-3-031-71713-0_8

Mohanty, B. S., Shaikh, Z. H., Mahapatra, D. M., Ratnakaranm, S., & Manikeswari, D. (2025). Wearable technologies in education: Advantages, limitations, and technical difficulties. In *Wearable devices and smart technology for educational teaching assistance* (pp. 309–330). IGI Global Scientific Publishing.

Mollick, E., & Mollick, L. (2023). Assigning AI: Seven Approaches for Students with Prompts. *SSRN*. DOI: 10.2139/ssrn.4475995

Moravec, H. P. (1983). The Stanford cart and the CMU rover. *Proceedings of the IEEE, 71*(7), 872–884. DOI: 10.1109/PROC.1983.12684

Moravec, J. W., & Martínez-Bravo, M. C. (2023). Global trends in disruptive technological change: Social and policy implications for education. *On the Horizon, 31*(3–4), 147–173. DOI: 10.1108/OTH-02-2023-0007

Morgan, S. D., & Stewart, A. C. (2019). Teams in Management Education. *Journal of Management Education, 43*(5), 573–582. DOI: 10.1177/1052562919864377

Morris, D. S. (2003, November). Automatic grading of student's programming assignments: an interactive process and suite of programs. In *33rd Annual Frontiers in Education, 2003. FIE 2003.* (Vol. 3, pp. S3F-1). IEEE. DOI: 10.1109/FIE.2003.1265998

Mudrinić, D., & Šoda, I. (2024, November). The Rise of Generative Artificial Intelligence in Business. In *2024 IEEE 17th International Scientific Conference on Informatics (Informatics)* (pp. 493-498). IEEE. DOI: 10.1109/Informatics62280.2024.10900880

Mukherjee, S., Sharma, V., & Singh, S. (2021). Cybersecurity challenges in AI-driven business applications. *Journal of Business Ethics, 171*(3), 647–662.

Munir, H., Vogel, B., & Jacobsson, A. (2022). Artificial intelligence and machine learning approaches in digital education: A systematic revision. *Information (Basel), 13*(4), 203. DOI: 10.3390/info13040203

Mu, Q., & Zhao, Y. (2024). Transforming entrepreneurship education in the age of artificial intelligence. *Resources Data Journal, 3*, 2–20.

Murphy, R. F. (2019). Artificial intelligence applications to support K-12 teachers and teaching. *Rand Corporation, 10*(1), 1–20.

Napier, N. K., Harvey, M., & Usui, K. (2008). Management Education in Emerging Economies: The Impossible Dream? *Journal of Management Education, 32*(6), 792–819. DOI: 10.1177/1052562908319994

Nasr, A., Kamalov, F., & Balogun, A. O. (2022). Fraud detection in finance using machine learning. *Journal of Risk and Financial Management, 15*(2), 1–22.

National University of Singapore Business School. (2022). *The NUS MBA: Programme structure and curriculum overview* [Web page].https://mba.nus.edu.sg/the-programme/

Nedungadi, P., Tang, K. Y., & Raman, R. (2024). The Transformative Power of Generative Artificial Intelligence for Achieving the Sustainable Development Goal of Quality Education. *Sustainability (Basel), 16*(22), 9779. Advance online publication. DOI: 10.3390/su16229779

Newell, A. (1962). The processes of creative thinking. *Contemporary approaches to creative thinking/Atherton*.

Nguyen, A., & Henderson, M. (2022). AI-powered peer learning: The role of intelligent systems in shaping professional development. *International Journal of Educational Technology in Higher Education, 19*(1), 23. PMID: 35434266

Nguyen, A., Kremantzis, M., Essien, A., Petrounias, I., & Hosseini, S. (2024). Enhancing Student Engagement Through Artificial Intelligence (AI): Understanding the Basics, Opportunities, and Challenges. *Journal of University Teaching & Learning Practice, 21*(6). Advance online publication. DOI: 10.53761/caraaq92

Nguyen, A., Ngo, H. N., Hong, Y., Dang, B., & Nguyen, B.-P. T. (2023). Ethical principles for artificial intelligence in education. *Education and Information Technologies, 28*(4), 4221–4241. DOI: 10.1007/s10639-022-11316-w PMID: 36254344

Nguyen, T. N., & Truong, H. T. (2025). Trends and emerging themes in the effects of generative artificial intelligence in education: A systematic review. *Eurasia Journal of Mathematics, Science and Technology Education, 21*(4), em2613. DOI: 10.29333/ejmste/16124

Nicolae, M., & Nicolae, E. E. (2018). Leadership in higher education–coping with AI and the turbulence of our times. In *Proceedings of the International Conference on Business Excellence* (Vol. 12, No. 1, pp. 683-694). Sciendo. DOI: 10.2478/picbe-2018-0061

Niu, S. J., Luo, J., Niemi, H., Li, X., & Lu, Y. (2022). Teachers' and students' views of using an AI-aided educational platform for supporting teaching and learning at Chinese schools. *Education Sciences, 12*(12), 858. DOI: 10.3390/educsci12120858

Nordhoff, S., Lee, J. D., Calvert, S. C., Berge, S., Hagenzieker, M., & Happee, R. (2023). (Mis-) use of standard Autopilot and Full Self-Driving (FSD) Beta: Results from interviews with users of Tesla's FSD Beta. *Frontiers in Psychology, 14*, 1101520. DOI: 10.3389/fpsyg.2023.1101520 PMID: 36910772

Nord, V. P. N. https://nordvpn.com/cybersecurity/glossary/autonomous-intelligence/#:~:text=Autonomous%20intelligence%20is%20artificial%20intelligence,care%20robots%20for%20the%20elderly., Retrieved 7:25, February 21, 2025.

Novaes, A. L. (2025). Enhancing sustainability education in higher education through simulation-based learning: Integrating sustainable development goals. *International Journal of Sustainability in Higher Education*. Advance online publication. DOI: 10.1108/IJSHE-08-2024-0571

Nowani, D. (2020, September 25). *Old education policy*. The Indian Express, p. 6.

Nyaaba, M. (2024). *Transforming Teacher Education in Developing Countries: The Role of Generative AI in Bridging Theory and Practice*.

Nyaaba, M., Zhai, X., & Faison, M. Z. (2024). Generative AI for Culturally Responsive Science Assessment: A Conceptual Framework. *Education Sciences*, *14*(12), 1325. Advance online publication. DOI: 10.3390/educsci14121325

Nyoko, A. E., & Hanafiah, M. H. (2024, May). A Systematic Literature Review on Entrepreneurial Intention: PRISMA Method. In *Proceedings of the International Conference on Economic Management, Accounting and Tourism (ICEMAT 2023)* (pp. 254-273). Springer Nature. DOI: 10.2991/978-94-6463-411-2_21

OECD. (2023). *Digital Education Outlook 2023: Towards an effective digital education ecosystem*. OECD Publishing.

Ogunleye, B., Zakariyyah, K. I., Ajao, O., Olayinka, O., & Sharma, H. (2024). A Systematic Review of Generative AI for Teaching and Learning Practice. In *Education Sciences* (Vol. 14, Issue 6). Multidisciplinary Digital Publishing Institute (MDPI). DOI: 10.3390/educsci14060636

Omran Zailuddin, M. F. N., Nik Harun, N. A., Abdul Rahim, H. A., Kamaruzaman, A. F., Berahim, M. H., Harun, M. H., & Ibrahim, Y. (2024). Redefining creative education: A case study analysis of AI in design courses. *Journal of Research in Innovative Teaching and Learning*, *17*(2), 282–296. DOI: 10.1108/JRIT-01-2024-0019

On EdTech Newsletter. (August 6, 2024). Leading use cases for artificial intelligence (AI) tools in schoolwork among higher education students worldwide as of July 2024 [Graph]. In *Statista*. Retrieved January 16, 2025, from https://www.statista.com/statistics/1498323/use-cases-ai-by-students-worldwide/

Onesi-Ozigagun, O., Ololade, Y. J., Eyo-Udo, N. L., & Ogundipe, D. O. (2024). Revolutionizing education through AI: A comprehensive review of enhancing learning experiences. *International Journal of Applied Research in Social Sciences*, *6*(4), 589–607. DOI: 10.51594/ijarss.v6i4.1011

Ooi, K. B., Tan, G. W. H., Al-Emran, M., Al-Sharafi, M. A., Capatina, A., Chakraborty, A., Dwivedi, Y. K., Huang, T.-L., Kar, A. K., Lee, V.-H., Loh, X.-M., Micu, A., Mikalef, P., Mogaji, E., Pandey, N., Raman, R., Rana, N. P., Sarker, P., Sharma, A., & Wong, L. W. (2025). The potential of generative artificial intelligence across disciplines: Perspectives and future directions. *Journal of Computer Information Systems*, *65*(1), 76–107. DOI: 10.1080/08874417.2023.2261010

Open AI research Dactyl. https://openai.com/index/learning-dexterity/, Retrieved 7:27, February 24, 2025

Open AI research. Five, https://openai.com/index/openai-five/, Retrieved 7:27, February 24, 2025

Open, A. I. DALL·E, https://openai.com/index/dall-e/, Retrieved 7:10, February 24, 2025

Ouyang, F., Wu, M., Zheng, L., Zhang, L., & Jiao, P. (2023). Integration of artificial intelligence performance prediction and learning analytics to improve student learning in online engineering course. *International Journal of Educational Technology in Higher Education*, *20*(1), 4. DOI: 10.1186/s41239-022-00372-4 PMID: 36683653

Owoseni, A., Kolade, O., & Egbetokun, A. (2024). Generative AI and Its Implications for Higher Education Students and Educators. In *Generative AI in Higher Education: Innovation Strategies for Teaching and Learning* (pp. 1–25). Springer Nature Switzerland. DOI: 10.1007/978-3-031-60179-8_1

Owoseni, A., Kolade, O., & Egbetokun, A. (2024). *Generative AI in Higher Education*. Springer Books. DOI: 10.1007/978-3-031-60179-8

Padovano, A., & Cardamone, M. (2024). Towards human-AI collaboration in the competency-based curriculum development process: The case of industrial engineering and management education. *Computers and Education: Artificial Intelligence*, *7*, 100256. DOI: 10.1016/j.caeai.2024.100256

Paliwal, S., & Sharma, S. (2022). Stock prediction using neural networks and evolution algorithm. [IJRASET]. *International Journal for Research in Applied Science and Engineering Technology*, *10*(4), 661–671. DOI: 10.22214/ijraset.2022.41331

Palmer, N. J., Davies, J., & Viney, C. (2023). *Growth Patterns of Business and Management Doctorates Around the World, Business and Management Doctorates World-Wide: Developing the Next Generation*. Emerald Publishing Limited., DOI: 10.1108/9781789734997

Paluch, M., & Jackowska-Strumiłło, L. (2018). Hybrid models combining technical and fractal analysis with ANN for short-term prediction of close values on the Warsaw Stock Exchange. *Applied Sciences (Basel, Switzerland)*, *8*(12), 2473. DOI: 10.3390/app8122473

Pan, X., Wang, W., Zhang, X., Li, B., Yi, J., & Song, D. (2019). How you act tells a lot: Privacy-leakage attack on deep reinforcement learning. *arXiv preprint arXiv:1904.11082*.

Panda, R. (2024). Artificial Intelligence in Educational Systems: From Early Computational Tools to Contemporary AI-Enhanced Learning Environments. *International Journal of Research Publication and Reviews*, *5*(8), 3756–3760. DOI: 10.55248/gengpi.5.0824.2213

Pang, W., & Wei, Z. (2025). Shaping the future of higher education: A technology usage study on generative AI innovations. *Information (Basel)*, *16*(2), 95. DOI: 10.3390/info16020095

Panigrahi, R. R., Dash, M., Shaikh, Z. H., & Irfan, M. (2023). Review of Machine Learning Techniques in the Supply Chain Management of Indian Industry: A Future Research Agenda. In Irfan, M., Elhoseny, M., Kassim, S., & Metawa, N. (Eds.), *Advanced Machine Learning Algorithms for Complex Financial Applications* (pp. 199–219). IGI Global., DOI: 10.4018/978-1-6684-4483-2.ch013

Patil, D. (2024). *Artificial intelligence-driven supply chain optimization: Enhancing demand forecasting and cost reduction. SSRN* https://doi.org/DOI: 10.2139/ssrn.5057408

Pattanayak, S. (2021). Leveraging Generative AI for Enhanced Market Analysis: A New Paradigm for Business Consulting. *International Journal of All Research Education and Scientific Methods*, *9*(9), 2456–2469.

Patwardhan, B., & Mittal, P. (2020, September 10). *An academic bank of credit will transform Indian education*. The Hindustan Times, p. 11.

Pawar, S., & Dhumal, V. (2024). The role of technology in transforming leadership management practices. *Multidisciplinary Reviews*, *7*(4), 2024066–2024066. DOI: 10.31893/multirev.2024066

Pendy, B. (2023). Role of AI in business management. *Brilliance: Research of Artificial Intelligence*, *3*(1), 48–55. DOI: 10.47709/brilliance.v3i1.2191

Perriton, L., & Reynolds, M. (2018). Critical Management Education in challenging times. *Management Learning*, *49*(5), 521–536. DOI: 10.1177/1350507618795090

Poet, H., & Aston, K. (2025, June 9). *Teachers' use of ChatGPT in lesson preparation can save time*. Chartered College of Teaching. https://my.chartered.college/impact_article/teachers-use-of-chatgpt-in-lesson-preparation-can-save-time/#:~:text=Saving%20time,not%20to%20use%20any%20GenAI

Polakova, P., & Klimova, B. (2024). Implementation of AI-driven technology into education – a pilot study on the use of chatbots in foreign language learning. *Cogent Education*, *11*(1), 2355385. Advance online publication. DOI: 10.1080/2331186X.2024.2355385

Portuguez-Castro, M. (2024). Reimagining the future of business education through educational innovation. *International Journal of Markets and Business Systems*, *5*(2), 192–208. DOI: 10.1504/IJMABS.2024.10069258

Portuguez-Castro, M., & Marchena Sekli, G. (2025). Empowering educators: A multi-case study investigating the transformative integration of generative AI tools for teaching in business education. *Journal of Education for Business*, *100*(4), 1–11. DOI: 10.1080/08832323.2025.2470731

Prabha, D., Subramanian, R. S., Dinesh, M. G., & Girija, P. (2024). Sustainable Farming Through AI-Enabled Precision Agriculture. In *Artificial Intelligence for Precision Agriculture* (pp. 159–182). Auerbach Publications. DOI: 10.1201/9781003504900-8

Priatna, T., Maylawati, D., Sugilar, H., & Ramdhani, M. (2020). Key success factors of e-learning implementation in higher education. [iJET]. *International Journal of Emerging Technologies in Learning*, *15*(17), 101–114. DOI: 10.3991/ijet.v15i17.14293

Puffer, S. M. (1993). The Booming Business of Management Education in Russia. *Journal of Management Development*, *12*(5), 46–59. DOI: 10.1108/02621719310038962

Quinlan, J. R. (1986). Induction of decision trees. *Machine Learning*, *1*(1), 81–106. DOI: 10.1023/A:1022643204877

Radford, A., Wu, J., Child, R., Luan, D., Amodei, D., & Sutskever, I. (2019). Language models are unsupervised multitask learners. *OpenAI blog, 1*(8), 9.

Raghavendran, C. V., Pavan Venkata Vamsi, C., Veerraju, T., & Veluri, R. K. (2021). Predicting student admissions rate into university using machine learning models. In *Machine Intelligence and Soft Computing* [Springer Singapore.]. *Proceedings of ICMISC, 2020*, 151–162.

Rahiman, H. U., & Kodikal, R. (2024). Revolutionizing education: Artificial intelligence empowered learning in higher education. *Cogent Education*, *11*(1), 2293431. DOI: 10.1080/2331186X.2023.2293431

Rajput, J. S. (2020, August 27). *Education makes the man*. The Pioneer, p. 8.

Ramaiah, M. S., Nagarajan, S. K. S., Whig, P., & Dutta, P. K. (2025). AI-Powered Innovations Transforming Adaptive Education for Disability Support. In *Advancing Adaptive Education: Technological Innovations for Disability Support* (pp. 73-100). IGI Global Scientific Publishing.

Ramesh, A., Dhariwal, P., Nichol, A., Chu, C., & Chen, M. (2022). Hierarchical text-conditional image generation with clip latents. *arXiv preprint arXiv:2204.06125, 1*(2), 3.

Rana, S. (2023). AI and GPT for Management Scholars and Practitioners: Guidelines and Implications. *FIIB Business Review, 12*(1), 7–9. DOI: 10.1177/23197145231161408

Rane, N. (2023). ChatGPT and similar generative artificial intelligence (AI) for smart industry: role, challenges and opportunities for industry 4.0, industry 5.0 and society 5.0. *Challenges and Opportunities for Industry, 4*.

Rane, N., Choudhary, S., & Rane, J. (2024). Gemini or ChatGPT? Capability, performance, and selection of cutting-edge generative artificial intelligence (AI) in business management. *Capability, Performance, and Selection of Cutting-Edge Generative Artificial Intelligence (AI) in Business Management (February 19, 2024)*.

Rane, N. (2023). Role and challenges of ChatGPT and similar generative artificial intelligence in business management. *Available at SSRN* 4603227. DOI: 10.2139/ssrn.4603227

Ranoliya, B. R., Raghuwanshi, N., & Singh, S. (2017, September). Chatbot for university related FAQs. In *2017 International Conference on Advances in Computing, Communications and Informatics (ICACCI)* (pp. 1525-1530). IEEE. DOI: 10.1109/ICACCI.2017.8126057

Ransbotham, S., Kiron, D., Gerbert, P., & Reeves, M. (2017). Reshaping business with artificial intelligence: Closing the gap between ambition and action. *MIT Sloan Management Review, 59*(1).

Raphael, B. (1972). *Robot Research at Stanford Research Institute*. Stanford University.

Rasche, A., Gilbert, D. U., & Schedel, I. (2013). Cross-disciplinary ethics education in MBA programs: Rhetoric or reality? *Academy of Management Learning & Education, 12*(1), 71–85. DOI: 10.5465/amle.2011.0016a

Ratnakaram, S. P. K., Manikeswari, D., Shaikh, Z. H., & Mahapatra, D. M. **Mohanty, B. S.**, & Soni, A. (2025). Wearables and AI-smart technologies: Transforming the education sphere. In Wearable devices and smart technology for educational teaching assistance (pp. 27-52). IGI Global Scientific Publishing.

Ratten, V., & Jones, P. (2023). Generative artificial intelligence (ChatGPT): Implications for management educators. *International Journal of Management Education*, *21*(3), 100857. DOI: 10.1016/j.ijme.2023.100857

Redcay, E., & Schilbach, L. (2019). Using second-person neuroscience to elucidate the mechanisms of social interaction. *Nature Reviews. Neuroscience*, *20*(8), 495–505. DOI: 10.1038/s41583-019-0179-4 PMID: 31138910

Reicher, H. (2010). Building inclusive education on social and emotional learning: Challenges and perspectives – a review. *International Journal of Inclusive Education*, *14*(3), 213–246. DOI: 10.1080/13603110802504218

Reidenberg, J. R., & Schaub, F. (2018). Achieving big data privacy in education. *Theory and Research in Education*, *16*(3), 263–279. DOI: 10.1177/1477878518805308

Rekha, K., Gopal, K., Satheeskumar, D., Anand, U. A., Doss, D. S. S., & Elayaperumal, S. (2024, May). Ai-Powered Personalized Learning System Design: Student Engagement and Performance Tracking System. In *2024 4th International Conference on Advance Computing and Innovative Technologies in Engineering (ICACITE)* (pp. 1125-1130). IEEE.

Renz, A., & Hilbig, R. (2020). Prerequisites for artificial intelligence in further education: Identification of drivers, barriers, and business models of educational technology companies. *International Journal of Educational Technology in Higher Education*, *17*(1), 14. DOI: 10.1186/s41239-020-00193-3

Riapina, N. (2024). *Unleashing the Potential of Every Child.*, DOI: 10.4018/979-8-3693-1022-9.ch002

Risang Baskara, F. X. (2024). *British Journal of Teacher Education and Pedagogy Generative AI as an Enabler of Sustainable Education: Theoretical Perspectives and Future Directions*. https://doi.org/DOI: 10.32996/bjtep

Rosenblatt, F. (1961). *Principles of neurodynamics. perceptrons and the theory of brain mechanisms*. Cornell Aeronautical Lab Inc Buffalo NY. DOI: 10.21236/AD0256582

Rouabhia, R. (2025). Ethical Implications of AI: Examining Bias and Fairness in AI-Powered Education. In *Using AI Tools in Text Analysis, Simplification, Classification, and Synthesis* (pp. 411-438). IGI Global Scientific Publishing.

Rouchy, P. (2006). Aspects of PROLOG History: Logic Programming and Professional Dynamics. *Blekinge Institute of Technology, Sweden).(English). TeamEthno-Online*, (2), 85-100.

Ruiz-Rojas, L. I., Acosta-Vargas, P., De-Moreta-Llovet, J., & Gonzalez-Rodriguez, M. (2023). Empowering education with generative artificial intelligence tools: Approach with an instructional design matrix. *Sustainability (Basel), 15*(15), 11524. DOI: 10.3390/su151511524

Ruiz-Rojas, L. I., Salvador-Ullauri, L., & Acosta-Vargas, P. (2024). Collaborative Working and Critical Thinking: Adoption of Generative Artificial Intelligence Tools in Higher Education. *Sustainability (Basel), 16*(13), 5367. Advance online publication. DOI: 10.3390/su16135367

Rumelhart, D. E., Hinton, G. E., & Williams, R. J. (1985, September). *Learning internal representations by error propagation.*

Russell, S., & Norvig, P. (2021). *Artificial intelligence: A modern approach* (4th ed.). Pearson.

Rust, R. T., & Huang, M. H. (2022). The AI marketing canvas: A five-stage roadmap to implementing artificial intelligence in marketing. *Journal of Business Research, 140*, 781–789.

Ryzhko, O., Krainikova, T., Vodolazka, S., & Sokolova, K. (2024). Generative AI changes the book publishing industry: Reengineering of business processes. *Communicatio Socialis*, •••, 255–271.

S. C. V., V. P., A., & Vidhyapriya, P. (2025). Enhancing R&D Success in Entrepreneurship Education With Industry: Academia Collaboration and Simulation Tools. In A. N. Masouras, S. Anastasiadou, G. A. Deirmentzoglou, H. Ph. Sophocleous, & E. E. Anastasopoulou (Eds.), *Integrating Simulation Tools Into Entrepreneurship Education* (pp. 213–238). IGI Global. DOI: 10.4018/979-8-3693-9040-5.ch011

Saeger, K. J., Finley, L. R., & Wickam, M. J. (2024). The AI revolution: Awareness of and readiness for AI-based digital tools and technologies in business education. *The Journal of Research In Business Education, 64*(1).

Salesforce. (2024). *Discover how AI is transforming education.* https://www.salesforce.com/campaign/experience/edu-ai-data/

Salinas-Navarro, D. E., Palma-Mendoza, J. A., & Vilalta-Perdomo, E. (2024). Integrating Circular Supply Chains into Experiential Learning: Enhancing Learning Experiences in Higher Education. *Sustainability (Basel), 16*(23), 10789. DOI: 10.3390/su162310789

Salinas-Navarro, D. E., Vilalta-Perdomo, E., Michel-Villarreal, R., & Montesinos, L. (2024). Designing experiential learning activities with generative artificial intelligence tools for authentic assessment. *Interactive Technology and Smart Education, 21*(4), 708–734. DOI: 10.1108/ITSE-12-2023-0236

Samala, A. D., Rawas, S., Wang, T., Reed, J. M., Kim, J., Howard, N. J., & Ertz, M. (2024). Unveiling the landscape of generative artificial intelligence in education: A comprehensive taxonomy of applications, challenges, and future prospects. *Education and Information Technologies*, •••, 1–40.

Samarawickrama, A. J. P., & Fernando, T. G. I. (2017, December). A recurrent neural network approach in predicting daily stock prices: An application to the Sri Lankan stock market. In *2017 IEEE International Conference on Industrial and Information Systems (ICIIS)* (pp. 1–6). IEEE. DOI: 10.1109/ICIINFS.2017.8300345

Samuel, A. L. (1960). Programming computers to play games. [). Elsevier.]. *Advances in Computers, 1*, 165–192. DOI: 10.1016/S0065-2458(08)60608-7

Sandhu, R., Channi, H. K., Ghai, D., Cheema, G. S., & Kaur, M. (2024). An introduction to generative AI tools for education 2030. *Integrating generative AI in education to achieve sustainable development goals*, 1-28.

Sandhu, V. (2020, December 4). *Ad Council report has a message for celebs, education sector*. Business Standard, p. 14.

Sarea, A., Subramanian, S., Alareeni, B., Shaikh, Z. H., Hawaldar, I. T., & Elshaker, A. H. (2021). Financial Disclosures by Using Machine Learning Analysis. In Alareeni, B., Hamdan, A., & Elgedawy, I. (Eds.), *The Importance of New Technologies and Entrepreneurship in Business Development: In The Context of Economic Diversity in Developing Countries. ICBT 2020. Lecture Notes in Networks and Systems* (Vol. 194). Springer., DOI: 10.1007/978-3-030-69221-6_5

Sarker, M. S., Khan, F. S., & Roon, S. L. (2024). The Impact of Artificial Intelligence (AI) on Business Operations in Bangladesh.

Satia, J. K. (1992). Reshaping Management Education. *Vikalpa, 17*(4), 25–28. DOI: 10.1177/0256090919920405

Sax, M. (2025, June 24). *Custom AI tutor bots are transforming learning at HBS: Here's how students are using them.* Harvard Business Publishing. https://hbsp.harvard.edu/inspiring-minds/ai-tutor-bots-harvard-business-school

Schindler, L. A., Burkholder, G. J., Morad, O. A., & Marsh, C. (2017). Computer-based technology and student engagement: A critical review of the literature. *International Journal of Educational Technology in Higher Education, 14*(1), 25. DOI: 10.1186/s41239-017-0063-0

Schmidhuber, J. (1993). Habilitation thesis: System modeling and optimization. *Credit assignment across the equivalent of 1200 layers in an RNN*, 150.

Schmidhuber, J. (2015). Deep learning in neural networks: An overview. *Neural Networks, 61*, 85–117. DOI: 10.1016/j.neunet.2014.09.003 PMID: 25462637

Sedkaoui, S., & Benaichouba, R. (2024). Generative AI as a transformative force for innovation: A review of opportunities, applications and challenges. *European Journal of Innovation Management*. Advance online publication. DOI: 10.1108/EJIM-02-2024-0129

Selwin, S., Saseendran, H., Vemavarapu, K. R., Shaikh, I., Shaikh, Z. H., & Harris, S. B. (2024). AI-Driven Employee Engagement: Transforming Banking Workforce Dynamics Using the BEULA Model. In Awwad, B. (Ed.), *The AI Revolution: Driving Business Innovation and Research. Studies in Systems, Decision and Control* (Vol. 525). Springer., DOI: 10.1007/978-3-031-54383-8_32

Selwyn, N. (2023). *Should robots replace teachers? AI and the future of education*. Polity Press.

Shah, R., Patel, A., & Mehta, P. (2022). AI in risk management: Predictive analytics in financial decision-making. *Journal of Risk and Financial Management, 15*(4), 108–124.

Shaikh, Z. H., Irfan, M., Nomran, N. M., & Ratnakaram, S. P. (2024). Unlocking the Potential of AI for Efficient Governance: Innovative Approaches of Bahrain. In Irfan, M., Elmogy, M., Gupta, S., Khalifa, F., & Dias, R. (Eds.), *AI-Driven Decentralized Finance and the Future of Finance* (pp. 115–142). IGI Global Scientific Publishing., DOI: 10.4018/979-8-3693-6321-8.ch005

Shaikh, Z. H., Irfan, M., Nomran, N. M., Ratnakaram, S. P., Abey, J., & Anto, M. L. (2025). Measuring Vital Sign: A Case Study of India's Emerging Wearable Technology (EzeCheck) for Mass Screening and Health Monitoring. In Ul Rehman, S. (Ed.), *Wearable Devices and Smart Technology for Educational Teaching Assistance* (pp. 285–308). IGI Global Scientific Publishing., DOI: 10.4018/979-8-3693-7817-5.ch011

Shaikh, Z. H., Irfan, M., Vemavarapu, K. R., Sadayan, S., Hawaldar, I. T., & Rehman, S. U. (2024). Assessing the Effectiveness of Learning Outcomes: In Achieving Quality Education at Higher Learning Institutions in Bahrain. In Naim, A., Saklani, A., Khan, S., & Malik, P. (Eds.), *Evaluating Global Accreditation Standards for Higher Education* (pp. 50–65). IGI Global Scientific Publishing., DOI: 10.4018/979-8-3693-1698-6.ch004

Shaikh, Z. H., Sarea, A., & Irfan, M. (2022). *Islamic Banking Strategies in the World of Fintech: Success Story of Bahrain* (Vol. 423). Springer., DOI: 10.1007/978-3-030-93464-4_10

Shaikh, Z., Irfan, M., Sarea, A., & Panigrahi, R. R. (2024). *The Emergence of Islamic Fintech and Bahrain: Prospect for Global Financial Sectors* (Vol. 503). Springer., DOI: 10.1007/978-3-031-43490-7_52

Sharma, R. R. (2017). A Competency Model for Management Education for Sustainability. *Vision (Basel), 21*(2), x–xv. DOI: 10.1177/0972262917700970

Sharma, R., Gupta, N., & Rathore, H. (2022). Data security risks in artificial intelligence applications. *Information Systems Frontiers, 24*(4), 887–901.

Sharma, R., Gupta, N., & Verma, S. (2022). AI-driven forecasting models for business decision-making. *Expert Systems with Applications, 189*, 116048.

Shortliffe, E. H., Davis, R., Axline, S. G., Buchanan, B. G., Green, C. C., & Cohen, S. N. (1975). Computer-based consultations in clinical therapeutics: Explanation and rule acquisition capabilities of the MYCIN system. *Computers and Biomedical Research, an International Journal, 8*(4), 303–320. DOI: 10.1016/0010-4809(75)90009-9 PMID: 1157471

Shukla, B. (2020, December 2). *HEIs have their task cut out*. The Pioneer, p. 9.

Siemens, G., & Baker, R. S. (2023). The state of learning analytics in 2023. *Computers & Education, 203*, 104624.

Silver, D., Huang, A., Maddison, C. J., Guez, A., Sifre, L., Van Den Driessche, G., ... & Hassabis, D. (2016). Mastering the game of Go with deep neural networks and tree search. *nature, 529*(7587), 484-489.

Silver, D., Schrittwieser, J., Simonyan, K., Antonoglou, I., Huang, A., Guez, A., ... & Hassabis, D. (2017). Mastering the game of go without human knowledge. *nature, 550*(7676), 354-359.

Singh, A., Bhardwaj, G., Srivastava, A. P., Bindra, A., & Chaudhary, P. (2022, April). Application of neural network to technical analysis of stock market prediction. In *2022 3rd International Conference on Intelligent Engineering and Management (ICIEM)* (pp. 302–306). IEEE. DOI: 10.1109/ICIEM54221.2022.9853162

Singh, J. (2025) The Trust challenge in the Age to AI, IT NEXT January - February 2024, Pp:8-9.

Singh, J., & Praneeta (2025) Balancing fresh talent with Experienced experts is key to AI success, CIOs Leader, March 2025, Pp. 28-31.

Singh, N., Chaudhary, V., Singh, N., Soni, N., & Kapoor, A. (2024). Transforming Business with Generative AI: Research, Innovation, Market Deployment and Future Shifts in Business Models. *arXiv preprint arXiv:2411.14437.*

Singh, E., Vasishta, P., & Singla, A. (2025). AI-enhanced education: Exploring the impact of AI literacy on generation Z's academic performance in Northern India. *Quality Assurance in Education*, *33*(2), 185–202. DOI: 10.1108/QAE-02-2024-0037

Sircar, S. (2009). Business intelligence in the business curriculum. *Communications of the Association for Information Systems*, *24*(1), 17.

Slavin, A. (2023, March 19). *How AI can support educators to make their lives easier* [Blog post]. Jasper.https://www.jasper.ai/blog/amanda-slavin-how-ai-can-support-educators-to-make-their-lives-easier

Smolansky, A., Cram, A., Raduescu, C., Zeivots, S., Huber, E., & Kizilcec, R. F. (2023, July). Educator and student perspectives on the impact of generative AI on assessments in higher education. In Proceedings of the tenth ACM conference on Learning@ Scale (pp. 378-382). DOI: 10.1145/3573051.3596191

Sollosy, M., & McInerney, M. (2022). Artificial intelligence and business education: What should be taught. *International Journal of Management Education*, *20*(3), 100720. DOI: 10.1016/j.ijme.2022.100720

Southgate, E., Blackmore, K., Pieschl, S., Grimes, S., McGuire, J., & Smithers, K. (2019). *Artificial intelligence and emerging technologies in schools: Research report.* University of Newcastle. https://www.dese.gov.au/supporting-family-school-community-partnerships-learning/resources/ai-schools-report

Sreelakshmi, S., Babu, A. A., Lakshmipriya, C., Gracious, L. A., Nalini, M., & Subramanian, R. S. (2024, October). Enhancing Intrusion Detection Systems with Machine Learning. In *2024 2nd International Conference on Self Sustainable Artificial Intelligence Systems (ICSSAS)* (pp. 557-564). IEEE. DOI: 10.1109/ICSSAS64001.2024.10760341

Sridevi, K. B. (2021). Filling the quality gaps for a futuristic management education. *Journal of Economic and Administrative Sciences*, *37*(4), 393–400. DOI: 10.1108/JEAS-09-2018-0097

Sridharan, S., & Iyengar, S. (2020, November 16). *Gig work & India's Gen-Z challenge: Melding this subset of millennials to the workforce*. Business Line, p. 13.

Startari, A. V. (2025). AI, Tell me your protocol: The Intersection of Technology and Humanity in the Era of Big Data. SSRN *Electronic Journal*. DOI: 10.2139/ssrn.5260083

Steele, G. L., & Gabriel, R. P. (1996). The evolution of Lisp. In *History of programming languages---II* (pp. 233-330). DOI: 10.1145/234286.1057818

Stevens, A. O., & He, Y. (2022). Benchmarking the accuracy of AlphaFold 2 in loop structure prediction. *Biomolecules*, *12*(7), 985. DOI: 10.3390/biom12070985 PMID: 35883541

Stine, J., Trumbore, A., Woll, T., & Sambucetti, H. (2019). Implications of artificial intelligence on business schools and lifelong learning. *Final Report at Academic Leadership Group*, 19-2.

Strielkowski, W., Grebennikova, V., Lisovskiy, A., Rakhimova, G., & Vasileva, T. (2024). AI-driven adaptive learning for sustainable educational transformation. *Sustainable Development*.

Strielkowski, W., Grebennikova, V., Lisovskiy, A., Rakhimova, G., & Vasileva, T. (2025). AI -driven adaptive learning for sustainable educational transformation. *Sustainable Development (Bradford)*, *33*(2), 1921–1947. DOI: 10.1002/sd.3221

Subha, S., Balakrishnan, C., & Anish, T. P. (2024, August). Optimizing Machine Learning Algorithms for Heart Disease Prediction in Healthcare: A Comparative Study. In 2024 5th International Conference on Electronics and Sustainable Communication Systems (ICESC) (pp. 866-872). IEEE. DOI: 10.1109/ICESC60852.2024.10689877

Suen, H. Y., Hung, K. E., & Lin, Z. P. (2019). AI-powered recruitment and hiring: Challenges and future directions. *Computers in Human Behavior*, *99*, 224–234.

Sundermeyer, M., Schlüter, R., & Ney, H. (2012, September). LSTM neural networks for language modeling. *Interspeech*, *2012*, 194–197.

Sun, J., Li, H., & Wang, Q. (2021). AI-powered self-service business intelligence: A review and future directions. *Journal of Information Technology*, *36*(2), 184–201.

Suryanarayana, K. S., Kandi, V. P., Pavani, G., Rao, A. S., Rout, S., & Krishna, T. S. R. (2024). Artificial intelligence enhanced digital learning for the sustainability of education management system. *The Journal of High Technology Management Research*, *35*(2), 100495. DOI: 10.1016/j.hitech.2024.100495

Taddy, M. (2019). The technological singularity: A business leader's guide to artificial intelligence. McGraw-Hill Education. Goyal, K., Aggarwal, P., & Garg, R. (2022). AI applications in supply chain management: A systematic literature review. *Operations Research Perspectives*, *9*, 100244.

Tafrihah, U., Utanto, Y., & Pristiwati, R. (2024). Optimizing Digital Literacy Integration in Early Childhood Education: A Case Study of Tarbiyatul Athfal Bulumanis Kidul Kindergarten. *Golden Age: Jurnal Ilmiah Tumbuh Kembang Anak Usia Dini*, *9*(4), 757–770. DOI: 10.14421/jga.2024.94-14

Talaei Khoei, T., Ould Slimane, H., & Kaabouch, N. (2023). Deep learning: Systematic review, models, challenges, and research directions. *Neural Computing & Applications*, *35*(31), 23103–23124. DOI: 10.1007/s00521-023-08957-4

Tambe, P., Cappelli, P., & Yakubovich, V. (2019). Artificial intelligence in human resources management: Challenges and a path forward. *California Management Review*, *61*(4), 15–42. DOI: 10.1177/0008125619867910

Tan, C. Y., & Heng, S. H. (2021). Integrating AI in business education: A Singapore perspective. *Asian Journal of Management Education*, *18*(2), 77–89.

Tapalova, O., & Zhiyenbayeva, N. (2022). Artificial intelligence in education: AIEd for personalised learning pathways. *Electronic Journal of e-Learning*, *20*(5), 639–653. DOI: 10.34190/ejel.20.5.2597

Tariq, M. U. (2024). Generative AI in Curriculum Development in Higher Education. In Fields, Z. (Ed.), *Impacts of Generative AI on Creativity in Higher Education* (pp. 227–258). IGI Global., DOI: 10.4018/979-8-3693-2418-9.ch009

Tariq, M. U. (2025). AI and the Ethical Crossroads: Navigating Privacy, Personhood, and Autonomy in the Digital Age. In Chakraborty, S. (Ed.), *Human Values, Ethics, and Dignity in the Age of Artificial Intelligence* (pp. 49–72). IGI Global Scientific Publishing., DOI: 10.4018/979-8-3693-9035-1.ch003

Tariq, M. U. (2025). Bridging Cultures and Languages: Innovative Literacy Strategies for Inclusive and Engaged Classrooms. In Tussey, J., & Haas, L. (Eds.), *Supporting Cultural Differences Through Literacy Education* (pp. 257–282). IGI Global Scientific Publishing., DOI: 10.4018/979-8-3693-9271-3.ch010

Tariq, M. U. (2025). Empowering Patients With AI-Ethical Digital Tools for Health Data Management and Decision. In Pesqueira, A., & de Bem Machado, A. (Eds.), *Navigating Privacy, Innovation, and Patient Empowerment Through Ethical Healthcare Technology* (pp. 197–216). IGI Global Scientific Publishing., DOI: 10.4018/979-8-3693-7630-0.ch008

Tariq, M. U. (2025). Integrating ICT for Enhanced Organizational Resilience: Strategies and Case Studies. In Carvalho, L., Reis, L., Neves de Almeida Baptista Figueiredo, A., & Russo, N. (Eds.), *Leveraging Technology for Organizational Adaptability* (pp. 59–80). IGI Global Scientific Publishing., DOI: 10.4018/979-8-3693-6045-3.ch004

Taye, G., Sharma, S., Shah, P., & Nuriye, Y. G. (2023, October). Exploring the Role of Artificial Intelligence in Class Scheduling and Management: A Comprehensive Survey and Review. In *2023 International Conference on Computer Science and Emerging Technologies (CSET)* (pp. 1-11). IEEE. DOI: 10.1109/CSET58993.2023.10346898

Team, G., Georgiev, P., Lei, V. I., Burnell, R., Bai, L., Gulati, A., . . . Batsaikhan, B. O. (2024). Gemini 1.5: Unlocking multimodal understanding across millions of tokens of context. *arXiv preprint arXiv:2403.05530.*

Terblanche, N. H. D. (2024). Artificial intelligence coaching: Redefining people development and organizational performance. *The Journal of Applied Behavioral Science*, *23*(1), 384–393. DOI: 10.1177/00218863241283919

Tesauro, G. (2002). Programming backgammon using self-teaching neural nets. *Artificial Intelligence*, *134*(1-2), 181–199. DOI: 10.1016/S0004-3702(01)00110-2

Thaper, N. (2023, July 9th). Good B-school Builds credibility. *Business Today (Norwich)*, •••, 106–107.

Thottoli, M. M., Cruz, M. E., & Al Abri, S. S. S. (2025). The incubation revolution: Transforming entrepreneurial education with artificial intelligence. *Asia Pacific Journal of Innovation and Entrepreneurship*, *19*(1), 2–23. DOI: 10.1108/APJIE-11-2023-0221

Thrun, S., Montemerlo, M., Dahlkamp, H., Stavens, D., Aron, A., Diebel, J., Fong, P., Gale, J., Halpenny, M., Hoffmann, G., Lau, K., Oakley, C., Palatucci, M., Pratt, V., Stang, P., Strohband, S., Dupont, C., Jendrossek, L.-E., Koelen, C., & Mahoney, P. (2006). Stanley: The robot that won the DARPA Grand Challenge. *Journal of Field Robotics*, *23*(9), 661–692. DOI: 10.1002/rob.20147

Tiwari, R. (2023, February). *The integration of AI and machine learning in education and its potential to personalize and improve student learning experiences. International journal of scientific research in engineering and management, 7*(2)

Tiwari, R. (2023). The integration of AI and machine learning in education and its potential to personalize and improve student learning experiences. *International Journal of Scientific Research in Engineering and Management*, *7*(2). Advance online publication. DOI: 10.55041/IJSREM17645

Touvron, H., Lavril, T., Izacard, G., Martinet, X., Lachaux, M. A., Lacroix, T., . . . Lample, G. (2023). Llama: Open and efficient foundation language models. *arXiv preprint arXiv:2302.13971.*

Trajkovski, G. (2024). Bridging the public administration-AI divide: A skills perspective. *Public Administration and Development*, *44*(5), 412–426. DOI: 10.1002/pad.2061

Turing, A. M. (2009). *Computing machinery and intelligence*. Springer Netherlands. DOI: 10.1007/978-1-4020-6710-5_3

Twabu, K., & Nakene-Mginqi, M. (2024, December). Developing a design thinking artificial intelligence driven auto-marking/grading system for assessments to reduce the workload of lecturers at a higher learning institution in South Africa. [). Frontiers Media SA.]. *Frontiers in Education*, *9*, 1512569. DOI: 10.3389/feduc.2024.1512569

UNESCO. (2023). *Technology in education: A tool on whose terms? Global Education Monitoring Report*.https://unesdoc.unesco.org/ark:/48223/pf0000385723

Upasana (2023) AI: Harbinger of unprecedented wave of Automation", Business world, 16th December 2023, Pp 110-111.

Uzumcu, O., & Acilmis, H. (2024). Do innovative teachers use AI-powered tools more interactively? A study in the context of diffusion of innovation theory. *Technology. Knowledge and Learning*, *29*(2), 1109–1128. DOI: 10.1007/s10758-023-09687-1

Van Busum, K., & Fang, S. (2023, March). Analysis of AI models for student admissions: a case study. In *Proceedings of the 38th ACM/SIGAPP Symposium on Applied Computing* (pp. 17-22). DOI: 10.1145/3555776.3577743

van Lehn, K., & Chi, M. (2012). Adaptive expertise as acceleration of future learning. *Adaptive technologies for training and education*, 28-45.

Van Nuland, H. J. (2023). The role of AI in transforming leadership and organizational management. *Journal of Organizational Change Management*, *36*(2), 123–139.

Vardhan, S. (2020, August 29). *Hits and misses of NEP 2020 and its impact on legal education*. The Daily Guardian, p. 8.

Varona, D., & Suárez, J. L. (2022). Discrimination, bias, fairness, and trustworthy AI. *Applied Sciences (Basel, Switzerland), 12*(12), 5826. DOI: 10.3390/app12125826

Vecchiarini, M., & Somia, T. (2023). Redefining entrepreneurship education in the age of artificial intelligence: An explorative analysis. *International Journal of Management Education, 21*(3), 100879. DOI: 10.1016/j.ijme.2023.100879

Verma, M. (2018). Artificial intelligence and its scope in different areas with special reference to the field of education. *Online Submission, 3*(1), 5–10.

Viant Technology. (2024, January 15). *Understanding AI in programmatic advertising*. [Blog post]. Viant Technology Blog.https://www.viantinc.com/blog/understanding-ai-in-programmatic-advertising/

Viera Trevisan, L., Leal Filho, W., & Ávila Pedrozo, E. (2024). Transformative organisational learning for sustainability in higher education: A literature review and an international multi-case study. *Journal of Cleaner Production, 447*, 141634. DOI: 10.1016/j.jclepro.2024.141634

Vijh, M., Chandola, D., Tikkiwal, V. A., & Kumar, A. (2020). Stock closing price prediction using machine learning techniques. *Procedia Computer Science, 167*, 599–606. DOI: 10.1016/j.procs.2020.03.326

Vinuesa, R., Azizpour, H., Leite, I., Balaam, M., Dignum, V., Domisch, S., & Nerini, F. F. (2020). The role of artificial intelligence in achieving the Sustainable Development Goals. *Nature Communications, 11*(1), 1–10. DOI: 10.1038/s41467-019-14108-y PMID: 31932590

Vujović, D. (2024). Generative AI: Riding the new general purpose technology storm. *Ekonomika preduzeća, 72*(1-2), 125-136.

Walck, C. (2009). Integrating Sustainability Into Management Education: A Dean's Perspective. *Journal of Management Education, 33*(3), 384–390. DOI: 10.1177/1052562908323091

Walkington, C., & Bernacki, M. L. (2019). Personalizing algebra to students' individual interests in an intelligent tutoring system: Moderators of impact. *International Journal of Artificial Intelligence in Education, 29*(1), 58–88. DOI: 10.1007/s40593-018-0168-1

Wang, R. E., & Demszky, D. (2023). Is ChatGPT a good teacher coach? Measuring zero-shot performance for scoring and providing actionable insights on classroom instruction. *arXiv*.https://doi.org//arXiv.2306.03090DOI: 10.18653/v1/2023.bea-1.53

Wang, T., Bi, Z., Zhang, Y., Liu, M., Hsieh, W., Feng, P., . . . Niu, Q. (2024). Deep Learning Model Security: Threats and Defenses. *arXiv preprint arXiv:2412.08969*.

Wang, H., Dang, A., Wu, Z., & Mac, S. (2023). *Generative AI in Higher Education: Seeing ChatGPT Through Universities' Policies*. Resources, and Guidelines., DOI: 10.1016/j.caeai.2024.100326

Wang, T., Lund, B. D., Marengo, A., Pagano, A., Mannuru, N. R., Teel, Z. A., & Pange, J. (2023). Exploring the potential impact of artificial intelligence (AI) on international students in higher education: Generative AI, chatbots, analytics, and international student success. *Applied Sciences (Basel, Switzerland)*, *13*(11), 6716. DOI: 10.3390/app13116716

Wang, Y. (2021). Artificial intelligence in educational leadership: A symbiotic role of human-artificial intelligence decision-making. *Journal of Educational Administration*, *59*(3), 256–270. DOI: 10.1108/JEA-10-2020-0216

Wang, Z. (2024). Artificial intelligence in dance education: Using immersive technologies for teaching dance skills. *Technology in Society*, *77*, 102579. DOI: 10.1016/j.techsoc.2024.102579

Warburton, K. (2003). Deep learning and education for sustainability. *International Journal of Sustainability in Higher Education*, *4*(1), 44–56. DOI: 10.1108/14676370310455332

Watkins, C. J. C. H. (1989). Learning from delayed rewards.

Weizenbaum, J. (1966). ELIZA—A computer program for the study of natural language communication between man and machine. *Communications of the ACM*, *9*(1), 36–45. DOI: 10.1145/365153.365168

West, S. M., Whittaker, M., & Crawford, K. (2019). *Discriminating systems: Gender, race, and power in AI*[PDF]. AI Now Institute.https://ainowinstitute.org/wp-content/uploads/2023/04/discriminatingsystems.pdf

Wharton School. (2023). *AI for business*.https://ai.wharton.upenn.edu/

Whittaker, M., Alper, M., Brown, B., & Crawford, K. (2022). Addressing AI bias in practice. *AI Now Institute Report*.

Wijayati, T., Hayatie, M. N., & Safitri, Y. D. (2024). Enhancing Business Communication Skills in Vocational Education: A Generative Ai Approach for Personalized Learning. *Frontier Management Science*, *1*(2), 53–60. DOI: 10.53893/fms.v1i2.270

Wilson, H. J., & Daugherty, P. R. (2018). Collaborative intelligence: Humans and AI are joining forces. *Harvard Business Review*, *96*(4), 114–123.

Winkelhaus, S., & Grosse, E. H. (2020). Logistics 4.0: A systematic review towards a new logistics system. *International Journal of Production Research*, *58*(1), 18–43. DOI: 10.1080/00207543.2019.1612964

Winkler, R., & Söllner, M. (2018, July). Unleashing the potential of chatbots in education: A state-of-the-art analysis. In *Academy of management proceedings* (Vol. 2018, No. 1, p. 15903). Briarcliff Manor, NY 10510: Academy of Management. DOI: 10.5465/AMBPP.2018.15903abstract

Wirtz, B. W., Weyerer, J. C., & Geyer, C. (2022). Artificial intelligence and regulation. *Government Information Quarterly*, *39*(2), 101679.

Wollny, S., Schneider, J., Di Mitri, D., Weidlich, J., Rittberger, M., & Drachsler, H. (2021). Are we there yet?-a systematic literature review on chatbots in education. *Frontiers in Artificial Intelligence*, *4*, 654924. DOI: 10.3389/frai.2021.654924 PMID: 34337392

Wood, D., & Moss, S. H. (2024). Evaluating the impact of students' generative AI use in educational contexts. *Journal of Research in Innovative Teaching and Learning*, *17*(2), 152–167. DOI: 10.1108/JRIT-06-2024-0151

Xia, Q., Weng, X., Ouyang, F., Lin, T. J., & Chiu, T. K. F. (2024). A scoping review on how generative artificial intelligence transforms assessment in higher education. In *International Journal of Educational Technology in Higher Education* (Vol. 21, Issue 1). Springer Science and Business Media Deutschland GmbH. DOI: 10.1186/s41239-024-00468-z

Yadav, S. (2025). Leveraging AI to Enhance Teaching and Learning in Education: The Role of Artificial Intelligence in Modernizing Classroom Practices. In *Optimizing Research Techniques and Learning Strategies With Digital Technologies* (pp. 211-238). IGI Global Scientific Publishing.

Yadav, S. (2025). Leveraging AI to Enhance Teaching and Learning in Education: The Role of Artificial Intelligence in Modernizing Classroom Practices. In Basha, J. S., Alade, T. O., Al Khazimi, M. O. A., Vasudevan, R., & Khan, J. B. (Eds.), *Optimizing Research Techniques and Learning Strategies With Digital Technologies* (pp. 211–238). IGI Global., DOI: 10.4018/979-8-3693-7863-2.ch008

Yamijala, S. M. S., Chodisetty, R. S. C. M., Chakravorty, C., & Sai, K. P. (2024). *AI-Powered Learning Revolutionizing Smart Education With Personalized Learning Styles.*, DOI: 10.4018/979-8-3693-8151-9.ch007

Yawson, R. M., Johnson-Kanda, I., & Yarney, L. (2025), Participant journaling as a data collection method in management education research, Qualitative Research Journal, Vol. ahead-of-print No. ahead-of-print. https://doi.org/DOI: 10.1108/QRJ-01-2025-0021

Yelamarthi, K., Dandu, R., Rao, M., Yanambaka, V. P., & Mahajan, S. (2024). Exploring the potential of generative AI in shaping engineering education: Opportunities and challenges. *Journal of Engineering Education Transformations*, *37*(2), 439–445. DOI: 10.16920/jeet/2024/v37is2/24072

Yoon, S., & Rao, K. (2023). Personalized learning analytics and AI-driven MBA programs. *Journal of Management Education*, *47*(2), 188–207.

Young, N. T., & Caballero, M. D. (2019). Using machine learning to understand physics graduate school admissions. *arXiv preprint arXiv:1907.01570.*

Zawacki-Richter, O., Marín, V. I., & Bond, M. (2022). Systematic review of research on AI in higher education. *Educational Technology Research and Development*, *70*, 1345–1370.

Zawacki-Richter, O., Marín, V. I., Bond, M., & Gouverneur, F. (2019). Systematic review of research on artificial intelligence applications in higher education–where are the educators? *International Journal of Educational Technology in Higher Education*, *16*(1), 1–27. DOI: 10.1186/s41239-019-0171-0

Zhang, C., Zhang, C., Zhang, M., & Kweon, I. S. (2023). Text-to-image diffusion models in generative ai: A survey. arXiv preprint arXiv:2303.07909.

Zhang, K., & Aslan, A. B. (2021). AI technologies for education: Recent research & future directions. *Computers and education. Artificial Intelligence*, *2*, 100025.

Zheng, L., Fan, Y., Gao, L., Huang, Z., Chen, B., & Long, M. (2024). Using AI-empowered assessments and personalized recommendations to promote online collaborative learning performance. *Journal of Research on Technology in Education*, •••, 1–27. DOI: 10.1080/15391523.2024.2304066

Zhou, X., Zhang, J., & Chan, C. (2024). Unveiling students' experiences and perceptions of Artificial Intelligence usage in higher education. *Journal of University Teaching & Learning Practice*, *21*(6), 126–145. DOI: 10.53761/xzjprb23

Zohuri, B., & Mossavar-Rahmani, F. (2024). The symbiotic evolution: Artificial intelligence (AI) enhancing human intelligence (HI) an innovative technology collaboration and synergy. *Journal of Material Sciences and Applied Engineering*, *3*(1).

Zou, Y., Zhong, N., Chen, Z., & Zhao, W. (2024). Bridging digitalization and sustainability in universities: A Chinese green university initiative in the digital era. *Journal of Cleaner Production*, *469*, 143181. DOI: 10.1016/j.jclepro.2024.143181

# About the Contributors

**Manjunath B R** holds a Ph.D. in Finance with a specialization in the performance evaluation of Indian and Australian mutual fund schemes, awarded by Davangere University in 2019. He currently serves as the Professor of Finance & Analytics and Director of Academic Affairs at the School of Business Management, Shoolini University, Solan, Himachal Pradesh, India. Dr. Manjunath is also a Global Visiting Professor at Tecnológico de Monterrey, Mexico, where he lectures on finance and analytics. With over 16 years of combined academic and industry experience, Dr. Manjunath has made significant contributions to the fields of business analytics, finance, and management education. His research interests include data science applications in finance, econometrics, and business analytics. He has authored over 88 peer-reviewed research papers indexed in ABDC, Scopus, and UGC journals, focusing on applied finance, analytics, and business decision-making. Dr. Manjunath has designed and delivered various workshops, faculty development programs, and management development programs on topics such as financial econometrics, data visualization, and advanced business analytics. He has extensive expertise in using tools like Python, R, Tableau, and EViews for business and financial data analysis. His innovative teaching approaches emphasize experiential learning and bridging the gap between academic theory and industry practice. Dr. Manjunath's academic excellence has been recognized with several accolades, including the MTC Global Award for Global Education Ambassador and multiple best research paper awards. He is also the author of an upcoming textbook, Machine Learning and Deep Learning, slated for publication in 2024. His commitment to advancing education and research makes him a valuable contributor to the ongoing discourse on integrating AI, machine learning, and analytics in business and management education.

**Sunil Kumar** is an Associate Professor at the Faculty of Management Sciences, Shoolini University, India, brings over 15 years of experience in teaching, academic research, eLearning, and educational quality management. Dr. Kumar's teaching repertoire spans various subjects, including Human Resource Management (HRM), HR Analytics, Organizational Behavior, and Industrial Psychology. His research portfolio features 50 publications in prominent journals like the International Journal of Educational Management and the Journal of Workplace Learning, with his studies often revolving around employee competencies, mindfulness in the workplace, and the impact of technology on organizational efficiency. He has presented his research at international conferences and received awards for his contributions. Dr. Kumar has authored several book chapters and edited volumes on topics such as healthcare management and organizational behavior. He has also secured copyrights for various research models, including frameworks for e-training and AI-based tools for organizational development. His ongoing research interests include AI in recruitment and employee resilience, and he is actively involved in supervising PhD candidates. Furthermore, Dr. Kumar's editorial and reviewer roles in academic journals highlight his influence in the broader academic community.

***

**Shyam Sunder Agrawal**, Assistant Professor, Mittal school of Business, Lovely Professional University, Phagwara, Punjab. He has been associated with the education industry since 2015. He has presented papers in various reputed IIM conferences and published several research papers in UGC CARE, SCOPUS and ABDC Journals. His field of interest are Behavioral finance, Sustainable finance, Capital Market, Banking and Insurance, Fintech. He has published and granted 2 patents from Govt of India. He got International Case Study award in 2022. He is reviewer of Emerald, Springer and UGC care Journals.

**Balaraman Premkumar** is currently serving as Associate Professor in the Faculty of Management, SRM Institute of Science & Technology, Kattankulathur, India. He completed his Ph.D degree in 2013 in Human resource management focused on Occupational Stress from SRMIST. A committed academician and administrator with 20 years of experience, 16 years especially in teaching students from various social and cultural backgrounds and also with a strong industry exposure of 4 years in Production / IT & Banking organizations, possessing excellent administrative, verbal communication and written skills along with constructive and effective teaching methods that promote a stimulating learning environment. He has published and presented papers in peer reviewed journals and conferences. Currently handles funded research and guides research scholars in the domain of management. His research interests includes HRM, Entrepreneurship, Information Systems, Supply Chain Management and Strategy.

**Ramya H P** holds an MBA in finance and is pursuing a Ph.D. in investments from VTU. Currently, she works as an assistant professor at the Department of Management Studies at DSCE, with 15 years of experience. She has conducted workshops and seminars on topics such as financial management using Excel, financial accounting and taxation, and financial statement analysis, and has presented and published research papers in various national and international journals. Additionally, she is trained in personal finance, data processing using Python, taxation, financial modelling, trading strategies, portfolio optimization using the Markowitz model, and investment management. She is also an AICTE-nominated innovation ambassador for the Institute Innovation Council.

**R. Kennady** is an Assistant Professor in the Department of Artificial Intelligence and Data Science at Rajalakshmi Institute of Technology, Chennai. His areas of interest include artificial intelligence, machine learning, and data science. He is committed to academic excellence and innovative research in emerging technologies.

**Sunil Kumar**, currently an Associate Professor at Faculty of Management Sciences, Shoolini University, possesses extensive academic and research experience. With a background in Business Administration, Sunil's research endeavors span multiple domains, including human resource management, e-training, and the application of artificial intelligence in business. His prolific contributions are evidenced by numerous research papers, book chapters, copyrights, and patents. Dr. Kumar has a knack for teaching with expertise in subjects like HR Analytics, Talent Management, Industrial Psychology, and more. He has also successfully guided PhD students and actively contributes to various academic administrative roles. Dr. Kumar's vast research landscape includes topics like AI-based chatbots in recruitment, e-training impact, and more. His papers have been published in esteemed journals like Journal of Workplace Learning and International Journal of Law and Management. Moreover, he has authored books and edited volumes touching upon themes related to the contemporary business environment. Dr. Sunil has been a dynamic participant in numerous workshops, ranging from data analysis to stress

**Rakshith Kumar R** is a finance and business analytics practitioner affiliated with the Department of Management Studies, Dayananda Sagar College of Engineering. His academic interests lie in data-driven decision-making, financial modeling, and business intelligence. He has worked on various analytical projects, blending statistical tools with business insights to solve real-world problems.

**L. A. Anto Gracious** is an accomplished academic professional in Information Technology and Computer Science, known for his dedication to education, technology, and research. He holds a B.Tech in IT from C.S.I Institute of Technology (2006), an MBA in Technology Management, and an M.Tech in IT from Francis Xavier Engineering College (2011). He began his career as a Programmer at Software Solutions Integrated Limited, later transitioning to academia in 2011 as an Assistant Professor at Marthandam College of Engineering and Technology. Over eight years, he excelled in teaching, led the Software Development Cell, and earned multiple awards for his contributions. He later served at St. Xavier's Catholic College of Engineering and currently holds a position at R.M.K. College of Engineering and Technology. A prolific researcher, Anto focuses on machine learning, wireless sensor networks, and healthcare technologies. His work is widely published, and he has received accolades such as the Best Paper Award and multiple Best Faculty Awards.

**Bhabani Shankar Mohanty** is currently working as an Assistant Professor in the Department of Statistics and Applied Mathematics, School of Mathematics and Computer Sciences, Central University of Tamil Nadu, Tamil Nadu. He has an M.Phil and a Doctorate (Ph.D.) in Statistics from the P.G. Department of Statistics, Utkal University, Bhubaneswar. He has completed a Master's Degree in Statistics from Utkal University and worked for one year as a Project-JRF at IIT-Bhubaneswar. He has presented research papers at National/ International conferences in India and has published papers in indexed international journals of repute. He has over 10 years of teaching and research experience. His research interests are inventory control, fuzzy logic, optimization techniques, and sustainable supply chains. He also has command over analyzing high-dimension data generated from different real-life phenomena.

|**Indranil Mutsuddi** is PhD in Management Studies from Amity University Uttar Pradesh. He is presently associated with the Faculty of Management, JIS University, Kolkata as HOD and Associate Professor in HR. Dr. Indranil has more than 20+ years of teaching experience as a faculty member in Human Resources Management, Organizational Behaviour and Behavioural Sciences. He had published 62 research papers, authored 3 text books in Human Resource Management and contributed 16 chapters in edited books.

**P. Rashmi** is working at Velammal Engineering College, Surapet, Chennai. She is actively engaged in teaching and research, with interests in emerging technologies and their practical applications. Her academic contributions include participation in research projects, paper publications, and technical events. She is committed to fostering innovation and knowledge-sharing within the academic and research community. Ms. Rashmi continues to enhance her expertise through workshops, faculty development programs, and collaborative initiatives.

**P. Vinitha Baby** is an Assistant Professor in the Department of Artificial Intelligence and Data Science at Vel Tech Multi Tech Dr. Rangarajan Dr. Sakunthala Engineering College, Avadi, Chennai. She specializes in AI and data-driven technologies in engineering education. Her work includes academic teaching and research in emerging tech domains.

**Priya K** is currently working as Associate Professor at SRM Institute of Science & Technology, Faculty of Management, Ramapuram, Chennai, India. She completed her Ph.D degree in 2021 in Finance focused on behavioral finance from SRMIST. Her research interests include financial modeling, Entrepreneurship, strategy, small business and technology management. She has presented papers in International conferences and published in peer reviewed journals in varied areas of management.

**K. Saranya** is an Assistant Professor in the Department of Artificial Intelligence and Data Science at Panimalar Engineering College, Chennai. She is engaged in teaching and research in the areas of AI, machine learning, and data analytics. Her academic contributions support the advancement of intelligent systems and technology-driven education.

**Barsha Baishali Sahoo** is currently working as Asst. Prof in MBA dept in College of Engineering Bhubaneswar, Odisha under BPUT University. She has 6 years of teaching experience, and her research domain are AI, ML integrated education system, HRM etc

**Partap Singh** is committed to teaching and research in Finance and Investment domain since last 18 years+. His qualification is PhD (Commerce), M. Com (Finance& Accounting), and MBA(Finance). He has rich work experience in the field of Teaching, administration and research as well. He held various responsibilities like Editor, Co-editor, and Editorial Board member, Associate Editor in number of national and international journals. He has been regularly been receiving offers for writing books from the top publishing houses of India and received many letter of thanks& compliments for giving valuable suggestions and commendable views concerning improvement of many leading Publications/Books. He has written and published 5 books namely Financial Management, Risk Management, working capital Management, Management Accounting and Analysis of Financial Statements. Further, he has published more than 68 papers and book chapters in good reputed journals and he has also contributed numerous research papers in national and international conferences or seminars. He has good participation in MDPs. FDPs and STCs as well as Life Membership of reputed academic bodies. His future interest area of research is Financial Market, Financial Derivatives, Technological innovations in Finance& Investment, Artificial Intelligence and Its Impact on Finance and Investment. " Dr Partap Singh has act as Associate Professor in School of Management &Commerce, Lovely Professional University, Punjab, India. " Dr Partap Singh is currently working as Professor in MMIM, MMU Mullana, Ambala, Haryana, India."

**Siva Subramanian R** is working in the School of Computing at SRM Institute of Science and Technology, Trichy. His research interests span across computing technologies and their real-world applications. He is actively involved in academic and research initiatives in the field of computer science.

**Amanjot Singh Syan** is a dynamic and accomplished Business Analyst with over five years of IT experience, delivering business value through data-driven decision-making. Skilled in Rational Unified Process (RUP) and Agile methodologies, he excels in gathering and analyzing business requirements, creating functional specs (BRD, FRD, SRS), and designing workflow diagrams using UML tools. Proficient in Tableau and Power BI, he develops dashboards and conducts cost-benefit analyses. Experienced in software testing, process mapping, and project management, he collaborates with IT teams to implement solutions aligned with industry best practices while ensuring projects meet deadlines and budgets.

**T. Venketbabu** is an Assistant Professor (SG) in the Department of Computer Science and Engineering, School of Computing at Vel Tech Rangarajan Dr. Sagunthala R\&D Institute of Science and Technology, Chennai. His academic focus includes teaching, research, and development in computer science. He contributes to scholarly activities and technological advancements in his field.

**Muhammad Usman Tariq** has more than 16+ year's experience in industry and academia. He has authored more than 200+ research articles, 110+ case studies, 130+ book chapters and several books other than 4 patents. He is founder and CEO of The Case HQ, a unique repository for courses, narrative and video case studies. He has been working as a consultant and trainer for industries representing six sigma, quality, health and safety, environmental systems, project management, and information security standards. His work has encompassed sectors in aviation, manufacturing, food, hospitality, education, finance, research, software and transportation. He has diverse and significant experience working with accreditation agencies of ABET, ACBSP, AACSB, WASC, CAA, EFQM and NCEAC. Additionally, Dr. Tariq has operational experience in incubators, research labs, government research projects, private sector startups, program creation and management at various industrial and academic levels. He is Certified Higher Education Teacher from Harvard University, USA, Certified Online Educator from

HMBSU, Certified Six Sigma Master Black Belt and has been awarded PFHEA, SFSEDA, SMIEEE, and CMBE.

**Vinayak Anand Teli** is an aspiring finance professional pursuing MBA from Dayananda Sagar College of Engineering, Bengaluru. He has completed his under graduation in commerce with first rank to Rani Channamma University, Belagavi.

**Komal Thakur** is a research scholar in the Faculty of Management Sciences at Shoolini University, currently pursuing her Ph.D. in Management.

**Roopa U** is an esteemed Assistant Professor at Dayananda Sagar College of Engineering, bringing over two decades of dedicated teaching experience in academia. Her academic journey includes the attainment of an M.Sc. and M.Phil. in Statistics, coupled with an MBA in Marketing. She is pursuing her Ph.D. from Visvesvaraya Technological University in the field of exploring the transformative impact of social media applications on higher education further enhancing her expertise and contributions to the field. Areas of Expertise • Business Analytics using Python, R, Excel, and SPSS tools. • Machine Learning, Quantitative Techniques, Operations Research, Business Mathematics. • Research Methodology and Statistical Analysis for interdisciplinary applications. • Curriculum design and facilitation of innovative teaching methods.

# Index

## A

## B



## C



## D



## E



## F

## R



## S



## T

www.ingramcontent.com/pod-product-compliance
Lightning Source LLC
LaVergne TN
LVHW062326300926
849161LV00007B/1587
*9798337321509*